Y0-BCI-695

VEHBİ KOÇ FOUNDATION

Encyclopedia

VEHBİ KOÇ FOUNDATION
ENCYCLOPEDIA

RENAN AKMAN   GÜREL TÜZÜN

FOREWORD

Why an Encyclopedia?

In 2014, we began preparing to celebrate the 50th anniversary of the establishment of the Vehbi Koç Foundation. In addition to organizing special events, we all wanted to create a publication that would provide a lasting record of our 50 years of activity. Bülent Erkmen, the designer of our *Forty Year Book* published in 2009, suggested, "This time let's make an encyclopedia rather than a book." When our President Erdal Yıldırım first shared the idea with us, we were not immediately convinced. However, the more we thought about it, the more we all warmed to the idea. Before long, we were excited about the idea of an encyclopedia describing the people, organizations, events and activities that have been part of our 50-year journey since 1969, even including the concepts behind the establishment of the foundation. We were similarly thrilled that there would be a digital version which could be continually updated.

During the process of assembling this encyclopedia, we remembered things we had forgotten, learned things we didn't know and felt both moved and proud of our achievements. In other words, the encyclopedia found a place in our hearts even before it was published.

Our dream was that this book would be a resource that you will always keep to hand; I hope that our dream comes true. I am grateful to the people and organizations who worked so hard to bring this project to fruition and labored over the content, weaving it together article by article.

With my warmest regards,

SEMAHAT ARSEL

PREFACE

The *Vehbi Koç Foundation Encyclopedia* was created as part of a series of work to commemorate the foundation's fiftieth year. Its aim was to provide a definitive source of information on the people, organizations, activities, projects, awards, scholarships, places and publications associated with the Vehbi Koç Foundation. At the preparatory stage, Editorial Board meetings deliberated the general approach, principles and methods to be adopted and also collated the list of subject headings. Great care was taken to ensure that the list of subjects to be accommodated in the encyclopedia was neither superfluous nor deficient. The information for the text was gathered by researching both material resources and through direct contact with the relevant bodies and individuals. At the next stage, the compiled information was scrutinized for inconsistencies and omissions, while work also began to identify appropriate visual content for the encyclopedia. Zeynep Otluoğlu Dursun and Nazlı Başak Örgüt made a huge contribution to this work, particularly in the collation of information, documents and visual materials.

With these preparations completed, work began on composing the text in accordance with the finalized list of subject entries and the agreed writing conventions. The preparation stage took almost three years, during which the written content was reviewed and updated on numerous occasions. Much of the text was sent out to the individuals or bodies concerned and their feedback informed the writing process.

Throughout this long period, both the subject headings list and written content was continually amended and updated to reflect recent developments. This review process continued after the written and graphic content was at the page-setting stage and even after the first draft of the book was ready. We are greatly indebted to the team at BEK Tasarım for their patience and understanding, particularly at this latter stage.

Lastly, we would like to thank Erdal Yıldırım, Seçil Kınay and all the employees of VKV for their help and support in completing this project.

With our sincerest regards,

RENAN AKMAN GÜREL TÜZÜN

Notes on the Encyclopedia

Arrangement of entries

The names of individuals are listed with the surname first followed by the forename separated by a comma.

Within the text, works are written with their original name in italics and publication date in parentheses. The works translated to and published in English appear in italics inside parentheses together with their publication date, otherwise, English translations of the titles are provided in regular inside parentheses.

Alphabetical order

The alphabetical order is arranged by word rather than letter. Words that may consist of one or more letters are separated from the following word by a space; slashes (/) and hyphens (-) qualify as spaces.

The headings of entries about individuals, places, concepts and organizations are arranged according to the Turkish alphabet. Letters that do not exist in the Turkish alphabet are in the order of the Latin alphabet; apostrophes, accents or other punctuation marks are ignored.

If the only difference between two headings is a punctuation mark, the title without any punctuation mark will be listed first. Hyphenated words (-) are considered as two separate words and listed according to the first word.

Headings that begin with numbers are listed alphabetically according to the spelt version of the number.

Identical headings are listed in the order of individuals, places, concepts and objects.

References

References have been added to help readers understand the text or direct them towards further information. The symbol (*) is used to indicate words or proper nouns in the text that constitute an entry in their own right. The source of further information is shown within the text or at the end of the entry preceded by *see* or *see also*. Different written forms of standard words and proper nouns have also been added as reference headings.

Abbreviations

AD	Anno Domini *(After Christ)*
AO	Anonim Ortaklık *(Joint Stock Partnership)*
AŞ	Anonim Şirket *(Joint Stock Company)*
b.	born
BCE	Before Common Era
Co.	Company
d.	death
Dr.	Doctor
e.g.	exempli gratia *(for example)*
ed.	Edited by
et al.	et alia *(and others)*
etc.	et cetera
EU	European Union
Inc.	Incorporated
Jr	Junior
km	kilometer
Ltd.	limited
nd	no date
No.	number
p.	page
Prof.	Professor
pp.	pages
r.	the term of reign
TAO	Türk Anonim Ortaklığı *(Turkish Joint Stock Partnership)*
TAŞ	Türk Anonim Şirketi *(Turkish Joint Stock Company)*
TGNA	Turkish Grand National Assembly
UK	United Kingdom
UN	United Nations
USA	United States of America

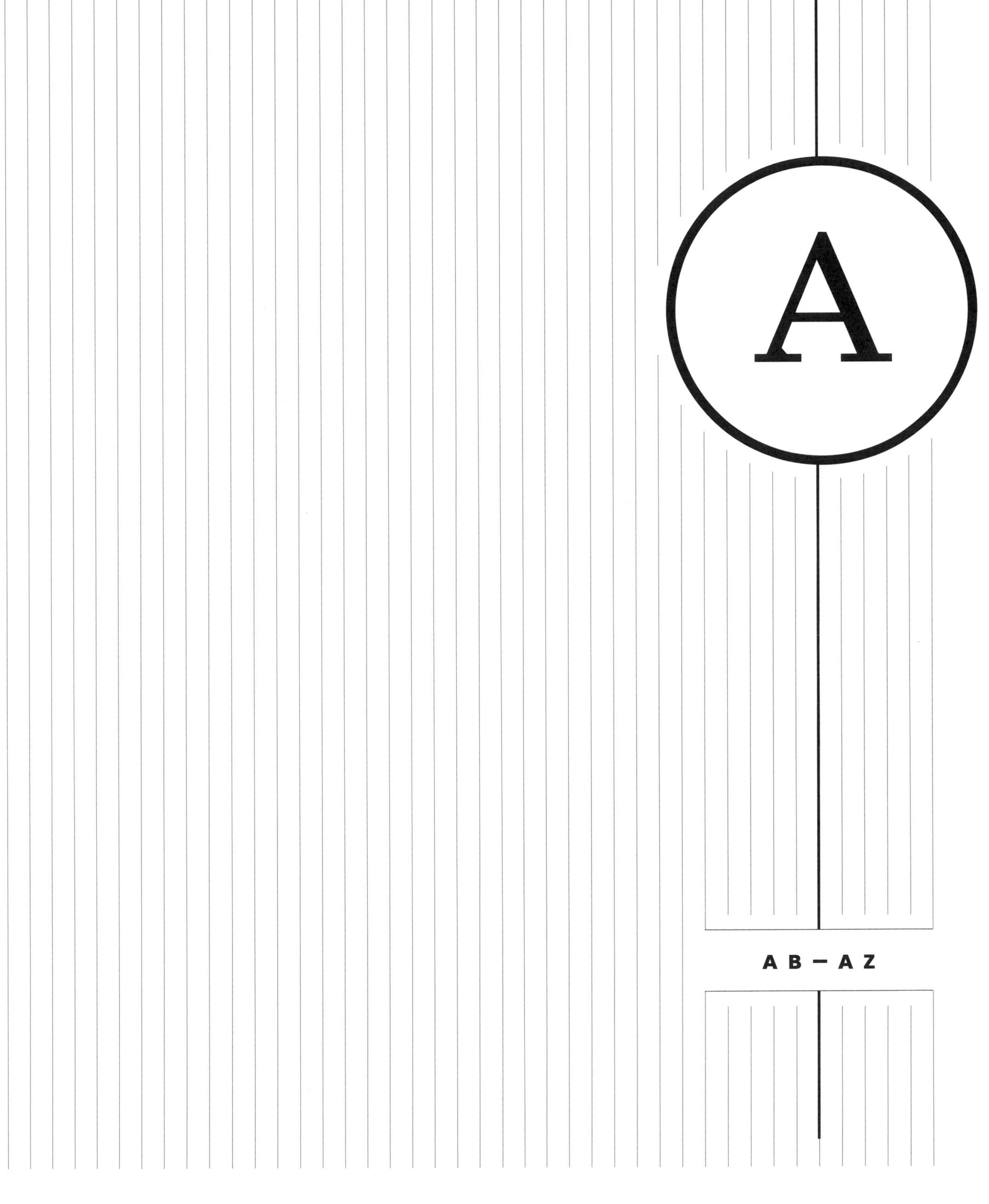

A

AB — AZ

Abadan Unat, Nermin *(b. September 18, 1921, Vienna)*, political scientist who received the Vehbi Koç Award(*) for education in 2012. She has gained recognition for her work on external migration and women in Turkey.

The daughter of Izmir businessman Mustafa Süleymanoviç and Baroness Elfriede Karwinsky from Hungary, she graduated from Izmir High School for Girls (1940) and Istanbul University Faculty of Law (1944). After working at *Ulus* newspaper between 1944 and 1950, she studied for a master's degree at Minnesota University (1952-53). She was appointed as an academic assistant at Ankara University Faculty of Political Sciences (Mülkiye) in 1954, then became associate professor in 1958 and professor in 1966, when she founded the Chair of Political Behavior. Prof. Abadan Unat served in various academic

and administrative roles throughout the 1970s and was a guest professor at Berlin, Munich, New York City, Denver and Georgetown Universities. She participated in a variety of conferences as expert consultant on migrant workers. She served on the Turkish National Commission for UNESCO. She was vice president of the International Political Science Association (IPSA) between 1967 and 1970. From 1978 to 1984, she was the president of the Turkish Social Sciences Association. In 1980, she represented Turkey at the United Nations World Conference on Women and was vice president of the Council of Europe Gender Equality Commission from 1978 to 1984. She sat in the Turkish Grand National Assembly as a senator appointed by the President of Turkey (1978-80). In 1981, she returned to the Ankara University Faculty of Political Sciences. After retiring in 1989, she continued to lecture at Boğaziçi University and Istanbul University Women's Research and Education Center.

As well as publishing numerous articles in French, German and English, Prof. Abadan Unat has also edited books in these languages. Her principal works are *Halk Efkârı Mefhumu ve Tesir Sahaları* (1957; Public Opinion, Concepts and Areas of Influence), *Bürokrasi* (1959; Bureaucracy), *Social Change and Turkish Women* (1961), *Batı Almanya'daki Türk İşçileri ve Sorunları* (1964; Turkish Workers in West Germany and Their Problems), *Anayasa Hukuku ve Siyaset Bilimi Açısından 1965 Genel Seçimlerinin Tahlili* (1966; 1965 General Election's Analysis in the Light of Constitutional Law and Political Science), *Göç ve Gelişme* (1976; Migration and Development), *Turkish Workers in Europe* (1976), *Türk Toplumunda Kadın* (1979; Women in Turkish Society), *Türk Dış Göçü 1960-84, Yorumlu Bibliyografya* (1986; Turkish External Migration 1960-84, Annotated Bibliography), *Women in the Developing World: Evidence from Turkey* (1986) and *Bitmeyen Göç: Konuk İşçilikten Ulus-Ötesi Yurttaşlığa* (2002; Endless Migration: From Guest Workers to Transnational Citizenship). Prof. Abadan Unat published her memoirs in a book entitled *Kum Saatini İzlerken* (1997; Watching the Hour Glass) and co-edited the works of her first husband Prof. Yavuz Abadan under the title *Kırım'dan Gelen Bir Aydının Seçilmiş Yazıları* (Selected Essays of an Intellectual from Crimea) in 2017. The book *Hayatını Seçen Kadın* (The Woman Who Chose Her Life), based on her conversations with Sedef Kabaş was published in 2010.

Prof. Abadan Unat was granted the Vehbi Koç Award in 2012 for her "outstanding contribution in the field of education". At the awards ceremony, Prof. Abadan Unat was acknowledged as a pioneer female political scientist who "had raised thousands of students and hundreds of academicians in the fields of political science and sociology, was considered as an exemplary lecturer and 'teacher of teachers' for her leading work on women and migration, and was an instigator, manager and participant in many educational projects."

Prof. Abadan Unat received the Mülkiye Alumni Association's Grand Award in 2016, followed by the Sakıp Sabancı International Research Awards Jury Special Prize in 2017.

Prof. Daron Acemoğlu (MIDDLE) **at the award ceremony with president of Koç University, Prof. Umran İnan** (LEFT) **and Rahmi M. Koç**

Acemoğlu, K(amer) Daron *(b. September 3, 1967, Istanbul)*, world-famous economist, who was awarded the Rahmi M. Koç Medal of Science(*) by Koç University(*) in 2017 for his "trailblazing contribution in the fields of macroeconomic growth and development, labor economics, and political economy."

He completed his elementary education at Kadıköy Aramyan Uncuyan Armenian Elementary School and secondary education at Galatasaray High School (1986) in Istanbul. After graduating from York University Department of Economics (1989), he received a master's degree at the London School of Economics (LSE) Department of Mathematical Economics and Econometrics (1990) and a PhD from the Department of Economics of the same university (1992). In 1993, he went to the USA to pursue an academic career at the Massachusetts Institute of Technology (MIT). He became a professor in 2000 and is currently serving in the MIT Department of Economics as Elizabeth and James Killian Professor.

Acemoğlu's main fields of interest are political economy, economic development, economic growth, economic theory, technology, income and wage inequality, human capital and education, labor economics and network economics. His numerous articles were published in international peer-reviewed economics journals and collective works. He wrote the *Economic Origins of Dictatorship and Democracy* with James A. Robinson, which was published in 2006. His book *Why Nations Fail: Origins of Power, Poverty and Prosperity*, also co-written with Robinson, was published in 2012 and was on the *New York Times* bestseller list. As well as these multi-award winning works, he also wrote *Introduction to Modern Economic Growth* (2009) and *Economics* (together with David Laibson and John List, 2014).

Among the many awards that Daron Acemoğlu has won are Chicago University T. W. Schultz Prize (2004), American Society of Labor Economics Sherwin Rosen Prize (2004), American Economic Association John Bates Clark Medal (2005), Turkish Academy of Sciences (TÜBA) Academy Prize (2006), Rajk László College for Advanced Studies John von Neumann Award (2007), Galatasaray Prize (2012), Northwestern University Erwin Plein Nemmers Prize in Economics (2012), Kadir Has University Kadir Has Lifetime Contribution to Science Award (2013), Turkish Presidential Culture and Arts Grand Award (in the field of social sciences, 2013) and the BBVA Foundation Frontiers of Knowledge Award (2016). He has been awarded with honorary doctorate degrees by the École Normale Supérieure in Paris and by Utrecht, Bilkent, Bath, Boğaziçi and Athens Universities.

Acıman, Eli *(b. 1919, Istanbul - d. January 13, 2011, Istanbul)*, businessman who was founder of the modern advertising sector in Turkey. He served as member (1964-96) and president (1985-89) of the board of directors of the American Hospital(*).

https://www.pinterest.com.au/pin/321585848090911186/

After graduating from Istanbul Saint-Joseph French High School in 1936, Acıman went abroad to study journalism in 1939. On his return to Turkey, he started work in Mahmutpaşa in Istanbul. He made his debut in the advertising world in 1943 with the commercial campaign for Vitali Hakko's hat business "Şen Şapka". In 1944, he set up an advertising agency called Faal Reklam with Vitali Hakko and Mario Beghian, but his business partners left a short time later. After meeting Vehbi Koç(*) in 1946, he took charge of the publicity for Koç Ticaret. When Arif Erdemir and Nesim Matan joined Faal Reklam in 1957, it was incorporated and renamed Faal Ajans. Acıman went to the USA in the same year and worked as a copywriter and account representative at J. Walter Thompson advertising agency. Faal Ajans grew rapidly after his return from the USA in 1960. Following the breakup of the partnership in 1965, Acıman set up Manajans and Erdemir set up Yeni Ajans. Manajans played a crucial role in the development of the modern advertising sector in Turkey and served as a school for the new generation of advertising professionals. In 1985, following the partnership with J. Walter Thompson, the name of the agency was changed to Manajans/Thompson.

Acıman played a major role in founding the National Association of Advertising (Ulusal Reklamcılık Derneği) in 1972 and the Association of Advertising Agencies (Reklamcılar Derneği) in 1985. He was also the first president of the latter. He was one of the founding members of the Quincentennial Foundation (1989) of Turkish Jews. In 1990, he was awarded a gold medal by the European Association of Advertising Agencies. He retired in 2001.

His biography *Eli Acıman*, written by Nil Baransel, was published in 2003.

AÇEV, full name ANNE ÇOCUK EĞİTİM VAKFI (MOTHER CHILD EDUCATION FOUNDATION), civil society organization that aims to improve preschool education. In 2003, AÇEV received the Vehbi Koç Award(*) for education.

AÇEV began with a research project on preschool education, which was undertaken by professors Sevda Bekman, Çiğdem Kağıtçıbaşı and Diane Sunar from Boğaziçi University, Istanbul (1982-86). The research revealed that there was a major lack of work in the field and that many children received no education in their early childhood years. The academics who carried out the research set about improving the situation by developing and implementing an alternative "home-centered preschool education program" called the Mother Child Education Program (MOCEP). This work later developed into a more formal structure, leading to the establishment of AÇEV in Istanbul in 1993.

Since its foundation, AÇEV has developed and managed numerous projects and programs for adult and child education. In addition to MOCEP, which was transferred to the Ministry of Education in 2003, other significant projects and programs are: Mother Support Program, Father Support Program, Rural Education Program, Preschool Education, Family Letters, Preschool Parent Child Education Program, First Step to the Future, Educating Fathers for Violence-Free Families, All-Round Empowerment for Women, Functional Adult Literacy Program, and Advanced Literacy and Access to Knowledge. Other important campaigns are "7 is Too Late" and "You're My Dad". The organization also runs two online adult education campaigns, called "Me As well" and "Literacy at AÇEV", and a TV campaign entitled "Our Class". The Mother Support Program and MOCEP have been implemented in various other countries, such as Bahrain, Belgium, France, Germany, Jordan, Saudi Arabia and Switzerland. AÇEV is also a founding partner of the Center on the Developing Child at Harvard University. The organization was also one of the partners in a campaign with the theme "I Support Gender Equality", which took place in 2015-17 as part of a project called "For My Country" started by Koç Holding(*) in 2006.

AÇEV's activities are supported by numerous national and international public organizations, private companies and NGO's. In addition to a Family and Child Education Center, an Education and Cultural Center and a Child Development Center, AÇEV has offices in other cities such as Adana, Ankara and Izmir.

AÇEV President Ayşen Özyeğin at the award ceremony

In 2001, AÇEV received the Millennium Award from the National Women's Health Commission, followed in 2003 by the Vehbi Koç Award for its "work and contribution in the field of education". The Foundation's Functional Adult Literacy Program earned the UNESCO King Sejong Literacy Award in 2006 and the Qatar Foundation World Innovation Summit for Education (WISE) Award in 2010.

Adalya, annual history and archaeology journal published in Antalya by AKMED(*) since 1996. This peer-reviewed journal, denominated after an ancient name of the city, contains original articles in Turkish, English, French and German, about the history and archaeology of the region stretching from Fethiye to Antioch, including Ancient Lycia, Pamphylia, Pisidia and Cilicia. Along with publishing scholarly research, the journal also serves to document and protect the region's history and consider its relationship with the coastal cultures of the Mediterranean basin.

Adalya is indexed in the international citation indexes A&HCI (Arts & Humanities Citation Index) and CC/A&H (Current Contents/Arts & Humanities).

Adar, Yasemin, *(b. December 6, 1991, Balıkesir),* European and World Champion national wrestler, who received the Mustafa V. Koç Sports Award(*) in 2018.

Adar, who came from a family of wrestling enthusiasts, first became involved in sport at school, when she joined the school athletics team. After finishing high school, she studied at the Balıkesir University College of Physical Education and Sports and began wrestling at the Balıkesir Municipal Sports Center. While competing professionally as a wrestler with the Edirne Trakya Sports Club, Adar also worked as a physical education teacher in Niğde. In 2013, she won the gold medal in the 72 kg category at the Mersin Mediterranean Games. In Riga in 2016, she became the first Turkish female wrestler to win a gold medal at the European championships. She also won the European Championship in 2017 and 2018. At the World Wrestling Championships in Paris in 2017, Adar won a gold medal in the 75 kg category, becoming the first Turkish female wrestler to be world champion.

Adıyaman University Faculty of Education Vehbi Koç Building, faculty building constructed by the Vehbi Koç Foundation(*) (VKV). The faculty first opened as part of Gaziantep University in 1997-98. It moved to the new building built by VKV in the academic year 2006-07, when it became affiliated to Adıyaman University. Education programs in the fields of Classroom, Social Sciences, and Mathematics Teaching are conducted in the Vehbi Koç Building that can accommodate around 1,000 students.

http://egitim.adiyaman.edu.tr/Files/egitim/Resimler/5.JPG

Admiral Bristol Hospital Vehbi Koç Cancer Pavilion *see* **American Hospital**

The **Admiral Bristol Nursing School,** formally known as the ADMIRAL BRISTOL VOCATIONAL HIGH SCHOOL IN HEALTHCARE between 1981 and 1994, is a school established within the American Hospital(*) in 1920, management of which was transferred to the Vehbi Koç Foundation(*) (VKV) in February 1995, before being transferred again to Koç University(*) (KU) in 1999.

Nursing School students (1931-32)
Gülsevim Çeviker, *Amiral Bristol Hastanesi Hemşirelik Okulu Tarihi: 1920-1999* (The History of the Admiral Bristol Hospital Nursing School: 1920-1999), Koç University Publications, SANERC Books, No. 2, Istanbul, 2012, p. 51

When Admiral Mark L. Bristol(*) founded the American Hospital in May 1920, there was great difficulty in recruiting nurses. There were almost no nurses in Turkey, nor were there any educational institutions offering training for nurses. As a result of this, a school of nursing was opened in the hospital on August 20, 1920. One floor of the hospital building, located on Çarşıkapı Caddesi in Beyazıt, was reserved for the nursing school and Dr. Alden R. Hoover and Annie E. Rothrock assumed the posts of chief physician and chief nurse respectively. At the time, the school's course of study, formally known as the American Hospital Nursing Course, lasted two and a half years.

Producing its first graduates in 1923, it moved—together with the American Hospital—into the German Hospital on Taksim's Sıraselviler Caddesi that same year; in 1928, it moved to the Bedrettin Bey Apartments on Teşvikiye Caddesi, the modern-day home of the Istanbul Fashion Academy. In 1931, the school's course of study was extended to three years. Its name was formally changed to the American Hospital Nursing Training Course.

In 1945, following the death of Admiral Bristol in 1939, the school's name was changed to the Admiral Bristol Nursing School in his memory. In 1950, the school, which had been operating from the first floor of the east wing of the American Hospital in Nişantaşı throughout the 1940s, moved into a new building next door, built based upon a project organized by Sedad Hakkı Eldem(*). The four-story building provided space for training, teaching units, offices, student dormitories, bedrooms for executives and a range of other living and work spaces. That same year, together with three other nursing schools, including the Kızılay School of Nursing, the school received accreditation from the Ministry of Education (ME).

Management of the school had been undertaken by foreign nationals since its foundation. In 1948, a Turkish citizen was appointed chief deputy director alongside the foreign director. Esma (İbrahim) Deniz, who graduated from the school in 1924, held the post of chief deputy director from 1948 to 1952, later becoming the school's first Turkish director between 1952 and 1954.

The school extended its course of study to four years in 1957, becoming a vocational high school, and became known as the Admiral Bristol Hospital Private Nursing Health College. In February 1976, the school was bestowed with private school status by the ME and was registered as the Admiral Bristol Vocational High School in Private Nursing. In 1981, the ME changed its name to the Admiral Bristol Vocational High School in Healthcare.

From its foundation, the School of Nursing had operated with the support of various foreign and local institutions; it began to struggle as a result of a reduction in available funds, stopping its four-year nursing courses in 1994. Despite this, beginning in the 1992-93 academic year, a two-year post-high school Finishing Course in Nursing came into effect with approval from the ME. The Semahat Arsel Nursing Education & Research Center (*see* SANERC) was established within the American Hospital in 1992.

Thus, the Admiral Bristol Nursing School, which had been acquired by the VKV in February 1995, attained a management structure which was independent from the American Hospital. In September 1996, it moved into a new building on Teşvikiye Büyükçiftlik Sokak. The school affiliated with KU in 1999 and became the Koç University School of Nursing (*).

SANERC and the KU School of Nursing began

Admiral Bristol Nursing School, Nişantaşı, Istanbul (1950-96) Warren H. Winkler and George D. Rountree, *American Hospital* (1920-2007), American Hospital Publications, İstanbul 2012, p. 93

operating from the new Semahat & Dr. Nusret Arsel School of Nursing building, built on the former site of the Güzelbahçe Hospital and completed in 2002 with the help of a 10 million dollar endowment from Semahat Arsel(*) and Dr. Nurset Arsel(*). The former School of Nursing on Büyükçiftlik Sokak was transformed into a dormitory for students of the KU School of Nursing. The academy moved to the Koç University Health Sciences Campus(*) in Topkapı in July 2015 and gained college status, keeping its name as the Koç University School of Nursing (*see* Koç University) in 2016.

Adolescent Days Congress, conference that took place on December 13, 2017 with the support of the Vehbi Koç Foundation(*). The congress, held at Koç University Hospital(*) in Istanbul, was organized by the Turkish Association for Child and Adolescent Psychiatry in cooperation with the Koç University School of Medicine Department of Child and Adolescent Mental Health and Illness. The congress, with the theme of Psychotherapeutic Approaches for Adolescents, debated the specific adaption of psychotherapeutic approaches to the psychological features of adolescents.

Advan, Satia *(b. October 15, 1966, Diyarbakır),* physician and administrator. Served as acting chief physician of the American Hospital(*) between 2006 and 2008.

Advan graduated from Diyarbakır Anatolian High School in 1983 and Istanbul University Faculty of Medicine in 1990. Following her compulsory service in Adıyaman (1991), she worked as a general practitioner at various public hospitals in Istanbul. In 1998, she completed her residency in public health at Istanbul University Faculty of Medicine. After joining the staff of the American Hospital in 1999, Dr. Advan went on to become the responsible director in 2003 and deputy chief physician in 2006. After leaving the American hospital in 2008, she worked at the Jinemed Medical Center (2008-09; chief physician), Acıbadem Hospital (2009-10; assistant medical director), Istanbul Cerrahi Hospital (2010-12; chief physician) and Anadolu Health Center (2012-15; chief physician). In 2016, she was appointed medical director of MedAmerikan Health Center(*).

Adventure İstiklal Contemporary Art Exhibition Series, contemporary art exhibitions held in the Yapı Kredi Kâzım Taşkent Art Gallery between 2007 and 2010.

Curated by René Block(*) with the consultancy of Melih Fereli(*), the project encompassed 11 exhibitions of works by artists who were influential on the contemporary art scene in Turkey. The Contemporary Art in Turkey Series(*), containing monographs of artists who have taken part in the project, was published by Yapı Kredi Culture Arts and Publishing in parallel with the exhibitions.

EXHIBITIONS HELD UNDER THE HEADING "ADVENTURE İSTİKLAL"

- **Lâhavle** *(April 5–May 5, 2007)* Hale Tenger
- **Erratum Musicale** *(September 7–October 6, 2007)* Füsun Onur
- **sineması/cineması** *(October 26–November 25, 2007)* Gülsün Karamustafa
- **Ups and Downs** *(May 16–July 15, 2008)* Ayşe Power
- **I'm not sure if this is an exhibition** *(September 18–October 5, 2008)* Halil Altındere
- **Elina Brotherus** *(October 11–November 29, 2008)* Elina Brotherus
- **What time is it?** *(December 18, 2008–January 31, 2009)* Cengiz Çekil
- **Collective Notice** *(May 15–July 31, 2009)* Nasan Tur
- **Olga Çernişeva** *(September 9–October 11, 2009)* Olga Çernişeva
- **Passengers** *(May 13–June 20, 2010)* Esra Ersen
- **An Icon** *(September 3–October 20, 2010)* Sarkis

Ahunbay, Zeynep *(b. June 20, 1946, Ünye, Ordu),* architect and architectural historian who received the Vehbi Koç Award(*) for culture in 2017. She is known for her work on the conservation of cultural heritage and restoration.

Ahunbay completed her secondary education at Arnavutköy American College for Girls (*see* Robert College) in Istanbul in 1965 and received her bachelor's and master's degrees as a civil engineer-architect from Istanbul Technical University's (ITU) Faculty of Architecture in 1970. In 1971, she became an academic assistant in the same faculty's Department of Architectural History and Restoration. She received a PhD in 1975 with her work on the Sultanahmet Complex. She completed specialist training on conservation at York University in England in the academic year 1977-78 with her work on the archaeology and conservation of the ancient city of Side. She became associate professor in 1980, and professor in December 1988 with her work on "The Educational Buildings of the Architect, Sinan". She retired from ITU Faculty of Architecture Department of Restoration in 2013.

Prof. Ahunbay has directed conservation and restoration projects in numerous places, from Istanbul to Edirne, Bursa, Gaziantep, Safranbolu, Tarsus, Samsat and Hasankeyf. These included the Temple of Apollo in Side, the Marmara University Rectorate Building, Istanbul land walls between T1 and T5, Zeyrek Mosque, Bursa Green Tomb and the Uzunkemer restoration projects. Her restoration work on the southwest corner of Istanbul's Hagia Sophia, which she carried out with her husband, Prof. Metin Ahunbay, was given the Restoration Merit Award in the 8th National Architectural Awards program of the Chamber of Architects of Turkey.

The selection committee of the Vehbi Koç Award, which she received in 2017 for her work on the conservation and restoration of cultural assets, said: "Professor Ahunbay is a scholar who has developed a unique approach to protect a vast range of cultural heritage from archaeological sites to Ottoman buildings, and exemplified it in the restoration projects she has undertaken. She is one of the top experts in conservation in the world. A vanguard of architectural heritage conservation in Turkey, Ahunbay has trained numerous students and thereby contributed to the development of this field as a solid discipline."

Prof. Ahunbay served two terms as chairperson of the International Council on Monuments and Sites (ICOMOS) Turkey National Committee from 1999 to 2005. She is also a member of the Chamber of Architects of Turkey and Europa Nostra-Turkey. She currently plays an active role on the advisory boards for monuments such as Hagia Sophia and the Great Mosque of Diyarbakır.

In addition to many articles, Prof. Ahunbay has also published several books. These include *Tarihi Çevre Koruma ve Restorasyon* (1966; Conservation and Restoration of the Historical Environment), the section on Istanbul in *Dünya Mirasında Türkiye* (2006; Turkey in the World Heritage), and *Cultural Heritage of Turkey* (2009).

Prof. Zeynep Ahunbay at the award ceremony with Ömer M. Koç

Akgül, Taha *(b. November 22, 1990, Sivas)*, Olympic and world champion national wrestler. Received the Mustafa V. Koç Sports Award(*), together with national archer Gizem Girişmen(*) in 2017, the year of the award's introduction.

Akgül, who began wrestling in 2003, is a graduate of the Karamanoğlu Mehmetbey University College of Physical Education and Sports and completed his master's degree at Sivas Cumhuriyet University.

He won a gold medal in the freestyle 120 kg category at the European Wrestling Championships in 2012 and 2013. In 2014 and 2015, he won gold medals in the European Wrestling Championships and World Wrestling Championships freestyle 125 kg category. He was an Olympic winner in 2016 in the same category. In 2017, he was the European Champion and came second in the World Championships. He became the European Champion once again in 2018.

He received the Sedat Simavi Sports Award in 2016, followed in 2017 by the Mustafa V. Koç Sports Award, which he received together with Paralympic Games and world champion national archer Gizem Girişmen. They were nominated for "their embodiment of all the Olympic values and worldwide sporting success, achieved through the determination, discipline and commitment shown in their work."

Akın, İlhan *(b. 1927, Izmir)*, lawyer and academician. He was a member of the Vehbi Koç Foundation(*) Board of Directors between 1978 and 1996.

He graduated from Istanbul University (IU) Faculty of Law in 1950. After completing a PhD at Paris Faculty of Law, he began working at Istanbul University Faculty of Law, in the Departments of Public International Law and Public Law. He became professor in 1966. He was elected dean of IU Faculty of Law in 1972. After being elected for three consecutive terms, he held the post until 1980, while at the time lecturing at the IU Faculty of Political Sciences. He was elected dean of the Faculty of Law again in 1986 and stayed in post until 1994. Prof. Akın served as a member in the presidential contingent of The Council of Higher Education (YÖK) General Board and Supervisory Board (1993-95). He also sat on the Press Advertising Council and the board of directors of the Turkish Radio and Television Corporation (TRT).

He published several books, including, *Türk Devrimi Tarihi* (1966; History of the Turkish Revolution), *Kamu Hukuku* (1979; Public Law), *Siyasi Tarih 1870-1914* (1983; Political History 1870-1914) and *Devlet Doktrinleri* (2013; State Doctrines).

AKMED, until 2016 known by its full name of THE SUNA AND İNAN KIRAÇ RESEARCH CENTER FOR MEDITERRANEAN CIVILIZATIONS, an international cultural organization set up to support research, documentation, restoration and conservation work related to the history, archaeology, ethnography and culture of Antalya and the surrounding area and encourage scholarly studies into the interrelations in the region of the Mediterranean shores. It was founded by the Vehbi Koç Foundation(*) in 1996 in Kaleiçi, Antalya. As Turkey's first and only dedicated research body based in the Mediterranean area, AKMED has operated in conjunction with Koç University since 2016.

İnan (LEFT) **and Suna Kıraç opening AKMED, 1996**
AKMED Archive

AKMED was established in Antalya's Kaleiçi area, which is under protection as an archaeological and historical site, after Suna Kıraç(*) and İnan Kıraç(*) restored a traditional Antalya house with an old adjoining church in the same building complex between 1993 and 1995. When the existing building became insufficient for current needs, another adjoining historical building became part of the organization's premises in 1999. In 2014, another Kaleiçi house was restored to meet the requirements of the AKMED library.

The first two of these buildings house the Kaleiçi Museum(*), which is run as part of AKMED. The third building, which houses the institute center and library, is a late example of an L-shaped, two-story traditional Turkish house with an external anteroom. A large part of the house had been destroyed before it was renovated, both in keeping with traditional Kaleiçi architecture and in line with the requirements of a contemporary library. The top floor of the building is given over to periodicals, rare books and study rooms, while the lower floor contains the library galleries, office and cafe. On the upper level of the building that was annexed later, there is an exhibition room and the lower level houses a conference area. As well as containing libraries, the last building added to the AKMED complex also includes work spaces, archives and a pioneering numismatic book collection of national significance.

Researchers can make use of the AKMED's collection of 25,000 works, one of the most important specialist collections on the history and archaeology of the Anatolian Mediterranean area, as well as its valuable, ever-growing collection of rare books and archives of documents, photographs and dia-positives. The organization's annual program covers a wide variety of academic and cultural events, such as congresses, symposiums, conferences, seminars, public viewings of archaeological films, exhibitions and concerts. The center provides education and research grants to many undergraduate and postgraduate students. It also supports excavation, restoration and ground surveys in the Anatolian Mediterranean area.

AKMED organized the First International Congress on Monetary History and Numismatics in February 2013 and a second one in January 2017. As well as publishing the annual periodicals *Adalya*(*) and *ANMED*(*), AKMED has also published a number of books.

General view of AKMED
AKMED Archive

AKMED PUBLICATIONS

- Abut, Ahmet (ed.), *Fotoğraflarla Atatürk/ Atatürk en Photos/Atatürk with Photos*, Istanbul, 1998
- Akalın, Şebnem and Bilgi, Hülya Yılmaz, *Suna ve İnan Kıraç Koleksiyonunda Kütahya Seramikleri: Yadigâr-ı Kütahya* (Kütahya Ceramics in the Suna and İnan Kıraç Collection: Delights of Kütahya), Istanbul, 1997
- Alçıtepe, Galip, *Antalya'da İki Öncü Dergi* (Two Leading Journals in Antalya), Antalya, 2005
- Altun, Ara et al., *Çanakkale Seramikleri/ Çanakkale Ceramics*, Istanbul, 1996
- Atay, Çınar, *19. Yüzyıl İzmir Fotoğrafları* (19th Century Izmir Photos), Istanbul, 1997
- Aydın, Ayşe, *Lahit Formlu Rölikerler/Reliquaries of the Sarcophagus Type*, Antalya, 2011
- Aygün, Çakır Afşin, *Andriake Mureks Boya Endüstrisi/Andriake Murex Dye Industry*, Istanbul, 2016
- Bayburtluoğlu, Cevdet, *Lykia* (Lycia), Istanbul, 2004
- Beaufort, Francis, *Karamanya* (Karamania, Turkish translation), Istanbul, 2002
- Belli, Oktay, *Anadolu'da Kalay ve Bronzun Tarihçesi* (History of Tin and Bronze in Anatolia), Istanbul, 2004
- Borchhardt, Jürgen et al., *Kerththi oder der Versuch, eine antike Siedlung der Klassik in Zentrallykien zu identifizieren* (Kerththi or the Attempt to Identify an Ancient Classical Settlement in Central Lycia), Istanbul, 2005
- Borchhardt, Jürgen and Bleibtreu, Erika, *Strukturen lykischer Residenzstädte im Vergleich zu älteren Städten des Vorderen Orients* (Comparison of Lycian Central Administrative Cities with Early Cities of Asia Minor), Antalya, 2013
- Çevik, Nevzat et al. (ed.), *Trebenna: Tarihi, Arkeolojisi ve Doğası/Trebenna: History, Archaeology and Natural Environment*, Istanbul, 2005
- Çevik, Nevzat, *Lykia Kitabı* (The Book of Lycia), Istanbul, 2015
- Çokay-Kepçe, Sedef, *Antalya Karaçallı Nekropolü/ The Karaçallı Necropolis near Antalya*, Istanbul, 2006
- Danieloğlu, Dimitri E., *1850 Yılında Yapılan Bir Pamphylia Seyahati* (A Trip to Pamphylia in 1850), Antalya, 2010
- Delemen, İnci et al. (ed.), *Prof. Dr. Haluk Abbasoğlu'na 65. Yaş Armağanı - Euergetes/ Festschrift für Prof. Dr. Haluk Abbasoğlu zum 65. Geburtstag – Euergetes* (65th Birthday Present for Prof. Haluk Abbasoğlu), Istanbul, 2008
- Dostoğlu, Neslihan Türkün, *Osmanlı Döneminde Bursa. 19. Yüzyıl Ortalarından 20. Yüzyıla Bursa Fotoğrafları*/Bursa à l'Époque Ottomane,

Photographies de Bursa Milieu du XIXéme au XXéme siècle/Bursa in the Ottoman Period, Photographs of Bursa from Mid-19th to the 20th Century, *Istanbul, 2001*

- **Dörtlük, Kayhan et al. (ed.),** ***III. Uluslararası Likya Sempozyumu: Sempozyum Bildirileri/ III. International Lycia Symposium: Proceedings 2 Vol.,*** *Istanbul, 2007*
- **Dörtlük, Kayhan and Boyraz, Remziye,** ***Çanakkale Seramikleri Kolokyumu Bildirileri*** **(Çanakkale Ceramics Colloquium Proceedings),** *Antalya, 2008*
- **Dörtlük, Kayhan and Boyraz, Remziye,** ***Gezginlerin Gözüyle Antalya/Aus dem Blickwinkel von alten Reisenden*** **(Antalya through the Eyes of Travelers),** *Antalya, 2008*
- **Dörtlük, Kayhan et al. (ed.),** ***Uluslararası Genç Bilimciler Buluşması I: Anadolu Akdenizi Sempozyum Bildirileri 4-7 Kasım 2009/International Young Scholars Conference I: Mediterranean Anatolia Symposium Proceedings 4-7 November 2009,*** *Antalya, 2012*
- **Dörtlük, Kayhan et al. (ed.),** ***Birinci Uluslararası Anadolu Para Tarihi ve Numismatik Kongresi. Bildiriler/First International Congress on Monetary History and Numismatics Proceedings,*** *Istanbul, 2014*
- **Duru, Refik,** ***MÖ 8000'den MÖ 2000'e Burdur-Antalya Bölgesinin Altıbin Yılı*** **(6000 Years of the Burdur-Antalya Region from 8 BC to 2 BC),** *Istanbul, 2008*
- **Duru, Refik,** ***Elli Yıllık Bir Arkeoloji Öyküsü: Hacılar*** **(A Fifty Year Archaeology Tale: Hacılar),** *Antalya, 2010*
- **Durugönül, Serra (ed.),** ***Dağlık Kilikia'da Bir Antik Kent Kazısının Sonuçları: Nagidos/Nagidos: Results of an Excavation in an Ancient City in Rough Cilicia,*** *Istanbul, 2007*
- **Eschbach, Norbert and Martini, Wolfram,** ***Akropolis von Perge*** **(The Perga Acropolis),** *Antalya, 2017*
- **Işık, Fahri,** ***Doğa Ana Kubaba. Tanrıçaların Ege'de Buluşması*** **(Mother Nature Kubaba. Meeting of the Goddesses in the Aegean),** *Istanbul, 1999*
- **Kavas, Kemal Reha,** ***Akdeniz Dağlık Yerleşimindeki Kırsal Mimari Gelenekte Çevre Estetiği: Ürünlü (Akseki-İbradı Havzası)/Environmental Aesthetics of the Rural Architectural Tradition in the Mediterranean Highlander Settlement: Ürünlü (Akseki-İbradı Basin),*** *Istanbul, 2016*
- **Kaymak, Gamze,** ***Antalya Cumanın Camii: Mimari Tarihi ve Bizans Kökeni Rölöve-Yapı Analizi - Anıt Koruma ve Bakımı/Die Cumanın Camii in Antalya: Ihre Baugeschichte und ihre byzantinischen Ursprünge Bauaufnahme-Bauforschung – Denkmalpflege*** **(Antalya Cumanın Mosque: Architectural History and Byzantine Origin Relevé–Structural Analysis – Conservation and Maintenance of the Monument),** *Antalya, 2009*
- **Koch, Guntram,** ***Türkiye'deki Roma İmparatorluk Dönemi Lahitleri/Sarkophage der Römischen Kaiserzeit in der Türkei*** **(Roman Tombs/Sarcophagi in Turkey),** *Antalya, 2010*
- **Kürkman, Garo,** ***Anadolu Ağırlık ve Ölçüleri/ Anatolian Weights and Measures,*** *Istanbul, 2003*
- **Lanckoronski, Karl Graf,** ***Pamphylia ve Pisidia Kentleri. 1. Cilt: Pamphylia*** **(The Cities of Pamphylia and Pisidia, Vol. 1: Pamphylia),** *Istanbul, 2005*
- **Lanckoronski, Karl Graf,** ***Pamphylia ve Pisidia Kentleri, 2. Cilt: Pisidia*** **(The Cities of Pamphylia and Pamphylia, Vol. 2: Pisidia),** *Istanbul, 2015*
- **Nollé, Johannes,** ***Sikkeler, Ağaçlar ve Alimler: Selge. Pisidia'nın Dağ Şehrinde Bir "Doğa Tapınağı"*** **(Coins, Trees and Scholars: Selge. A 'Temple to Nature' in the Mountain City of Pisidia),** *Istanbul, 2015*
- **Onur, Bekir,** ***Müze Eğitimi Seminerleri I: Akdeniz Bölgesi Müzeleri*** **(Museum Education Seminars I. Museums of the Mediterranean Region),** *Antalya, 2003*
- **Öney, Gönül,** ***Akdenizle Kucaklaşan Osmanlı Seramikleri ve Günümüze Ulaşan Yansımaları/ Ottoman Ceramics Embracing the Mediterranean and Their Reflections to the Present,*** *Antalya, 2009*
- **Özdizbay, Aşkım,** ***Perge'nin M.S. 1.-2. Yüzyıllardaki Gelişimi/Die Stadtentwicklung von Perge im 1-2. Jh. N.Chr.*** **(The Growth of Perge 1-2 AD),** *Antalya, 2012*
- **Özüsağlam-Mutlu, Zeynep,** ***Principatus Devri'nde Lykia ve Pamphylia Kökenli Roma Senatörleri*** **(Roman Senators of Lycian and Pamphylian Origin during the Principate),** *Antalya, 2013*
- **Recke, Matthias,** ***In loco Murtana, ubi olim Perge sita fuit: Der Beginn archaologischer Forschungen in Pamphylien und die Kleinasien-Expedition Gustav Hirschfelds 1874/ Pamphylia'daki Arkeolojik Araştırmaların Başlangıcı ve Gustav Hirschfeld'in 1874 Yılı Küçük Asya Araştırma Gezisi*** **(The Start of Archaeological Study in Pamphylia and the Asia Minor Expedition of Gustav Hirschfield 1874),** *Antalya, 2007*
- **Redford, Scott and Leiser, Gary,** ***Taşa Yazılan Zafer: Antalya İçkale Surlarındaki Selçuklu Fetihnamesi/ Victory Inscribed: Seljuk Fetihname on the Citadel Walls of Antalya,*** *Istanbul, 2008*
- **Soustiel, Laure and Garnot, Nicolas Sainte Fare,** ***Osmanlı Seramiklerinin Görkemi, XVI.-XIX. Yüzyıl*** **(The Grandeur of Ottoman Ceramics, 16th to 19th centuries),** *Istanbul, 2000*
- **Spratt, T.A.B. and Forbes, Edward,** ***Milyas, Kibyratis ve Likya'da Yolculuklar*** **(Journeys in Milyas, Kibriyatis and Lycia)** ***2 Vol.,*** *Istanbul, 2008*
- **Şahin, Hamdi et al. (ed.),** ***Özsait Armağanı: Mehmet ve Nesrin Özsait Onuruna Sunulan Makaleler/Studies Presented to Mehmet and Nesrin Özsait,*** *Antalya, 2011*
- **Şahin, Nuran,** ***Zeus'un Anadolu Kültleri*** **(Anatolian Cults of Zeus),** *Istanbul, 2001*

- Tansel, Oğuz, *Zakkum Çiçeği Tan Yerinde: Antalya Dolayları Üzerine Şiirler/At the Dawn of Oleander Blossoms: Poems on Antalya Environs*, Antalya, 2011
- Tekin, Oğuz and Tekin, Nil Türker, *Mülteci Bir Akdemisyenin Biyografisi, Clemens Emin Bosch (1899-1955)/Biography of a Refugee Academician, Clemens Emin Bosch (1899-1955)*, Istanbul, 2007
- Tekocak, Mehmet (ed.), *K. Levent Zoroğlu'na Armağan/ Studies in Honor of K. Levent Zoroğlu*, Istanbul, 2013
- Türker, Ayşe Ç., *Demre-Myra Aziz Nikolaos Kilisesi Bizans Dönemi Sırsız Seramikleri/ Byzantine Unglazed Pottery of Saint Nicholas Church at Demre-Myra*, Antalya, 2009
- Uçkan, B. Yelda Olcay (ed.), *Olympos 1, 2000-2014 Araştırma Sonuçları* (Olympos 1, 2000-2014 Research Findings), Antalya, 2017
- Urfalıoğlu, Nur, *Antalya, Isparta ve Burdur Evlerinde Cephe Biçimlenişi* (Facade Formation of Antalya, Isparta and Burdur Houses), Antalya 2010
- Winiewicz-Wolska, Joanna, *Jacek Malczewski'nin Anadolu'ya Yolculuğu/Jacek Malczewski's Journey to Anatolia*, Antalya, 2014

TWO LETTERS FROM İNAN KIRAÇ

June 3, 1991

My Dear Suna,

Today is June 3, 1991... The day you become 50. You have spent 24 of those years with me. I love you and have shared my finest memories, all my happiness with you.

Having looked at my financial situation, this year I am able to buy you a historical church in the Barbaros district of Antalya.

The name of your dear mother lives on today through the Sadberk Hanım Museum and many works of our cultural heritage are protected under its roof. You and her other children have done everything you can to ensure that these works survive.

My only wish is that this house of God is turned into a museum named after you. You can be absolutely sure that I will do whatever is necessary to get the required permission for this and for the building's restoration.

My dear Suna, I am writing a letter to our daughter İpek along with this letter. Just like you, she will be a child worthy of her mother and will look after the institution established in your name; she will make it even more perfect and leave it to her children.

Suna, I wish you a happy birthday and wish us many more happy years together.

With all my love,

İnan Kıraç

June 3, 1991

My Dear İpek,

Today is June 3, 1991... Your mother's 50th birthday. On June 7, you will have finished the first grade of elementary school.

I've bought your mother a church in Barbaros Street in Kaleiçi, Antalya. We have loved it for a long time but not had the opportunity to buy it until now. As I wrote to her in a letter attached to this one, I am giving her the building as a birthday present. I will also do my utmost to restore the building and have it turned into a museum.

What I ask of you is that you give your material and moral support to keeping it going and making it even grander for as long as you live.

My dear İpek, your mother played a huge role in the growth of the Sadberk Hanım Museum; I have absolutely no doubt that you will do the same for the place named after her and work as hard as possible to keep it alive and develop it further.

İnan Kıraç

Suna Kıraç, *Ömrümden Uzun İdeallerim Var* (My Ideals, Longer Than My Lifetime), Suna and İnan Kıraç Foundation Publications, Istanbul, 2006, pp. 230-31

AKMED: THE FULFILLMENT OF A COMMITMENT...

Suna Kıraç considered the Research Center for Mediterranean Civilizations as her "first sweetheart", founding it in Antalya, a place of incomparable cultural heritage and the cradle of Mediterranean Civilization. Suna Kıraç discussed the idea for the institute with archaeologists, historians and academics while visiting excavations at important archaeological sites in Antalya. Believing that the institute should be "not local but universal" she finally decided on a name that alluded to the Mediterranean in general rather than just Antalya.

The concept of the research center was inspired by an institute in Marseille. In fact, the true response to the historical call of the Marseillais should have risen from the ancient cultural heritage of Antalya and the lands that gave birth to the Ottoman Empire. The Marseillais, who drove Mediterranean trade and acted as ambassadors on behalf of the king, called for a common Mediterranean history through their chambers of commerce:

"All the countries bordering the Mediterranean should establish an institute of Mediterranean civilization in order to unite our histories. Through mutual exchanges of information, we can break new ground on the shared history of the Mediterranean

and strengthen each other through academic solidarity between the institutes."

This call was answered by the major cities of the Mediterranean, following which institutes established in Morocco, Egypt, Dubai, Lebanon, Spain, former Yugoslavia, and Italian cities such as Venice, Florence and Pisa played a prominent role in the research of Mediterranean civilization. All the while, as a large part of the historical archives of the Mediterranean countries had previously been brought to the Ottoman capital, the main resource lay in the state archives of Istanbul. It was Turkey that had given the idea to the Marseillais, so it was all the more strange that this proposal, that met with a response in other Mediterranean countries, did not get off the ground in Turkey. The founding of AKMED was, in some part, the fulfillment of this commitment several years later.

Suna Kıraç, *Ömrümden Uzun İdeallerim Var* (My Ideals, Longer Than My Lifetime), Suna and İnan Kıraç Foundation Publications, Istanbul, 2006, pp. 232-33

Aksoy, Erdal M(ehmet) *(b. May 11, 1974, Istanbul)*, physician and director. Chief physician and medical director at the Koç University Hospital(*) since 2015.

Aksoy graduated from the Beşiktaş Atatürk Anatolian High School in Istanbul (1988-92), before receiving medical training at Istanbul University Faculty of Medicine (1992-98). He received a master's degree in Health Management from Istanbul Bilgi University (2011) and is still (2018) continuing his residency at the Istanbul University Institute of Forensic Sciences.

After beginning his working life as the workplace physician at Emlak Bank in 1999, Dr. Aksoy went on to work at Motorola Turkey and the Özel Haznedar Hospital. In 2003, he started work at the Koç University(*) Health Center as responsible director. Moving to the American Hospital(*) as deputy responsible director in 2008, he later served as responsible director (2010-14). In 2015, he was appointed chief physician and medical director at Koç University Hospital.

Aktar, Emin *see* **Koç Family**

Aktar, Hüsniye *see* **Koç Family**

Aktar, Sadullah *see* **Koç Family**

Ali, Filiz *(b. September 30, 1937, Istanbul)*, pianist, musicologist, music critic and writer who won the Vehbi Koç Award(*) for culture in 2011, together with the Ayvalık International Music Academy(*) (AIMA) of which she was a founder.

The daughter of Aliye and Sabahattin Ali, one of the greatest authors of Turkish literature, Filiz Ali studied in the Ankara State Conservatory Piano Department, graduating from the class of Ferhunde Erkin in 1958. She went to the USA on a Fulbright Scholarship to continue her musical education at the New England Conservatory of Music in Boston and the Mannes College of Music in New York. After receiving a Chevening Scholarship, she studied for a master's degree at the Musicology Department of King's College at London University (1985-86).

She worked at the Ankara State Conservatory as piano and accompaniment lecturer (1962-65), the Istanbul City Opera and Istanbul State Opera as repetiteur (1965-72), and the Mimar Sinan University State Conservatory as piano and accompaniment lecturer (1972-85). She became head of Mimar Sinan University State Conservatory Musicology Department in 1990, remaining in post there until her retirement in 2005. She later taught at Sabancı University.

Alongside her academic work, Filiz Ali also produced programs for TRT, including World Folk Songs, Piano Literature, Vocal Music and Jazz Today. She wrote on music for the newspapers *Cumhuriyet*, *Hürriyet*, *Yeni Yüzyıl*, *Radikal* and *Milliyet*. She was general arts manager at the Cemal Reşit Rey Concert Hall (1989-92) and has been musical advisor for the Eskişehir International Festival since 1995. In 1998, she founded the Ayvalık International Music Academy with the aim of providing master classes for conservatory level students from Turkey and abroad, giving talented young people the chance to work with renowned leading musicians from Europe and Turkey.

She is a member of the Balkan Music Forum and Turkey's representative on the International

Prof. Filiz Ali at the award ceremony with Semahat Arsel

Music Council and European Music Council. She has also written a number of books on music and musicians: *Müzik ve Müziğimizin Sorunları* (1987; Music and the Problems of Our Music), *Dünyadan ve Türkiye'den Müzisyen Portreleri* (1994; Portraits of Musicians from Turkey and the World), *Cemal Reşit Rey Unutulmaz Marşın Büyük Bestecisi* (1996; Cemal Reşit Rey: The Great Composer of the Unforgettable Anthem), *Ferhunde Erkin Tuşlar Arasında...* (2000; Ferhunde Erkin, Among the Keys), *Elektronik Müziğin Öncüsü Bülent Arel* (2002; Bülent Arel: Electronic Music Pioneer), *Mitos Diyarında Çağdaş Bir Müzik Odağı: Ayvalık'tan Bir Masterclass Öyküsü* (2008; A Modern Music Focus in the Land of Myths: Tale of a Masterclass from Ayvalık), *Müzikli Geziler* (2012; Musical Travels). She has written two books about her father: *Sabahattin Ali* (1979), written together with Atilla Özkırımlı, followed by an expanded new edition, *Sabahattin Ali; Anılar, İncelemeler, Eleştiriler* (2014; Sabahattin Ali; Memoirs, Studies, Criticisms) written with Atilla Özkırımlı and Sevengül Sönmez; and *"Filiz Hiç Üzülmesin" Sabahattin Ali'nin Objektifinden, Kızı Filiz'in Gözünden BirYaşamöyküsü* (1995; "Filiz, Don't be Sad" A Life-Story Written from the Objective of Sabahattin Ali in the Eyes of His Daughter Filiz). Filiz Ali's memoirs, *Yok Bi'şey, Acımadı ki...* (It's Nothing, It Didn't Hurt...), were published in 2017.

In 1995, the French Ministry of Culture made Filiz Ali a Knight of the Order of Arts and Letters (Chevalier de l'Ordre des Arts et des Lettres). In 2015, she received an Award of Honor at the 43rd Istanbul Music Festival, organized by the Istanbul Foundation for Culture and Arts (İKSV), in appreciation of her work on polyphonic Western music.

Alisbah, Hulki *(b. 1903, Sivas - d. May 1, 1985, Istanbul)*, director who played an important role in the establishment of Koç Holding(*) and the Vehbi Koç Foundation(*) (VKV), working in various roles across the Koç companies. He served on the Vehbi Koç Foundation(*) Board of Directors between 1969 and 1985.

After graduating from the Mekteb-i Mülkiye (today's Ankara University Faculty of Political Sciences), he was appointed to the district administration in Edirne. In 1925, after passing the necessary exam, he became assistant auditor at the Divan-ı Muhasebat (today's Turkish Court of Accounts). He left in 1931, going on to work in various roles at Ziraat Bank (1932-40) and ultimately rising to the post of assistant general manager. In early 1941, he was appointed general manager of the Turkish Grain Board. He also served as general manager of Sümerbank (1942-44) and of İller Bank (1948-49). After leaving his last position for political reasons, he accepted the offer of Vehbi Koç(*), an acquaintance from previous years, to take the position of general manager at Koç Ticaret AŞ. When Koç Holding was formed in 1963, he was brought in as general coordinator and continued in that role until his retirement in 1975. He continued to serve on the boards of Koç Holding companies and VKV until his death on May 1, 1985.

"HULKİ ALİSBAH WAS AN INCREDIBLE PERSON..."

As well as being a close friend, Hulki Alisbah was an exemplary manager, who I knew to be industrious and efficient with a meticulous and thorough work ethic. We worked together for 26 years from 1949 to 1975. In the following years, he served on the boards of directors of companies in the Koç Group as well as in the Foundation management; we were together without a pause until his death. Our friendship had begun much earlier. Before coming to us, Hulki Alisbah had given 26 years of service to the state. He came to us as an extremely experienced and knowledgeable bureaucrat who had distinguished himself as Ziraat Bank Assistant General Manager, and

as General Manager of the Turkish Grain Board, Sümerbank and İller Bank. In our early founding years, when there was a shortage of experienced people, Hulki Alisbah was one of the advisors from whom I derived the most benefit. It was a huge boon to have at my side someone of such maturity who had vast experience of the highest echelons of government financial bodies. I consulted Hulki Alisbah on all my major initiatives and followed his advice. During the second half of the 1940s, I discussed every economic issue I took to the Party Caucus with him and Cafer Tüzel beforehand so I didn't upset İsmet Pasha [İsmet İnönü]. In those days, he was still working for the state and he was one of the few people whose opinions I could rely on. I used to invite him to my house and he'd come along; we were at most three to four people. We would talk at length about the economic woes of our country and discuss the remedies. Right back then, he drew my attention for his ability to view matters from a wide perspective and offer consistently rational and practical suggestions.

He came to us in 1949 after his retirement and became general manager of Koç Ticaret AŞ. Over the 26 years that we worked together, he made a huge contribution to the growth of the Koç Group. He did the preparatory work on the Koç Holding project and was also instrumental in giving its final shape. He supported and developed my idea to set up a foundation to institutionalize our social endeavors, preparing the Foundation's deed of trust himself. We always benefited from his knowledge and experience when we were setting up our large industrial enterprises; in short, Hulki Alisbah had been an inseparable part of us. Our companionship lasted until 1975, the year he completed his 52nd year of work. We lost him on May 1, 1985. He was still one of my closest friends and his death brought me great pain. Something of yourself is buried and disappears whenever someone you love dies.

Vehbi Koç, *Hatıralarım Görüşlerim Öğütlerim (Recollections, Observations, Counsel, 1973-1987)*, Vehbi Koç Foundation Publications, Istanbul, 1987, pp. 40-41

The **American Hospital,** officially known as the VEHBİ KOÇ FOUNDATION AMERICAN HOSPITAL, was founded in 1920 in Istanbul, before being taken over by the Vehbi Koç Foundation(*) (VKV) and established as a private medical institution in 1995.

The history of American hospitals in Turkey goes back to the nineteenth century. Beginning in the mid-century, the American Board of Commissioners for Foreign Missions (ABCFM) founded dispensaries and hospitals in towns and cities with missionary centers, such as Adana, Merzifon, Sivas, Talas (Kayseri), Harput, Van, Mardin and Diyarbakır; these were established close to schools and were typically referred to as American hospitals. According to some sources, there were nine American hospitals in Anatolia in 1914.

Istanbul's first American Hospital was founded in 1905 by Dr. Thomas (Spees) Carrington (1868-1940), who was affiliated with the ABCFM. The American Hospital of Constantinople and School of Nursing Studies in Üsküdar, founded by Dr. Carrington—formerly employed at the hospital in Merzifon (1898-1904)—operated under the supervision of a USA-based committee. The purpose of this organization was to provide the poor with free medical and surgical services and to train nurses. However, Dr. Carrington struggled to acquire the funds required to keep the hospital running, leaving the ABCFM in 1909 and returning to the USA. The hospital was subsequently closed.

Efforts to reestablish an American Hospital in Istanbul began following the posting of Mark L. Bristol(*), admiral of the US Eastern Mediterranean Fleet, to Istanbul in 1918, where he assumed the role of High Commissioner in an attempt to "resolve ongoing conflicts and protect American interests". To all intents and purposes, Admiral Bristol also served as the US ambassador to Turkey during this period.

The concept of founding an American Hospital in Istanbul was discussed during a meeting in Admiral Bristol's office on November 8, 1919, after which planning began in earnest. American businessmen held a meeting with a number of organizations and representatives of foundations, such as the American Red Cross, the Near East Relief Committee, the American Board for Foreign Missions, Constantinople College for Girls and the US Consulate, with the aim of securing their places as founding members and receiving support in this enterprise. In the meeting, the decision was made to build a school of nursing at once due to the total lack of nurses in Turkey at that time. The hospital was to be directed by an advisory board composed of representatives from the five American foundations mentioned above.

On May 20, 1920, the American Hospital opened its outpatient clinic; on August 20, 1920, the American Hospital of Constantinople—as it was then known—held its official opening. The hospital was located in a wooden villa at 67 Tramvay Yolu, Çarşıkapı Caddesi. The villa was owned by the son-in-law of Sultan Abdülaziz, Mehmed Şerif Pasha. The villa comprised three stories, featuring a garden surrounded by a wall measuring six meters in height and which contained several small annexes. Patients' families were permitted to bring their horses and donkeys into the garden and were able to set up camp for several days until the patient recovered.

Admiral Bristol clearly stated the hospital's aims in the speech he gave at its opening, namely to provide all races, religions and peoples with health services on an equal basis; to establish a school of nursing to train nurses in order to attend to Turkey's urgent needs in this area and to ensure the provision of American-standard health services to Americans, Turks and all peoples. The hospital entered into operation with 78 beds and five nurses obtained from the US Navy and the American Red Cross; Dr. Alden R. Hoover(*) and Annie E. Rothrock were appointed to the roles of chief physician and chief nurse respectively. The first class to enter the American Hospital School of Nursing comprised 12 students, who began their studies in September 1920.

American Hospital, 1939

Winkler and Rountree, *American Hospital (1920-2007)*, p. 64

THE CHANGING NAMES OF THE AMERICAN HOSPİTAL

While its ideals and spirit remain constant, the hospital's official name has changed considerably over the course of history. The American Hospital was founded as the *American Hospital of Constantinople* by Admiral Mark L. Bristol on August 20, 1920, bearing this name through the final years of the Ottoman sultanate and the early years of the Turkish Republic until 1931. In 1930, in the era of the Turkish Republic, the decision was taken to replace the title Constantinople with Istanbul, the city's Turkish name. For this reason, the organization became known as the *American Hospital of Istanbul*. In 1945, following the death of its founder Admiral Mark L. Bristol, the hospital was renamed the *Admiral Bristol Hospital* in his memory. ... However, this name was never accepted by the people of Istanbul and thus the hospital was once again renamed the *American Hospital of Istanbul* in 1968. Ultimately, when the Vehbi Koç Foundation assumed ownership of the hospital in 1994, it became known by its official title, the *Vehbi Koç Foundation American Hospital* and still bears the name to this day.

Warren H. Winkler and George D. Rountree, *American Hospital (1920-2007)*, American Hospital Publications, Istanbul, 2012, p. 9

In 1923, when the building was deemed to have insufficient capacity for the hospital's quickly growing staff and increasing scope of activities, the American Hospital moved into the former site of the German Hospital on Sıraselviler Caddesi in Taksim, once used by the British occupying forces. In 1927, the hospital's advisory board became board of managers. In the first meeting of the board of managers, comprising 12 American members all domiciled in Istanbul, the decision was taken to create a board of trustees in New York in an effort to open an official agency in the USA and raise money for the hospital.

After Dr. Hoover returned to the USA for personal reasons, Dr. Wilfred M(cIlvaine) Post(*) assumed the role of chief physician. Dr. Post returned to the USA in 1926 following the death of his wife and Dr. Lorrin Andrews Shepard(*) took up the role. After the tenancy period at the German Hospital expired, the American Hospital moved into a four-story apartment block at 19 Silahhane (Teşvikiye) Caddesi on March 12, 1928. The new site of the nursing school was directly across the street at the Bedrettin Bey Apartments.

On June 17, 1931, the government agreed to recognize the American Hospital as an organization with land-ownership and construction rights. In New York, on October 30 of the same year, the American Hospital was formally registered as a non-profit organization under the name American Hospital of Istanbul, Inc. Resources secured by the US drive for donations played a big role in reducing the running deficits, particularly during the Great Depression in the early 1930s. In March 1938, construction was able to begin on a new hospital building in Nişantaşı thanks to funds secured in the same way. The new building was completed in less than two years and opened for business on November 14, 1939. In 1945, the names of the hospital and the school of nursing were changed respectively to the Admiral Bristol American Hospital and the Admiral Bristol Nursing School(*) in memory of their founder. The Nursing School was built next to the hospital, opening in 1950. The American Hospital Philanthropic Association was founded in 1956.

Following the retirement of Dr. Shepard, who had been the chief physician since 1927, Dr. Wilson Swanker(*) took up the post at the beginning of 1957. In 1962, Dr. Rolf Lium(*) took up the post of chief physician. In July 1964, the United States Agency for International Development (USAID) provided 250,000 dollars of aid to support works carried out to modernize and expand the hospital. In the same year, the government of the Turkish Republic approved plans to increase the hospital's bed capacity to 250. In 1966, Vehbi Koç(*) donated 70,000 dollars to set up a cancer (cobalt) pavilion within the hospital. Following Dr. Lium's departure from his post due to personal and family reasons, Dr. Warren H. Winkler(*) assumed part-time responsibility for the roles of chief physician and director in August 1967, switching to full-time the following year.

Lila Acheson Wallace, owner of *Reader's Digest*, provided the American Hospital with a donation of 540,000 dollars to fund the construction of a six-story building; work began in July 1971 and the Barclay Acheson Building opened in late March 1973. The new foyer building, financed by USAID, opened in April 1983. At the end of January 1985, work began on a ten-story outpatient building, also funded by USAID. In May 1985, Eli Acıman(*) was elected director of the board of managers, becoming the first Turkish citizen to hold the post. A collaborative practice agreement was signed with Houston Methodist Hospital in the US the same year.

VEHBİ KOÇ KANSER MERKEZİ AÇILDI

Vehbi Koç, merkezin açılışını yapıyor.

Amerikan Bristol Hastanesinde Vehbi Koç Kanser Merkezi 14 Haziran 1991 Cuma günü açıldı. Bu arada aynı gün, Vehbi Koç tarafından Amerikan Bristol Hastanesi Kobalt Servisine bağışlanan Kobalt cihazı tanıtıldı.

Vehbi Koç onuruna verilen törende açılış konuşmasını Amerikan Bristol Hastanesi Yönetim Kurulu üyesi Eli Acıman yaptı. Ardından V.K.V. Başkanı Vehbi Koç, Amerikan Bristol Hastanesi Yönetim Kurulu Başkanı Rahmi M. Koç, Genel Müdür George D. Rountree, Başhekim Dr. Warren H. Winkler, Vehbi Koç Kanser Merkezi Genel Koordinatörü Dr. Cemalettin Topuzlu, Kobalt Servisi Şefi Dr. Oktay İncekara birer konuşma yaptılar. Törende işadamları, hastane doktorları, yöneticiler ve basın mensupları bulundular.

Eli Acıman, açılış konuşmasını yaparken

Davetlilerden bir görünüm

Rahmi M. Koç ve George D. Rountree Vehbi Koç Kobalt Merkezi'nde

Genel Müdür George D. Rountree konuşmasını yaparken

Amerikan Bristol Hastanesi Genel Müdürü George D. Rountree törende yaptığı konuşmada şunları söyledi : "Amerikan Bristol Hastanesinde hasta bakım uygulamalarında kusursuzluğu getiren bir sağlık bakım ortamı yaratmakla bize yardımcı olan gerekli pek çok imkana sahip olduğumuz için şanslıyız. Vehbi Koç Kanser Merkezi hastanenin daha çok insana hizmet verebilmesini sağlayacak olan ve hastanede şu anda mevcut bulunan birimlerin (Laboratuvar, Röntgen, Cerrahi, Nükleer Tıp, Kobalt ve diğerleri), kanser hastalarının taranması, teşhisi tedavisi ve izlenmesi amacıyla bir merkezde toplanması yoluyla gerçekleştirilen en yeni programımızdır. Böylece Amerikan Bristol Hastanesinde hasta bakım hizmetlerine yeni bir boyut kazandırılmış olacaktır.

Sayın Vehbi Koç'un cömert bağışı geleceğe yönelik bu adımın atılmasına olanak sağlamıştır. Hastane Yönetimi adına Sayın Vehbi Koç'a teşekkürlerimizi sunmaktan şeref duyuyor, ayrıca, yeni merkezde ve Kobalt Ünitesinde kanser tedavisi görecek olan binlerce hasta adına, en samimi şükran ve takdirlerimi iletiyorum.

Bu önemli olaya ve hastanemize yardıma katıldığınız için buradan hepinize teşekkür ediyor ve büyük dostumuz ve velinimetimiz Sayın Vehbi Koç'a saygılarımı sunuyorum."

Bu sayıyı hazırlayanlar :
Dr. Halil Arpacıoğlu (Tıbbi Koordinatör)
Sibel Engin (Halkla İlişkiler Md.)

News on the opening of the Vehbi Koç Cancer Center
VKV Archive

The new outpatient building opened in July 1988. Following Eli Acıman's departure from his post in 1989, Rahmi M. Koç(*) was elected to the position. The American Hospital Foundation was founded in March of the same year. November saw the opening of Turkey's first Preventative Healthcare Center.

In 1990, changes were made to the hospital's governing structure and Dr. Winkler continued in his role as chief physician while George D. Rountree assumed the role of administrative director (in 1991 he became general director and CEO). The Vehbi Koç Cancer Center was opened in June of the following year. The Semahat Arsel Nursing Education and Research Center (*see* SANERC) was opened as part of the American Hospital in 1992. Following Dr. Winkler's departure, Dr. Engin Bazmanoğlu(*) assumed the vacant role of chief physician in 1995.

The VKV assumed ownership of the hospital in order to resolve its ever-growing financial problems. Administrative powers of American Hospital of Istanbul, Inc. were legally transferred to the VKV when the agreement was signed on June 20, 1994. The agreement included conditions stipulating, among other things, that the hospital property was not to be sold or transferred and that it would continue to be used as a hospital for years to come. Following sale and transfer, all legal rights and powers formerly belonging to the New York Board of Trustees and the Board of Directors in Istanbul were transferred to the VKV Board of Directors. The hospital and the Admiral Bristol Nursing School were formally transferred to the VKV on February 27, 1995. The name of the hospital was changed to the Vehbi Koç Foundation American Hospital.

THE AMERICAN HOSPITAL IN THE WORDS OF RAHMİ KOÇ

My late father worked for many years as a dealer for Socony Vacuum (Mobil), so he was always close friends with the managers.

The board of managers of the American Hospital was composed of general managers from foreign firms such as Mobil, which was based in Istanbul, as well as Pan American, Uniroyal, J. P. Morgan, American Express and the American consul general.

One day, the director of Mobil asked Vehbi Koç to join the board of directors of the American Hospital, to which he replied, "I have neither the language skills nor the time, but my son Rahmi M. Koç could take my place". And thus, I took up my role on the board of directors of the American Hospital in 1966. To this day, I continue to take a close interest in the hospital and its concerns.

Today's American Hospital, general view, entrance hall and reception
Amerikan Hospital Archive

As a general rule, the chairman of the board of managers would be chosen from among foreign candidates. In 1985, the advertising guru Eli Acıman became the first Turkish head of the managing board and in 1989 I assumed the role after him.

The American Hospital's Board of Trustees was based in New York, together with a fund, USAID (United States Agency for International Development) also provided the hospital with financial support every year. Aside from this, the money to purchase equipment, etc. was provided by the fund in New York. As living standards in Turkey rose, the funds provided by USAID decreased year on year and ultimately stopped.

The hospital continued to run for a while on the donations it had received within Turkey and with the help of the New York fund. Following a case brought against it in New York, the fund—which had lasted for years—was all but spent and went bankrupt. As a result, the Vehbi Koç Foundation took over the American Hospital in 1994, due largely to my insistence.

At the end of the agreement made with the Board of Trustees in New York, several strict conditions—stipulating that the hospital's

property could not be sold or transferred and that it would remain in use as a hospital for years to come—were accepted and the hospital was transferred to the Vehbi Koç Foundation.

Since then, the Vehbi Koç Foundation has invested hundreds of millions of dollars in the hospital. It purchased the hospital next door, carried out new construction work, modernized the equipment and brought in young, dynamic doctors. It also took over the School of Nursing, bringing the hospital into the present day.

Koç University took over the administration of the School of Nursing and the Semahat Arsel Nursing Education and Research Center in 1999 and 2004 respectively. In 2009, the hospital became a joint-stock company.

Winkler and Rountree, *American Hospital (1920-2007)*, p. 7

The neighboring Güzelbahçe Hospital was purchased in November 1995 with the aim of securing sufficient space for an expansion of the American Hospital and School of Nursing. Güzelbahçe Hospital was renovated and connected to the main hospital building by a corridor before being re-opened as the Semahat Arsel and Dr. Nusret Arsel Building; several of the units in the American Hospital moved into this new building. The School of Nursing and SANERC were taken over by Koç University(*) in 1999 and 2004 respectively.

In 1998, the American Hospital became a member of the American Hospitals Association. An agreement was signed that same year by the American Hospital, New York Presbyterian Hospital and the medical faculties of Cornell and Columbia universities, covering collaboration on topics such as medical training and patient care, as well as exchanges for doctors, directors, nurses and students.

The MedAmerican Outpatient Clinic (now MedAmerican Medical Center[*]) opened in Kadıköy in December 1997 with the aim of providing medical services on behalf of the American Hospital on Istanbul's Asian side. Based in Tophane, the Italian Hospital(*) was leased in March 1998 following an agreement between the Italian Consulate and the American Hospital and, following renovation work funded by contributions from the Agnelli Foundation, was reopened as the Giovanni Alberto Agnelli Building, a health center focusing primarily on providing cancer diagnosis and treatment. The hospital opened on November 18, 1999, however, it was closed again due to new legal barriers and did not reopen until July 2005. The Italian Hospital closed in August 2006 following financial troubles.

The American Hospital's new wing, constructed on the former site of the School of Nursing, opened in October 1999. The Güzelbahçe Hospital building was demolished in 2000; work was completed on its replacement, the Semahat and Dr. Nusret Arsel School of Nursing building, in 2002.

In October 1999, George D. Rountree departed from his role as general director, continuing his work as business development advisor and director. Talat Pekelman(*) assumed the role of general director. As the hospital's financial problems worsened, changes were made to senior management and, in May 2001, Dr. Serdar Savaş was appointed acting general director. But in the face of growing financial problems, Dr. Savaş departed from his post in October of the same year and was replaced by George D. Rountree. Dr. Ömer Arıkan(*) assumed the role of chief physician. The "culture of profitability" program, which was gaining legitimacy at the hospital, soon bore fruit, making important progress towards overcoming financial issues.

In 2002 and 2005, the hospital received accreditation papers documenting conformance to Joint Commission International (JCI) standards. (The JCI papers were renewed for the fifth time in 2015.) In March 2005, the American Hospital became the first private hospital to receive ISO 14001 accreditation, valid for three years. The ISO 9001 it had previously received was also renewed for a further three years.

Zekeriyaköy Family Health Center(*) opened in March 2003 with the aim of providing health services to people living in Zekeriyaköy, Kilyos, Maslak, Sarıyer and the surrounding districts and continued to run until 2014.

Following the departure of George D. Rountree from the role of general director in late 2006, Dr. Evren Keleş(*) took his place. Dr. Keleş also took on the role of chief physician in 2008.

The American Marine Outpatient Clinic(*) which was opened by the VKV in Göcek in conjunction with the American Hospital in August 2007—in cooperation with Göcek Municipality and the DenizTemiz Association/ TURMEPA(*)—ceased operations at the end of 2013. In July 2018, Bodrum American Hospital has opened.

Today (2018), the American Hospital is a full-fledged health organization providing health services to over 220,000 patients every year, presiding over a 60,500 square meter site, featuring 261 rooms, 41 of which are reserved for intensive care, as well as 31 observation beds and 12 operating rooms. Since 2014, Dr. Erhan Bulutcu(*) has held the role of general director and İsmail Bozkurt(*) the role of chief physician.

THE AMERICAN HOSPITAL ART GALLERY, "THE OPERATION ROOM"

"The Operation Room", which has been in place in the American Hospital since 2008, is the first art gallery to be established within a hospital in Turkey. The gallery space, covering an area of 150 square meters, hosts works by local and foreign artists from different branches of the art world.

EXHIBITIONS OPENING AT THE GALLERY*

- **Emissaries of Divine Power: Medical Instruments in Ancient Medicine** *(March-May 2008)*
  Erdoğan Yalav
- **Camouflage** *(June-September 2008)*
  Ekrem Yalçındağ
- **Daylife** *(November-December 2008)*
  Sandra Mann
- **Still Men Out There** *(February-April 2009)*
  Björn Melhus
- **Material Picture** *(May-June 2009)*
  Various Artists
- **Peter Kogler Exhibition** *(September-October 2009)*
  Peter Kogler
- **New Approaches** *(December 2009-February 2010)*
  İzzet Keribar
- **A/B** *(February-March 2010)*
  Selçuk Artut
- **Vacuum** *(April-June 2010)*
  Metehan Özcan
- **Shoot** *(June-August 2010)*
  Karolin Fişekçi
- **No Where** *(October-November 2010)*
  Burcu Perçin
- **Professore** *(December 2010-January 2011)*
  Stephane Graff
- **Minus Feld** *(February-March 2011)*
  Refik Anadol
- **Looking back at you** *(May-July 2011)*
  Gözde Türkkan
- **Undefined** *(July-September 2011)*
  Engin Konuklu
- **I Discovered Joy on the Road** *(November-December 2011)*
  Akgün Akova
- **Spatial memory** *(February-March 2012)*
  Canan Dağdelen
- **Wild is the Wind** *(April-May 2012)*
  Hayal İncedoğan
- **deus ex machina** *(November-December 2012)*
  Korhan Karaoysal
- **Untitled** *(March-April 2013)*
  Osman Kerkütlü
- **Borrowed Togetherness** *(December 2013-January 2014)*
  Eda Gecikmez

- **A Moment in the Shadow of the Image** *(April-May 2014)*
  Burcu Orhon
- **Curious Moments** *(September-November 2014)*
  Ferhat Özgür
- **Turnaround** *(January-March 2015)*
  İrem Sözen
- **Placebo Effect** *(April-May 2015)*
  Ali Cabbar
- **In Fog: Floating Glaciers and Wild Boar** *(June-August 2015)*
  Ülgen Semerci and Burcu Yağcıoğlu
- **Savage Humanchine** *(December 2015-February 2016)*
  Bora Başkan
- **Sami, the beautiful angel** *(March-April 2016)*
  Sami Baydar
- **Drawings from Sainte-Anne** *(June-August 2016)*
  Fikret Muallâ
- **Aesthetical Interference** *(November 2016-January 2017)*
  Özgül Arslan
- **The Ambiguous Whiner** *(March-May 2017)*
  Metin Üstündağ
- **Surface Heap or Metal Mountain** *(June-August 2017)*
  Furkan Temir
- **in-finite** *(October-December 2017)*
  Julie Upmeyer
- **Oblique** *(February-April 2018)*
  Pavlos Nikolakopoulos
- **Not/Not There** *(June-July 2018)*
  Kadir Has University Department of Visual Communication Design faculty and students

*All exhibition catalogs have been published.

AMERICAN HOSPITAL ADMINISTRATION

CHIEF PHYSICIAN

1920-1924	Dr. Alden R. Hoover(*)
1924-1926	Dr. Wilfred Post(*)
1927-1957	Dr. Lorrin A. Shepard(*)
1957-1961	Dr. Wilson Swanker(*)
1962-1966	Dr. Rolf Lium(*)
1967-1994	Dr. Warren H. Winkler(*)
1995-2001	Dr. Engin Bazmanoğlu(*)
2001-2003	Dr. Ömer Arıkan(*)
2003-2006	Dr. Teoman Dal(*)
2006-2008	Dr. Satia Advan(*) (Acting)
2008-2010	Dr. Evren Keleş(*)
2010-2014	Dr. Ömür Erçelen(*)
2014-	Dr. İsmail Bozkurt(*)

GENERAL DIRECTOR

1967-1990	Dr. Warren H. Winkler
1990-1999	George D. Rountree(*)
1999-2001	Talât Pekelman(*)
2001	Serdar Savaş (Acting)
2001-2006	George D. Rountree
2007-2014	Dr. Evren Keleş
2014-...	Dr. Erhan Bulutcu(*)

RESPONSIBLE DIRECTOR

1938-1947	Dr. Aziz Fikret Derlen
1947-1964	Dr. Nevzat Yeğinsu
1964-1978	Dr. Erotoklis Prifti
1978-1985	Dr. Haluk Aker
1985-1994	Dr. Gürhan Ünlütürk
1995-2002	Dr. Engin Bazmanoğlu
2002-2003	Dr. Ömer Arıkan
2003-2008	Dr. Satia Advan
21.01-17.10.2008	Dr. Evren Keleş
2008-2010	Dr. Ömür Erçelen
2010-2014	Dr. Erdal M. Aksoy(*)
2014-...	Dr. İsmail Bozkurt

SOME OF THE AMERICAN HOSPITAL'S PUBLICATIONS

- Bahar, Mois, *Amerikan Hastanesi Yoğun Bakım Tarihi* (History of American Hospital's Intensive Care Unit), 2018
- Çerezci, Önder et al., *El Rehabilitasyonu* (Hand Rehabilitation), 2013
- Ergin, N. Tan, *Kulak Burun Boğaz Hastalıklarında İleri Teknoloji* (Cutting-edge Technology in the Ear, Nose and Throat Diseases), nd.
- Eroğlu, Egemen, *Erkek Sünneti, İnsanlık Tarihindeki Hikâyesi* (Male Circumcision: The Story of Human History), 2011
- Güllüoğlu, Bahadır, Elvin Aydın and Vivi Soryano, *Meme Kanseriyle Baş Etme Rehberi* (A Guide to Coping with Breast Cancer), 2011
- Koç, Rahmi M., *Alaska*, 2013
- Koç, Rahmi M., *Around the World with Nazenin IV* (Nazenin IV ile Devr-i Âlem), 2009
- Koç, Rahmi M., *Sergüzeştir Seyahatnamem* (My Travelogue is an Adventure), 2009
- Özer, Ali Fahir, *Lomber Dejeneratif Disk Hastalığı ve Dinamik Stabilizasyon* (Lumbar Degenerative Disc Disease and Dynamic Stabilization), 2011
- Winkler, Warren H. and Rountree, George D., *American Hospital (1920-2007)*, 2012
- Yalav, Erdoğan, *Yaratıcı Gücün Sanatkarları "Cerrahlar"* (Artists of the Creative Power "Surgeons"), 2018
- Yeşilada, Erdem, *Doğadan Gelen Sağlık, Bitki Çayları* (Natural Health, Herbal Teas), 2011
- Yıldırım, Ferda Maden, *Çifte Mucize Çifte Sorumluluk, Çoğul Gebelik* (Double the Miracle Double the Responsibility, Multiple Pregnancies), 2007

American Hospital Art Gallery "Operation Room" *see* **American Hospital**

The **American Marine Outpatient Clinic**, full name THE PRIVATE AMERICAN MARINE OUTPATIENT CLINIC, the health center opened by the Vehbi Koç Foundation(*) in August 2007 in Muğla Göcek, in cooperation with Göcek Municipality and the DenizTemiz Association/ TURMEPA(*), in conjunction with the American Hospital(*). At the outpatient clinic, which provided diagnostic services and treatments

in Göcek Municipal Marina, there was also a fully-equipped patient transport boat. Health screenings were also carried out on children from elementary schools in Göcek and the surrounding villages in cooperation with the Muğla Directorate of Education.

The outpatient clinic closed at the end of 2013.

ANAMED, full name KOÇ UNIVERSITY RESEARCH CENTER FOR ANATOLIAN CIVILIZATIONS, an international cultural organization which was founded in 2005 with the aim of supporting academic research into the history, art, architecture and archeology of civilizations in Turkey and developing and increasing public awareness of cultural heritage management and museum studies. It carries out its work in the renovated historical building, Merkez Han(*), situated on İstiklal Caddesi in Istanbul. In the building's three blocks there are three separate libraries, one belonging to ANAMED itself and the other two belonging to the Netherlands Institute of Turkey (NIT) and the Turkish Institute of Prehistory (TEBE); there are also the office of the Turkish Foundation for Underwater Archeology (TINA), guest rooms for research fellows, an auditorium for public conferences, seminar rooms and a gallery. ANAMED's main activities include securing fellowships for researchers specializing in the cultural heritage of Anatolia, providing library services, arranging symposiums, conferences, workshops and exhibitions on Anatolian civilizations and publishing scientific manuscripts.

ANAMED provides fellowships for doctoral students and postdoctoral researchers, some of which include accommodation, travel expenses and a monthly allowance, with the aim of supporting the academic work of an average of 30 researchers from Turkey and other countries every year. As well as the annual symposiums, ANAMED has held the International Sevgi Gönül Byzantine Studies Symposium(*) every three years since 2007 (2013 and 2016) with the support of the Vehbi Koç Foundation(*). The center also prepares publications as lasting records of symposiums and exhibitions and in order to be able to share its work with a wider public audience.

THE STORY OF ANAMED, AS TOLD BY ERDAL YILDIRIM*

In the early 2000s, Beyoğlu was like a marketplace from Taksim Square to the Galatasaray High School, and it was as if every day was Sunday from there to Tünel. For this reason, when the idea of founding ANAMED arose, none of us thought of Merkez Han as a possible location. We looked at various places, like Cihangir, then an old villa used in a TV series and a building in Galata (which, I think, used to belong to the Kamondo family), thinking they might be more suitable. We had no idea of the precious jewel that lay right in front of our noses.

I can't remember who first suggested Merkez Han. But we embraced it at once. We had a bit of difficulty evicting the previous tenants. While we were busy deciding, Asmalımescit was getting lively and every stretch of Cadde-i Kebir had become very popular. We subsidized the Nazim Hikmet Cultural Center to move out and were able to see off the branch of Şekerbank thanks to a bilateral friendship—the president is an old friend of mine from university.

Fahrettin Ayanlar had long since started work on the project. It was agreed upon then that the top floor would be an alumni club. At the time, I was head of the Koç School Alumni Association and I realized how beneficial it would be to have a space like this, which could be shared by high school and university alumni associations.**

Fahrettin Ayanlar developed a wonderful project, as ever. The project was presented at a meeting of the Koç University Board of Trustees at Koç Holding. We

managed to successfully dismiss the suggestion not to build a conference room and have a car park instead. And thank goodness we did.

The construction process was a difficult one, as is to be expected. It wasn't easy to build an earthquake-proof building, keep its functions as broad as possible, and satisfy aesthetic concerns. Thanks to Fahrettin Ayanlar and his team, we were able to achieve an outcome that we could all be proud of.

Merkez Han was the first building our founder, Vehbi Koç, bought when he decided to move his company to Istanbul, a building with special significance for the Koç family, Koç Holding and the Vehbi Koç Foundation and is now a vibrant culture and research center every day of the week and every hour of every day thanks to its on-site academic accommodation.

Lucky us!

ANAMED, Special, June 2015, p. 4
* President of the Vehbi Koç Foundation
** Fahrettin Ayanlar's ANAMED project won the Chamber of Architects 11th National Building Achievement Awards in 2008.

Affiliated with the Koç University Suna Kıraç Library(*), the ANAMED Library offers a variety of materials such as CD-ROMs, DVDs, cassettes, maps and reprints, as well as books and magazines. At the library, it is also possible to access electronic resources such as online databases, e-books and e-magazines. In cooperation with the Suna Kıraç Library, the ANAMED Library runs digitization projects to protect, keep safe and record Turkey's cultural heritage and to pass these precious collections on to future generations. The internationally-renowned photographer, ethnographer and connoisseur of Turkish textiles, Josephine Powell(*), features among the ANAMED Library's special collections with a collection showcasing thousands of books, travel notes, slides, negatives and photographs detailing Anatolian cities, lives, cultures and nomadic lifestyles (*see* Josephine Powell Collection).

ANAMED, IN THE WORDS OF DR. ALESSANDRA RICCI*

This is the first Turkish research centre of its kind. Until now these kinds of activities were exclusively in the hands of foreign research centres like the German Archaeological Institute, the French Institute and so on. Research institutes like us are not moneymaking establishments, but they produce something that is much more valuable than money: they produce cultural messages and cultural growth, which are extremely important not only for this country but for its reputation abroad. So, looking at these establishments as simply philanthropic establishments is somewhat reductive... they produce the cultural level and cultural interest that can only be positive for this country.

This research centre functions as a bridge between the international community we are bringing here, the larger community of scholars here in Turkey and everyone who is genuinely interested in pursuing these research themes. We are also helping to build a connection between past and present, helping to create a harmonious dialogue between the past and the

directions this country will be taking in the future.

This research centre represents for many of us a dream turned into reality. It is a very important cultural message. Instead of only sending Turkish scholars abroad, we are inviting foreign scholars to come here to research. It is totally unique for this country and I hope other universities will follow this example.

*Associate Director at ANAMED (2008)
Suna Dokur (ed.), *Forty Year Book*, Vehbi Koç Foundation Publications, Istanbul, 2009, p. 214

ANAMED EXHIBITIONS*

- **What Josephine Saw** *(June 11–October 21, 2012)*
  Curator: Kimberly Hart
- **Imagining History: Sagalassos**
  (March 9–June 10, 2013)
  Curators: Bruno Vandermeulen, Danny Veys
- **Stories from the Hidden Harbor: Shipwrecks of Yenikapı** *(June 25, 2013–January 25, 2014)*
- **A Capital's Waterways**
  (November 9, 2012–February 18, 2013)
  Curators: James Crow, Derya Maktav
- **Artamonoff: Images of Byzantine Istanbul, 1930-1947** *(June 26–November 10, 2013)*
  Curator: Günder Varinlioğlu
- **Robertson, Photography and Carving in the Ottoman Capital** *(November 27, 2013–February 20, 2014)*
  Curator: Bahattin Öztuncay

- **Antioch on the Orontes, Early Explorations in the City of Mozaics** *(February 28–April 20, 2014)*
  Curator: Murat Akar
- **Nazlı's Guestbook, Osman Hamdi Bey's Circle**
  (April 30–July 10, 2014)
  Curator: Edhem Eldem
- **An Innocent City** *(July18–September 3, 2014)*
  Curator: Ian Alden Russell
- **The Forgotten Kingdom**
  (September 13–December 7, 2014)
  Curators: Murat Akar, Hélène Maloigne
- **War and Propaganda on the Allied Front in World War One** *(December 24, 2014– April 2, 2015)*
  Curator: Bahattin Öztuncay
- **Camera Ottomana: Photography and Modernity in the Ottoman Empire, 1840-1914**
  (April 21–August 19, 2015)
  Curators: Zeynep Çelik, Edhem Eldem, Bahattin Öztuncay
- **John Garstang's Footsteps Across Anatolia**
  (September 17–December 20, 2015)
  Curator: Alan M. Greaves
- **Everyday Sounds: Exploring Sound Through Daily Life** *(January 9–March 20, 2016)*
  Editing and design: PATTU
- **Scent and the City** *(April 14–June 8, 2016)*
  Curator: Lauren Nicole Davis
- **Byzantium's Other Empire: Trebizond**
  (June 24–September 30, 2016)
  Curator: Antony Eastmond
- **On the Fringe** *(October 19, 2016–January 2, 2017)*
  Curator: Figen Kıvılcım Çorakbaş
- **The Characters of Yusuf Franko: An Ottoman Bureaucrat's Caricatures** *(January 26–June 1, 2017)*
  Curator: Bahattin Öztuncay
- **The Curious Case of Çatalhöyük**
  (June 21–February 18, 2018)
  Curator: Duygu Tarkan
- **Ottoman Arcadia: The Hamidian Expedition to the Land of Tribal Roots (1886)**
  (May 10–September 30, 2018)
  Curators: Bahattin Öztuncay, Ahmet Ersoy, Deniz Türker
- **Picturing a Lost Empire: An Italian Lens on Byzantine Art in Anatolia, 1960-2000**
  (June 1-September 30, 2018)
  Curator: Livia Bevilacqua, Giovanni Gasbarri

*All exhibition catalogs have been published.

ANAMED offers summer programs on Byzantium and Post-Byzantine Cappadocia, Istanbul through the Ages, The Ancient Languages of Anatolia and Ottoman Turkish.

ANAMED ANNUAL SYMPOSIA

- **Looking at the Past in the Republican Era,** *December 2006*
- **Bathing Culture in Anatolian Civilizations: Architecture, History and Imagination,** *December 2007*
- **The Challenges of Conservation in Archeology, Architecture and Museums: Turkey and Beyond,** *November 2008*
- **Cities and Citadels,** *December 2009*

- **Istanbul and Water,** *December 2010*
- **Of Vines and Wines: The Production and Consumption of Wine in Anatolian Civilizations Through the Ages,** *December 2011*
- **Ephesos: From Late Antiquity to the Later Middle Ages,** *November-December 2012*
- **The Palimpsest of the House: Re-Assessing Roman, Late Antique, Byzantine, Early Islamic Living Patterns,** *November-December 2013*
- **Crossroads: Konya Plain from Prehistory to the Byzantine Period,** *December 2014*
- **Spolia Reincarnated: Second Life of Spaces, Materials and Objects in Anatolia from Antiquity to the Ottoman Period,** *December 2015*
- **Sacred Spaces+Urban Networks,** *December 2016*
- **Spatial Webs,** *29-30 November 2017*

From the exhibition "On the Fringe" (October 19, 2016-January 2, 2017)

ANAMED PUBLICATIONS

- **Çelik, Zeynep and Eldem, Edhem (ed.),** ***Camera Ottomana: Photography and Modernity in the Ottoman Empire, 1840-1914,*** 2015
- **Eastmond, Anthony (ed.),** ***Byzantium's Other Empire: Trebizond,*** 2016
- **Greaves, Alan M. (ed.),** ***Anadolu'da John Garstang'ın Ayak İzleri/ John Garstang's Footsteps Across Anatolia,*** 2015
- **Hart, Kimberly (ed.),** ***What Josephine Saw,*** 2012
- **Kızıltan, Zeynep and Çelik, Gülbahar Baran (ed.),** ***Stories from the Hidden Harbor: Shipwrecks of Yenikapı,*** 2013
- **Maloigne, Hélène and Akar, Murat (ed.),** ***Unutulmuş Krallık/The Forgotten Kingdom,*** 2014
- **Ödekan, Ayla et al. (ed.),** ***The Byzantine Court: Source of Power and Culture,*** 2013
- **Redford, Scott (ed.),** ***Asi'deki Antakya/ Antioch on the Orontes,*** 2014
- **Varinlioğlu, Günder,** ***Artamonoff: Images of Byzantine Istanbul, 1930-1947,*** 2013

"Anatolia is Reading" Book Project,

a book donation project developed by the Vehbi Koç Foundation(*) in response to high demand for books. The project, which has been running since 2011, aims to send library packs—composed from among 100 fundamental works appropriate for school-age readers—to school libraries in elementary and middle schools based in the city which scores the lowest in the National Competitiveness Report. In 2011, books were sent to 200 elementary schools and 29 high schools in Hakkâri; in 2012, to help overcome educational problems arising in the aftermath of the earthquake in Van, books were sent to 83 high schools and 200 elementary schools; in 2013, books were sent to 42 high schools and 200 middle schools in Şırnak; in 2014, books were sent to 261 schools in Ağrı; in 2015, books were sent to 44 high schools and 197 middle schools in Muş; in 2016, books were sent to 218 schools in Bitlis and in 2017, books were sent to 49 high schools and 136 middle schools in Siirt. The number of schools receiving books within the seven-year period amounted to 1,658.

Anatolian Civilizations Research Center *see* ANAMED

The **Anatolian Scholarship Program**

is Koç University's (KU) scholarship program, which aims to provide the opportunity to study at KU to highly talented young people who have been unable to access quality higher education due to financial disadvantages. 2017 saw scholarships on the program—which began in 2011 with the support of Arçelik, Ford Otosan, Tofaş, Tüpraş, Turkish Economy Bank and Yapı Kredi Bank—awarded to 376 students from 75 cities, with more than 180 benefactors supporting the program.

Evaluation of applications to the Anatolian Scholarship Program takes many factors into account, such as candidates' scores in

the university entrance exam, family income, social activities, teachers' references, written composition pieces and the socioeconomic situation in their home district. Candidates coming within the first 10,000 in the relevant category of the Undergraduate Placement Exam (UPE) and achieving at least four out of five in their high school diploma are given priority. School of Medicine candidates are expected to come within the first 1,500 in the relevant UPE category.

Files provided by candidates are scrutinized by the committee at KU for preliminary screening. Candidates who pass this preliminary stage are invited to a "24 Hours at Koç" event, where they are hosted on campus to help them get to know the university up close.

As part of the Anatolian Scholarship Program, students are entirely exempted from paying tuition fees and gain the right to free accommodation in dormitories; the cost of their textbooks is also fully covered, and they receive a monthly allowance. The scholarships are non-repayable as part of the program and continue throughout the course of education and training. Students attending the foreign language proficiency program will receive scholarships for the duration of this program plus their standard four-year course; students beginning at the freshman year will receive scholarships for the standard four-year course. For students studying for a double major, the scholarship will cover the language program plus a five-year course. If students receiving the Anatolian Scholarship are studying at the School of Medicine, they will benefit from a seven-year scholarship including the language program. Students with a good attendance record will not lose their scholarships in the event of academic failure. Students who receive scholarship places on KU programs will continue to receive their scholarship if they transfer to another program.

The program is supported by a large number of institutions, organizations and individuals, including the American Hospital(*), The Anadolu Group, Aygaz, BASF, Bosch, Coca Cola, Denizbank, Enka Foundation, Garanti Bank, Koç Holding(*), The Koç University Alumni Association, Koçtaş, Limak, Migros, MNG, Opet, Otokar, Otokoç, Sütaş, Tat, Türk Traktör, Tüyap, Unilever, Yapı Kredi and Yıldız Holding.

The Anatolian Scholarship Program received the Gold Award in the category of "Emerging Programs in Fundraising" by The Council for Advancement and Support of Education (CASE), one of the world's respected educational associations, in 2015.

Ankara Orchard House, also known as SEMAHAT-NUSRET ARSEL ANKARA ORCHARD HOUSE, historic house museum and cultural center connected to VEKAM(*). The building, situated in the Keçiören district of Ankara, is one of the few remaining examples of Ankara's civil architectural heritage.

The Orchard House was built in the early 1900s by Ali Gedikoğlu, Vehbi Koç's uncle-in-law and a distinguished member of Ankara society. After Gedikoğlu's death, his wife sold the house to Vehbi Koç(*). Semahat Arsel(*) later inherited the somewhat dilapidated house from her father and donated it to the Vehbi Koç Foundation(*) so it could be restored and used to teach future generations about the way of life and culture of the period in which it was built. It was restored in keeping with its original form in 2006 and opened up to visitors in the following year.

Maintaining the authentic architectural and decorative characteristics of its era, the Orchard House has been endowed with the legal status of a Priority Protected Immovable Cultural Asset. The outer walls of the ground and middle floors are constructed from andesite and Ankara stone, while the interior loadbearing walls from ground level upwards are timber.

The dining room, living room and bedroom are designed to reflect life in the Orchard House during the transition from the Ottoman Empire to the new Republic, with furnishings such as low copper tray tables, divans, rattan chairs, brass bedsteads and embroidered linen curtains. The other rooms are used by small groups for cultural activities, documentary presentations and meetings.

Ankara Orchard House, in partnership with the Contemporary Drama Association, has organized drama-based educational and awareness raising projects such as "The Changing Face of Womanhood in Ankara" and "Growing up in Ankara in the Early Days of the Republic." An exhibition set up in the garden in a Mongol tent from May 22, 2015 to March 1, 2016, showed aspects of the Mongol lifestyle.

Ankara Rahmi M. Koç Museum, a museum of industry run under the auspices of the Rahmi M. Koç Museology and Culture Foundation(*). The museum first opened to the public in 2005, situated opposite the main entrance to Ankara Castle in a historical caravansary called Çengelhan(*). Another caravansary in the same area, Safranhan(*), was bought in 2012 and opened as a second museum building in 2016 after its restoration. Today the museum covers an area of 7,000 square meters. This is the second museum of industry to open under the auspices of the Rahmi M. Koç Museology and Culture Foundation. The first was the Rahmi M. Koç Museum (*see* Istanbul Rahmi M. Koç Museum) in the Golden Horn area of Istanbul, which opened in 1994.

Rented from the Ankara Regional Directorate of Foundations, the museum at Çengelhan collects and exhibits items from across the globe relating to all eras of industry and engineering, supporting their protection and conservation, as well as further research. As part of the restoration work during the years 2003 and 2005, the structure was reinforced while remaining faithful to the original architectural characteristics; as part of this work, the courtyard was conserved with a glass roof.

Vehbi Koç Shop in the museum

The museum's collections and resources aim to be both interesting and informative to the public, increase museum attendance across Turkey, and support the research of industrial history. Most of the works are compiled from the personal collection of Rahmi M. Koç(*). The museum's collections are exhibited under the categories: Ankara and Atatürk, Road Transportation, Rail Transportation, Maritime, Aviation, Craftsman Street, Machinery, Scientific Instruments, Communication, Toys, Agriculture, Medicine and Pharmacy, and Everyday Life.

The shop where Vehbi Koç(*), founder of Koç Holding, first went into business has been set up in Çengelhan's courtyard as a special focal point called the "Vehbi Koç Shop". Other special points of interest in the museum are the Workshop of Uncle Ismail, Model Machinery Workshop and Ali Rıza Pharmacy. "Weekend Workshops" and the "Elementary School Education Project" are educational programs devised and provided to schools by the museum.

Ankara University Medal of Philanthropy, award granted by Ankara University (AU) Rectorate to the Koç family(*) in 2015 for their contribution to society, education and the university. The Ankara University Vehbi Koç Student Dormitory, built in 1949–50, was the first major social contribution made by Vehbi Koç(*), who donated the building to the university in 1951. The Vehbi Koç Eye Bank affiliated to Ankara University School of Medicine was built in 1963, also by Vehbi Koç. Forty years after its inauguration, it was thoroughly renovated and expanded by the Vehbi Koç Foundation(*) (VKV), opening in 2007 with the new name, Ankara University School of Medicine Vehbi Koç Eye Hospital(*). The financial support of VKV also led to the establishment of Turkey's first underwater archaeology research and application center, the Ankara University Mustafa V. Koç Research Center for Maritime Archaeology(*), which opened in June 2015 in the Urla district of Izmir. The VKV continues to provide support for numerous departments of AU.

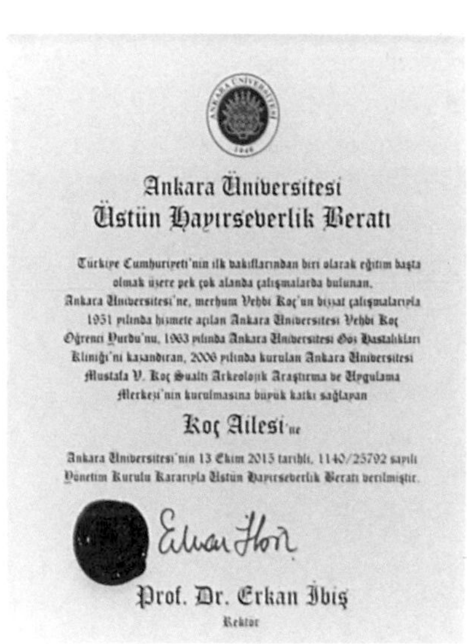
Ankara Üniversitesi
Üstün Hayırseverlik Beratı

Türkiye Cumhuriyeti'nin ilk vakıflarından biri olarak eğitim başta olmak üzere pek çok alanda çalışmalarda bulunan, Ankara Üniversitesi'ne, merhum Vehbi Koç'un bizzat çalışmalarıyla 1951 yılında hizmete açılan Ankara Üniversitesi Vehbi Koç Öğrenci Yurdu'nu, 1963 yılında Ankara Üniversitesi Göz Hastalıkları Kliniği'ni kazandıran, 2006 yılında kurulan Ankara Üniversitesi Mustafa V. Koç Sualtı Arkeolojik Araştırma ve Uygulama Merkezi'nin kurulmasına büyük katkı sağlayan

Koç Ailesi'ne

Ankara Üniversitesi'nin 13 Ekim 2015 tarihli, 1140/25792 sayılı Yönetim Kurulu Kararıyla Üstün Hayırseverlik Beratı verilmiştir.

Prof. Dr. Erkan İbiş
Rektör

Ankara University Mustafa V. Koç Research Center for Maritime Archaeology, Turkey's first underwater archaeology research and application center. Situated in the Urla district of Izmir, the center was established by Ankara University Underwater Archaeology Research and Application Center with financial support from the Vehbi Koç Foundation(*) and help from the Turkish Foundation for Underwater Archaeology (TINA).

In 2009, Urla Municipality allotted an area of 11,000 square meters for the center in the Çeşmealtı district of Urla. Construction began in 2013 and the center opened in June 2015. The site is made up of five different units: a main building hosting administrative offices, conference room and library; indoor and outdoor restoration laboratories and storerooms; a 30-bed dormitory section for project participants; a five-room guest house and lodging buildings; and a 4,000-square-meter open exhibition area displaying the developments in maritime technology from ancient times until the present day.

Ankara University School of Medicine Vehbi Koç Eye Hospital, known by the full name of ANKARA UNIVERSITY SCHOOL OF MEDICINE DEPARTMENT OF OPTHALMOLOGY VEHBİ KOÇ EYE HOSPITAL, a specialist center located on the Ankara University (AU) School of Medicine Cebeci Research and Application Hospital Campus. The center has carried out pioneering ophthalmological work in Turkey.

It stemmed from the country's first Eye Bank, established by Vehbi Koç(*) in 1963, in connection with AU School of Medicine. Vehbi Koç became involved after receiving a request for help in setting up an eye bank in 1957. With his financial support, the 90-bed capacity Vehbi Koç Eye Bank was built in 1959–63 and opened for service in the final year. Vehbi Koç was awarded a Golden Plaque by Ankara Eye Bank in 1968.

Demand for its services soon outgrew the site and, once more with the financial help of Vehbi Koç, a second section was added in 1972. As well as supporting its construction, the Vehbi Koç Foundation(*) also gave ongoing support to the hospital in the form of medical equipment, research grants and donations. Forty years after its opening, VKV renovated the entire facility from treatment rooms to offices, doubling the size of the premises. In 2007, it reopened as the School of Medicine Vehbi Koç Eye Hospital.

Covering an area of almost 4,000 square meters, the hospital has 49 beds, 38 rooms and four operating rooms, all equipped with state-of-the-art technology. The hospital offers a 24-hour service, performing around 100 operations per week and providing outpatient services for approximately 500 patients a day in its retina, tumor, uvea, strabismus, glaucoma, oculoplastic, cornea-contact lens, trauma and neuro-ophthalmological units.

In 2012, AU Vehbi Koç Eye Hospital became accredited by the European School for Advanced Studies in Ophthalmology, a body set up to advance the postgraduate clinical and surgical training of eye doctors. It was only the sixth center in the world to receive the accreditation.

THE STORY OF ANKARA UNIVERSITY VEHBİ KOÇ EYE HOSPITAL

My business was progressing and so were my profits. Once more, my mind turned to thinking of new services I might be able to provide for the good of all. I'm not sure why, but I had a great interest in blindness. I can never forget how important an organ the eye is to human beings. The renowned professor, late Süreyya Gördüren, and his colleagues were working on the mezzanine floor of Ankara University School of Medicine's old building. Both Süreyya and his deputy, the young and talented Professor Cahit Örgen, who eventually took over from him, had considered establishing an eye bank but not been able to get the idea off the ground. The two professors were successfully correcting blindness in some patients with an operation called keratoplasty. As they explained to me, the basis of this operation was altering the transparent part of the eye, the cornea, with a piece taken from another eye. Obtaining material from a healthy cornea was essential for the operation. If an eye bank could be established, people could pledge to donate their eyes while still alive, meaning that after their death they could be stored in the eye bank to be used in future operations. Following the establishment of the world's first eye bank in New York in 1945, the idea rapidly caught on across the globe. Eye banks were established in Tunisia, Morocco, Syria and Egypt before ours.

The Eye Bank Association of Turkey arose from the efforts of Professor Süreyya Gördüren to set up an eye bank, and Refik Koraltan, Speaker of the Grand National Assembly, was made honorary president. Acting upon the advice of Refik Koraltan, Prof. Süreyya Gördüren wrote to me requesting help on April 1, 1957. Deeply moved by the sincerity and heartfelt concern with which the letter was written, I wrote the following words to our general manager, Hulki Alisbah, on April 4, 1957, asking him to look into the situation:

"The subject is very important. On the other hand, we do have other commitments to meet. I would be overjoyed if there is any possibility of supporting this important endeavor, but I don't know anything about it—the nature of support it would require or what else it might necessitate."

Hulki Alisbah did some research and wrote back to me with his findings on April 8, 1957:

"For 15 years, it hasn't been possible to remove the outer cataract attached to the clear part [of the eye]. Instead, the cataract is removed along with the clear part and replaced with the clear, round part of a cataract-free eye removed in the same way from a deceased person. It fuses with the eye 30–35 days after the operation, restoring sight to the patient. According to the professor, this process cannot be completed at the University Eye Clinic because the entire facility only contains 45 beds. To develop the skills of their students and assistant doctors, they need to fill the beds with a wide variety of eye patients, but for this operation each patient needs to be in hospital for 30–35 days. If they assign five of the beds for this operation, and those beds change

over six times a year, that still means they can only restore sight to 30 people. Trachoma damage is really widespread in our country. There are already hundreds of patients waiting. Therefore, a hospital needs to be built and furnished with all kinds of equipment so that these patients can be treated separately from other eye patients, but still in conjunction with the university."

This letter really moved me and I decided to help. On April 25, 1957, I wrote to Dr. Süreyya Gördüren and the Ankara University rector of the time, Professor Hikmet Birand, informing them of my decision. Professor Gördüren was one of the most energetic people I have met in my life. He immediately spoke to those concerned and we donated 1,200,000 Turkish lira. That's how work on the Eye Bank in Cebeci next to the University Hospital began. Assistance was obtained from the army. The German government helped to bring equipment. The Red Crescent and Eye Bank Association also helped immensely. In no more than one and a half years, on Monday December 3, 1963, the new building and its clinics opened for service.

Three years after the first section had opened, Süreyya Gördüren passed away. One day, his successor, Professor Cahit Örgen, came to me to say that the Eye Bank wasn't able to meet the demand and asked if I would help them to build a second section. I told him that the first section had provided a great service to the country and that I would give the same help, 1,200,000 Turkish lira, for another section. Work began after I donated the money in 1970 and the second section opened at the end of 1972.

Vehbi Koç, *Hayat Hikâyem* (*My Life Story*), 4th Edition, Vehbi Koç Foundation Publications, Istanbul, 1983, pp.115–17

Ankara Vehbi Koç Eye Hospital

see **Ankara University School of Medicine Vehbi Koç Eye Hospital**

Ankara University Vehbi Koç Student Dormitory,

also known as ANKARA UNIVERSITY VEHBİ KOÇ MALE DORMITORY, is located in the Maltepe area of Ankara and accommodates students from Ankara University (AU). The facility was built in 1949–50 by Vehbi Koç(*) and donated to the university in 1951. It was the first major social contribution made by Vehbi Koç and one of the primary educational projects supported by the Vehbi Koç Foundation(*) (VKV) from its inception.

Situated on land owned by Vehbi Koç on a street called Gazi Mustafa Kemal Bulvarı in Maltepe, the building's foundations were laid in 1949 and it was completed towards the end of 1950. Donated to AU in early 1951, Ankara's first modern student dormitory initially accommodated 150 people, 86 in single rooms and the remainder in four-bed dorms. In response to increasing demand, the dormitory building was expanded almost twofold between 1956 and 1957. The VKV has carried out renovations on the dormitory at regular intervals since its opening, also giving support for fixtures and fittings.

Today, as well as single, double, three-bed and four-bed rooms, the dormitory also contains common service areas such as a restaurant, cafeteria, tailor, barber, laundry and study rooms. The students housed in the dormitory are normally in their senior year and chosen according to their level of achievement. The building is also sometimes used to host inter-university congresses and symposiums, as well as accommodating Turkish and international PhD students and students on language courses.

The plaque in the dormitory entrance hall contains a quote from the speech given by Vehbi Koç at the opening ceremony in 1951.

VEHBİ KOÇ: "HOW DID I FIRST GET INVOLVED IN PHILANTHROPY?"

I thought it was time that businesses started doing charitable work for the public good on a systematic basis and wanted to set a pioneering example... The first time I went to the USA, two things left a lasting impression on me: one was Columbia University's student dormitories and the other was the hospital at Johns Hopkins University in Baltimore. When you go into the hospital, you see two plaques, each on the left and right, explaining that the hospital was a foundation endowed by the businessman Johns Hopkins. Most of the universities and hospitals in America are charitable foundations.

When I got back home, I set my heart on following that example and using my available funds to build a facility. I just didn't know where or what I could do, so I started to discuss it with various people I trusted... For my first enterprise, I had in mind a budget of between 500,000 and one million Turkish lira. Some of my friends thought I should build a mosque or library, while others thought it should be a student dormitory...

I settled on building a student dormitory on the land I owned on Gazi Mustafa Kemal Caddesi in Maltepe and donating it to Ankara University... An agreeable deed of donation was prepared. We made an agreement with the university, marked the occasion with a celebration and the building began. The building work was completed on time without a hitch and the building was

kitted out. The first part of the student dormitory had 150 beds: 86 single rooms and the remainder four-bed dorms. The Vehbi Koç Student Dormitory was ready to hand over to Ankara University in May 1950.

In 1949, a new law was introduced stating that higher education dormitories were to fall under the remit of the Ministry of Education. I didn't want to transfer the dormitory to the ministry. I insisted on donating the building to the university because the ministry was a political institution.

Adnan Menderes became president after the Democrat Party came to power in the 1950 general election. I told him my wishes and he accepted them. In March 1951, Law No. 5744 was introduced, allowing "universities and faculties to take on student dormitories that have been bequeathed or donated, on condition that they are under their own management."

The late Tevfik İleri, Minister of Education at the time, agreed to do the official opening and the dormitory opened with a nice ceremony on April 30, 1951. The Ankara University rector at the time, the now deceased Professor Hikmet Birand, accepted the dormitory on behalf of the university. I'll never forget my excitement that day, nor the speech I gave to the guests and the young students who filled the dormitory.

The opening day of the dormitory was one of the best days in my life.

My words, like a legacy to the students, were written on a marble plate and placed in the dormitory entrance hall:

"Ankara has grown along with the Republic. Ever since it became a new educational center for our country, I have willed God to give me an opportunity to support this tide of enlightenment with my own means, because I believe that tomorrow depends on education, science and technology. The joy of attaining this wish is one of the proudest moments of my life.

I believe that any endeavor that helps to better nurture the young people, in whose hands Atatürk entrusted the country and Republic, is the greatest form of benevolence in the revolution we are living through. This facility arose from that belief.

Dear Young Resident,

You inspired this work. It is yours. I am just a humble means to an end. I am donating it to Ankara University so it can nurture you and your successors. All I ask of you is to do everything you can to help the realization of this great aim. Never forget the principle of working for the good of the country and nation with wisdom and an upright character.

This dormitory gives you a start in that direction, small though it may be, and if it sets an example, that will be my sole reward.

Vehbi Koç"

The dormitory was opened and the students settled in. It was the most modern dormitory built in Ankara at the time. Now and again, I would go to the dormitory, eat with the students, and follow their revelry and academic successes. It gave me a great deal of moral strength...

The need for student dormitories was growing every day. The municipal authorities had not given us permission for all the floors we wanted. In fact, they fined us for the fourth floor, which they said was illegal. The dormitory could take 150 students. In 1956, I wanted to expand it and the university accepted the idea. Intending to increase the capacity to 285 students, we started building in 1956 and the work was completed in 1957.

Vehbi Koç, *Hayat Hikâyem*, 4th Edition, Vehbi Koç Foundation Publications, Istanbul, 1983, pp. 111–14

Anlağan, Çetin *(b. March 17, 1938, Urfa)* archeologist and museologist. He was director of the Sadberk Hanım Museum(*) between 1985 and 2005.

Çetin Anlağan graduated from Ankara University Faculty of Languages, History and Geography Department of Protohistory and Asia Minor Archeology. After working at the Museum of Anatolian Civilizations in Ankara, he served as a museum inspector (1970–72). He went on to work at the Ministry of Education, General Directorate of Antiquities and Museums, fulfilling the role of assistant general manager from 1978 until his retirement in 1982. While working as director of Sadberk Hanım Museum (1985–2005), Anlağan published the following works: *Protohistorik Çağ Silahları/Weapons of the Protohistoric Age* (with Önder Bilgi, 1989) and *Bir Arkeolog Müzecinin Anıları: Suyun İki Yakasında* (Memoirs of an Archaeologist Curator: At Both Shores of the Sea; 2011).

ANMED, full name NEWS BULLETIN ON ARCHAEOLOGY FROM MEDITERRANEAN ANATOLIA, an annual journal of archeological reports in Turkish and English published by AKMED(*) since 2003. It has been published only as an e-journal since 2017. The journal contains details of archaeological digs and ground surveys in the regions of ancient Lycia, Pamphylia, Pisidia and Cilicia, in addition to news on restoration and conservation projects.

Aphrodisias Excavations *see* **Geyre Foundation**

Arçelik "Standing United for Education" Project, initiated in 2004 by Arçelik AŞ, in partnership with the Ministry of Education, with the aim of "improving the education and development of children at regional elementary boarding schools and creating exemplary individuals for the benefit of society". It receives sponsorship from the Arçelik Corporate Social Responsibility Project Fund set up under the auspices of the Vehbi Koç Foundation(*) (VKV).

One of several projects supported by VKV in the educational field, it is managed by Greenactive, an Arçelik public relations company. Its ultimate objective is to reach all of around 300 regional elementary boarding schools, which teach 200,000 rural children of limited financial means. The project remit includes: creating "Voluntary Family Unions" in the provinces to give children a warm family environment and meet their clothing and book needs; opening spaces called "Our Rooms" equipped with interactive educational and play materials to help cognitive, personal and social development; managing a program called "Support for Teachers and Education" which gives in-service training to a number of teachers chosen from each school, focusing on new developments in education and technology; running the "They Were Kids Too" campaign which enables children to meet famous role models from the business, media and arts world; and providing unconditional education grants to top students who have graduated from the regional boarding schools and are in need of financial support.

It is a multi-agency project, run through the collaboration of civil society groups such as the Educational Volunteers Foundation of Turkey (TEGV[*]), the Mother Child Education Foundation (AÇEV[*]), and the Private Sector Volunteers Association, together with the families of local Arçelik dealers and local administration in the cities.

Arıkan, Ömer *(b. ?),* physician and director. Served as chief physician and responsible director of the American Hospital(*) between 2001 and 2003.

He graduated from Dicle University Faculty of Medicine in 1982 and, after completing his compulsory service, underwent his general surgery residency at the SSK Samatya Hospital (1984–88). After completion, he worked as a surgeon at various state hospitals from 1988 to 1994, following which he was appointed chief physician at the Kadıköy Şifa Hospital. He was chief physician and responsible director of the American Hospital between 2001 and 2003. Dr. Arıkan has worked freelance for some time and is currently working at the MedEra Hospital in Baku, Azerbaijan.

Arman, Gürsen *(b. June 16, 1943, Diyarbakır),* economist and director. He served as president of the Vehbi Koç Foundation(*) (VKV) from 1988 to 1997.

Arman completed secondary education at Ziya Gökalp High School in Diyarbakır and graduated from Ankara Academy of Economic and Commercial Sciences in 1968. He worked at Elginkan Holding, before starting at Otoyol, a Koç Group(*) company, in 1975. From 1983 to 1988, he worked as the general accounting manager at Arçelik AŞ. He became president of VKV in 1988 and continued until 1997, finally retiring from the Koç Group in 2002.

Arsel, Nusret *(b. October 9, 1922, Adana – d. January 18, 2014, Istanbul),* lawyer and businessman who worked in the senior management of Koç Holding(*) companies between 1953 and 2014. He was married to Semahat Arsel(*), the eldest daughter of Vehbi Koç(*) and Sadberk Koç(*).

Born in Adana as the second son of Mehmet and Zeynep Arsel, he started elementary school in Antalya in 1929. His family moved to Ankara in 1932, when his father began working at Koçzade Ahmet Vehbi Firması, a company belonging to Vehbi Koç. After finishing elementary school there (1934), he continued his secondary education at Gazi High School (1942), before enrolling at Ankara University Faculty of Law. While still at university, he worked for the State Railway and Central Bank, respectively. A year after graduating in 1946, Arsel went to Paris to study for a doctorate in law, which he received in April 1951 after completing his thesis, "Working Conditions in Sweeden after World War I."

Returning to Turkey in the same year, he worked for two months as a translator at the Joint United States Military Mission for Aid to Turkey (JUSMMAT). After completing a legal practice internship in Ankara and Izmir, he completed his military service in Ankara. Following his military discharge, in March 1953 he accepted Vehbi Koç's proposal to work as the assistant of Hulki Alisbah(*) at Koç Ticaret. On January 5, 1956, he married Semahat Koç.

STARTING WORK AT KOÇ TİCARET IN THE WORDS OF NUSRET ARSEL...

[When I heard that the application I had made for a job equivalent to my education had been rejected by the Ministry of Labor] I dejectedly walked from the area where all the ministries were located onto the main street. I walked towards Kızılay, slowly and with great despondence. All the years of hard work and considerable stress flashed in front of my eyes like a cinema strip. About 15 minutes later, I heard a voice in the distance calling, "Nusret, Nusret..." The voice was coming from a black car on my right, facing towards Çankaya. I realized that the person waving his hand from the driver side window was Mr. Koç. I went over to him. He was driving the car himself.

I remember very well, even today, the perforated leather gloves he was wearing. In an endearing and affectionate voice, he said, "Nusret, what's the matter? What's eating you? You look really upset." It was as if he had woken me up from a sleep full of nightmares. I pulled myself together. Standing by the car, I explained that my application to the Ministry of Labor had been rejected and that's why I was upset.

He invited me into the car. After explaining that he had a half hour meeting at the Ministry of Commerce, but would like to talk to me in more detail, he asked me to wait in the car for him. I think it was about 20 minutes later when he came back and we went together to his office at Koç Ticaret in Ulus Square. It was noon. Recalling that the last time we had met was about four or five years ago, Vehbi Koç said, "If I'm not mistaken, at that time you were working for the Central Bank as well as studying at the Faculty of Law. Then you disappeared. I thought you must have gone off to do military service, got married, or found a job outside Ankara."

I told him briefly what I had done since leaving the faculty. Mr. Koç listened with great care; it was clear that my story interested him more than his ministerial visit. Now and then, he scribbled a few brief notes. Then, he invited me to eat at the Zevk Restaurant, at the same time letting İlhan (Arsel) know. The three of us had a very enjoyable meal and the positive atmosphere instantly dispelled my stress.

After the meal, we went back to the office. He said, "Nusret, now let's talk to you about work." (İlhan was with us during the conversation.) "You can start work with me tomorrow for a monthly salary of 500 lira." I was completely taken aback by this unexpected offer, but quickly pulling myself together, I replied, "Mr. Koç, you must be feeling sorry for me. You probably felt upset and made the offer just to cheer me up." I continued by saying, "I'm really grateful, but could you first of all put down in writing how I can be useful and what my duties and responsibilities will be. Then, I'll try to satisfy your requirements accordingly." He listened patiently to me and advised me to meet with the general manager of Koç Ticaret, Hulki Alisbah, to talk in more detail about the job before making my final decision.

Of course, that's what happened and a week later I went to see Mr. Alisbah. He gave me a warm welcome and we talked for about an hour. That's how, in March 1953, I began working at Koç Ticaret as Mr. Alisbah's assistant and second-degree authorized signatory. My office was between Hulki Alisbah and Vehbi Koç's offices, my salary was 500 Turkish lira and I had 15 days annual leave.

Nusret Arsel, *Ana Duası* (A Mother's Blessing), Yapı Kredi Publications, Istanbul, 2012, pp. 61–62

At the end of 1958, he became deputy general manager of Simko Ticaret ve Sanayi AŞ, a Koç-Siemens partnership, which he founded together with Vehbi Koç(*). After Simko began operations in early 1959, he went to Munich for an internship at Siemens, returning to Istanbul in 1960. In January 1964, he was appointed general manager of Simko. In early August of the same year, foundations were laid in Mudanya for a cable factory, which was completed and went into operation one year later as Türk Siemens Kablo ve Elektrik Sanayii AŞ.

In 1982, he received the National Order of Merit from the President of France for "improving relations between Turkey and France and contributing, along with his wife, to the development of culture and art." In 1984, his 20th year at the Simko head office, he was awarded with the Grand Order of Merit of the German Federal Republic for "his contribution to the consolidation of Turkish-German relations." In 1982, he was appointed honorary consul general of Malaysia, which he continued until his death. In 1991, he received the Dato title and medal granted by the Sultanate of Malaysia.

From the end of 1986 until his retirement, Nusret Arsel was chair of the board of directors and general manager at Etmaş and Hataş, both companies affiliated to Simko and Türk Siemens Kablo. He also served on the boards of other Koç Group companies, such as Migros, Beko Elektronik, Tat Konserve, Tat Tohumculuk, Maret, Pastavilla, SEK, Simtel, Ram Foreign Trade, İzocam and Türk Demir Döküm. As a member of the Istanbul Chamber of Commerce Energy Committee, he attended the International Chamber of Commerce (ICC) annual conferences for 12 years as Turkey's representative and served on the ICC Energy Commission. A founding member of both the Turkish Education Foundation(*) (TEV) and Turkish Lions, Arsel set up an insurance brokers company, Aransem, after his retirement and continued to serve on the board of directors at some Koç Holding companies.

He was interested in developing agricultural production, particularly in relation to soy, and wrote several newspaper articles expounding his views and suggestions on the topic. He became chair of the Tat Tohumculuk Board of Directors in 1987 and continued in the role for many years.

Semahat and Dr. Nusret Arsel donated 10 million dollars for the building of a nursing school on the site of the old Güzelbahçe Hospital in Nişantaşı, Istanbul. The building, which was completed in 2002, was named after them. A one million dollar fund, also created by the couple, went into the establishment of NASAMER(*) as part of the Koç University Law School (*see* Koç University). The center opened in 2007 and deals with matters of international trade law.

Arsel was also an art and music enthusiast. His foray into amateur painting began in 1976 and lasted about 25 years. A selection of his work was published in 2009 in his book, *Çizgilerimdeki Çizgilerim!* (The Lines in My Drawings!). His memoirs, entitled *Ana Duası* (A Mother's Blessing), were published in 2012. He passed away in Istanbul, on January 18, 2014, leaving a large proportion of his assets to the Vehbi Koç Foundation(*).

Arsel, (Sevim) Semahat *(b. September 8, 1928, Keçiören, Ankara),* née KOÇ, businesswoman and philanthropist. Among her other roles, she is the chair of the Vehbi Koç Foundation(*) (VKV) Executive Committee and Board of Directors, member of the Koç Holding(*) Board of Directors and Koç University(*) (KU) Board of Overseers.

At the Arnavutköy American College for Girls, 1949

The eldest child of Vehbi Koç(*) and Sadberk Koç(*), she was born in the family Orchard House in Keçiören, Ankara, which is today used as VEKAM(*) operational center. Along with her brother Rahmi M. Koç(*), she grew up under the care of Australian and German nannies. After completing elementary education at the TED Ankara College, she went to board at the Arnavutköy American College for Girls (*see* Robert College[*]), graduating in 1949. She moved to Ankara after marrying Dr. Nusret Arsel(*) on January 5, 1956. Her husband was at the time working as an assistant to Hulki Alisbah(*) at Koç Holding. She lived in Germany in 1959–60, together with her husband who was doing an internship in Siemens, and attended the Goethe Institute in order to improve her German.

Joining the Koç Holding Board of Directors in 1964 and the VKV Board of Directors in 1969, Arsel made a valuable contribution to Koç Holding with her work in the tourism and service sectors. In 1972, she took a keen interest in renovation work at the Divan Hotel in the Elmadağ district of Istanbul and from then on took part in the management of the hotel. She was a key figure in building and transforming the "Divan" name into an internationally renowned, luxury brand and is currently chair of the board of directors of Divan Group. Arsel was also one of the founders of the Tourism Development and Education Foundation (TUGEV)(*), a body set up to develop tourism in Turkey, help provide training, and create more qualified employees for the sector. In 1996, she became chair of the board of directors at SETUR, a travel and tourism company connected to Koç Holding.

From an early age, she underwent a large number of operations and witnessed firsthand the important role played by the nursing profession. She subsequently became involved in numerous initiatives in the field. She became chair of the Nursing Committee, which manages the Nursing Fund(*) established in 1974, under the auspices of VKV. The Nursing Fund provided grants for thousands of nursing students, compiled and published much-needed nursing books, and

organized numerous academic meetings and conferences. Semahat Arsel was a leading figure in setting up Turkey's first and only postgraduate nursing training center, which aimed to raise health sector standards and expand service coverage. It was founded in 1992 as part of the American Hospital, and named in her honor (*see* SANERC [Semahat Arsel Nursing Education and Research Center]). The nursing school on the site of the old Güzelbahçe Hospital in Nişantaşı, Istanbul, was built with donations from Semahat Arsel and her husband, Dr. Nusret Arsel. The building, finished in 2002, was named after the couple. She also served as the second chair of the Florence Nightingale School of Nursing Foundation, and in 2012 she received the accolade of honorary doctor from Istanbul University Florence Nightingale Faculty of Nursing for her contribution to advancement in the nursing profession.

Along with her husband, Semahat Arsel created a one million dollar fund for the establishment of NASAMER(*), a center that deals with matters of international trade law. The center opened in 2007 as part of the Koç University Law School. In the same year, the Semahat–Dr. Nusret Arsel Education Park(*) opened in association with the Foundation of Educational Volunteers (TEGV[*]). The park is situated in Etimesgut, the district with Ankara's highest population of children and young people. The sports hall on the KU Rumelifeneri Campus bears the name of Semahat Arsel and the Science and Technology Building is named after both her and her husband.

In 2010, she played a leading role in the setting up of KOÇ-KAM(*), a research and application center for gender and women's studies operating as part of Koç University. In 2015, KOÇ-KAM introduced the Semahat Arsel Honorary Award, to be awarded to "women of high international standing and those working in gender and women's studies" (*see* KOÇ-KAM).

To mark the 40th birthday of the Divan Hotel, Arsel initiated the creation of the book *Eskimeyen Tatlar: Türk Mutfak Kültürü/Timeless Tastes: Turkish Culinary Culture*, which was published by VKV in 1996.

IN THE WORDS OF SEMAHAT ARSEL...

I finished the American College for Girls. Then, as I was preparing for the university exams, I caught a serious illness. It was an illness caused by parasites spread by dogs. I had to have nine operations. I stayed in many different places and saw very different hospitals in Japan, America, Switzerland, Germany and Turkey. Because of that experience, I knew how important the nursing profession was. That means God gave me an ideal, a duty, saying, "You [should] advocate for nurses." In 1974, with the support of Mr. Koç, I set up a fund at the Vehbi Koç Foundation and from that day onwards, I devoted a lot of attention to the nursing profession. It became my ideal.

http://www.capital.com.tr/is-dunyasi/sirketler-ve-yoneticiler/%E2%80%9Cvehbi-bey-yasasaydi--simdi-cok-mektup-yazardi%E2%80%9D-haberdetay-5018

Of course, the eldest child in any family takes on different responsibilities by necessity. Right from my childhood, I was raised with responsibilities within the family. After my mother's death, I tried wholeheartedly to fill her place, to keep my father from feeling lonely and longing for her. In actual fact, my father and I both thought along similar lines. Afterwards, I tried hard to be a grown-up for my siblings and to maintain family unity.

http://www.capital.com.tr/is-dunyasi/sirketler-ve-yoneticiler/%E2%80%9Cvehbi-bey-yasasaydi--simdi-cok-mektup-yazardi%E2%80%9D-haberdetay-5018

As Semahat Koç grew older, she took priority place in joining her father on his business trips: "Sometimes my mother couldn't keep up with my father's fast pace. When that happened, it was over to me. As my father's foreign trips were always related to business, someone with a good knowledge of both the business and the language of the country we are visiting would accompany the group... Kenan İnal was his constant companion in English-speaking countries and Adnan Berkay fulfilled the same role in the Germanic nations."

Can Kıraç, *Anılarımla Patronum Vehbi Koç* (Memories of My Boss, Vehbi Koç), Milliyet Publications, Istanbul, 1995, p. 162

Mrs. Arsel! As Vehbi Koç's inseparable friend, how do you manage the "cash" when you're travelling? "My father doesn't like carrying money on him. He thinks it's dirty and worries about losing it! When we travel, he gives all the money to me, never forgetting to add the caveat, 'You manage it for us and then give me the accounts!' He asks the price of everything... I don't tell him the real hotel room prices any more. He doesn't know about giving tips, he wouldn't like it... He used to say, 'Look how cheap our country is, it's great,' every time we returned from a trip."

Kıraç, *Anılarımla Patronum Vehbi Koç*, p. 376

ADVICE AND COUNSEL FROM VEHBİ KOÇ TO HIS CHILDREN

The Family Committee that I set up in 1972 should carry on.

My eldest child, Semahat Arsel, should be the committee's chair. Pay heed to the advice of Semahat Arsel and rally round her. It is her action up until this day that has maintained your unity, and I trust her opinions. Argue matters, and keep disagreements between yourselves. Try to make decisions by consent. When that isn't possible, go with the majority and make sure you all comply with it. Try to prevent any of your issues becoming public.

Suna Kıraç, *Ömrümden Uzun İdeallerim Var* (My Ideals, Longer than My Lifetime), Suna and İnan Kıraç Foundation Publications, Istanbul, 2006, p. 294

Artam, (Mehmet) Evren *(b. June 5, 1937, Istanbul – d. April 23, 2008, Istanbul)*, director. Represented Koç Holding(*) on the Vehbi Koç Foundation(*) Board of Directors between 1997 and 2002.

After completing his secondary education at Galatasaray High School in 1957, Artam continued his education at the Istanbul Academy of Economic and Commercial Sciences until 1961. He joined Uniroyal, one of the Koç Holding companies, in 1964 on completion of his military service. He was accounting manager at Uzel (1965–76) and deputy general manager at Asil Çelik (1976–79). Artam subsequently served as general manager of Mavi Çelik and was appointed president of Garanti Bank (1981). After working as financial coordinator at Koç Holding (1983–84), he went on to serve as executive director of Ram Foreign Trade Inc. (1984–89). He was general manager of Ram from 1989 to 1992 and Koç Yatırım from 1992 to 1997, following which he became president of Koç Holding Foundations in 1997, continuing in the post until his retirement in 2000.

Artam also served as chair of the board at both the Swiss Chamber of Commerce in Turkey (1988–90) and TURKTRADE (1990–92), as well as vice president of the Foreign Economic Relations Board Turkish-American Business Councils (1990–92).

Arter, contemporary arts institution of the Vehbi Koç Foundation(*) (VKV). Arter was opened in May 2010 on Istanbul's İstiklal Caddesi in the historical building known as Meymaret Han, with the aim of providing a sustainable infrastructure for producing and exhibiting contemporary art.

Arter opened with an exhibition called "Starter", which showcased 160 works from the VKV Contemporary Art Collection created by 87 artists from Turkey and across the globe. Between 2010 and 2018, Arter hosted solo exhibitions, collaborative events with other international institutions, and group exhibitions focusing on new productions. As part of the exhibitions of this period, Arter presented 35 solo and group exhibitions with accompanying publications, talks, performances and workshops; and provided support for the production of 183 artworks in the framework of these exhibitions.

Arter also served as a preparatory research and learning environment for the contemporary art museum, which is VKV's single major project in the field of contemporary art. Due to open in September 2019, Arter's new building is designed by London-based Grimshaw Architects, whose design concept was selected through a paid competition. Covering a space of 18,000 square meters, the museum is envisaged as both a cultural and educational hub. At its new home in Dolapdere, Arter will present exhibitions from but not limited to the VKV Contemporary Art Collection, as well as performances and events across disciplines, expanding the range of its programmes. As well as exhibition spaces, the museum includes performance spaces, meeting and activity rooms, a library, conservation lab, bookstore focused on art publications, and refreshment areas.

Melih Fereli(*) is the founding director and Emre Baykal(*) leads the museum's team of curators. As of the end of 2018, the museum's collection, started through the initiative of Ömer M. Koç(*) in 2007, contains more than 1,300 works of more than 350 artists from Turkey and its neighboring countries, as well as Europe and North America. It combines the work of leading artists that started out in the 1960s with that of later generations.

Arter Contemporary Art Museum (project)

Arter, 2014
Photo: Serkan Taycan

ARTER EXHIBITIONS*

- **Starter. Works from the Vehbi Koç Foundation Contemporary Art Collection** *(May 8–October 31, 2010)*
  Curator: René Block
- **Second Exhibition** *(November 28, 2010–March 13, 2011)*
  Artists: Halil Altındere, Burak Arıkan, Volkan Aslan, Vahap Avşar, Banu Cennetoğlu – Yasemin Özcan Kaya, Ayşe Erkmen, Hafriyat (Murat Akagündüz, Antonio Cosentino, extramücadele, İnci Furni, Mustafa Pancar), Ali Kazma, Aydan Murtezaoğlu – Bülent Şangar, Ahmet Öğüt, İz Öztat, Cengiz Tekin, Canan Tolon
  Curator: Emre Baykal
- **Tactics of Invisibility** *(April 9–June 5, 2011)*
  Artists: Nevin Aladağ, Kutluğ Ataman, Cevdet Erek, Ayşe Erkmen, Esra Ersen, İnci Eviner, Nilbar Güreş, Hafriyat, Ali Kazma, Ahmet Öğüt, Füsun Onur, Sarkis, Hale Tenger, Nasan Tur, xurban_collective
  Curators: Daniela Zyman and Emre Baykal
- **Hold Me Close to Your Heart** *(June 22–August 21, 2011)*
  Patricia Piccinini
  Curator: Başak Doğa Temür
- **5 Person Buffet** *(July 8–September 25, 2011)*
  Deniz Gül
  Curator: Emre Baykal
- **Mesopotamian Dramaturgies** *(September 15–December 11, 2011)*
  Kutluğ Ataman
  Curator: Emre Baykal
- **Freedom to the Black** *(February 10–26, 2012)*
  Erdem Helvacıoğlu
  Curator: Melih Fereli
- **Stage** *(April 6–May 27, 2012)*
  Nevin Aladağ
  Curator: Başak Doğa Temür
- **You Are Still Here** *(March 17–May 27, 2012)*
  Mona Hatoum
  Curator: Emre Baykal
- **The Silent Shape of Things** *(June 21–August 26, 2012)*
  Sophia Pompéry
  Curator: Ece Pazarbaşı
- **The Wound** *(June 21–August 26, 2012)*
  Berlinde De Bruyckere
  Curator: Selen Ansen
- **The Move** *(October 5–November 18, 2012)*
  Artists: Adel Abidin, Rosa Barba, Runa Islam
  Curator: Başak Şenova
- **Envy, Enmity, Embarrassment** *(January 24–April 7, 2013)*
  Artists: Selim Birsel, Hera Büyüktaşçıyan, CANAN, Aslı Çavuşoğlu, Merve Ertufan & Johanna Adebäck, Nilbar Güreş, Berat Işık, Şener Özmen, Yusuf Sevinçli, Erdem Taşdelen, Hale Tenger, Mahir Yavuz
  Curator: Emre Baykal

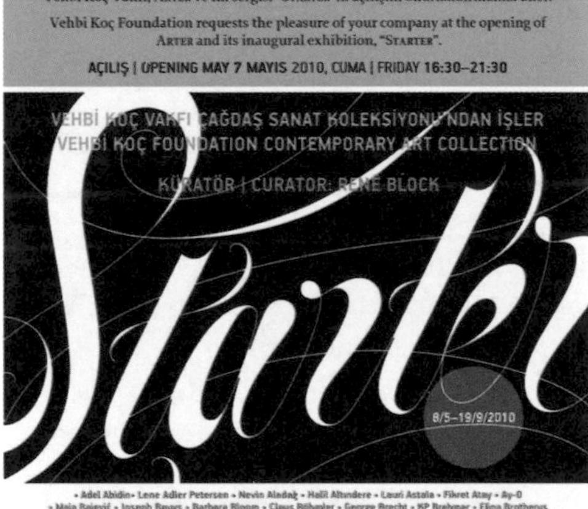

- **Don't Forget to Remember** *(May 2–August 11, 2013)*
  Volkan Aslan
  Curator: Emre Baykal
- **Afterimage** *(May 2–August 11, 2013)*
  Mat Collishaw
  Curator: Başak Doğa Temür
- **Interpretation of Cage/Ryoanji** *(November 15, 2013–January 12, 2014)*
  Sarkis
  Curator: Melih Fereli

- **Yet Another Story About the Fall**
  (November 15, 2013–January 12, 2014)
  Fatma Bucak
  Curator: Başak Doğa Temür
- **The Stones Talk** *(November 15, 2013–January 12, 2014)*
  Aslı Çavuşoğlu
  Curator: Özge Ersoy
- **The Sleep of Reason** *(February 8–April 27, 2014)*
  Marc Quinn
  Curator: Selen Ansen
- **Through the Looking Glass** *(May 28–August 17, 2014)*
  Füsun Onur
  Curator: Emre Baykal
- **The Roving Eye: Contemporary Art from Southeast Asia** *(September 18, 2014–January 4, 2015)*
  Artists: Alwin Reamillo, Araya Rasdjarmrearnsook, Aung Ko, Aung Myint, Bui Cong Khanh, Chris Chong Chan Fui, Dinh Q. Le, Duto Hardono, FX Harsono, Heri Dono, Isabel & Alfredo Aquilizan, Ise Roslisham, Jakkai Siributr, Jason Lim, Josephine Turalba, Krisna Murti, Lee Wen, Luong Hue Trinh & Nguyen Xuan Son, Manit Sriwanichpoom, Melati Suryodarmo, Mella Jaarsma, Michael Shaowanasai, Nguyen Van Cuong, Restu Ratnaningtyas, Srey Bandaul, Sutee Kunavichayanont, Tawatchai Puntusawasdi, Tay Wei Leng, Vasan Sitthiket, Vertical Submarine, Vu Dan Tan, Yee I-Lann
  Curator: Iola Lenzi
- **timemaker** *(January 30–April 5, 2015)*
  Ali Kazma
  Curator: Emre Baykal
- **Spaceliner** *(May 15–August 2, 2015)*
  Artists: Peter Anders, Sandra Boeschenstein, Pip Culbert, İnci Eviner, Monika Grzymala, Nic Hess, Gözde İlkin, Harry Kramer, Pauline Kraneis, Hans Peter Kuhn, Zilla Leutenegger, Pia Linz, Christiane Löhr, Ulrike Mohr, Jong Oh, Nadja Schöllhammer, Heike Weber
  Curator: Barbara Heinrich
- **When the Heart Goes Bing Bam Boom**
  (December 11, 2015–February 28, 2016)
  Šejla Kamerić
  Curator: Başak Doğa Temür
- **Flow Through** *(March 30–May 15, 2016)*
  Bahar Yürükoğlu
  Curator: Duygu Demir
- **Vertigo** *(March 30–May 15, 2016)*
  Murat Akagündüz
  Curator: Aslı Seven
- **Unfiltered** *(March 30–May 15, 2016)*
  Şener Özmen
  Curator: Süreyyya Evren
- **Not All That Falls Has Wings**
  (June 9–September 18, 2016)
  Artists: Bas Jan Ader, Phyllida Barlow, Cyprien Gaillard, Ryan Gander, Mikhail Karikis, Uriel Orlow, VOID, Anne Wenzel
  Curator: Selen Ansen
- **Words, Numbers, Lines** *(October 14, 2016–January 15, 2017)*
  Bilge Friedlaender
  Curators: Mira Friedlaender and Işın Önol
- **Off the Record** *(October 14, 2016–January 15, 2017)*
  Nil Yalter
  Curator: Eda Berkmen
- **In the Realm of the Senseless** *(February 10–May 7, 2017)*
  Jake & Dinos Chapman
  Curator: Nick Hackworth
- **Ways of Seeing** *(June 2–August 13, 2017)*
  Artists: Ghada Amer, Chris Bond, Ulisse Cantagalli, David Claerbout, Jojakim Cortis & Adrian Sonderegger, Hayri Çizel, Salvador Dali, Hans-Peter Feldmann, Andreas Gursky, Mona Hatoum, Jeppe Hein, Paul & Marlene Kos, Alicja Kwade, Gustav Metzger, Shana Moulton, Vik Muniz, Grayson Perry, Walid Raad, Edouard Frederic, Wilhelm Richter, Fred Sandback, Markus Schinwald, Hassan Sharif, Cindy Sherman, Kim Tschang-Yeul, James Turrell, Kara Walker, James Webb, Frederik de Wit, *and anonymous artists*
  Curators: Sam Bardaouil and Till Fellrath
- **Behind Mount Qaf** *(September 12–February 18, 2018)*
  CANAN
  Curator: Nazlı Gürlek
- **Isle** *(March 16–July 15, 2018)*
  Ali Mahmut Demirel
  Curator: Başak Doğa Temür
- **Empty House** *(March 16–July 15, 2018)*
  Can Aytekin
  Curator: Eda Berkmen

*All exhibition catalogs have been published.

Starter exhibition, 2010
Photo: Murat Germen

Aşkar, Attila *(b. September 1943, Bolvadin, Afyonkarahisar),* scientist. He was president of Koç University(*) (KU) between 2001 and 2009.

After finishing Saint Joseph High School in 1961, Aşkar studied civil engineering at Istanbul Technical University, graduating with a master's degree in 1966. He completed his PhD at Princeton University in the USA and after graduating in 1969 began working as a postdoctoral researcher at Brown University. In 1971 he returned to Turkey, working for a while at the Scientific and Technological

Research Council of Turkey (TÜBİTAK), where he taught a PhD class. He was appointed as a lecturer at the Department of Mathematics of Boğaziçi University in 1972, later serving as vice dean of the Faculty of Basic Sciences, Senate member, and Intercollegiate Board representative. He was also guest professor at Princeton and Paris VI Universities, the Göttingen Max-Planck Institute in Göttingen, and the Royal Swedish Institute of Technology in Stockholm. Aşkar is currently professor in the KU Department of Mathematics. As well as lecturing, he was also founding dean of the College of Arts and Sciences (1993–98) and vice president for academic affairs (1998–2001).

A member of both the Turkish Academy of Sciences (TÜBA) and TÜBİTAK, he has received the TÜBİTAK Incentive Award, TÜBİTAK Science Award and Ministry of Culture Information Age Award. Almost 100 of his articles have appeared in international journals and he has written two books on mathematics: *Methods in Applied Algebra and Analysis* (1981) and *Lattice Dynamical Foundations of Continuum Theories of Solids* (1986). He also developed the "Aşkar Theory" in mathematics, which was named in his honor.

ATARC BOUN Cultural Heritage Project, full name I KNOW THE CULTURAL HERITAGE OF MY DISTRICT AND MY CITY ISTANBUL AND SHARE MY KNOWLEDGE WITH MY FRIENDS, project conducted by the Boğaziçi University's Applied Tourism Administration and Research Center (ATARC) to encourage appreciation of cultural heritage at a young age. It was launched with support from several institutions at the start, including the Vehbi Koç Foundation(*).

The project, conducted between October 2012 and December 2014, studied the effects of a multi-dimensional education program created to develop and measure cultural heritage awareness in elementary school pupils of 2nd through to 4th grades. A total of 286 pupils from three state elementary schools in the Fatih district of Istanbul took part in the project. As part of the project, story books with visual and audio appeal were developed, workshops organized, and field trips arranged. The six story books produced as a result were distributed in partnership with municipalities; this was further supported by practical activities.

Atatürk Library, also known by its full name of ISTANBUL METROPOLITAN MUNICIPALITY ATATURK LIBRARY and TAKSIM ATATURK LIBRARY, public library connected to Istanbul Metropolitan Municipality (IBB) Directorate of Libraries and Museums. The library is situated on the street Mete Caddesi in Taksim, Istanbul. The library building was constructed by the Vehbi Koç Foundation(*) on behalf of the Koç Group and to mark the 50th anniversary of the foundation of the Turkish Republic and was transferred to the Istanbul Municipality in 1976. Enriched by personal donations, the historical significance and diversity of its collection have made it into an important center frequently used by national and international researchers.

Istanbul's first municipal library was established in 1924 in a building known as Şehremaneti Dairesi. The collection began in 1929 at the Atatürk House Museum in Şişli and moved to Beyazıt Madrasa in 1931. The madrasa was opened to the public as the Municipal Museum and Library in 1939. Due to the collection eventually expanding beyond the limits of its location, in 1981 it was moved to its current site constructed by the Koç Group in 1973–76. Vehbi Koç(*) received a plaque from

IBB in 1996 in appreciation for constructing the library.

Designed by the architect Sedad Hakkı Eldem(*), the Atatürk Library covers an area of 5,000 square meters, overlooking the Bosporus from Taksim. It is a three-story concrete structure created from hexagonal elements, reflecting Eldem's desire to synthesize traditional Turkish architecture with modernism. The hexagonal book depository on the bottom floor has the capacity to hold around 600,000 books. Reading and study rooms are situated on the top two floors. There is a large reading hall and periodical room on the highest level beneath hexagonal pyramid-shaped domes in the roof. The exhibition and conference hall are situated in the wings on either side of the entrance. A marble plaque on the front of the library bears the words, "This library building was donated to the people of Istanbul and the Turkish nation by Koç Holding AŞ and associated companies on the 50th anniversary of the Republic."

Containing the vast majority of Ottoman books published from the printing of the first books on the Müteferrika press through to the alphabet reform, the Atatürk Library has one of the country's richest collections of Turkish books written in Arabic script. Together with the first Ottoman newspapers, the library collection also contains the only copies of publications such as *Enîn-i Mazlûm* (The Howl of the Wronged), *Bâdiye* (Desert) and *Varlık* (Existence). The rare books foreign language collection includes thousands of manuscripts, including travel books about Istanbul and others containing historic, geographic, demographic and folkloric information. Istanbul's largest archive of old city maps is also part of the library collection. Work on digitalizing the collection has been ongoing since 1998.

Open 24 hours a day to meet heavy demand, it was chosen as Turkey's best library in 2007 and 2011.

https://kultursanat.ibb.istanbul/KulturMd_CultureCenter/Index/12

Atay, Temel K(amil) *(b. September 17, 1940, Istanbul),* engineer, director. He has represented Koç Holding(*) on the Vehbi Koç Foundation(*) (VKV) Board of Directors since 1998.

After graduating with a BSc in Mechanical Engineering from Istanbul Technical University, Atay completed an MBA at Wayne State University in Detroit, USA. He was product development engineer at Chrysler Istanbul (1965–66), product development manager at Otosan (1966–69), and product development engineer at Ford Motor Co. in the USA (1969–72). After working as Koç Holding assistant coordinator in the automotive department (1972–74), he served as general manager at Otoyol Sanayi AŞ in 1974 and at Tofaş in 1981. From 1992 to 1994, he was Koç Holding vice president of technical projects, and from 1994 to 1996, he served as Tofaş Group president.

In 1996, he joined the Koç Holding Board of Directors and also served as vice chair of the Group Executive Committee and president of Other Automotive Companies. He became a member of the Koç Holding Management Committee in 1998 and served as vice chair of the board of directors until 2016. He was CEO in 2000 and 2001 and took over responsibility for the Family Office in 2003. He is still on the board of directors at Koç Holding and the executive committee of VKV, as well as serving on the Tüpraş Board of Directors.

Ayanlar, (Ramazan) Fahrettin *(b. August 20, 1944, Ankara - d. 13 Ocak 2015, İstanbul),* architect who carried out many of the Vehbi Koç Foundation's(*) (VKV) architectural projects while serving as coordinator of projects and construction at the VKV from 1997 to 2010.

He graduated with a master's degree from Middle East Technical University Faculty of Architecture in 1967. After working for a while with architects Toğrul Devres and Doruk Pamir, in 1973 he went to Venezuela and worked at Arquitectura Beckhoff in Caracas as a designer and manager. In 1981, he established his own architectural office, Ayanlar & Siebert. Returning to Istanbul in 1987, he began working on the design and application of architectural projects for organizations connected to the Koç Group(*). After his appointment as coordinator of projects and construction at the VKV in 1997, Ayanlar undertook numerous architectural projects for the foundation, including the Koç Private School (see Koç School), Koç University(*) Rumelifeneri Campus, the American Hospital(*) and ANAMED(*). After leaving the VKV in 2010, he set up Ayanlar Mimarlık and also served as a consultant for the L35 AS/OS architectural company. In 2008, he received the Building Category Award as part of the Chamber of Architects of Turkey 11th National Architecture Awards in recognition for his ANAMED design project.

Ayvalık International Music Academy (AIMA), a music training center founded in 1998 in Balıkesir, Ayvalık. It received the Vehbi Koç Award(*) for culture in 2011, along with its founder, Filiz Ali(*).

AIMA provides opportunities for young musicians to work alongside distinguished international teachers, helping to broaden their educational experience as well as their horizons. At its center in Ayvalık, the academy holds annual summer and spring master classes, which last 8–10 days and primarily focus on bowed string instruments. It has diversified considerably since its foundation and now offers composition workshops, together with master classes in creative writing, piano, flute, guitar, singing and opera. Ayla Erduran, Suna Kan, Lukas David, Peter Bruns, Valery Oistrakh and İdil Biret are among the considerable number of internationally renowned virtuoso musicians who have participated in the Academy's work.

AIMA organizes the Ayvalık Music Festival, which has been held every July since 2013 and strives to enrich the cultural life of Ayvalık with film screenings that showcase classic cinema.

Ayvalık Rahmi M. Koç Museum, a museum run under the auspices of the Rahmi M. Koç Museology and Culture Foundation(*). It is located in the historical Taxiarches Church on Alibey (Cunda) Island on the coast of Ayvalık in Balıkesir province and was Ayvalık's first private museum when it opened in 2014.

The Taxiarches Church, the first in Ayvalık, was originally built as a small sanctuary in the fifteenth century. In 1873, it was rebuilt over the old foundations and reopened as a metropolitan church. The church's design, on a rectangular plan with a single-dome basilica, reflects the neoclassical architectural style of the time. The masonry walls were built using the famous local limestone known as "sarımsaktaşı" and the four loadbearing columns are constructed from brick with lime plaster and stucco cladding. The interior is decorated with icons of the saints and depictions of the apostles as well as botanic and geometrical motifs.

From 1927 to 1928, it was converted into a mosque with no minaret and was used as a Tekel depot for some time afterwards. It was severely damaged in the 1944 earthquake

and again later by other natural causes. Due to this, and the added effect of illegal excavations in search of treasure, the building was largely left in ruins. In May 2012, the Rahmi M. Koç Museology and Culture Foundation rented it from the General Directorate of Foundations, for use as a cultural and arts facility, on a 49-year lease. The building was restored and opened as a museum on May 31, 2014.

The museum has a broad range of exhibits based on the collections in the Rahmi M. Koç Museums in Istanbul and Ankara, including tin toys, prams, steam models, and timekeeping devices.

Azaryan Mansion, a historical mansion located on the street Büyükdere Piyasa Caddesi in the Sarıyer district of Istanbul. The building, which currently houses the Sadberk Hanım Museum(*), was built at the start of the twentieth century on the site of an old burnt-out dwelling. The architect was Andon Kazazyan, who was commissioned by Armenian businessman Bedros Azaryan. Bought by Vehbi Koç(*) in 1950, the mansion continued to be used as the family's summer residence until 1978. Between 1978 and 1980, it was converted into a museum as part of a restoration project devised by the architect Sedad Hakkı Eldem(*) and opened as the Sadberk Hanım Museum in 1980.

According to rumor, locals dubbed the building Vidalı Yalı, meaning literally "house of screws," due to materials being brought from outside and mounted onto the facade. The building covers an area of 400 square meters and is located in a garden of 4,280 square meters, which borders the grounds of the Russian Summer Embassy behind. As in many other residences on the Bosporus, the garden is landscaped and enclosed by trees.

Built using the *bagdadi* technique (wattle and daub) over stone, the building layout is in the style called *karnıyarık* (literally "split belly"). The building, which consists of five floors including a basement and attic level, contains 33 rooms, four anterooms and three entrances, one on the façade and two on each side of the house. The ceilings are 4.2 meters high. The x-shaped timber ornamentation between the windows of the facade distinguishes it from other mansions. The projecting terrace, referred to as *cihannüma* in Ottoman residences, is in a balcony form. The street-side entrance opens into a large anteroom with parquet floors and two wooden staircases on either side lead to the upper floors.

The interior is decorated in an imperial style, reflecting central European architecture with various hand-carved features, imitation marbleized interior plastering and stucco ceilings. The ceiling of the now unused main entrance is decorated with carton-pierre coffers in a style evocative of Ancient Rome.

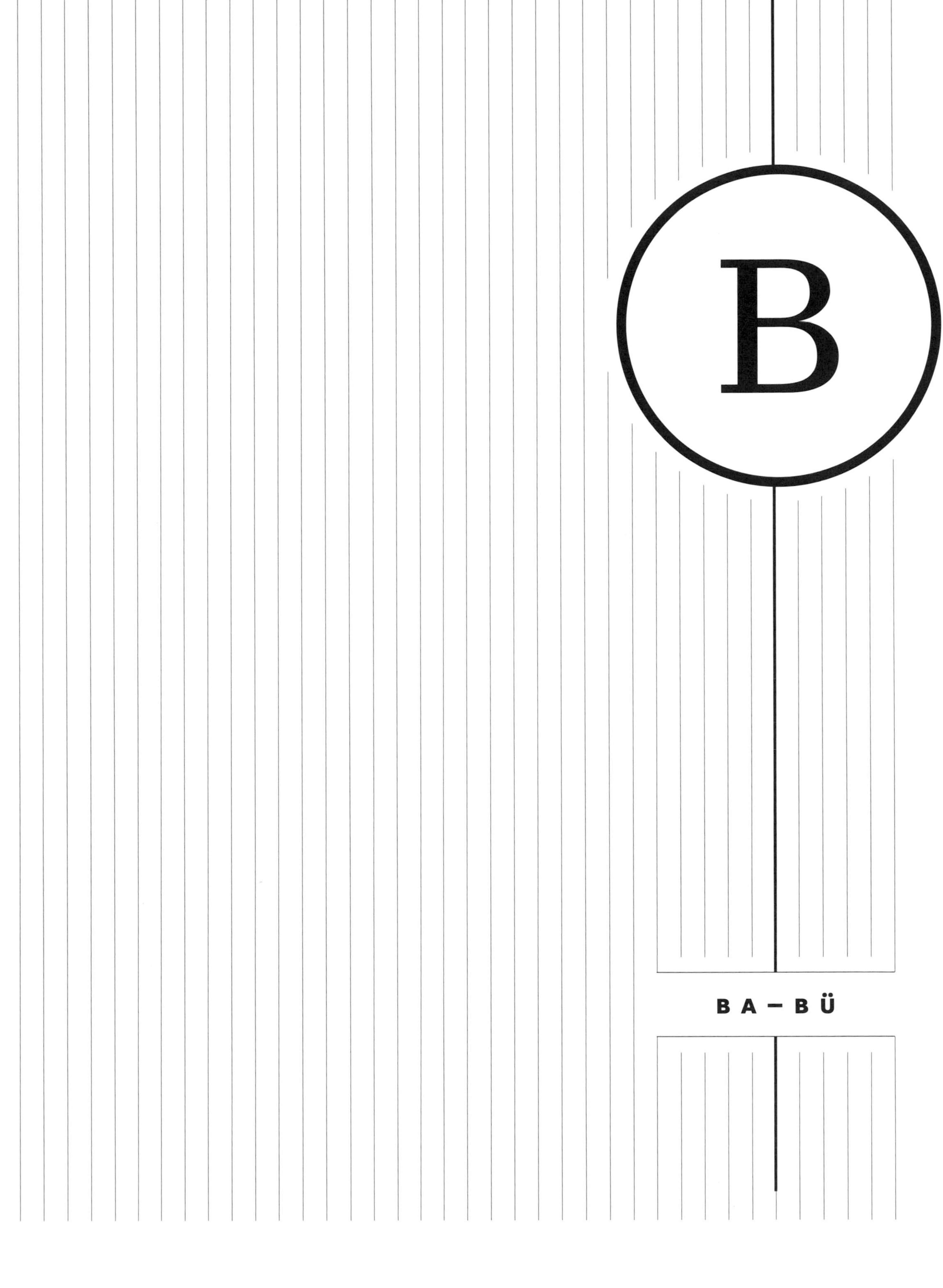

BA—BÜ

BAGEP Scholarship Award *see* **Science Academy Young Scientists Program (BAGEP) Scholarship Award**

Bali, Adnan *(b. April 23, 1962, Islahiye, Gaziantep),* banker and director. He serves on the Vehbi Koç Foundation(*) Board of Directors, representing Türkiye İş Bankası A.Ş., where he has been chief executive officer since 2011.

After completing his secondary education at Islahiye High School in 1980, Bali studied at the Middle East Technical University Faculty of Economics and Administrative Sciences Department of Economics, graduating in 1986. In the same year, he assumed the role of assistant inspector on the Türkiye İş Bankası A.Ş. Board of Inspectors. He was appointed assistant manager at the Fund Management Directorate in 1994, group manager in 1997 and division head in 1998. He served as manager of the bank's branches in Şişli and Galata in 2002 and 2004 respectively. In 2006, he was made deputy chief executive in charge of corporate and commercial banking. On April 1, 2011, he became the 16th chief executive officer of Türkiye İş Bankası A.Ş. As well as being a member of the Banks Association of Turkey Board of Directors, president of the Türkiye İş Bankası A.Ş. Credit Committee and a member of the Risk Committee, Bali has also been employed as chairman of the board of directors at the Industrial Development Bank of Turkey since 2011 and Türkiye İş Bankası A.Ş. AG since 2012.

Batur, Sabahattin *(b. August 1, 1920, Devrek, Zonguldak - d. January 19, 2012, Aydın),* literary scholar, librarian and museologist. He was director of the Sadberk Hanım Museum(*) between 1980 and 1985.

After graduating from Kastamonu High School in 1940, he studied at Istanbul University, firstly in the Department of Philosophy at the Faculty of Letters and then in the School of Advanced Teacher Training (1947). After working as a philosophy teacher at a number of schools, he began working as a librarian in 1951. In Istanbul, he was employed as the head of a number of libraries (1960-77), as the director of Istanbul Provincial Directorate of Culture (1977-78) and director of Topkapı Palace Museum (1978-80). In 1980, he retired from his post as advisor to the Ministry of Culture. In the following period, he was director of the Sadberk Hanım Museum between 1980 and 1985 and managed a number of cultural institutions from 1985 to 1995.

Sabahattin Batur (RIGHT) **with Vehbi Koç**

Batur began writing poems in high school, a number of which were published in magazines before being published as a collection in *Akçakuşlar* (2002; Whitish Birds). He also published an anthology, *Yeni Şiirimiz* (Our New Poetry) in 1960 and an intellectual study, *Topkapı. Architecture: The Harem and Other Buildings* (together with Kemal Çığ and Cengiz Köseoğlu, 1988).

Baykal, Emre *(b. May 12, 1965, Istanbul)* curator. He has worked as director of exhibitions and curator at Arter(*) since 2008 and currently manages the curatorial team of the contemporary art museum scheduled to open in September 2019.

He graduated from Işık High School in Istanbul in 1983 and completed an English Language and Literature degree at Boğaziçi University in 1991. Baykal served as editor at *Anons Journal of Plastic Arts* (1992-94), assistant director (1994-2000) and director (2000-05) at the Istanbul Biennial(*), and director of exhibitions at santralistanbul (2005-07). He has also curated various exhibitions at different institutions home and abroad. In 2008, he became director of exhibitions and curator at Arter. In 2013, he curated the Pavilion of Turkey at the Venice Biennale 55th International Art Exhibition. He has also contributed to numerous publications and exhibition catalogs. Among the exhibitions Baykal curated at Arter are solo exhibitions of Deniz Gül (2011), Kutluğ Ataman (2011), Mona Hatoum (2012), Volkan Aslan (2013), Füsun Onur (2014) and Ali Kazma (2015).

Bazmanoğlu, Engin *(b. 1946, Istanbul),* physician and director. He was chief physician at the American Hospital(*) between 1995 and 2001.

Bazmanoğlu graduated from Vefa High School in Istanbul before going on to receive his medical training at Istanbul University Faculty of Medicine. He completed his residency in urology at Haydarpaşa Numune Hospital in 1978. Dr. Bazmanoğlu was responsible director and chief physician of the American Hospital between 1995 and 2001 and is still working at the hospital.

Bequest *see* **Vehbi Koç Foundation**

Beyazıt Ford Otosan Koç Elementary School *see* **17 Schools Project**

Beylikdüzü Koç Middle School
see **17 Schools Project**

Bilgi, Hülya *(b. November 7, 1967, Adana)*, art historian and museum director. She has been the director of the Sadberk Hanım Museum(*) since 2007.

She graduated from Atatürk High School in Beşiktaş, Istanbul in 1984, going on to receive an undergraduate degree from the Department of Art History at Istanbul University in 1988 and a master's degree in 1991. In 1988, she began working at the Sadberk Hanım Museum as a specialist in the Turkish-Islamic Art Section, continuing in this role until 2005 when she became deputy director of the museum for two years from 2005 to 2007. In 2007, she became director. Bilgi still holds this role today and has compiled catalogs for numerous exhibitions at the museum. A special catalog, *Iznik, The Ömer Koç Collection* was published in 2015.

Bilgin, Selçuk *(b. January 30, 1964, Eskişehir)*, financier and director. He has held the role of assistant general manager of the Vehbi Koç Foundation(*) (VKV) since 2001.

After completing his studies at Eskişehir Anatolian High School in 1982, he studied business administration at the Faculty of Economics and

Administrative Sciences at Boğaziçi University, graduating in 1987. That same year, he began working as an external affairs specialist at Yapı Kredi Bank. He subsequently served as vice president of credits at Credit Lyonnais (1989-95), finance director at Söğüt Seramik (1996-97), director of finance and risk management at Eti Marketing (1997-98) and finance director at Compaq (1999-2001). Bilgin assumed the role of assistant general manager at the VKV in 2001 and still holds this position today.

Bilkent University Faculty of Science Department of Molecular Biology and Genetics, higher education and scientific research institution. In 2004, it received the Vehbi Koç Award(*) for health in recognition for its pioneering efforts to train scientists working in molecular biology in Turkey, research into the molecular foundations of some genetic conditions and cancers, and studies into diagnostic genetic testing.

The foundations for the Department of Molecular Biology and Genetics, the first academic entity in Turkey to bear this name, were laid by the world-renowned genetics expert Professor Mehmet Öztürk. The department, which opened in September 1995, had its first intake of students studying at bachelor's, master's and doctorate levels in the 1995-96 academic year. In his speech at the Vehbi Koç Award ceremony, departmental head Professor Öztürk remarked that research in Turkey was underfunded and that the money

Prof. Mehmet Öztürk (RIGHT) at the award ceremony with Semahat Arsel

from this first award of them would go towards a pioneering project on molecular cell biology. He added that their future goal would be to study cellular treatments. With its high-end laboratory facilities, the department researches areas such as genes linked to diseases, the genetic foundations and molecular biology of cancer, structural and operational analysis of genes and proteins, molecular mechanisms for resisting cell death and cell aging, the immune system, hereditary conditions, the biology of reproduction and development, biocomputing, epigenetics, identifying biomarkers, operational genomics, and the production of recombinant protein and monoclonal antibodies.

Birsel, Mahmut (Tevfik) *(b. September 15, 1929, Karşıyaka, Izmir)*, lawyer and academic. He served on the Vehbi Koç Foundation(*) Board of Directors between 1996 and 2013.

He completed his studies at Izmir Atatürk High School in 1946 and graduated from Ankara University Faculty of Law in 1950. After completing his doctoral studies at Paris Law Faculty, he was registered to the bar in Izmir in 1955. He taught agricultural law at Ege University Faculty of Agriculture and worked as a commercial law assistant at Izmir School of Economics and Commerce (Izmir Academy for Economics and Commercial Sciences, IAECS, as of 1959). He became associate professor at IAECS in 1962, before becoming professor of law at Ege University Faculty of Economics and Commercial Sciences in 1970.

Professor Birsel served on the Ege University Senate as member (1972-74) and vice rector (1973-74). Following the foundation of the Ege University Faculty of Law in 1978, he was appointed chair of international law and lectured in commercial law and international private law. He was director of the Ege University College of Justice from 1981 to 1982 and retired of his own volition in 1983.

Until 2017, Professor Birsel worked as a lawyer at Birsel Law Offices, which he co-founded in 1976. He served on the Koç University(*) Law School Advisory Board, the International Chamber of Commerce Arbitration Council and Arbitration Commission. He has produced numerous publications on different branches of commercial law, predominantly in the fields of commercial enterprise, corporations and international arbitration.

Block, René *(March 15, 1942, Velbert, Germany)*, German art dealer, collector and curator. From 2008 to 2013, he was director of the non-profit gallery TANAS(*) in Berlin, entirely funded by the Vehbi Koç Foundation(*) (VKV). He also curated Arter's first exhibition at its venue on İstiklal Caddesi. The exhibition, entitled “Starter: Works from the Vehbi Koç Contemporary Art Collection”, opened to the public in 2010.

Block was Germany’s youngest art dealer when he opened the Grafische Cabinet René Block gallery in 1964 in Berlin, forming a close bond with Joseph Beuys and the Fluxus group. In 1966, he founded Edition Block, which publishes limited edition reproductions of artifacts and printed works by artists, in Berlin. In 1974, he went to New York with Beuys and opened a gallery in Manhattan, which remained active until 1977.

In 1979, Block closed his gallery in Berlin to concentrate on his independent curatorial activities, organizing exhibitions for a number of art and culture organizations. He worked on the Berlin Artist in Residence Program as the director in charge of visual artists and composers from 1982

to 1992. From 1985 to 2007, he curated a number of biennials, including the 4th Istanbul Biennial in 1995, which bore the title, *Orientation: A Perspective on Art in a Paradoxical World.*

Block worked as director at the Fridericianum Museum in Kassel between 1997 and 2006. He also curated the Adventure İstiklal Contemporary Art Exhibition Series(*), which was on show at the Yapı Kredi Kâzım Taşkent Gallery (2007-10), working with Melih Fereli as advisor, and edited the Contemporary Art in Turkey Series(*) published in parallel to the exhibitions. He has contributed to the establishment of the VKV Contemporary Art Collection as advisor and has been serving as a member of the acquisition committee since 2007. In 2008, he established the Kunsthal 44 Møen art gallery on Denmark's Møen island. He was also director of TANAS (2008-13), the non-profit gallery entirely funded by the Vehbi Koç Foundation(*) with the aim of exhibiting works by mainly Turkish artists.

Block published *Grafik des Kapitalistischen Realismus* (Graphics of Capitalist Realism; 2 vol., 1971-76). He was the recipient of the German Critics' Award in visual arts (1974), the Arthur Køpcke Award (1994), the Cologne Art Prize (2005) and the Hessen Culture Award (2007).

BNP Paribas Grand Prix for Individual Philanthropy, award given by the Paris-based global and financial services foundation, BNP Paribas, to entrepreneurs of philanthropic initiatives that set a good example to its own customers and philanthropists worldwide. The Koç family(*) received the annual award in 2011 for "pioneering and exemplary initiatives across the globe". In 2012, BNP Paribas published the book, *Koç: Une Saga Philantrophique Dans La Turquie Moderne/ Koç: A Story of Philanthropy in Modern Turkey*. The book celebrated the activities of the award-winning Koç family and Vehbi Koç Foundation(*) in the fields of education, health and culture and was written by Guy-Pierre Chomette with photography by Ahmet Sel.

Mustafa Koç (THIRD ON THE LEFT), at the launch of the book, *Koç: A Story of Philanthropy in Modern Turkey*, 2012
https://www.flickr.com/photos/bnpparibas/7420257072

Boğaziçi European School of Politics, education program that brings together young people aged 25-35 from different regions of Turkey and with different political views, introducing them to European standards and institutions, the opportunity to debate different political alternatives and giving them the basic skills to realize their goals. It was founded in Istanbul in 2014 as part of the Council of Europe Schools of Political Studies network. The school works in collaboration with Boğaziçi University and has received support from the Vehbi Koç Foundation(*) since 2017.

The program comprises an eight-day series of seminars presented twice a year (in summer and winter) by leading academics, experts and politicians from Turkey and across the world. Candidates who work or are keen to work in political parties, civil society organizations, or public institutions and organizations are given precedence during registration and a certificate of participation is awarded to students at the end of the program. Graduate gatherings and meetings with academics and experts are also organized in Istanbul and elsewhere with the aim of furthering dialogue with participants. Selected graduates carry out working visits to European countries and take part in the annual World Democracy Forum held in Strasbourg, France, in November every year.

Boğaziçi University Foundation (BUVAK), a non-governmental organization (NGO) founded with the aim of providing material and moral support for academic studies, teaching staff, students, graduates and staff of Boğaziçi University (BU). BUVAK was founded in 1978 by BU Rector Professor Aptullah Kuran together with Prof. Nedim Bilgen, member of the university teaching staff, and Ertuğrul Zekai Ökte. It is one of the NGOs supported by the Vehbi Koç Foundation(*) (VKV).

BUVAK first began its social aid and scholarship programs in 1981, later supporting the university by contributing towards academic activities, as well as establishing the Graduate Fund, Environmental Protection Fund, Atatürk Institute for Modern Turkish History Support Fund and the Student Activities Fund in 1984. This was followed in 1989 by academic incentive scholarships and awards.

BUVAK, which received its first in-kind donation in 1992, was granted tax exemption in 1995. Following this development, the foundation expanded its efforts, using resources secured from previous campaigns to support academic studies as well as making significant contributions to the restoration of the university's historical buildings. It pioneered a large number of projects providing BU with new buildings, laboratories, cultural centers and social space, also providing funds to complete the projects.

The foundation is a partner and founding member of Boğaziçi Education Tourism Technopark Application and Consultancy Services Industry and Trade Inc. (BÜTEK AŞ), BUVAK Commercial Enterprise and Boğaziçi University Technopark Inc.

Boğaziçi University Graduates Association, Boğaziçi University & Robert College International Alumni Association (BURCIN), Turkish Philanthropy Funds (TPF) and the Third Sector Foundation of Turkey (TÜSEV)(*) are BUVAK stakeholders.

The VKV and the Suna and İnan Kıraç Foundation(*) feature on BUVAK's Platinum Benefactors list.

Boğaziçi University Superdorm, private dormitory located at the Boğaziçi University Uçaksavar Culture and Sports Facility. It was built by the Boğaziçi University Foundation(*), with the support of a number of people and institutions including the Vehbi Koç Foundation(*) and Yapı Kredi Bank, before being transferred to the university.

Construction work began on the Superdorm in 1995 and the building was opened in the 1998-99 academic year. It was designed with the aim of creating a cozy living space, which differed from a classic student dormitory, with private rooms and common recreational rooms for students to socialize in.

The dormitory comprises five blocks, 127 apartments and 478 student rooms. The number of rooms in each apartment ranges from two to five and each room is single occupancy. The Superdorm also meets the basic needs of students with a small supermarket, a cafeteria, and a laundry for washing, drying and ironing clothes. These services run independently of Superdorm management and are overseen by the university.

Bokova, Irina (Georgieva) *(b. July 12, 1952, Sofia, Bulgaria)*, politician, diplomat and the first female director-general of UNESCO. She received the Semahat Arsel Honorary Award in 2015, its inaugural year. The award was founded by KOÇ-KAM(*) to reward the "women of high international standing and those working in gender and women's studies".

Bokova completed her university education in Sofia in 1971 and received a master's degree from the Moscow State Institute of International Relations in 1976. She continued her studies in the USA at Maryland University and the John F. Kennedy School of Government at Harvard University.

She began her career in 1977 in the United Nations office at the Ministry of Foreign Affairs in Bulgaria, holding posts at a number of levels within the ministry. She served in the National Assembly in 1990-91, joining as a member of the Bulgarian Socialist Party. She served under Jan Videnov's government from January 1995 to February 1997 as deputy foreign minister, before becoming acting minister. In 2001, she was re-elected to the National Assembly. After leaving the National Assembly in 2005, she served as general secretary at the European Union, as well as Ambassador of Bulgaria to France, Monaco and UNESCO.

She was elected director-general of UNESCO on November 15, 2009. In 2013, Bokova was re-elected and also held the post of executive secretary of the Steering Committee of the UN Secretary-General's Global Education First Initiative (2011-15). During her time as director, UNESCO's priorities were to ensure a quality education for all, promote gender equality and protect the world's cultural heritage. She led efforts to harness education to increase global awareness of hate speech, discrimination and racism. The safety of journalists and efforts to ensure freedom of expression also gained significance during this period.

In 2015, Bokova received the Semahat Arsel Honorary Award for her "global contribution to gender equality as the first female president of UNESCO". Bokova has received honorary doctorates from a large number of universities and was awarded the Légion d'honneur by France before ending her tenure at UNESCO in 2017.

Bolak, (Ahmet) Aydın *(b. August 13, 1925, Balıkesir - d. July 27, 2004, Istanbul)*, politician and businessman who served as deputy chair of the Vehbi Koç Foundation(*) (VKV) between 1969 and 2002.

After graduating from Istanbul University Faculty of Law in 1947, he entered the Ministry of Interior, serving as a ministerial assistant in Balıkesir and working as district governor in various districts including Kadirli throughout his time there. He later left to set up his own legal practice. He was one of the founders of the Liberty Party (Hürriyet Partisi) in 1955; following the dissolution of the party in 1958, he joined the Republican People's Party (Cumhuriyet Halk Partisi, CHP). He held a seat in the Turkish Grand National Assembly (TGNA) as the CHP representative for Balıkesir from 1961 to 1965 and played an important role in the introduction and enactment of Law No. 903, which changed the Civil Code to allow foundations to be re-established. He was involved in preparing the law as well as in its presentation to the TGNA and subsequent passage into law.

After 1965, Bolak left politics, moving into industry and trade. He was a founder, partner and manager of a wide range of companies, especially in the petroleum, tourism, shipbuilding, vegetable oils and nutrition industries. He served as the chair of the Türk Petrol Holding Board of Directors for a long time. Together with Vehbi Koç(*), he spearheaded the founding of the Turkish Education Foundation(*) (TEV) and was chair of the foundation's board of directors between 1993 and 2001. As well as contributing to the foundation of the TEV and VKV, he also helped establish and manage other foundations, such as the Turkish Petroleum Foundation, TÜSEV(*), TEMA(*), the Istanbul Traffic Foundation, the Turkish Heart Foundation, and the Foundation for Turkish Culture.

Bolak received honorary doctorates from Marmara University (1992) and Selçuk University (1995), and talks he delivered on TRT television were compiled into several books: *Söylediklerim ve Yazdıklarım* (1987; My Talks and Writings), *Sohbetler* (1994; Conversations), *Hayatın İçinden* (1996; Life: The Innerworkings), *Hayatın Öğrettikleri* (1998; What Life Teaches Us), *YüzYılınYetmişbeşi* (2000; Seventy-Five Years Out of a Hundred).

Bolu Koç Elementary and Middle School *see* **17 Schools Project**

Boyut *see* **Koç School**

Bozkurt, İsmail *(b. July 29, 1965, Esslingen, Germany)*, physician and director. He has worked at the American Hospital(*) as chief physician and responsible director since 2014.

After graduating from St George's Austrian High School in Istanbul in 1984, he studied medicine at the Medical University of Vienna. Following his graduation in 1993, he completed a residency in family practice at Istanbul's Şişli Etfal Hospital in 1996. In 2015, he received a master's degree in hospital management and excellence in healthcare from Berlin University.

Dr. Bozkurt began working as a specialist in family practice at the American Hospital in 2001, becoming deputy responsible director in 2011. In 2013, he became director for continuous quality improvement until his appointment as chief physician and responsible director in 2014.

Bristol, Admiral Mark L(ambert)

(b. April 17, 1868, Glasboro, New Jersey, USA - d. May 13, 1939, Washington DC, USA), American admiral who founded the American Hospital(*) in Istanbul. He continued to support the American Hospital and collect donations for the hospital until a few days before his death in 1939.

Mark L. Bristol graduated from the US Naval Academy and joined the US Navy in 1887. In 1898, he was an officer in the Battle of Santiago de Cuba during the Spanish-American War, serving on the USS Texas, the USS Connecticut and the USS Pittsburgh. As admiral, he commanded the USS Monterey, the USS Albany, the USS North Carolina and the USS Oklahoma.

Admiral Bristol was deputy commander- in-chief of the North Atlantic Fleet from 1901 to 1903, and also presided over the Naval Torpedo Station, Newport, Rhode Island, monitored the development of the fleet's air forces and was head of Naval Aeronautics and commander of the US naval base in Plymouth, England.

From 1919 to 1927, he served as the US Navy's commander in the Eastern Mediterranean, with headquarters in Istanbul. During the same period, he also held the position of high commissioner to Turkey in the US Department of State. He was one of the US delegates at the Lausanne Peace Conference. Correspondence from the time he spent in Turkey, along with his document collection and the report which bears his name, form a frequently referenced but controversial source for studies into Turkish-Armenian relations and the Great fire of Izmir in 1922.

On August 20, 1920, Admiral Bristol founded the American Hospital of Constantinople. This was followed by the foundation of a school of nursing in the same building. Until leaving Istanbul for other duties in 1927, he continued to personally support the hospital and take a close interest in ensuring the requirements of this important institution were met. As a result of his support for the hospital, which changed its name to the American Hospital of Istanbul in 1931, the American Hospital and the Nursing School were renamed the Admiral Bristol Hospital (1945-68) and the Admiral Bristol Nursing School(*) (1945-99) for a certain time period.

As rear admiral (upper half), Admiral Bristol led the US Navy's Asian Fleet (1927-29). His final role in the navy was as chair of the general board of the US Navy (1930-32). He received a commendation from the Chief of Naval Operations for protecting American interests during unrest in the city of Swatow (now Shantou), China. As well as receiving several medals and distinctions, he was also awarded the US Navy Distinguished Service Medal. Admiral Bristol died in Washington DC in 1939 following a short illness.

Bulgurlu, Bülent

(b. September 28, 1947, Ankara), engineer and director. From 2007 to 2009, he was a member of the Vehbi Koç Foundation(*) Board of Directors representing Koç Holding(*), where he held the position of CEO.

Bulgurlu graduated from the Ankara State Academy for Engineering and Architecture (now Gazi University Faculty of Engineering

and Architecture) in 1971 and began working as a civil engineer at Elliot Strómme in Oslo, Norway, that same year. He received a master's degree from the Norwegian University of Science and Technology Faculty of Civil Engineering in 1973, going on to receive a PhD in 1976; he taught at the university throughout this period. After returning to Turkey, he worked as a site manager for İntes Ticaret ve Sanayi A.Ş. from 1977 to 1979. In 1979, he began working at Garanti İnşaat, a Koç Holding company (Garanti Koza İnşaat from 1985, Garanti Koza since 2004). From 1982 to 1988, he worked as assistant general manager, going on to hold the post of general manager (1988-96). In 1996, he became vice president of the Koç Holding Tourism Group. From 2000 to 2004, he served as chair in the same group (known as the Tourism and Construction Group from 2003 onwards) and the Consumer Durables and Construction Group between 2004 and 2007. In May 2007, he joined the Koç Holding Board of Directors as CEO. In April 2010, Dr. Bulgurlu transferred the role to Turgay Durak(*) but continues to be a member of the board. Dr. Bulgurlu, who holds the position of life vice president of the Rahmi M. Koç Museology and Culture Foundation(*), is also a member of the boards of directors of companies in the Koç Group(*), including Arçelik, Beko, Tofaş, RMK Marine, Ford Otosan, and Aygaz.

Bulutcu, Erhan *(b. April 12, 1959, Bursa)*, physician and director. He has served as the CEO and member of the board of directors of the Vehbi Koç Foundation(*) (VKV) Healthcare Institutions since 2014.

Dr. Bulutcu graduated from Hacettepe University Faculty of Medicine and completed a residency in anesthesiology and reanimation in 1993. From 1994 to 1996, he worked as an academic in the same faculty and founded the Pain Unit together with Dr. Ömür Erçelen(*). In late 1997, he began working at the American Hospital(*), becoming deputy general director in 2009. Together with Dr. Evren Keleş(*) he played an active role in the foundation of the Koç University School of Medicine and the Koç University Hospital(*). In September 2014, Dr. Bulutcu assumed the role of CEO of the VKV Healthcare Institutions. Several of his articles have been published and he has contributed three book chapters for publications.

BÜVAK *see* **Boğaziçi University Foundation**

Büyükerşen, Yılmaz *(b. November 8, 1937, Eskişehir)*, academician and politician who received the Vehbi Koç Award(*) in 2018 for education. He is a former rector of Eskişehir Anadolu University and is currently serving as mayor of the Eskişehir Metropolitan Municipality.

Büyükerşen completed secondary education at Eskişehir Atatürk High School and in 1962 became one of the first to graduate from Eskişehir Academy of Economic and Commercial Sciences (EAECS). In the same year, he began as an assistant in the academy's Department of Finance. He completed his doctorate in 1966, became associate professor in 1968 and professor in 1973. In 1976, he became chair of EAECS, and in 1982 became rector of Eskişehir Anadolu University (AU), when it replaced the academy. Following two terms as

Prof. Yılmaz Büyükerşen (LEFT) **at the award ceremony with Ömer M. Koç**

rector, he assumed the roles of chair of the AU Department of Distance Learning and director of the Institute of Communication Sciences.

Professor Büyükerşen was a pioneer throughout his academic life, playing a pivotal role in the foundation of the distance learning system known in Turkey as "open education". The "Open Education Model for Turkey" that he developed was implemented in 1982 with the opening of the Open Education Faculty. Professor Büyükerşen contributed towards making AU one of Turkey's largest, most dynamic and innovative universities. He was also president of the Radio and Television Council (now the Radio and Television High Council, RTÜK) for two terms until 1993. He was one of the founders of TEGV(*), which began in 1995 with the aim of supporting children at elementary school by giving them the opportunity to receive free extra-curricular education, and served for four years as head of its first board of directors.

Professor Büyükerşen was elected mayor of the Eskişehir Metropolitan Municipality in 1999. In the course of his ongoing tenure, he has encouraged the development of significant infrastructure, making Eskişehir a model city of urbanization, changing the fabric and silhouette of the city and making it an attractive destination. He has developed practices based on the principle that education is not a job for educational institutions alone, but also requires support from museums, arts institutions and municipal centers, transforming the entire city into a vibrant educational center.

Professor Büyükerşen is also a sculptor, known for his Atatürk busts and sculptures, particularly his wax figures. A museum of wax figures bearing his name was opened in Eskişehir in 2013.

Professor Büyükerşen received the Vehbi Koç Award for education in 2018 in recognition for his work in distance learning his contribution to AU and TEGV, as well as his achievements as mayor of Eskişehir.

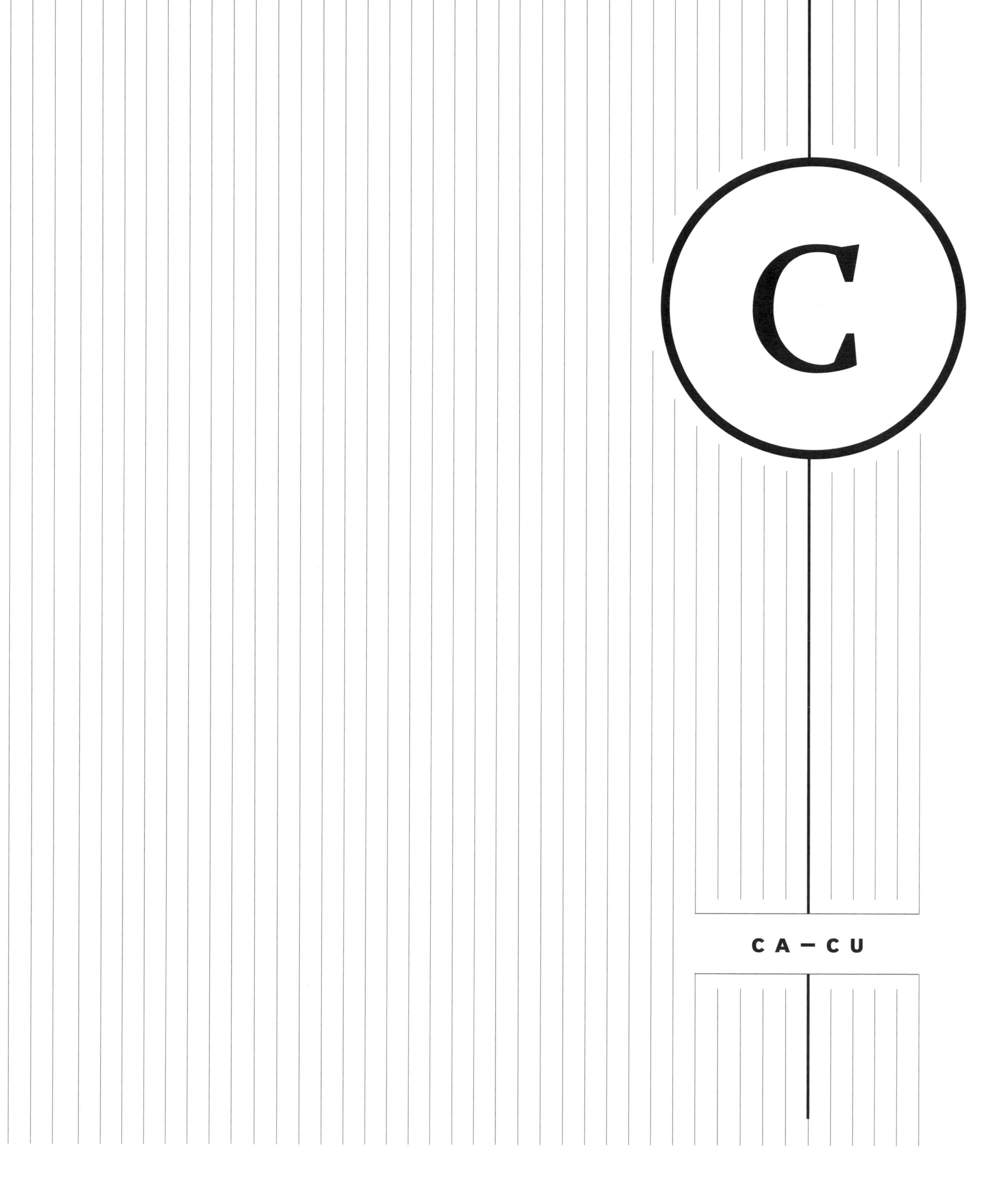

C

CA — CU

Carnegie Medal of Philanthropy, established in 2001 by representatives of over twenty institutions founded by Andrew Carnegie (1835-1919) in honor of the centennial of his career as a philanthropist. The medal is awarded every two years to one or more philanthropists who, like Andrew Carnegie, have contributed their personal wealth to exemplary initiatives for the benefit of society. The Koç family(*) received the medal in 2009 for its philanthropic contribution to culture,

2009 Carnegie Medal of Philanthropy holders award ceremony: (FROM LEFT TO RIGHT) **Sanford and Joan Weill, Gordon Moore, Rahmi M. Koç and Michael R. Bloomberg http://carnegiemedals.org/gallery/2009/**

education and health. Rahmi M. Koç(*) attended the award ceremony in New York in November 2009, on behalf of the family, accepting the prize which consists of a custom-made bronze bust of Andrew Carnegie and a bronze medal.

Center for Research on Globalization, Peace, and Democratic Governance *see* **GLODEM**

Chalfant, John C(lay) *(b. November 17, 1928, Oregon, USA)*, educator and director. From 1988 to 1992, he served as the first director of the Koç High School (*see* Koç School).

Chalfant completed his undergraduate education in literature and social sciences at Fresno State College in California between 1949 and 1952 and received an MA in American civilizations from Pennsylvania University in 1956. He began his professional career in 1955 as a teacher of English and physical education at Robert College(*). From 1956 to 1965, he taught physical education, history and English and performed administrative duties at a number of middle schools in the USA and Greece. Returning to Istanbul in 1965, he began working once again at Robert College, becoming its headmaster in 1971. Following his six-year tenure, he served as principal of The Sultan's School in Oman (1977-86). Chalfant served as project director for the foundation of the Koç High School (1987-88). In 1988, he became the school's first director, remaining in post until the high school produced its first graduates in 1992. In the 1992-93 academic year, he served as principal of Üsküdar American High School.

Chandler, John R(ussell) *(b. July 6, 1946, Massachusetts, USA)*, educator and director. He served as the third director of Koç High School (*see* Koç School) between 1996 and 1998. When the elementary school was added in 1998, he became the first general director of the new Koç Primary and High School, remaining in the post until 2005.

After studying language and literature at Yale College, affiliated with Yale University, he continued with a master's degree at the university's School of Theology in 1973-75. From 1968 to 1996, he worked as an English teacher at various middle schools in the USA, also serving as principal and vice principal. In 1996, he was appointed director of the Koç High School. During his tenure, along with the start of the application of nationwide eight-year compulsory elementary education, the Koç Primary School opened in 1998. In the same year, with a change in title, Chandler became the school's first general director and remained in post until 2005. He later served as headmaster of Robert College(*) from 2005 to 2012.

---

charity, a thought, behavior or voluntary action, which aims to improve the quality of people's lives by contributing to society. In the narrower sense, it is perceived as helping the poor and destitute and doing good to others. In this context, it is identified with aid supplied directly between individuals. The word *filantropi* (philanthropy), taken from English, is widely used in Turkish to express a similar concept, but actually originates from the Greek word meaning "love of humanity". Today, philanthropy expresses the concept of "volunteering one's time, expertise or wealth for the good of society". This includes financial aid provided by people, foundations and companies to non-profit organizations and generally covers more organized, systematic and strategic philanthropic activities. However it may be understood, charity is a form of behavior and action typical of people and organizations that tend towards altruistic acts for the benefit of others. Older examples of charitable organizations include Islamic foundations, Christian aid groups and the Platonic Academy in Ancient Greece.

Foundations played an important role in providing public services during the Ottoman era and were founded on the principle of charity. Traditionally, their basic function was to attend to specific needs of the public. When the Republic was founded, foundations largely stopped performing these functions as public services were covered by the state. Yet, it is still widely accepted that charitable efforts generally support social causes such as education, worship and poverty reduction.

The research reports, *Philanthropy in Turkey: Citizens, Foundations and the Pursuit of Social Justice* and *Individual Giving and Philanthropy in Turkey*, published by TÜSEV(*) in 2006 and 2016 respectively, revealed how the concept of charity is perceived in Turkey. According to research, the first thing people think of when asked about charity is helping the poor and destitute. Activities such as supporting students in their education, providing scholarships, building schools and dormitories, giving charity to the poor and building mosques are all generally considered charitable acts, and individuals focus their support on these areas. Conversely, activities in the fields of art, culture and even higher education and investments in civil society are not viewed as charity. In other words, these kinds of activities are not considered to be a response to societal needs. Equally, when people engage in forms of aid characterized as charity, they tend to choose family members, neighbors or fellow citizens, or people who share the same culture, language and religion as them.

The perception of charity as an individual and direct activity means that a relatively low proportion of people evaluate the donation of wealth to associations and foundations as charity. TÜSEV's research revealed that the view of charitable activities as those carried out for personal motives, such as religious obligation, duty to society and personal satisfaction, was widespread.

The slow development of corporate charity in Turkey is an indicator of the currently widespread understanding of charity. In addition, despite the long history of giving assistance, the legal and financial framework supporting corporate philanthropy remains weak. Donations are an important source of income for associations and foundations carrying out charitable works. The tax exemption associated with this type of charity is an important stimulus for individuals and corporations as the donations can be exempted from tax assessments. In priority regions for development, the tax reduction applied to donations made to tax-exempt foundations and public-interest associations is 10% of the taxable base; in other places, it is 5%. Together with this minimal tax reduction, only 389 of 110,420 existing associations and 268 of 5,083 foundations held this status in 2017. There is no exemption for donations made to other civil society organizations (CSOs). This restrictive practice limits the ability of CSOs to procure funds from private companies. Lack of established practices and donation mechanisms are also factors which negatively affect corporate charity with regard to fundraising and donations to CSOs. *See also* foundation.

Claros Excavations, a series of excavations carried out on the holy site of Claros, located close to the village of Ahmetli in the Menderes district of Izmir. Excavations in Claros, one of the most important centers of prophecy in ancient times, began in 2001. In 2016, the Vehbi Koç Foundation(*) sponsored work to document, preserve and restore the finds uncovered during the excavations.

Founded by the Myceneans at the end of the thirteenth century BCE, Claros served as a center of prophecy until it was abandoned in the fourth century AD. The Temple of Apollo at Claros is the only Doric temple built in Ionia. Construction began on the temple at the beginning of the third century BCE and was completed at the end of the second century BCE; it is the only holy site bearing inscriptions even on the steps. Twenty-seven meters to the east of the temple lies the Hellenistic altar to Apollo. The altar bears two sacrificial tables; one is dedicated to Apollo and the other to Dionysus. The 100 hecatombs at Claros provided the first archaeological proof of this sacrificial ritual. The site also features monumental, cult statues of Apollo, Artemis and Leto. Due to all these distinctive features, Claros holds a special place in Anatolian and world archeology.

The holy site was discovered by the German archaeologist Carl Schuchhardt in 1886 and the first surveys of the site were carried out in 1904 by the Ottoman archaeologist Teodor Makridi Bey. Makridi Bey carried out the first cycle of excavations together with Pierre-Charles Picard in 1913. The second cycle of excavations, begun in 1950 by Louis Robert, continued until 1961; the third cycle of excavations were begun in 1988 by Juliette de La Genière. The final cycle of excavations, which began in July 2001, are being led by Dr. Nuran Şahin from Ege University.

Life-size casts made from most of the statues found at Claros were used for an archeopark which opened in September 2011. The archeopark exhibits scale models of the Temple of Apollo and the altar.

Contemporary Art in Turkey Series, a series of books published by Yapı Kredi Culture Arts and Publishing between 2007 and 2011 with support from the Vehbi Koç Foundation(*). It consists of comprehensive monographs about artists from Turkey who have achieved success on an international level. It was compiled under the editorship of René Block(*), in consultation with Melih Fereli(*). In the series, each book cover features an authentic offset print prepared by the artist for his or her own monograph. A total 150 of the printed books have been numbered and signed by the artist. The series, which comprises 12 volumes, is published in Turkish and English. An exhibition of contemporary art titled "Adventure İstiklal" and comprising works by the artist or artists featured in each monograph was arranged at the Yapı Kredi Kâzım Taşkent Art Gallery to coincide with the publication of each monograph. (*See also* Adventure İstiklal Contemporary Art Exhibition Series)

WORKS FEATURED IN THE CONTEMPORARY ART IN TURKEY SERIES

- ***Hale Tenger: İçerdeki Yabancı / Hale Tenger: Stranger Within*** *(Ahu Antmen, 2007)*
- ***Gülsün Karamustafa: Güllerim Tahayyüllerim / Gülsün Karamustafa: My Roses, My Reveries*** *(Barbara Heinrich, 2007)*
- ***Füsun Onur: Dikkatli Gözler İçin / Füsun Onur: For Sharp Eyes*** *(Margrit Brehm, 2007)*
- ***Kutluğ Ataman: Sen Zaten Kendini Anlat! / Kutluğ Ataman: You Tell Me About Yourself Anyway!*** *(Emre Baykal, 2008)*
- ***Ayşe Erkmen:)>uçucu< / =şimdi=(/ Ayşe Erkmen:)>temporary< / =contemporary=(*** *(Friedrich Meschede, 2008)*
- ***Halil Altındere: Kayıplar Ülkesiyle Dans / Halil Altındere: Dance with the Land of the Lost*** *(Süreyyya Evren, 2008)*
- ***Cengiz Çekil: Bir Tanık / Cengiz Çekil: A Witness*** *(Necmi Sönmez, 2008)*
- ***Aydan Murtezaoğlu: Yakınlıklar Kaybolup Mesafeler Kapanırken / Aydan Murtezaoğlu: As Proximities Fade and Distances Disappear*** *(Erden Kosova, 2009)*
- ***Bülent Şangar: Gerilim İmgeleri / Bülent Şangar: Images of Tensity*** *(Ali Akay, 2009)*
- ***Sarkis: Ondan Bize / Sarkis: From Him to Us*** *(Elvan Zabunyan, 2010)*
- ***Esra Ersen: Yüz Yüze / Esra Ersen: Face to Face***

(Erden Kosova, 2011)
– ***Ahmet Öğüt et al.: Her Yerde, Evinde / Ahmet Öğüt et al.: At Home, Whereever*** *(kolektif, 2011)*

Cultural Awareness Foundation, a civil society organization which promotes the adoption of Turkey's cultural wealth and values as a common human heritage to be shared, protected and passed on to the future generations. One of the non-governmental organizations supported by the Vehbi Koç Foundation(*), its activities aim to increase social sensitivity and cultural awareness. It was founded in March 2003 by members of different professional groups, primarily academicians, businesspeople, artists, archaeologists, architects and art historians.

Since its foundation, the Cultural Awareness Foundation has run studies and projects with three main themes, one of which is the Culture Ants Project. As part of this initiative, sixth and seventh grade students spend a day touring significant places close to where they live, accompanied by guides and volunteers, encouraging them to get to know their town or city and teaching them how to protect its cultural heritage. The project received the European Union Europa Nostra Cultural Heritage Award (*see* Europa Nostra Awards) in 2009.

Since its establishment, the foundation has arranged seminars and conferences on history, archeology and art aimed at people of all ages and backgrounds as part of its activities under the theme Academy for Culture. Within the Cultural Heritage theme, a wide variety of projects are carried out in relation to archeology, art history, local history and tourism with the aim of protecting and sustaining the country's cultural assets.

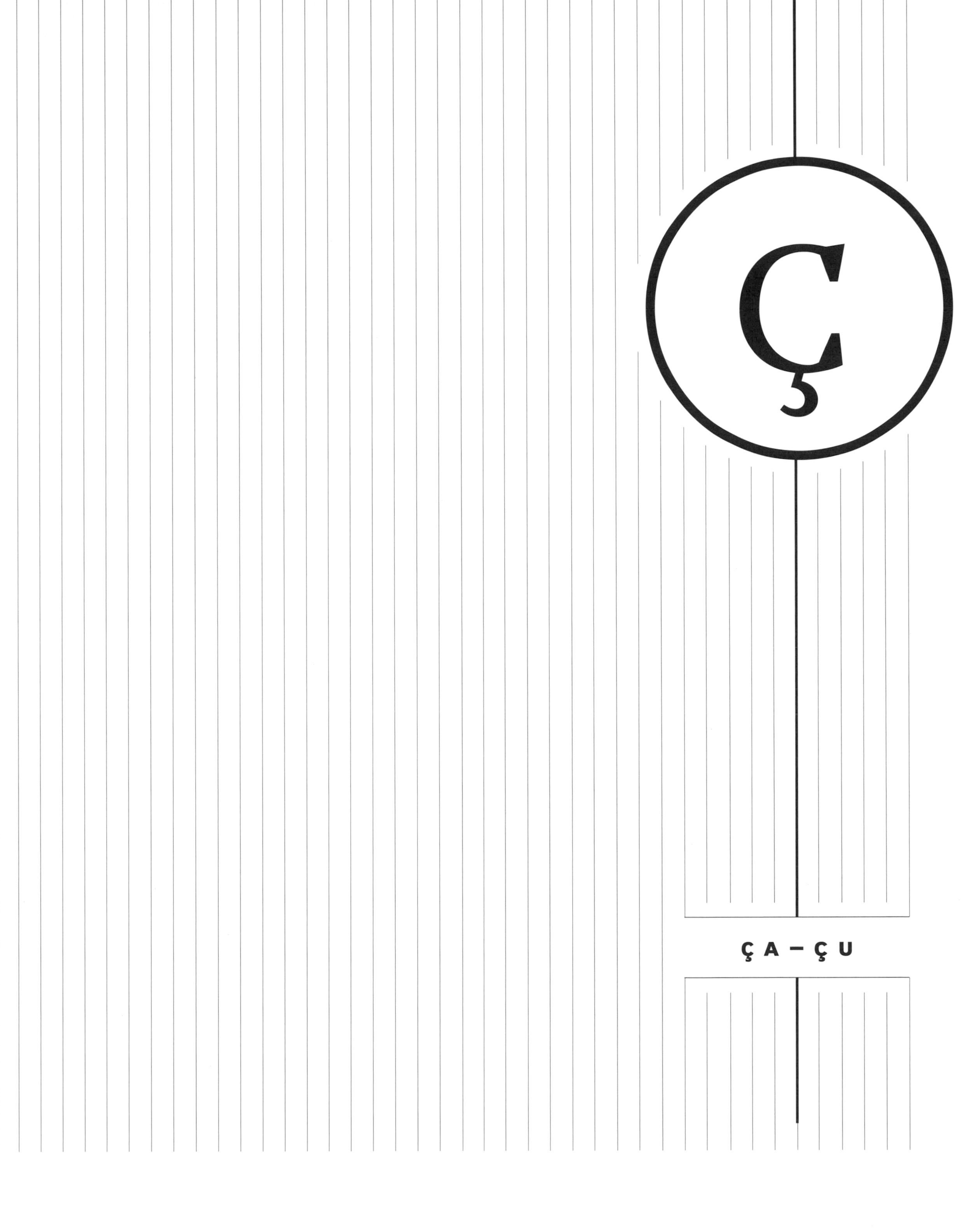

Ç

ÇA — ÇU

Çakıroğlu, Levent *(b. April 3, 1967, Ankara)*, director. Since 2015, he has served on the board of directors of the Vehbi Koç Foundation(*), representing Koç Holding(*), where he holds the position of CEO.

He graduated from the Ankara University Faculty of Political Science Department of Business Administration, before completing a master's degree in public finance at Illinois University. He started work as junior auditor at the Ministry of Finance in 1988, continuing as senior editor from 1991 to 1997. In 1997-98, Çakıroğlu was vice chair of the Ministry of Finance Financial Crimes Investigation Board and was also a part-time lecturer at Bilkent University. In 1998, he joined Koç Holding as financial coordinator. He was general manager of Koçtaş (2002-07) and Migros (2007-08). In 2008, he became general manager of Arçelik, assuming the role of president of Koç Holding Consumer Durables Group in 2010. In April 2015, he became CEO of Koç Holding, joining the Koç Holding Board of Directors in April 2016.

Prof. Zeynep Çelik at the award ceremony with Mustafa V. Koç

Çelik, Zeynep *(b. 1951?)*, Ottoman urban and cultural historian. In 2014, she received the Vehbi Koç Award(*) for culture.

After completing her secondary education at the Istanbul Arnavutköy American College for Girls (*see* Robert College) in 1970, Çelik studied at the Faculty of Architecture of the Istanbul Technical University, graduating in 1975. She received a master's degree from Rice University and completed her PhD at the University of California, Berkeley. She continues to teach at the New Jersey Institute of Technology College of Architecture and Design, which she joined in 1991.

Çelik received an honorary doctorate from Boğaziçi University in 2013 and received the thirteenth Vehbi Koç Award in 2014 for "unique and pioneering work in the fields of Ottoman urban, cultural and intellectual history". In her speech at the award ceremony, Çelik summarized her contribution to the field by saying: "My generation has played an important role in expanding the breadth of architectural history, in stretching and pulling it toward unexpected directions, and approaching from a critical point of view. A special contribution that my works have provided is to underline intercultural relationships. I believe I have established that the late period Ottoman Empire is an important part of modernity, which is always attributed to the West."

In 1987, Çelik received the Turkish Research Institute Book Award for the first serious and systematic work on the urban history of the Ottoman era, titled, *The Remaking of Istanbul, Portrait of an Ottoman City in the Nineteenth*

Century (1986).
In 2010, she won the Spiro Kostof Book Award, given by the Society of Architectural Historians (USA), for *Empire, Architecture, and the City: French-Ottoman Encounters*, 1830-1914 (2008).

Çelik's other works include *Displaying the Orient: Architecture of Islam at Nineteenth Century World's Fairs* (1992); *Urban Forms and Colonial Confrontations: Algiers under French Rule* (1997). From May 2009 to October 2009, she also co-curated an exhibition at the Getty Center in Los Angeles, "Walls of Algiers: Narratives of the City through Text and Image" and from November 2011 to March 2012, she again co-curated an exhibition at Istanbul SALT in Galata, "Scramble for the Past: A Story of Archeology in the Ottoman Empire, 1753-1914", also acting as one of the editors of the books published in parallel to the exhibition. Her book, *About Antiquities: Politics of Archaeology in the Ottoman Empire*, was published concurrently with the Turkish edition in 2016. From 2000 to 2003, Çelik edited the *Journal of the Society of Architectural Historians* and co-curated the exhibition "Camera Ottomana: Photography and Modernity in the Ottoman Empire, 1840-1914" held at ANAMED, Istanbul, on April-August 2015, also co-editing the exhibition catalog.

Çengelhan, historic caravansary on the old site of Atpazarı (horse market), opposite the main entrance to Ankara Castle. Çengelhan, which now hosts the Ankara Rahmi M. Koç Museum(*), was built in 1522-23 during the reign of Suleiman the Magnificent. The caravansary was attached to the foundation of Damat Rüstem Paşa, husband of the sultan's daughter, Mihrimah Sultan. At the time, Çengelhan was one of the four largest caravansaries in Ankara, with numerous rooms and the type of stable known as "develik". Before it was abandoned at the end of the twentieth century, it was used as a tannery and wool-shed, where

mohair, fleece and rawhide were sold wholesale.

With its rectangular, almost square structure, Çengelhan is a beautiful example of a classic urban Ottoman caravansary, with a central, open-air courtyard surrounded by vaulted porticoes. The shop where Vehbi Koç(*) began his business life was also located in this courtyard. Vehbi Koç referred to it in his memoirs: "At that time, commerce in Ankara was focused on the caravansary at Atpazarı and the surrounding shops. Çengelhan was very old and is still standing today, but in a very basic, dilapidated state... one summer I spent five months working there... I can't remember what year it was now, but between the ages of 13 and 15 I had a summer internship. At the end of the summer, I left and returned to school."

Çengelhan was restored in 2003-05 and reopened to the public as the Ankara Rahmi M. Koç Museum in April 2005.

Çengelhan Rahmi M. Koç Museum
see **Ankara Rahmi M. Koç Museum**

Çobanoğlu, Oral *(b. December 11, 1930, Izmir – d. December 18, 2017, Istanbul)*, banker and director. He served on the Vehbi Koç Foundation(*) Board of Directors, representing Türkiye İş Bankası A.Ş. between 1982 and 1985.

He graduated from St. Joseph French High School in Izmir in 1949 and completed his undergraduate studies in commerce in France in 1952. He began his career at Tutum Bank and then continued at Türkiye Kredi Bankası. From 1954 to 1958, he worked at Doğubank Türk AŞ, transferring to Türkiye İş Bankası A.Ş. in his final year there. After holding various posts, he retired from his role as deputy chief executive at Türkiye İş Bankası A.Ş. in 1985. From 1973 to 1976, Çobanoğlu also held the post of CEO at the Türk Dış Ticaret Bankası (Dışbank), a Türkiye İş Bankası A.Ş. enterprise.

Çukurhan, historic caravansary adjacent to the Ankara Rahmi M. Koç Museum(*) on the old site of Atpazarı (horse market) and opposite the main entrance to Ankara Castle.

The caravansary belonged to the foundation of Sheikh-ul-Islam Ankaravi Mehmet Emin Efendi and was built in the late sixteenth or early seventeenth century. The caravansary contained a central rectangular, open-air courtyard; the outside was built of stone brick with an interior wooden framework and a tiled roof. During the Ottoman period, the building was used as a typical urban caravansary, functioning as accommodation and as a place of commerce, which for many years contained numerous shops and businesses selling mohair, wool, grain, dried fruits and nuts, vegetables and other goods. After featuring on the World Monuments Fund's watch list of 100 heritage sites awaiting rescue, in 2006 Çukurhan was leased by the Rahmi M. Koç Museology and Culture Foundation(*) within the remit of the Ankara General Directorate of Foundations' "restore, manage, transfer" model. Following works carried out from October 2007 to May 2010, the caravansary was faithfully restored to its original state and a glass roof was added to protect the interior of the courtyard. Today, the building is in use as the Divan Çukurhan Hotel.

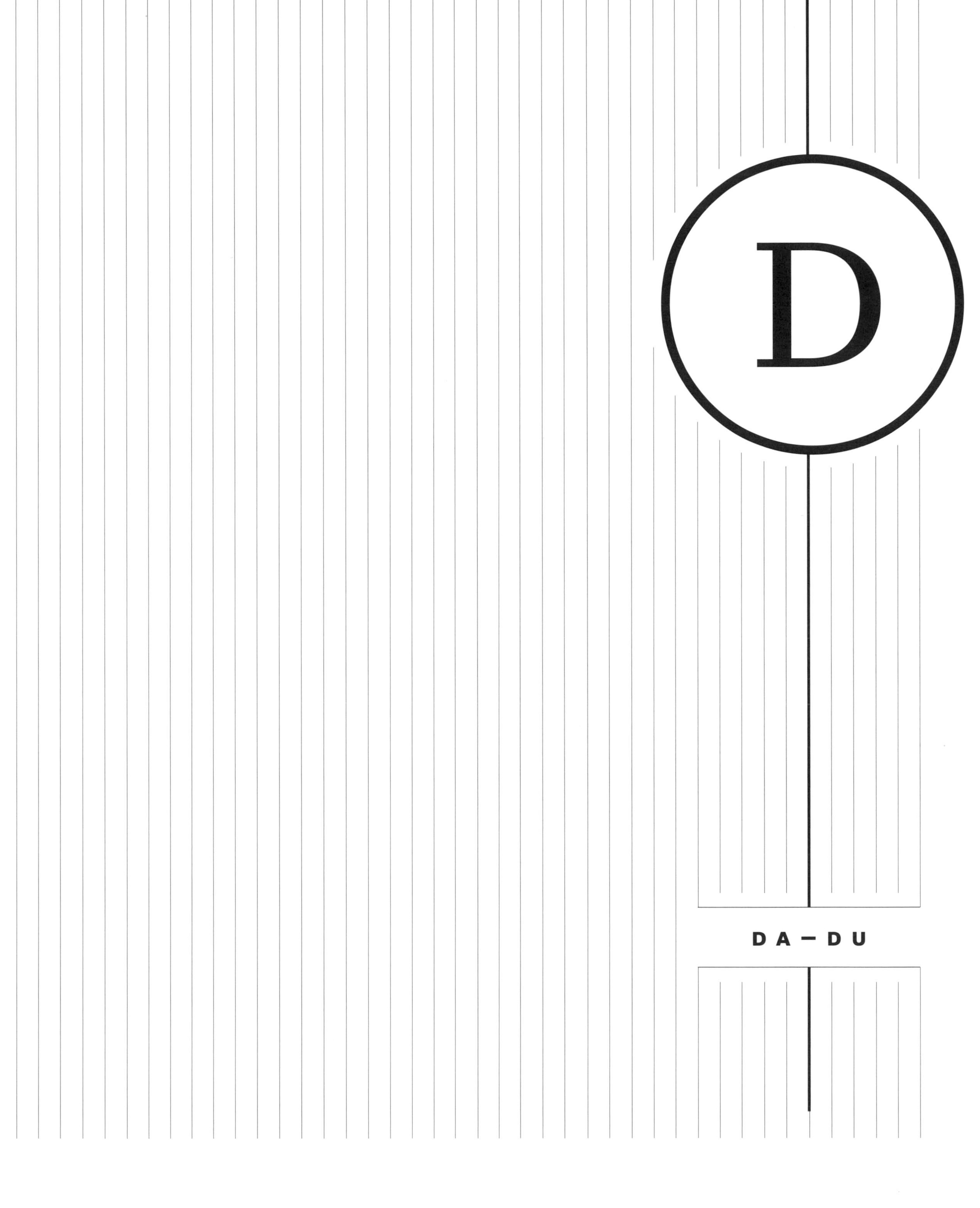

D

DA—DU

Dağlarca, Fazıl Hüsnü *(b. August 26 1914, Istanbul - d. October 15, 2008, Istanbul)*, real name MEHMET FAZIL, poet who received the Vehbi Koç Award(*) for culture in 2005. He is one of the leading names in contemporary Turkish poetry, following his own original path rather than identifying with any particular movement in Turkish literature. His book *Çocuk ve Allah* (1940; The Child and God) is considered to be one of the masterpieces of Turkish literature.

After graduating from Kuleli Military High School in 1933 and the Military Academy in 1935, Dağlarca joined the army as an infantry officer. He served in various parts of Anatolia and Thrace and left the army of his own accord in 1950. He worked for a time as a labor inspector and retired in 1959, opening a bookshop called "Kitap" ("Book") in Aksaray, Istanbul. Between January 1960 and July 1964, along with friends he published a monthly magazine, *Türkçe* (Turkish), with the aim of defending the purification of the language. After shutting down his bookshop in 1970, he focused exclusively on poetry.

Fazıl Hüsnü Dağlarca (MIDDLE) **at the award ceremony with Semahat Arsel and Mustafa V. Koç**

Dağlarca's first work, *Havaya Çizilen Dünya* (1935; The World Drawn in the Air), employed unique approaches previously unseen in Turkish poetry. In his later publication, *Çocuk ve Allah*, he achieved a greater finesse with regard to the integrity of language and structure. In *Çakır'ın Destanı* (1945; The Epic of Çakır) and *Taş Devri* (1945; The Stone Age), he continued along the same path, creating a language perfectly suited to the spirit of the poetry.

With *Üç Şehitler Destanı* (1949; The Epic of the Three Martyrs), Dağlarca entered a period of transition in his poetry, beginning to tackle humanistic relationships in nature. Following works such as *Toprak Ana* (1950; Mother Earth), *Aç Yazı* (1951; Hungry Writing), *Sivaslı Karınca* (1951; The Ant from Sivas), *İstanbul Fetih Destanı* (1953; The Epic of the Conquest of Istanbul), and *Anıtkabir* (1953), Dağlarca wrote *Asu* (1955), which heralded a new era in his poetry. He also participated in the debate surrounding the purification of the language during this period and employed a linguistic approach in his poems.

After publishing *Açıl Susam Açıl* (1967; Open Sesame!), his collection of poems for children, he focused more on children's poetry. Seeking to create a guileless sentimentality, this work encompassed themes such as the joy of living and the longing for union with the earth.

Due to his powerful use of language and imagery and the sincerity of his expression, Dağlarca's style has earned him a special place in contemporary Turkish poetry. In his thematically rich poems, he has always placed children center stage, using a child's perception of the world to tackle life's most important questions, as well as the relationships of humans and the natural world. In one of his last books, *Yapıtlarımla Konuşmalar (*1999-2000, 2 vols; Conversations with my Works), he adopted a new approach to the discussion of his works.

Many of Dağlarca's works have won awards; in 1967, he was voted "Greatest Living Turkish Poet" by the International Poetry Forum in Pittsburgh, USA, and in 1974 he was chosen as "Artist of the Year" by Milliyet Art Magazine. His work *Horoz* (1963; Cockerel) was awarded the 1977 Sedat Simavi Foundation Literature Award, which he shared with Peride Celal. In 1991, he declined the title of "State Artist" bestowed upon him by the Ministry of Culture.

In 2005, Dağlarca received the Vehbi Koç Award for culture and said in his acceptance speech: "The Vehbi Koç Award that I have received is a profound prize, to use a contemporary expression. By giving awards, literary institutions express 'the usual affection'. But this prize expresses an unusual affection. Through his philanthropic efforts and hard work over the years, Vehbi Koç became a true force. This is a demonstration of a businessman's respect for hard work. I wasn't close to Vehbi Koç myself, but he made me happy on at least two occasions. It's lovely to receive an award, but it's even better when that award comes from hard work. Now, it's as if this is the only prize I've ever won. I know that the Vehbi Koç Award comes from the heart, and that is why it's different from the others..."

Dağlarca's poetry has been translated into a number of languages, primarily English and French.

Dal, Teoman *(b. August 31, 1966)*, physician and director. From 2003 to 2006, he served as chief physician at the American Hospital(*) and medical director of the Vehbi Koç Foundation(*) (VKV) Healthcare Institutions.

He graduated from Hacettepe University Faculty of Medicine in 1989, before completing a residency in the Ear, Nose and Throat Department (ENT) of the same faculty (1989-93). From 1995 to 1999, he worked as an assistant professor at Ankara's Başkent University in the ENT Department of the Faculty of Medicine. He completed a master's degree in health administration at the same university in 1999. After his military service at Ankara Gülhane Military Medical Academy (1999-2000), he worked in the Faculty of Medicine at Başkent University in Ankara until September 2001. In November 2000, he became associate professor.

Dr. Dal worked at the American Hospital (2001-02) and at Acıbadem Kadıköy Hospital (2002-03). He served as chief physician at the American Hospital and medical director of the VKV Healthcare Institutions (2003-06). He was chief physician and director at Acıbadem Fulya Hospital (2008-10).

Dr. Dal, who became a professor in 2017, has contributed chapters to a number of books and published numerous scientific papers.

Dalkara, Turgay *(b. June 8, 1952, Çivril, Denizli)*, physician and scientist who received the Vehbi Koç Award(*) for health in 2010. He is known for his work on migraines, alleviation of cerebrovascular obstructions, Parkinson's and Alzheimer's disease.

Dalkara decided to become a scientist at just five years of age, while playing in the laboratory established by his father. After completing his elementary and secondary education in Denizli, he entered the Faculty of Medicine at Hacettepe University (HU) in 1968, graduating in 1975. Dr. Dalkara was already interested in the brain when he decided to specialize in neurology, considering the research possibilities presented by the CAT scan machinery obtained by the faculty at the time. From 1975 to 1979, he undertook his residency in neurology and completed a doctorate in pharmacology (1977-81). He carried out postgraduate research at McGill University Faculty of Medicine in Canada (1982-84).

After returning home, he began working in the Neurology Department at HU Faculty of Medicine, becoming a professor in 1993. Professor Dalkara is currently professor of neurology at the same faculty, while also serving as head of the Institute for Neurological Sciences and Psychiatry. Professor Dalkara also lectures on the Neuroscience and Neurotechnology Doctoral Program, jointly run by Middle East Technical University and HU, and is a member of staff at Massachusetts General Hospital connected to Harvard Medical School, generally working there during the summer months. From 2000 to 2004, he also held a number of posts on the Scientific and Technological Research Council of Turkey (TÜBİTAK).

In 2010, Professor Dalkara received the Vehbi Koç Award for "studies into diseases of the brain and vascular system". In his acceptance speech, he said: "Whatever I've achieved, I achieved it with my friends. Without their successes, none of my successes would have been possible. It would have been impossible for us to reach this point without their belief in our success." Dalkara has received many other awards, including the Atatürk Incentive Award for Scientific

Prof. Turgay Dalkara at the award ceremony with Semahat Arsel

Research (1981), the TÜBİTAK Incentive Award (1987), Eczacıbaşı Award for Medicine (1990), the Hacettepe University Award for Success in Science (1991), the Sandoz Grand Prize for Pharmacology (1996), the TÜBİTAK Science Award (2002), the World Academy of Sciences Award for Medical Sciences (2013) and the Kadir Has Award for Excellence (2014).

Professor Dalkara is a principle member of the Turkish Academy of Sciences (TÜBA), the Science Academy(*) and the European Academy for Science and Arts and is also a member of the editorial boards of the *Türk Beyin Damar Hastalıkları Dergisi* and *Türk Nöroloji Dergisi*. As well as publishing more than 100 scientific research papers in a number of journals, including *Nature Medicine* one of the most respected in the field, he also co-edited the book, *Neurological Basis of Migraine* (2017).

Darülaceze, officially known as THE DARÜLACEZE DIRECTORATE OF THE REPUBLIC OF TURKEY, a charitable institution which provides accommodation for orphans, almsmen and people with disabilities, cares for people who are unable to work and provides education and schooling to orphaned children. In accordance with the provisions of its formal deeds, the Vehbi Koç Foundation(*) has supported Darülaceze since 1969, providing aid, financial and otherwise, to cover the costs of building maintenance as well as food, nutrition and healthcare for those staying at the institution.

The foundations of Darülaceze were laid in 1892 and it opened its doors in 1896 in the Istanbul district of Okmeydanı, on a site measuring nearly 300,000 square meters. As people of all faiths made donations for the construction of the building, it was decided that it would serve everyone, regardless of their religious beliefs: space was allocated inside for a church and synagogue as well as a mosque. When Darülaceze was first founded, it comprised of four pavilions, a hospital, an orphanage, a pavilion for infants, a laundry, a hammam and a bakery. There were also studios for tailors, hosiers, cobblers, carpenters and ironmongers, carpet looms and an art school.

At its foundation, Darülaceze was connected to the Ministry of Interior, but after the Republic was founded, it transferred to the Ministry of Health and then to the Municipality of Istanbul in 1924. In 1999, it affiliated with the Ministry of Interior, before affiliating (under the name of the Darülaceze Directorate) with the Ministry of Family and Social Policy in 2011. All of the institution's needs and operational costs were covered by donations from benefactors, rental income from property belonging to the institution and a 10% share of municipal taxes.

The Darülaceze site now includes seven facilities for almsmen, an outpatient clinic, kindergarten, rehabilitation center with a library, a modern kitchen with the capacity to feed 3,000 people, a slaughterhouse, a cold room capable of preserving meat donations for up to one year, a laundry and a bakery. It runs its own printing press, cobblers, and iron-mongering and tailoring workshops to meet the needs of the institution.

Darülaceze shelters nearly 600 people and since its foundation has housed over 70,000 people, half of which were children.

Demirseren, Atakan *(b. July 7 1939, Mersin - d. May 13 1998, Istanbul),* educator and director. He served as chief deputy director of Koç High School (*see* Koç School) between 1988 and 1998.

After completing undergraduate studies in mathematics and physics at the Istanbul University Faculty of Sciences, he received a master's degree in educational sciences from the American University of Beirut. He worked at the Turkish Naval Academy in Istanbul as a teacher of mathematics and physics (1961-72), branch manager for education (1972-75), and planning and research manager and department head of sciences (1975-81). Following on from this, he worked as branch manager for education at the Turkish Naval Forces (1981-82) and head of teaching at the Naval Academy (1982-84). From 1985 to 1988, he was an educational consultant for the foundation of Koç High School. When the school opened in 1988, he became chief deputy director and continued in this role until his death in 1998. After his death, the school's auditorium was named after him and the Atakan Demirseren Mathematics Competition was established in his memory.

DenizTemiz Association/ TURMEPA (TURKISH MARINE ENVIRONMENT PROTECTION ASSOCIATION), non-governmental organization (NGO) that raises awareness of the importance of protecting the sea and beaches, aiming to ensure the seas surrounding Turkey are cleaner for future generations. It was founded in 1994 by the Chamber of Shipping together with committed volunteers and under the presidency of Rahmi M. Koç(*). Following a decision taken by the Council of Ministers in 2000, it acquired the status of a public interest association.

Following the publication of TURMEPA's "Declaration of Marine Protection" in 1995, it received the support of international institutions like the United Nations Environment Program, the International Maritime Organization (IMO), the International Chamber of Shipping (ICS), the International Union for Conservation of Nature (IUCN) and the Club of Rome, achieving ISO 14001, the international certification for environmental management in 2011. As Turkey's principal marine NGO, the organization has nearly 1,000 members, 350 of which are corporate; together with branch and regional coordinators and volunteers, it engages in work to sustain marine life in the 8,333-kilometer coastal strip which extends from Hopa to Iskenderun, including the islands.

Among the projects run by the association on protection, awareness and education is the Sea Ambassadors Community (DET), a network of student groups that promote environmental consciousness among young people. In 2017, the Vehbi Koç Foundation(*) provided support for DET programs carried out by TURMEPA at 13 universities in 10 cities.

From 2010 to 2012, TURMEPA held the presidency of INTERMEPA, an umbrella association for all MEPAs, founded in 2006. The association is a member of the Mediterranean Information Office for Environment, Culture and Sustainable Development (MIO-ECSDE), which is a federation of Mediterranean NGOs working in the field of environment and sustainable development. The association publishes educational material and its quarterly *DenizTemiz* (CleanSea) magazine has a circulation of 5,000 people.

A MESSAGE FROM THE ASSOCIATION'S FOUNDER AND HONORARY PRESIDENT RAHMİ M. KOÇ

Dear Friends of the Sea,

History and progress have shown that countries, in their efforts to industrialize, have pushed respect for the environment into second place, prioritizing construction of new factories, increasing manufacturing and rapidly improving standards of living. Indeed, Turkey has taken the same path. Our seas are polluted, many species of fish are facing the threat of extinction, marine plants have been lost, and now the sea and the environment are not too happy with us.

Alarm bells began to ring in our ears 21 years ago, when developed countries embraced care and protection of the environment, making it a priority. We founded TURMEPA with a handful of friends and marine enthusiasts. Our purpose was to inform and warn our fellow citizens of all ages and kindle a spark among the public.

We gave ourselves a 30-year deadline. Two thirds of that time has already passed. Despite this, we're still swimming against the tide but at the same time growing stronger. Have we managed to reach the point that we've been aiming for? We haven't reached it yet, but our fellow citizens, our government, our armed forces, our municipalities and those who rely on the sea for their livelihoods are gradually learning to respect the environment more.

It's not possible for us to tackle a matter like this on our own and we know that; but our supporters are increasing every day. We're pleased with this and are expanding the scope of our work as far as possible. If you too turn to the sea and give us your support, you can be another pinch of salt in this soup. And it's not just about you: we want you to encourage other people to join us too.

This is the only way that we will be able to leave behind a clean, healthy world that future generations can be proud of.

http://turmepa.org.tr/page/kurucu-ve-onursal-baskan_17

Diyarbakır Bağlar Vehbi Koç Elementary School *see* **17 Schools Project**

Diyarbakır Kayapınar Vehbi Koç Elementary School *see* **17 Schools Project**

Dörtlük, Kayhan *(b. 1945, Antakya),* archaeologist and director. He was director of AKMED(*) between 1996 and 2015.

After graduating from Ankara University Faculty of Languages, History and Geography with a degree in Classical Archeology in 1967, he began working at the Ministry of Tourism and Publicity (now Culture and Tourism). He served as an advisor, inspector and museum curator at the ministry's central and provincial sites. He retired from his final post at Antalya Museum after 17 years as director. In 1995, he was founding director of AKMED in Antalya and the affiliated Kaleiçi Museum(*). He managed AKMED until 2016, when it is affiliated to Koç University.

Dörtlük has also led a number of salvage excavations, edited various scientific publications and curated a number of exhibitions both at home and abroad.

Dr. Nusret and Semahat Arsel International Business Law Implementation and Research Center *see* **NASAMER**

Dreamstalk, a social enterprise platform encouraging and helping young people to realize their dreams, supporting user projects selected on criteria such as being innovative, fun, problem-solving, inspirational and bold. Founded in 2013, the platform's activities include dream-sharing seminars at universities and high schools, annual dream conferences and festivals, dream club activities, corporate dream conferences and training, dream classes at universities, dream coaching and dream competitions between high schools. Between November 2014 and April 2015, the Vehbi Koç Foundation(*) supported Dreamstalk in bringing their activities to nine universities in different regions of Turkey.

Durak, (Osman) Turgay *(b. January 17, 1952, Istanbul),* engineer and director. From 2010 to 2015, he served on the Vehbi Koç Foundation(*) Board of Directors, representing Koç Holding(*), where he held the position of CEO.

After graduating from Robert College(*) in 1970, Durak completed his undergraduate and master's studies in mechanical engineering at Northwestern University in the USA in 1974. In 1976, he began working as an application engineer at Ford Otosan. He became assistant general manager of marketing in 1986 and assistant general manager of purchasing in 1987. In 2000, he was appointed chief assistant general manager in charge of production, becoming general manager in 2002. From 2007 to 2010, he was president of the Koç Holding Automotive Group and was also a member of the Koç Holding Board of Directors and CEO from April 2010 to April 2015. He retired from the role on March 31, 2015.

From 2004 to 2010, Durak was chair of the Automotive Manufacturers Association Board of Directors and has been a member of the Tüpraş Board of Directors since April 2010.

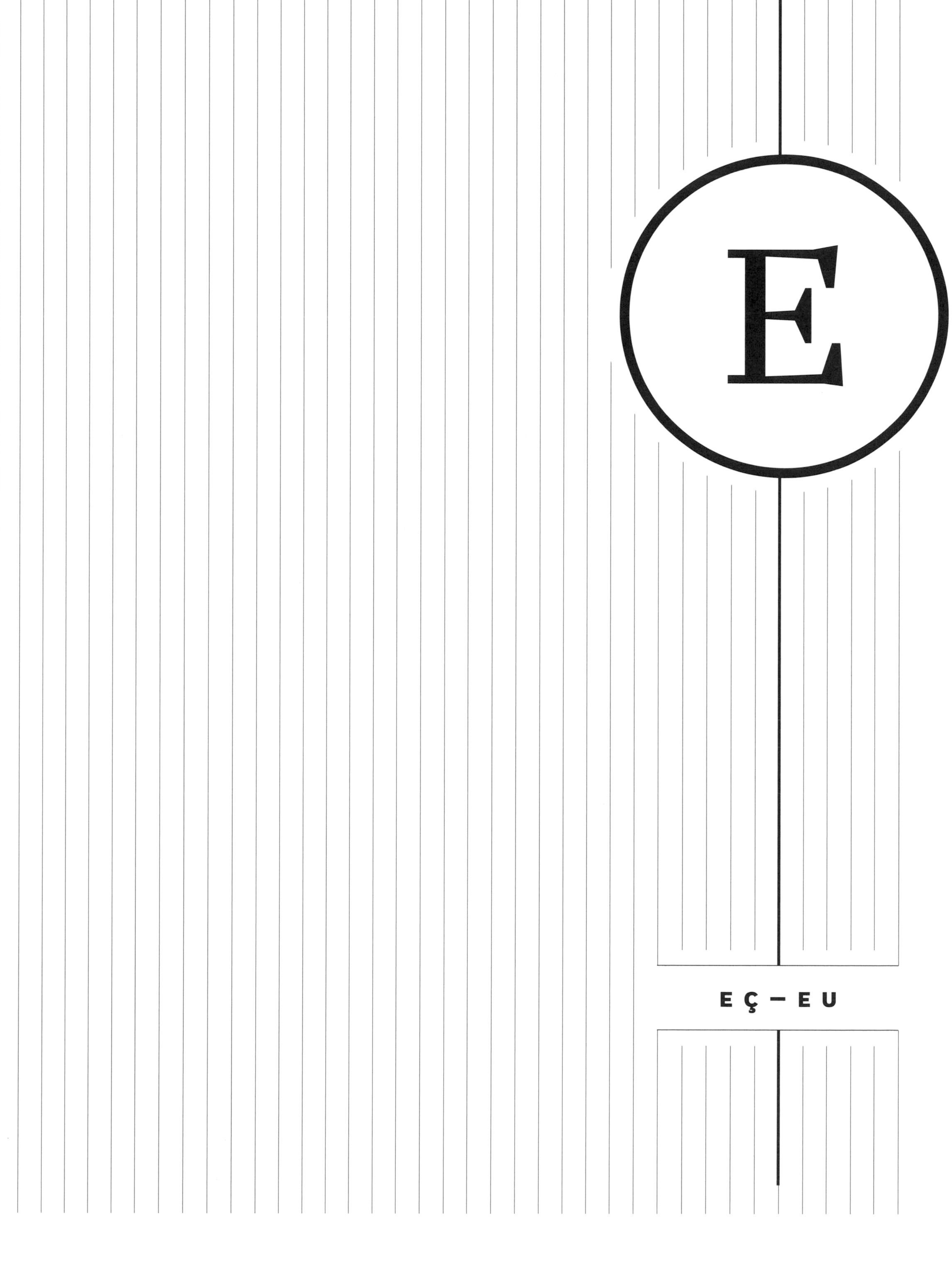
E
EÇ — EU

EÇADEM, full name ENGELLİ ÇOCUK VE AİLELERİNE DESTEK MERKEZİ (SUPPORT CENTER FOR DISABLED CHILDREN AND THEIR FAMILIES), a Koç University School of Nursing(*) initiative, offering material and moral support in partnership with Sarıyer Municipality and with financial help from the Istanbul Development Agency. It was founded in late 2014, in the Sarıyer district of Istanbul, to support the cognitive, physical, psychological and social development of children with learning disabilities and provide counseling and psychosocial support services to their mothers and siblings. In 2015, the center also organized a symposium, "A Multidisciplinary Approach to Disabled Children and Their Families", and a workshop, "Raising Disabled Children".

In 2016, EÇADEM received three awards at the 2016 NC Awards—including gold in the social media category—for its publicity film "A Smile is All It Takes to Change the World", which it produced for the International Day of Persons with Disabilities. In the same year, the center also won the Marmara Municipalities Union Golden Ant Award and the Association of Social Democratic Municipalities (SODEM) Award for Best Social Project.

Edge Jr – Math *see* **Koç School**

Education Reform Initiative *see* **ERG**

Elazığ Koç Elementary School *see* **17 Schools Project**

Eldem, Sedad Hakkı *(b. August 31, 1908, Istanbul – d. September 7, 1998, Istanbul),* architect. His work in design and application, architectural theory and education left a lasting mark on twentieth century Turkish architecture. He designed several buildings for the Koç Group(*) and Koç family(*), including the Admiral Bristol Nursing School(*), the Atatürk Library(*), the Kıraç Mansion and Rahmi Koç House, also devising restitution and restoration projects for the Azaryan Mansion housing the Sadberk Hanım Museum(*) and the Koç Holding AŞ Nakkaştepe Complex(*), where the Vehbi Koç Foundation(*) headquarters are based.

As his father was a diplomat, he attended elementary school in Geneva and completed the first years of his high school education in Munich. In 1924, aged only 16, he began his higher education in the Architecture Department of the Istanbul School of Fine Arts (later the Academy for Fine Arts [AFA], Istanbul State Academy of Fine Arts [ISAFA], Mimar Sinan University [MSU], now Mimar Sinan Fine Arts University), which did not stipulate a high school diploma for entrants. After graduating with a top grade in 1928, he worked in various architectural offices in Europe. After returning to Turkey in 1930, he exhibited his work at AFA and the Turkish Hearths Center in Ankara. In 1931, he was responsible for the design and erection of the Turkish Pavilion at the Budapest International Fair and also joined the teaching staff of the AFA as an assistant. In the same period, he opened his own architectural office, beginning a professional career which would last many years.

From 1941 to 1946, he was head of the architecture department at the academy and lectured on architectural projects and construction for 46 years. He was later appointed head of the Chair on Surveying and Restoration. He was also a member and president of various organizations in Istanbul, such as the Council for the Protection of Ancient Monuments (1941-45) and the High Council for Immovable Antiquities and Monuments (1962-78). After retiring from the academy due to an age limit in 1978, Eldem continued teaching design and in 1979 he was awarded the title of honorary doctor by ISAFA.

Eldem received many awards, among them the Turkish Ministry of Culture Award for Art and Culture (1983), the Aga Khan Award for Architecture (1986, for the Zeyrek Social Security Administration Buildings) and the Chamber of Architects Grand Award (1988). He also won first prize in many architectural project competitions.

A number of essays and books have been written about Eldem, including: *Sedad Hakkı Eldem: 50 Yıllık Meslek Jübilesi* (Sedad Hakkı Eldem: 50 Years in Architecture), which was published to mark 100 years since the foundation of MSU in 1983; and *Boğaziçi Yalıları*

https://archnet.org/authorities/338

(Mansions of the Bosphorus; 1993-94), which was compiled using materials from an archive left by Eldem and published in two volumes by the VKV.

Epic Authors *see* **Koç School**

Era *see* **Koç School**

Erçelen, Ömür *(b. December 4, 1964, Ankara),* physician and director. In 2015, he was appointed medical director of the Vehbi Koç Foundation(*) (VKV) Healthcare Institutions.

After attending TED Ankara College (1975-81), Erçelen studied medicine at Hacettepe University Faculty of Medicine (1981-87). He completed a residency in anesthesiology and reanimation in the same faculty in 1992. He worked at the Pain Clinic in the Memorial Sloan Kettering Cancer Center in New York from 1995 to 1996, before returning to Hacettepe University Faculty of Medicine, where he became associate professor in 1997.

In 1998, Dr. Erçelen joined the American Hospital(*) and from 2008 to 2010 held the positions of deputy chief physician and responsible director, later serving as chief physician between 2010 and 2014. In 2011, he joined Koç University Hospital(*) as a professor and, in 2015, became medical director of the Vehbi Koç Foundation(*) (VKV) Healthcare Institutions.

A member of the International Association for the Study of Pain and the European Society of Anesthesiology, and a member of the administration board of the Turkish Association for Anesthesiology and Reanimation, Erçelen has published a large number of scientific papers both at home and abroad.

ERG, full name EĞİTİM REFORMU GİRİŞİMİ (EDUCATION REFORM INITIATIVE), organization which aims to develop educational policies that underpin the social and economic development of Turkey. Established at Sabancı University in 2003 with the goal of promoting "a quality education for all", the organization brings together different stakeholders, supporting the development of participative processes for generating ideas and engaging in studies on research, advocacy and education. The Vehbi Koç Foundation(*) (VKV) provides regular support to the ERG, which is also sponsored by civil society organizations such as the Aydın Doğan Foundation, the Enka Foundation, the Elginkan Foundation and the Borusan Kocabıyık Foundation, companies such as Yapı Merkezi and Enerji-Su, as well as Sabancı, Istanbul Kültür and Istanbul Bilgi Universities.

The Good Practices in Education Conference, which ERG has organized every year since 2004, gathers together educational stakeholders, offering a platform of communication and cooperation to expand the reach of good practices. The "Education Monitoring Report", published annually since 2007, gives a comprehensive evaluation of the previous year's developments. From 2013 to 2015, ERG ran a project titled "Towards Democratic Schools: Participation Practices for Empowering Students and Schools", which was run in cooperation with Istanbul Bilgi University Child Studies Unit. The project set out to strengthen the culture of democracy in Turkey's schools, aiming to facilitate the participation of those with a stake in education, especially children, in educational procedures and decision-making mechanisms.

In 2012, ERG began holding Educational Policy Seminars, each focusing on a different theme, with the aim of diversifying the platforms on which education policies were discussed in Turkey. As part of the project "Vocational Education: A Crucial Matter for the Nation(*)", started in 2006 in partnership with the Ministry of Education (ME), Koç Holding(*) and the VKV, a cooperation agreement on improving the quality of vocational education in Turkey was signed in 2010 by Koç Holding and ERG. This led to the publication of four reports in 2012, containing research findings and policy recommendations resulting from the Collaborating for Quality in Vocational Education project run by ERG as part of the initiative; these included "Vocational and Technical Education Strategy Document" and "What Works in Vocational Education and Why? Policy Recommendations for School-Business Collaborations".

Another of ERG's important studies is the Rights in Education project, which first ran in 2007-09 and then again in 2009-10. "The Power of Thinking: Teaching Training Support Project for a Youth that Questions and Queries" was organized by ERG in collaboration with ME and Akbank; as part of the project, between January 2009 and May 2010, 4,250 teachers in eight cities were trained in skills for teaching and learning critical thinking.

The Teachers Network Project(*), which began as a result of the Teachers Research carried out by ERG in cooperation with VKV and ATÖLYE Labs, is supported by six leading foundations, including AÇEV(*), Enka Foundation, Sabancı Foundation and VKV. Starting in 2016, the project aimed to help raise the standards of education in Turkey and increase student success by collaborating with teachers to create an environment of continual interaction conducive to development and transformation.

ERG ranked among the top 50 "Top Education Policy Think Tanks" in the Global Go To Think Tank Index complied by the Think Tanks and Civil Societies Program of the University of Pennsylvania in 2013 and among the top 45 in 2014.

Ergüder, Üstün *(b. May 10, 1937, Istanbul)*, academician and foundation director. He has been a member of the Vehbi Koç Foundation(*) Board of Directors since 1997.

After graduating from Robert College(*) in 1957, Ergüder completed his undergraduate studies at University of Manchester School of Economic and Social Studies in England in 1960. From 1961 to 1962, he worked as an assistant at Middle East Technical University. In 1969, he received a doctorate in political sciences from Syracuse University in the USA before joining the teaching staff of the Robert College undergraduate department, now Boğaziçi University (BU). He was visiting lecturer at the University of Michigan (1974-75) and was head of the BU School of Foreign Languages (1978-81). During the same period, 1979-81, he was director of the Center for Applied Research at BU Faculty of Administrative Sciences, before serving as vice dean of the same faculty (1982-83). He was a visiting lecturer at New York State University in Binghamton (1983-84) and at Syracuse University in 1984. From 1986 to 1989, Ergüder was once again director of the BU School of Foreign Languages and became chair of the Department of Political Science and International Relations at the BU Faculty of Administrative Sciences in 1989. In 1992, he was appointed rector of BU. After leaving this role in 2000, he began teaching at Sabancı University (SU), also becoming director of the university-affiliated Istanbul Policy Center. He was a co-founder of the ERG(*) (Education Reform Initiative), which was affiliated to SU, becoming director in 2003. Professor Ergüder was made emeritus professor in 2010 and is the current president of the ERG Executive Board.

In addition to his academic responsibilities, Professor Ergüder has also held various administrative roles, including founding member of the Turkish Foundation for Economic and Social Studies (TESEV[*]) (1994), member of the TRT Executive Board (1996-2000), member of the European Cultural Foundation Executive Board (1996-2004), member of the Open Society Institute Advisory Committee (2001-03), member (1994-2014) and president (2001-16) of the administrative board of the Third Sector Foundation of Turkey(*) (TÜSEV), and member (2004-09) and president (2009-13) of the Magna Charta Observatory Council.

Professor Ergüder is an honorary member of the Turkish Academy of Sciences (TÜBA) and has published a number of essays and books, including *Türkiye'de Tarım Fiyat Destek Siyasası ve Siyaset* (1981; Politics and Agricultural Price Support Policy in Turkey), *Seçim Sistemleri ve Türk Demokrasisi* (1981; Electoral Systems and Turkish Democracy) and *Yükseköğretimin Fırtınalı Sularında* (2015; Higher Education in Crisis).

Erkut, (Fehmi) Celal *(b. December 1, 1958, Izmir)*, lawyer and academician. He has served on the board of directors of the Vehbi Koç Foundation(*) since 2014.

He graduated from Galatasaray High School in 1978 and Istanbul University (IU) Faculty of Law in 1982. From 1982 to 1984, he worked as a researcher in the Department of Administrative Law in the same faculty, while also studying for a master's degree. He began working on his doctorate at the IU Institute of Social Sciences, completing it in 1989. In 1993, he became an associate professor, joining the staff in the Department of Administrative Law at IU Faculty of Law.

In addition to being a faculty member, from 1994 onwards Erkut worked as a lawyer, co-founding the Soybay & Erkut Law Office, the country's first office of administrative law. In 1998, he took up a part-time post in the Department of Administrative Law at Galatasaray University Faculty of Law and was made head of department in the following year. Erkut became a professor in 2004 and retired in 2011. He has produced a large body of academic works in administrative law and administrative judicial legislation.

Eskinazis, Isak de *(b. September 6, 1909, Edirne – d. December 13, 2001, Istanbul)*, accountant and financier who worked with the Koç Group(*) companies between 1935 and 1986. From 1969 to 1986, he was a member of the Vehbi Koç Foundation(*) (VKV) Board of Directors representing Koç Holding(*).

Eskinazis completed his elementary and secondary education in Edirne and began his professional career at Osmanlı Bankası. While working at the bank's branch in Ankara, he was appointed assistant manager for the Çorum branch. As he preferred to stay in Ankara, he contacted Vehbi Koç(*) and as a result, on February 1, 1935, began working at Koçzade Ahmet Vehbi Firması as a book keeper.

İsak de Eskinazis (FRONT, LEFT) **with Vehbi Koç**

He later became accounting manager at Koç Ticaret AŞ. He was a founding partner of Koç Holding when it was inaugurated in 1963. As a member of the board of directors and head of the Finance Group, he played a leading role in the financial consolidation of the holding. In 1970, he became a member of the executive committee. He became a member of the VKV Board of Directors in 1969 and remained in the post until 1986, when he retired from the Koç Holding Board of Directors.

Eskişehir Academy of Economic and Commercial Sciences Vehbi Koç Library and Research Center Building, library commissioned by Vehbi Koç(*) at Eskişehir Academy of Economic and Commercial Sciences, which today forms the nucleus of the Anadolu University. Construction began in 1965 and the center opened in October 1968.

"Let's not forget that it's possible to pray under a tree. But teaching and scientific research are impossible without buildings, books, materials and equipment."
VEHBİ KOÇ

The year was 1963. I was invited to a seminar organized by the Economic and Social Studies Conference Board at the Çınar Hotel in Yeşilköy, Istanbul. One of those attending was Professor Orhan Oğuz, head of the Academy of Economic and Commercial Sciences, who I met at the cocktail party on the first day of the seminar. This passionate, young professor told me he was teaching in the academy's scattered rented buildings in Eskişehir and that his students were having to attend lessons in these difficult circumstances, roaming from place to place. When I opened the branch of Koç Teşkilatı in Eskişehir fifteen years earlier, I had said that I would serve Eskişehir in other ways. I promised Professor Orhan Oğuz that I would donate 1.5 million lira for a new building for the Academy of Economic and Commercial Sciences.

Meetings began with the relevant ministries and went on for a good while. Just at that time, Professor Orhan Oğuz managed to secure the necessary aid from the government, so construction began on the academy buildings. Professor Oğuz came to remind me about the support I had promised and asked me to build a library in the area allocated for the academy. I agreed, the library was built, and on October 21, 1968, it was formally opened at a ceremony attended by President Cevdet Sunay. In the speech I gave at the ceremony, I expressed my thoughts on education:

"If we look at advanced countries, we can see that well-educated people are working in every field and that talented, skilled people rise through the ranks of management. Our country has to develop quickly too, so it is vital that, as soon as possible, our country seriously focuses on training young people capable of working in a variety of fields. People take time to develop. Take a child who starts elementary school at seven years of age: if he continues his education in the normal manner, completing his higher education and then military service, he will not be productive until the age of 30. That's why these facilities have been established, so that our young people can work hard and have a proper education."

Vehbi Koç, *Hayat Hikâyem* (*My Life Story*), 4th Edition, Vehbi Koç Foundation Publications, Istanbul, 1983, pp 117-18

Europa Nostra Awards, award program which encourages excellence in conservation initiatives. It was established in 1978 by Europa Nostra, a federation of organizations working to protect cultural heritage, which includes 250 civil society organizations from 50 countries across Europe. Europa Nostra was founded in 1963 and was recognized by the European Commission as a European umbrella organization for conservation in 1998. The rewards system it has coordinated across Europe since 1978, was augmented by the European Union Prize for Cultural Heritage in 2002, following a decision of the European Commission.

Europa Nostra Award, Sadberk Hanım Museum, 1988

In 1988, Europa Nostra gave recognition to the Sadberk Hanım Museum(*) for the additional museum building, the Sevgi Gönül Building, which was "faithfully restored, renovated and reopened as a museum of archaeological works". In 1990, the Koç Holding AŞ Headquarters at Nakkaştepe(*) also received an honorable mention for being "faithfully restored and renovated".

European Association for Research on Adolescence (EARA) Çeşme Conference, international conference that took place in Çeşme, Izmir, on September 3-6, 2014. It was sponsored by Vehbi Koç Foundation(*) and Koç Holding(*).

While primarily attended by European psychologists working on adolescence, there were also researchers and professionals working in other fields such as education, sociology and

psychiatry. The conference included pre-conference workshops, invited symposiums, round-table talks, debates and poster presentations. The conference sessions covered themes such as adolescence from a cultural and intercultural perspective, youth participation in politics and society, interpersonal relationships, stress and stress management, identity, parent–adolescent relationships, becoming an adult, bullying and cyber-bullying.

European Association of Archaeologists (EAA) Congress 2014, science conference that took place on September 10–14, 2014, at Istanbul Technical University. The Vehbi Koç Foundation(*) was one of the sponsors for the congress, which attracted 2,065 scholars from 76 countries. There were 47 parallel sessions and 2,253 paper and poster presentations. The conference's main theme was "Connecting Seas – Across the Borders" and subthemes were: Managing Archaeological Heritage, Ancient Technologies in Social Context, Environment and Subsistence, Times of Change: Collapse and Transformative Impulses, and Retrieving and Interpreting the Archaeological Record. The congress was dedicated to the memory of Sevgi Gönül(*), in recognition for her interest and understanding of Byzantine archaeology.

European Foundation Centre (EFC), international body that aims to support social change by strengthening links and collaboration between charitable organizations. It was established in Brussels in 1989 and its membership has now reached 200 leading philanthropic organizations from across the world. The center has five members operating in Turkey: Vehbi Koç Foundation(*) (VKV), Anadolu Education and Social Assistance Foundation, Aydın Doğan Foundation, Sabancı Foundation and Third Sector Foundation of Turkey (TÜSEV[*]). In 2014, VKV was selected for the EFC General Assembly and Annual Conference Committee as well as the Grantmakers East Forum (GEF) Committee. The annual Grantmakers East Forum was held in Istanbul in 2015 with the theme of "Creating Equal Opportunities: Overcoming Divides."

European Youth Parliament (EYP), a civil society initiative that aims to increase political awareness and responsibility in young Europeans, encouraging them to be tolerant and free-thinking citizens. Since the organization began at a high school in the French city of Fontainebleau in 1987, it has rapidly grown into a network covering 40 European countries. It is Europe's largest youth platform for political debate, exchanging ideas, intercultural comparison, and European citizenship education. Thousands of young people offer their support in a voluntary capacity and its annual events attract almost 40,000 participants.

EYP Turkey joined the network in 1999, acquiring legal status as the European Youth Parliament Association (Avrupa Gençlik Parlamentosu Derneği) in 2011. The EYP's 69th International Session took place in Istanbul in 2012. The 78th International Session in Izmir in 2015 was sponsored by the Vehbi Koç Foundation(*). The Koç School(*) European Youth Parliament Club organizes an annual international meeting called the Koç Forum, in which students discuss current global issues and produce draft resolutions.

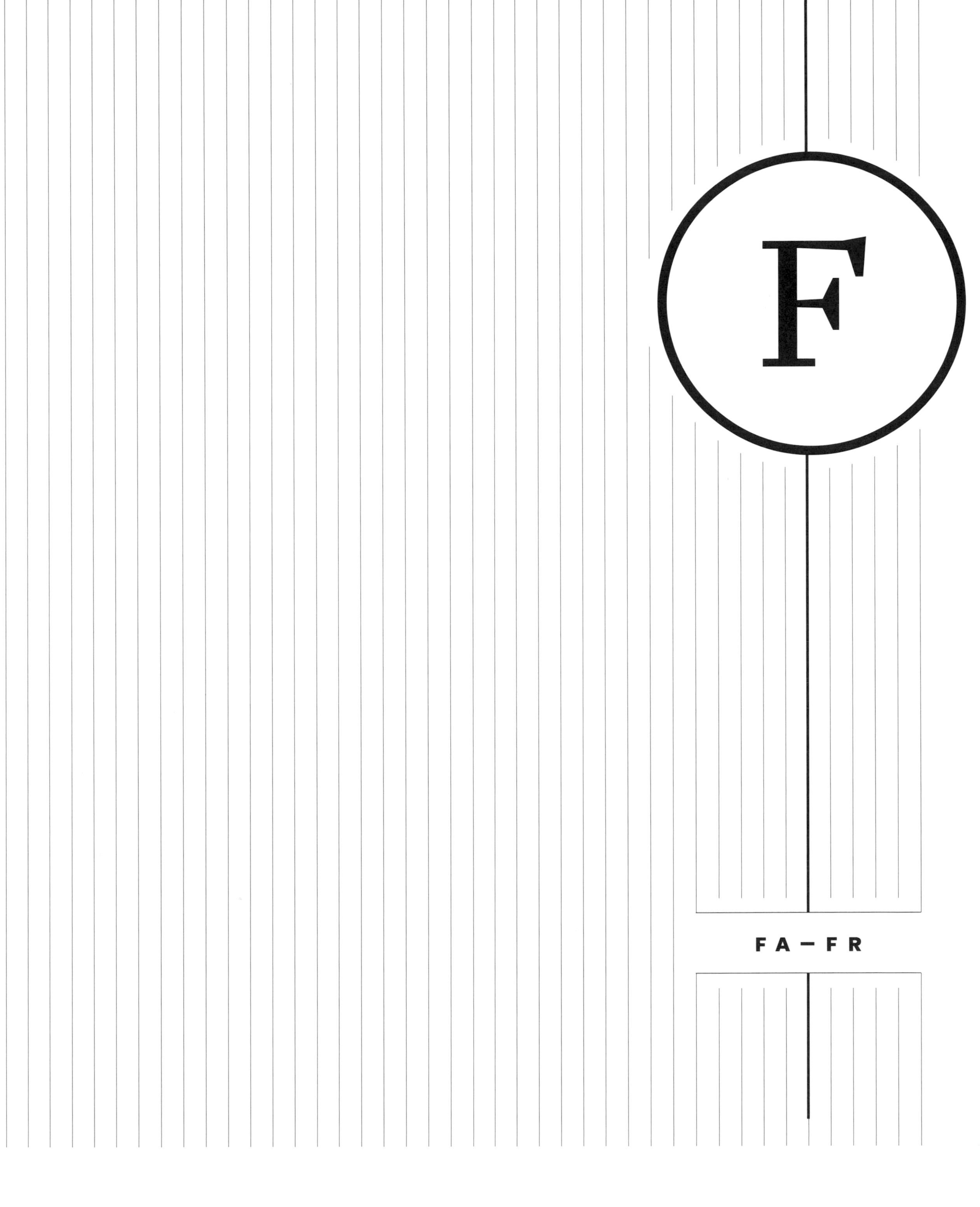

FA—FR

Family Committee, management mechanism established by Vehbi Koç(*) in 1972. The only committee members were Vehbi Koç and his children, Semahat Arsel(*), Rahmi M. Koç(*), Sevgi Gönül(*) and Suna Kıraç(*). The committee oversaw the development, vision and strategies of Koç Holding, agreeing on final decisions solely between the five members. All committee discussions, without exception, were recorded in official minutes and locked away in a secret safe. Suna Kıraç fulfilled the role of meeting secretary. When necessary, CEOs attended the meetings and informed the members. The essence of the committee was captured in the words of Vehbi Koç: "Argue matters between yourselves and keep your disagreements private. Try to make decisions by consent. When that isn't possible, you should go with the majority and everyone should comply. Try to prevent any of your issues becoming public."

VEHBI KOÇ ON THE FAMILY COMMITTEE...

I was driven to set up the FAMILY COMMITTEE in 1972 by my experiences talking to global companies and families and my subsequent observation that families, companies and peoples unravel because of inner conflicts that arise between their members. I served as chair until March 1984 and worked extremely hard to ensure the committee functioned smoothly. In setting up the committee, my aim was to create a space where matters concerning the family and the wider Koç Community could be discussed, along with various other issues, between either my children and I or just between the children; I wanted decisions to be agreed on or decided by majority and then complied with by all. I left the committee in March 1984 and Semahat Arsel is currently serving as chair. The FAMILY COMMITEE is still running, although not exactly in the form I had wished.

Vehbi Koç, *Hatıralarım Görüşlerim Öğütlerim (Recollections, Observations, Counsel)*, Vehbi Koç Foundation Publications, Istanbul, 1987, p. 16

Family Planning Foundation *see* **Turkish Family Health and Planning Foundation of Turkey**

Fatih Woodland TEMA Vehbi Koç Nature and Culture Center, today known as FATIH WOODLAND NATURE AND CULTURE CENTER a woodland and recreation area in Otağtepe in the Kavacık district of Beykoz in Istanbul. In 1995, after the site of 150,000 square meters was transferred to TEMA(*) by the General Directorate of Highways, the land was cultivated and transformed into a recreational area with financial support from the Vehbi Koç Foundation(*). A total of 2,645 trees, 12,355 plants and 20,655 square meters of lawn were planted at the center, which opened in 2000. As well as infrastructure facilities, the park also contains a small lake, stone bridge, viewing terraces, footpaths, hedges, and benches. At the entrance to the center, one of the best open spaces from which to glimpse the Bosporus in Istanbul, there is a statue of Vehbi Koç(*), one of TEMA's founding members. TEMA's remit expired in 2011 and the site was returned to the General Directorate for Highways in 2013.

Felsefe *see* **Koç School**

Fereli, Melih *(b. August 22, 1948, Istanbul),* arts manager. Melih Fereli, founding director of Arter(*), has been an arts and culture consultant for the Vehbi Koç Foundation(*) (VKV) since 2005.

Fereli attended the Istanbul High School for Boys until 1965, and completed his secondary education as an AFS fellow at Waynesboro Area High School in Pennsylvania State, USA, in 1966. He studied engineering in the undergraduate department of

Robert College (now Boğaziçi University) and graduated in 1970. In 1971, he completed an MSc in Fluid Mechanics at Virginia Tech (Virginia Polytechnic Institute and State University), USA. From 1973 to 1985, he worked at Lucas Industries in the UK. In addition to performing as a tenor member of the London Philharmonia Chorus, he also served on its executive board between 1985 and 1992, returning to Turkey in 1993 when he became director general of the Istanbul Foundation for Culture and Arts (İKSV). He continued in the post until 2001.

Between 2002 and 2005, Fereli worked as a freelance arts manager, before becoming culture and arts consultant at VKV in 2005. He was also founding director of Arter when it opened in 2010. He curated Erdem Helvacıoğlu's exhibition "Freedom to the Black" and Sarkis' "Interpretation of Cage/Ryoanji", organized by Arter. While still serving on the Arter Executive Board and as the founding director, Fereli is a member of the teaching staff at Istanbul Technical University Dr. Erol Üçer Center for Advanced Studies in Music. He is also a member of the TEGV Board of Trustees. In 1998, Fereli received an OBE (Officer of the Most Excellent Order of the British Empire) for services to Turkish-British cultural relations.

Fisherwomen of the Aegean Project, project helping women who fish in the Datça-Bozburun Special Environmental Protection Area to continue in their profession and also raising awareness of the principles of sustainable fishing and issues of conservation versus use. The project, started by the Mediterranean Protection Association in 2013 with support from the United Nations Development Program, is also supported by the Vehbi Koç Foundation(*).

As part of the project, local fisherwomen are given material support and education on topics

such as fishing in marine protected areas, marine ecosystems, fisherwomen in Turkey and the wider world, microcredit applications, safety on small fishing boats, and cooperatives.

Ford Otosan Gölcük Culture and Community Center *see* **Vehbi Koç Foundation Ford Otosan Gölcük Culture and Community Center**

Ford Otosan Koç Middle School *see* **17 Schools Project**

foundation *(vakıf)*, an organization or entity in law charged with the administration of assets—be they securities or real estate—designated by a person or institution for the benefit of another person or persons or to provide certain public services. Self-governing and non-profit, foundations are civil society organizations not constrained by membership requirements.

Every foundation has five indispensable elements:

(1) The owner of the assets in question (endower),

(2) The property, securities or source of income that are endowed,

(3) The person appointed to administer as directed the endowed assets or income source in question (trustee),

(4) The person, place or service that will benefit from the income stream to be generated under the trustee's governance,

(5) The unilateral contract or document where all the above are clearly detailed (foundation charter, deed of trust, pious foundation deed)

FOUNDATIONS IN HISTORY

Foundations first emerged in the Middle East, Ancient Greece and Rome. In Ancient Egypt, Greece and Rome, they served a single purpose, usually providing financial support to schools, libraries or a local charity. Medieval foundations in Europe usually operated in conjunction with the Church to fund monasteries, soup kitchens, orphanages or schools. Merchants established numerous private foundations during the Renaissance to support education and social aid. Foundations at the time shared a common trait in the close connection between the concepts of foundation, benevolence and almsgiving. This connection that declined in inverse relation to the advance of capitalism has been criticized as a factor preventing social stratification. As legal mechanisms, charitable foundations throughout history have strongly tended to sequester certain assets or sources

of income away from the existing property, audit and division systems and from creditors, other stakeholders or confiscation by the state. From the 1750s onwards, foundations confronted increasing allegations of poor governance, outdated purposes and triviality.

FOUNDATIONS IN ISLAMIC SOCIETIES AND STATES

The roots of philanthropic foundations providing major social functions in Islamic societies go back to pre-Islamic Arab society. Originally established exclusively for the benefit of temples or venues of collective worship, these foundations in time expanded to cover services that ought to have come from the public purse rather than provided by individuals, such as roads, wells, bridges and inns.

In Islamic jurisprudence *vakıf* (*waqf* in Arabic) means the irrevocable retention of a property for the benefit of the public to ensure the permanent availability of its proceeds always for a designated benevolent objective. Where the proceeds are earmarked for religious purposes, the institution is known as a *vakf-ı hayrî* (charitable foundations); *vakf-ı ehlî* (family foundations), on the other hand, is one where the income is channeled through the founder or his/her descendants.

A *vakıf* is only valid if the endower has donated the assets to the glory of God; the income or entitlement is thereafter given to the servants of God. The principal condition to create a *vakıf* is for the endower to declare his/her personal intent. The foundation charter called *vakfiye* enters into effect once its conformance to Islamic rules is certified. The lack of compulsion to name the beneficiaries in the charter would not validate a foundation that benefits solely the wealthy. In environments that offer no security of accumulation or bequest of personal wealth, such foundations did become instruments of safeguarding property especially for the benefit of future generations.

The earliest foundations in the history of Islam are generally dated to the 600s. The need for a public audit for the growing number of foundations first arose under the Abbasids. Soup kitchens and their endowments became popular after the Turks converted to Islam. By the middle of the sixteenth century, there were thousands of foundations in Anatolia.

The majority of foundations in the Ottoman Empire were alleged to have been established with the sole purpose of protecting personal property from the state in order to bequeath it to descendants, or to evade sharia inheritance rules.

MODERN FOUNDATIONS

In the early twentieth century, prominent foundations emerged from the fortunes of wealthy industrialists in the USA. The two most important were created in the early 1900s by Andrew Carnegie (1905) and John D. Rockefeller Jr. (1913). Just as in Canada and the United Kingdom, several other charities in Europe followed the American examples. Social charities proliferated rapidly in the USA after 1914, and a new wave of foundations developed in the 1940s, supported by individuals, families and companies. While these charities or non-profit entities in legal terms can provide services with their own staff, their principal purpose is to direct those funds to institutions that provide public services or conduct the relevant research. Anyone can bequeath or donate funds to a foundation, and a company or a family can establish a trust to provide a perpetual source of income to a charitable foundation.

Today, large charitable foundations, besides the Carnegie and Rockefeller foundations, include the Russell Sage Foundation (1907), the Commonwealth Fund (1918), the John Simon Guggenheim Memorial Foundation (1925), the Danforth Foundation (1927), the W.K. Kellogg Foundation (1930), Alfred P. Sloan Foundation (1934), the Ford Foundation (1936), the Robert Wood Johnson Foundation (1936), the Lilly Endowment, Inc. (1937), the Pew Memorial Trust (1948), the J. Paul Getty Trust (1953), the William and Flora Hewlett Foundation (1966), the Andrew W. Mellon Foundation (1969), the John D. and Catherine T. MacArthur Foundation (1970), and the Gordon and Betty Moore Foundation (2000). With assets totaling over 40 billion dollars, the Bill and Melinda Gates Foundation, established in 2000, is the largest philanthropic foundation in the world today.

Outside the United States some of the wealthiest foundations include the Wellcome Trust (1936) in the United Kingdom, the Robert Bosch Foundation (1964) in Germany, the Li Ka Shing Foundation (1980) in Hong Kong, the Stichting INGKA Foundation (1982) in the Netherlands, the MasterCard Foundation (2006) in Canada and the Mohammed Bin Rashid Al Maktoum Foundation (2007) in the United Arab Emirates.

FOUNDATIONS IN TURKEY

The greatest central philanthropic organization in the Ottoman Empire was the Foundations in

Mecca and Medina (*Haremeyn Evkafı*), which underwent restructuring as the Ministry of Imperial Foundations (Evkaf-ı Hümayun Nezareti) in 1826. In 1920 in the Republican era, foundations were first regulated by the Ministry of Religious Affairs and Pious Foundations until this particular department was abolished in 1924 and they came under the remit of the General Directorate of Foundations (Vakıflar Genel Müdürlüğü, VGM). In 1926, the Turkish Civil Code (Türk Medeni Kanunu, TMK) Act Number 743 was passed, intending to prevent the abuses of the foundation system in the past, to audit charitable foundations, to centralize their administration and to dissolve any found to be acting outside their charter. These regulations preferred the term "trust" *(tesis)* rather than "foundation" *(vakıf)* to designate "the allocation of certain properties to specific purposes for a limited period of time." The choice of terminology was motivated by concerns that vast fortunes of the foundations were denied the economy in Islamic societies, thereby stifling their economic potential, and causing the underdevelopment prevalent in these societies. "Trust" remained in force until the 1967 Foundations Act No. 903. (*see also* trust)

The foundations predating the TMK were classified as either *hayrî* (charitable) or *zurrî* (family) *vakıf*; foundations whose income was in part or in whole dedicated to charitable works were classed as *hayrî vakıf*. They either took the form of institutions serving the community, such as schools or mosques, or provided the funds for public services. The foundations whose proceeds were allocated to the endower's heirs, on the other hand, were known as *zurrî vakıf* or *evladiye vakfı*. The income of these foundations could only be used for charitable works after the death of the endower's heirs.

According to the most recent Foundations Act No. 5737 of 2008, foundations predating the effective date of the TMK No. 743, and whose administration is entrusted to the descendants of the endower are called *mülhak vakıf* (entailed trust fund). A *mazbut vakıf* (reverted foundation), on the other hand, is administrated by the state due to the lack of surviving trustees. Foundations predating the 1935 Foundations Act No. 2762 and administered by a board elected by merchants is known as an *esnaf vakfı* (merchants' foundation).

Cemaat vakıfları (community foundations) are established by non-Muslim citizens of the Republic of Turkey, chartered and registered by the VGM in 1936. These benevolent institutions belonging to communities therefore are certified as foundations, legal entities subject to special regulations and administered by elected boards from among their members. As the TMK does not sanction the establishment of a foundation designed to benefit a specific community, no legitimate new community foundation can be formed.

Foundations created after the 1967 Foundations Act are known as "new foundations". Nearly half of all new foundations are in Istanbul or Ankara, and the majority are active in education and social assistance.

Beyond the abovementioned legal definitions, foundations are classified as *family-*, *group-* or *company foundations* on the basis of their endowers. Those formed by an individual or a family are *family foundations*; foundations formed by a group of people like the Turkish Education Foundation(*), the TEGV(*) and TEMA(*) are *group foundations*, and the Turkish Vodafone Foundation and the Coca-Cola Life Plus Foundation, are classified as *company foundations*. Company foundations usually receive regular donations from the founding company.

There also are *public foundations* created by public institutions or organizations to support public services or personnel. Foundations created by charter like the social assistance and solidarity foundations, the Turkish Armed Forces Foundation and the Education Foundation are defined as *state foundations*.

Virtually all foundations in Turkey are self-governing and conduct their own projects; practically none has channeled the entirety of its budget to other institutions.

Important to foundations from a fundraising perspective is tax relief. Donations to listed charities are deductible at up to 5% of gross profit for individual and business taxpayers, making this a major incentive to donate to the foundations in question. As of the end of 2017, there were 268 foundations listed as tax exempt. The leading foundations in Turkey are the Vehbi Koç Foundation(*), the Sabancı Foundation (1974), the Anatolia Education and Social Aid Foundation (1979), the Enka Foundation (1983), the Hüsnü M. Özyeğin Foundation (1990), the Aydın Doğan Foundation (1996) and the Mehmet Zorlu Foundation (1998). Although they are essentially family foundations, the dividends they receive from the companies, owned in whole or in part by their founders, give them the company foundation status.

NUMBERS OF NEW FOUNDATIONS BY YEAR (1980-2018)

Year	Total	Year	Total
1980	604	1999	4508
1981	648	2000	4560
1982	689	2001	4566
1983	709	2002	4533
1984	738	2003	4503
1985	829	2004	4445
1986	1590	2005	4418
1987	1701	2006	4401
1988	1935	2007	4398
1989	2079	2008	4439
1990	2356	2009	4456
1991	2618	2010	4504
1992	2789	2011	4562
1993	2977	2012	4651
1994	3225	2013	4746
1995	3589	2014	4882
1996	4016	2015	5006
1997	4260	2016	5094
1998	4416	2017	5099
		(JULY 17) 2018	5158

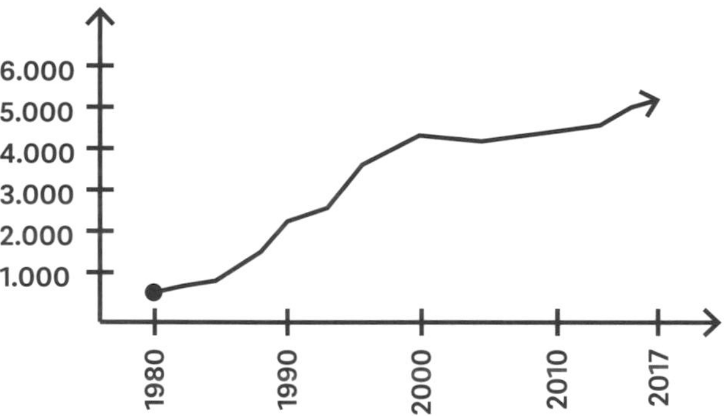

https://www.vgm.gov.tr/Documents/YEN%C4%B0%20VAKIFLARIN%20YIL%20BAZINDA%20DA%C4%9EILIMI%20(1980-28072017).pdf

TYPES OF FOUNDATIONS IN NUMBERS (JULY 17, 2018)

Entailed trust funds	260
Community foundations	167
Merchants' foundations	1
New foundations	5,158
Social assistance and solidarity foundations	1,002
Environmental protection foundations	15
Multi-purpose foundations	4,141

New foundations include	
Foundation universities	72
Foundation vocational colleges	5
Tax-exempt foundations	274
For profit organizations	1,425
Pension funds	21

https://www.vgm.gov.tr/Documents/VAKIFLARIN%20T%C3%9CRLER%C4%B0NE%20G%C3%96RE%20DA%C4%9EILIMI_31.12.2017.pdf

Foundation for Training and Protecting Children with Intellectual Disabilities (ZİHİNSEL YETERSİZ ÇOCUKLARI YETİŞTİRME VE KORUMA VAKFI, ZİÇEV), a non-governmental organization which aims to provide care, rehabilitation, adequate education and career development opportunities to children with intellectual disabilities. Established in Ankara by a group of volunteers led by Makbule Ölçen in 1982, ZİÇEV leads efforts to enable people requiring special education to be self-sufficient, independent and productive individuals. In 2016, the Vehbi Koç Foundation(*) covered part of the operational costs for ZİÇEV's Istanbul branch.

Frontier, officially KOÇ UNIVERSITY FRONTIER MAGAZINE, monthly magazine providing the community with information about the research activities of the students and faculties at Koç University(*) (KU), as well as promoting research opportunities and success stories. In publication since April 2006, *Frontier* aims to encourage communication and cooperation between KU, different academic institutions, public and private sector organizations and to support collaborative research.

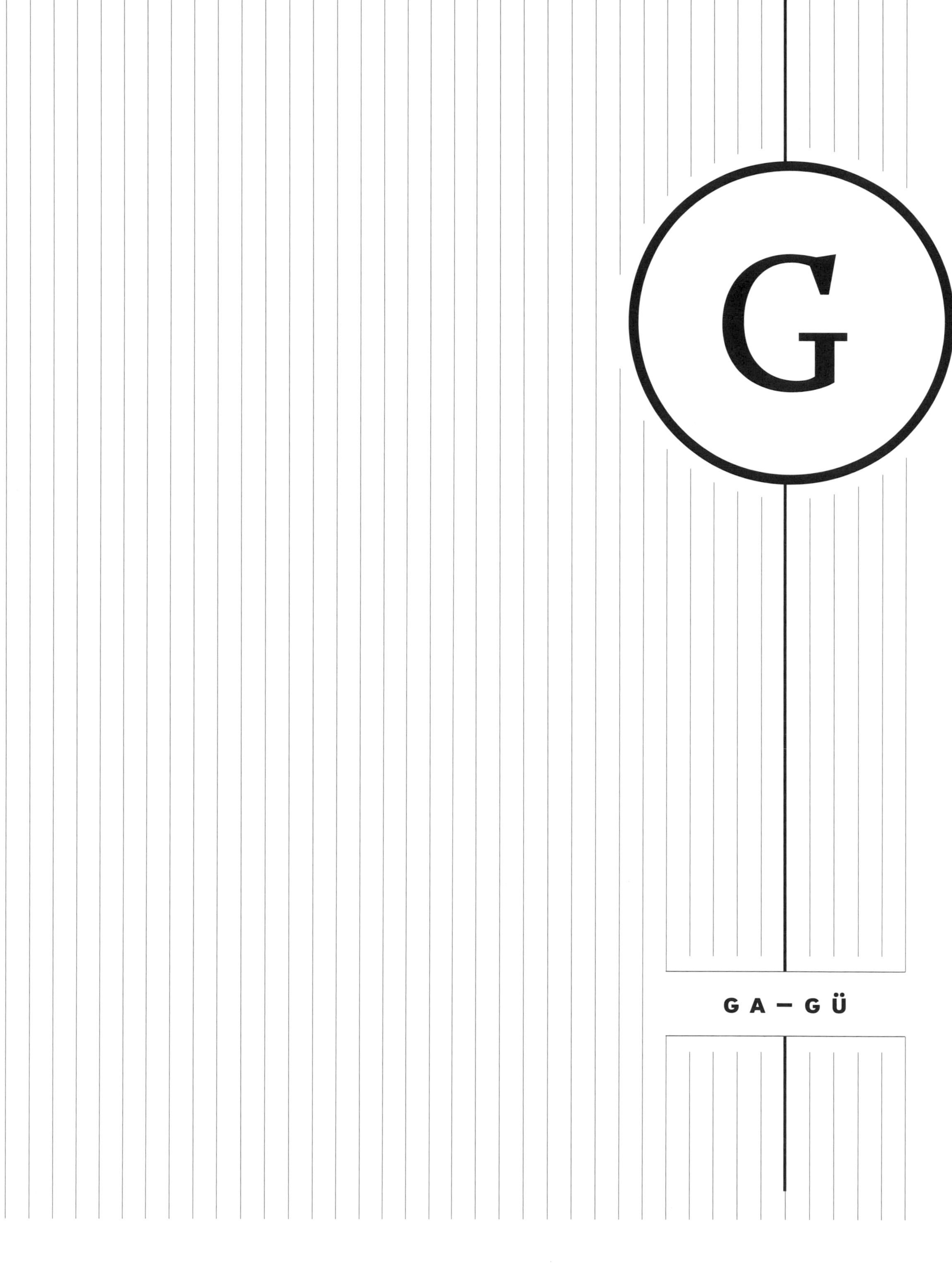

G

GA – GÜ

GABAM, full name KOÇ UNIVERSITY-STAVROS NIARCHOS FOUNDATION CENTER FOR LATE ANTIQUE AND BYZANTINE STUDIES, research center based at Koç University(*) (KU). Founded in 2015 with the support of KU and the Stavros Niarchos Foundation, which was established by ship-owner Stavros Niarchos. The center supports and partakes in academic research into the art, history and archeology of Late Antiquity and the Byzantine Era (approximately 300-1500 AD).

Christina Lambropoulou from the Stavros Niarchos Foundation with president of Koç University, Prof. Umran İnan, and Eva Polyzogopoulou at the GABAM opening ceremony, November 13, 2015

As the first academic research center in Turkey to focus on Byzantine art, history and archeology, GABAM supports research projects suited to its founding purpose, provides scholarships for doctoral and postdoctoral research, organizes conferences, symposiums and workshops, publishes scientific works and engages in initiatives to conserve and publicize the cultural assets of Byzantine civilization.

GABAM supports the International Sevgi Gönül Byzantine Studies Symposium(*), organized every three years by the Vehbi Koç Foundation(*) and ANAMED(*) (KU Research Center for Anatolian Civilizations). One of the center's first projects after it was established in 2015 was the Byzantine Monuments Photographs Archive. In 2016, a study was completed documenting Damatris Palace, the summer residence of Byzantine emperors, located on Istanbul's Asian side, and the archive opened for use in 2017. It comprises 1,173 photographs and can be accessed via GABAM's website and the Koç University Suna Kıraç Library(*) section of digital collections.

The Rhodiapolis Episcopal Church Mosaic Restoration and Architectural Documentation Project, the Archaeological Settlements of Turkey (TAY) Project and the Küçükyalı ArkeoPark Project are among those supported by the center.

Galatasaray University Suna Kıraç Library, opened in 1993 at the Galatasaray University (GSU) campus on the site of Feriye Palace in Ortaköy, Istanbul. Since May 2004, it has been housed in a modern building constructed on the Yiğit Okur Campus opposite the palace. Suna Kıraç(*) led efforts to found, equip and finance the library, which has received support from the Vehbi Koç Foundation(*) in the form of book purchases

and financial contributions since 1999. The Suna and İnan Kıraç Foundation(*) also supports the library with an annual grant.

In November 1995, Suna Kıraç received the Galatasaray Educational Foundation Medallion of Honor for her contribution to the library, and in February 2006, a bust of her was installed at the entrance to the new library building. At the award ceremony in November 1995, the foundation explained why Suna Kıraç was receiving the medal:

"Suna Kıraç sincerely believes that Turkey's capacity to create with a healthy social awareness will come through education, and that education must meet modern standards. This is not just something she believes, it is something she has physically and spiritually fought for over many years in various educational institutions. Kıraç is, above all else, someone who has committed herself to the cause of education. She donated a library to Galatasaray University, which was founded with the aim of training modern, secular, progressive and distinguished staff; she supported it with a 1.7 million dollar fund and equipped it with the latest facilities to ensure its continuity. In appreciation of her efforts, the executive board of the Galatasaray Educational Foundation have voted unanimously to award her the Galatasaray Educational Foundation Medallion of Honor and to name her a true 'Friend of Galatasaray'."

Gebze Koç Middle School
see **17 Schools Project**

Geyre Foundation, officially GEYRE FOUNDATION APHRODISIAS EXCAVATIONS, non-governmental organization (NGO) that supports academic research and analysis relating to the archeology of the ancient city of Aphrodisias, situated in the village of Geyre in Karacasu district of Aydın. The foundation helps to compile and repair findings from the excavations and promote tourism to the site. It was founded in January 1987 by the "Friends of Aphrodisias", who came together under the leadership of Sevgi Gönül, and in January 2008, the Council of Ministers proclaimed it a public interest foundation with tax exemption status. The NGO receives regular support from the Vehbi Koç Foundation(*). Sevgi Gönül was president from its foundation until her death in 2003, when the role was assumed by Ömer M. Koç(*).

Taking its name from the goddess Aphrodite, Aphrodisias was not just a place of worship in Ancient Greece, but also an important cultural center. It was a famous center of sculpture due to the local cream-colored, translucent Karya marble, which was especially easy to carve. The city enjoyed a golden era in the third and fourth centuries AD, but its fame and significance began to wane after the seventh century and it was completely abandoned by the beginning of the fourteenth century. Excavations at Aphrodisias were begun in 1961 by a team led by the archaeologist Kenan Erim (1929-90), who devoted almost his entire career to the site. Later work continued under the aegis of New York University. The excavations are currently

being carried out under the joint management of Professor R.R.R. Smith of Oxford University and Christopher Ratté of the University of Michigan.

Part of a high relief revealed by excavations at the city's Sebasteion complex, a center of worship famous for its reliefs, is on display at The Sebasteion Reliefs-Sevgi Gönül Hall, built by the Geyre Foundation and opened in 2008. The museum, founded in 1979 to exhibit the pieces excavated at Aphrodisias, was renovated by the Geyre Foundation and opened to visitors in 2009.

The ancient city of Aphrodisias was added to the UNESCO World Heritage site list in 2017.

Girişmen, Gizem *(b. November 25, 1981, Ankara)*, Paralympic and World Archery Champion. In 2017, together with national wrestling champion Taha Akgül(*), she received the Mustafa V. Koç Sports Award(*).

Girişmen was paralyzed following a traffic accident at the age of 11. She completed her secondary education at Tevfik Fikret Private High School in Ankara, before graduating from Bilkent University Faculty of Business Administration. In 2017, she received an MA in social policy from Middle East Technical University.

Girişmen began practicing archery in 2004, joining the National Archery Team for the Physically Disabled in the following year. In 2006, she came third in the 4th European Para-Archery Championships held in the Czech Republic. She received the gold medal in the individual recurve category at the 2008 Summer Paralympics in Beijing and was the first female Turkish athlete to achieve such success in the Paralympics. In 2009, she came first in the individual recurve category at the 7th Para-Archery World Championships held in the Czech Republic and was a member of the Turkish Women's Recurve Team, which came third.

In August 2009, Girişmen was voted "Athlete of the Month" by the International Paralympic Committee (IPC) and in 2010, she was the first Turkish athlete nominated for the Laureus World Sports Awards. From 2007 to 2010, she was first in her category in the IPC World Archery Rankings. In 2017, Girişmen and the Olympian and world champion wrestler, Taha Akgül, received the Mustafa V. Koç

http://www.kulturvarliklari.gov.tr/Resim/216757,afrodisias03jpg.png?0

Sports Award for "their embodiment of all the Olympic values and worldwide sporting success, achieved through the determination, discipline and commitment shown in their work."

Girişmen currently works at the Ministry of Youth and Sports and is a member of the Paralympic Games Preparation and Performance Monitoring Board. She is a member of the Archery Technical Board of the Physically Disabled Sports Federation of Turkey. From 2012 to 2017, she was also a member of the executive board of the European Paralympic Committee (EPC).

GLODEM, full name THE CENTER FOR RESEARCH ON GLOBALIZATION, PEACE, AND DEMOCRATIC GOVERNANCE, research center based at Koç University(*). It was formed in 2004 as a communication and discussion network

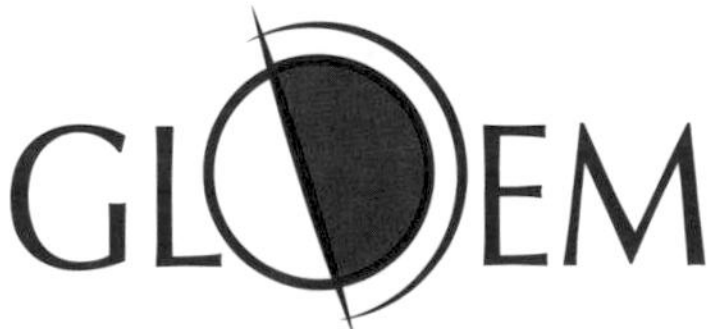

CENTER FOR RESEARCH ON GLOBALIZATION, PEACE, AND DEMOCRATIC GOVERNANCE

for teaching staff concerned with the effects of globalization on the dynamics and interactions of national and international politics and economics. In 2010, it received approval from the Higher Education Council (YÖK) to become a research center. At first, the center's two fundamental areas of expertise were: globalization and the political economy; democratic governance and administration. Peace and conflict resolution were added later. GLODEM leads research on topics in these areas of specialization, also organizing conferences and conventions.

SOME EVENTS ORGANIZED BY GLODEM

2011

- **The Global Financial Crisis and the European Periphery**
- **Politics of Ordinary People: Understanding the Revolutions in the Middle East**
- **Glodem Young Scholars Workshop: The Global Economic Crisis: Implications for Regional and Global Governance**
- **Glodem Panel Discussion: New Turkish Policy in Turbulent Times**
- **Glodem Panel Discussion: Eurozone Sovereign Debt Crisis and Global Implications**

2014

- **Stanford University Program on Arab Reform and Democracy Fifth Annual Conference: Political Change in the Arab World: Internal Dynamics and Regional Actors**
- **Crisis and Resilience of Neo-Liberalism: Lessons from the Great Financial Crisis**
- **Turkish International Political Economy Society (TIPES) Conference**
- **Koç University & Fudan University Joint International Conference: Turkey & China in the Age of Brics**

2015

- **MIKTA and Relevance of Regional Powers in Global Governance**
- **TIPES Interdisciplinary Workshop: The Political Economy of Contemporary Turkey**
- **International Workshop on Institutional and Policy Design in Financial Sector Reform**

2016

- **TIPES 2nd Interdisciplinary Workshop: Politics in Hard Times; Emerging Markets after the Global Recession**
- **Workshop on Turkish Multinational Corporations Abroad**
- **TIPES 2nd International Conference**

2017

- **China and the Future of International Relations Panel**

2018

- **Istanbul Workshop on Transnational Dimensions of Non-state Armed Groups**

Gönül, Erdoğan *(b. 1933 – d. July 15, 2003, Istanbul),* senior executive, businessman and collector who served the Koç Group(*) for many years. He was one of the founding partners of Koç Holding(*) and a member of the board of directors. He was married to Sevgi Gönül(*), middle daughter of Vehbi Koç(*) and Sadberk Koç(*).

He completed his secondary education at the English High School in Istanbul in 1952 and began working at Otosan, Turkey's first automobile factory, in 1959. He quickly proved his worth and became manager of production control. He was appointed deputy general manager of Otosan in 1963 and general manager in 1974, becoming vice president and then president of the Otosan Group in 1986 and 1992 respectively. He was part of a team breaking new ground in the Turkish automotive sector, including Otosan's production of Turkey's first assembly-line truck in 1960 and the first domestic passenger vehicle, the Anadol, which went into mass production in 1966. During his time with the company, 62,923 sedan and 49,964 pick-up Anadols were manufactured up until 1984. In 1977, while Erdoğan Gönül was general manager of Otosan, the first licensing agreement was signed with the Ford Motor Company, approving the right to produce and sell the Otosan D1210 Ford truck and Transit series in Turkey and permitting the engines to be manufactured domestically. Otosan's İnönü Engine Factory in Eskişehir also went into mass production in 1982 during his time as vice president of the Otosan Group, becoming the first establishment to produce diesel engines in Turkey. Gönül was a member of the Koç Holding Board of Directors from 1992 until his death in 2003.

Gönül, who married Sevgi Koç on January 4, 1962, had a great passion for classic cars. His favorite hobby was revamping classic cars he had bought, using parts imported from abroad. He donated his classic car collection to the Istanbul Rahmi M. Koç Museum(*) for exhibition. Comprising almost twenty of Gönül's classic automobiles, the collection is exhibited in the museum's largest and most popular gallery, the Erdoğan Gönül Gallery, where it is separated into two halves: pre-1950 and post-1950.

ERDOĞAN GÖNÜL'S PASSION FOR CARS AND THE STORY OF THE BUICK ON SHOW AT THE ISTANBUL RAHMİ M. KOÇ MUSEUM

The 1933 Buick was bought by my father as a present when my mother became pregnant with me in 1933. Only 152 of these were manufactured worldwide. Only three are thought to still be in existence. When war broke out in 1938, the government banned the use

of private cars. My father put the car up on blocks in the garage at the back of our apartment building. If I remember correctly, in 1945 my father was in the bathroom, listening to the radio while shaving. The presenter announced that the government would once again allow people to use private cars. So my father said, "Come on, son, let's get the car going". Just 11 years old, I went down to the garage with my father. He put the battery in its place underneath the front seat and connected it up. He tried the ignition and the car started on the first go. The exhaust fumes and smoke entered my lungs and body, and that's how my addiction began... Due to my experience at Otosan, I was made president of the Otosan Group and member of the board of directors of Koç Holding. But as someone who had become accustomed to spending every hour of the past 25 years occupied with plans, production and machine tools, I felt a little like a fish out of water after my appointment at Koç Holding. There's a big difference between being a senior manager and being on the front line. I'm a little nostalgic for my Otosan days. My passion Otosan had a new CEO, but this made me nostalgic for the smell of exhaust fumes, the scent of the cars and the glue. At which point, I turned to classic cars for entertainment. If I had continued in my roles at Otosan, I would never have considered such a hobby.

Erdoğan and Sevgi (Koç) Gönül

Within a month of our starting to use the Buick again, my father had ordered a 46 Ford Model. When the 46 Ford arrived, he sold the Buick to the owner of a farm in the area now called Ayazağa. The farm owner cut the car in half and turned it into a pick-up. He used it for many years to transport his goods. I say many years because I came across him using it in this way on the road 3-5 times over the years. But I didn't feel the slightest hint of nostalgia. Because the latest models were now in my life: the 46, 47 and 48. Although I was young, my father allowed me to drive. Later on, about seven years ago, my nephew brought me a photograph. In the photo, my mother and father were sitting in the car together. That really reignited my feelings of nostalgia. After about 4-5 years of research, I found the car in Canada. I called the owner and said that I would like to buy the car. At first, the owner didn't want to sell it. Later, I sent him the photo. A while afterwards, I received a phone call from Canada. The owner told me, "You've got a right to this car. I'll sell it to you".

"Kendi gitti, 'Gönül'ü otomobilde kaldı" (Gönül passed away, with automobiles on his mind), *Hürriyet*, July 17, 2003

The floor exhibiting the Orientalist Painting Collection at the Pera Museum(*), which opened in 2005, was renamed the Sevgi-Erdoğan Gönül Gallery in memory of the couple, who died after one another in close succession in 2003. The TEGV(*) education park, established in Şanlıurfa using the fund created by the Vehbi Koç Foundation(*) from Sevgi Gönül's will, was renamed the Sevgi-Erdoğan Gönül Education Park(*) in 2011.

Gönül, (Daime) Sevgi *(b. June 5, 1938, Keçiören, Ankara – d. September 12, 2003, Istanbul)*, née KOÇ, businesswoman, philanthropist and collector. She was a member of the Koç Holding(*) Board of Directors (1964-2003), member of the Vehbi Koç Foundation(*) (VKV) Board of Directors (1970-2003), president of the Sadberk Hanım Museum(*) Executive Committee (1980-2003), president of the Geyre Foundation(*) (1987-2003), a member of the Koç University(*) Board of Overseers (1993-2003), and president of the Turkish Numismatic Association (2003).

Born at the family's orchard house in Keçiören, Ankara (now the VEKAM[*] operational center), she was the third child of Vehbi Koç(*) and Sadberk Koç(*), after Semahat Arsel(*) and Rahmi M. Koç(*). She completed her elementary education in Ankara at the Turkish Education Association (TED) Elementary School, before attending Istanbul Arnavutköy American College for Girls (*see* Robert College). She attended boarding high school in London, followed by a year at finishing school in 1955. She said that if she had continued in education, she might have wanted to be an art historian and have an academic career.

"AS A CHILD OF THE REPUBLIC, I PLAYED WITH RAG DOLLS."

As a child of the Republic, I played with dolls made out of rags. When I was a little older, we began playing with paper dolls. My cousin Nezahat Aktar Hanif, who died a long time ago, used to draw beautifully. Suna and I would beg her to make us dolls and paint them for us. And dolls weren't enough for us, we would also ask for dresses and she would draw, paint and cut them out for us. I'm still surprised we didn't turn out to be fashion designers. Because Suna and I were of similar ages, we would each receive one of the same toy or just one that we would be asked to share. That's how we learned to share when we were young, though it took some noise and fighting to get there.

If I remember correctly, my father brought our first doll from Hungary and it had Hungarian clothes, blond hair and pigtails dangling on either side of its head. He also gave us a Nutcracker doll, though I don't know where he got it from. It had huge teeth, a black beard and mustache, and when it opened its mouth, it scared us out of our wits. My mother hid the Nutcracker in the dresser in the lounge because we were so afraid of it; I was almost too scared to go into that room. When I think about it now, I laugh, but I also feel annoyed that we were brought up to be such cowards.

At the Istanbul Arnavutköy American College for Girls, 1949

We would play tic-tac-toe and knucklebones at our orchard house. One of our greatest pleasures was to draw a grid with chalk and play the game with stones we found in the garden. Meanwhile Rahmi would labor away, making his own slingshot and try to hunt birds in the garden; my mother would get very angry at this habit of his and take the slingshots away and hide them. One day, Rahmi discovered the place where she had hidden his slingshots and was so happy when he saw hundreds of them that he didn't know what to do with himself.

Later on, lovely dolls and toys were brought from America. When I was 10, I was taken to America. It was Christmas time and I loved the lights, the Christmas decorations and the toys that I saw all around me. My mother didn't allow me to buy every toy, but that was where I first saw a jigsaw puzzle and thought it was amazing.

Sevgi Gönül, *Sevgi'nin Diviti* (From Sevgi's Pen), Vehbi Koç Foundation Publications, Istanbul, 2003, pp. 252-54; *Hürriyet*, April 27, 2003

Sevgi Gönül began her working life as a secretary at Bürokur, a subsidiary of the Koç Group(*). In 1962, she married Erdoğan Gönül(*), one of the managers of the Koç Group, who was also manager of production control at Otosan at that time.

Undoubtedly, Sevgi Gönül inherited her curiosity and interest in history and antiquities from her mother, Sadberk Koç, whose greatest wish was to establish a museum to preserve the pieces she had collected throughout her life, so they would be passed on for future generations. On October 12, 1980, seven years after her death, Sadberk Koç's dream became a reality with the opening of the Sadberk Hanım Museum(*), Turkey's first private museum, at the historic Azaryan Mansion(*) in Büyükdere, Istanbul. Sevgi Gönül played the chief role in the foundation of the Sadberk Hanım Museum and its development into an internationally renowned cultural institution. She was president of the executive committee and over time enriched Sadberk Koç's collection. The additional museum building, opened in 1988 to facilitate a more contemporary approach to exhibitions, was named the "Sevgi Gönül Building" and awarded a mention by Europa Nostra (*see* Europa Nostra Awards) in the same year.

In 1987, Sevgi Gönül spearheaded the establishment of the Geyre Foundation(*), which supports scientific research and analysis into the archeology of the ancient city of Aphrodisias, which is in the village of Geyre in the Karacasu district of Aydın province; the foundation also aims to develop a museum on the archaeological site. She remained president of the foundation until her death.

Aiming to popularize research into the Byzantine period in Turkey and encourage society to lay claim to its cultural heritage, Sevgi Gönül worked hard to encourage a tradition in Turkey similar to that which she had witnessed in other countries, where events sharing scientific studies in the field had been ongoing for many years. As a result of her efforts, the symposium, which is supported by VKV and has gathered every three years since 2007, was named the International Sevgi Gönül Byzantine Studies Symposium(*).

WHY ISN'T THERE A BYZANTIUM MUSEUM IN ISTANBUL?

The Eastern Roman Empire was established in 330 and ended in 1453 when Mehmet the Conqueror took Istanbul. This is a civilization that reigned for many years, but Istanbul seemingly has no museum to represent its artistic works and show them to the world; I don't understand why. That's not all; there's no department of the Byzantine era at Istanbul University either.

Art historians receive a class on Byzantine art as a mere formality. So it is the Greeks who lay claim to the history and art of the Byzantine era. Why are we leaving it to them? Why are we leaving the Greeks to lay claim to this history? I don't understand it. There isn't a proper Byzantine art historian in Turkey. The few that have existed didn't know Greek and failed to train others properly. I suspect that they were not doing the job out of enjoyment. A Byzantine Congress will be held in Paris soon, on August 19; I wonder how many keen Turkish scholars will go along to present papers and represent Turkey.

I once tried to organize a Byzantine Congress as part of the Sadberk Hanım Museum; especially the top academics working on Byzantium and the then Minister of Foreign Affairs did everything they could to stop it happening. If that had happened to me today, I wouldn't have listened to anyone, I'd have just gone ahead. Our society doesn't know how to appreciate its assets. If it were up to me, I'd do it twice a year: at Christmas I would decorate all of Haghia Sophia with oil lamps and play Byzantine music to attract the attention of the Christian world and collect donations; and at Laylat al-Qadr, I would light all the lamps, sing hymns and collect funds from Muslims. At least I could go some way towards lightening the financial burden of Haghia Sophia, an international masterpiece which requires constant care. If such a thing was achieved, the whole world would queue to witness it.

Sevgi Gönül, *Sevgi'nin Diviti,* p. 42; *Hürriyet,* August 5, 2001

Sevgi Gönül was a close follower of Turkey's domestic and foreign policy, and contrary to Koç family(*) custom, she played an active role in politics. In the 1994 local elections, she was elected city councilor for the Motherland Party (MP) for Beşiktaş district in Istanbul and remained active on the municipal council until her death.

In June 2001, Sevgi Gönül began a weekly column in the Sunday supplement of *Hürriyet* newspaper. In her columns, published under the title "From Sevgi's Pen", she discussed a wide range of topics from jewellery, painting, music, fashion, museums and collecting, to love, womanhood and manhood. She wrote with an ironic and witty tone, typically including thoughts from her travels and references to the lives of famous people who had made their name on the world stage through their contributions to art and culture. Her writing covered social, economic and political issues and compared the state of affairs in Turkey with positive examples from the Western world, evaluating it all with the eye of a businesswoman. Sevgi Gönül continued her column until the death of her husband in July 2003, writing her final column for him. She herself died in September of the same year, and some time later her writings were collected and published by the VKV as a book titled *Sevgi'nin Diviti* (From Sevgi's Pen).

The Sevgi Gönül Cultural Center, based on Koç University's Rumelifeneri Campus and in use since 2001, hosts a wide range of cultural events, including the Sevgi Gönül Theater Days and The Dance Festival. One of the Koç School's(*) traditional events is the Sevgi Gönül Art Night, which has been held annually since 2004. The floor exhibiting the Orientalist Painting Collection at the Pera Museum(*), which opened in 2005, was renamed the Sevgi-Erdoğan Gönül Gallery in memory of the couple. The TEGV(*) education park, established in Şanlıurfa using the fund created by the VKV from Sevgi Gönül's will, was renamed the Sevgi-Erdoğan Gönül Education Park(*) in 2011.

Greek–Turkish Youth Orchestra, an orchestra founded by Leni Konialidis in 2008 to foster friendship between Greece and Turkey through music. The orchestra is composed of 50–60 Greek and Turkish musicians aged 16–28, who are selected from Bilkent University and leading music academies in Athens. Since 2015, the Vehbi Koç Foundation(*) and the Stavros Niarchos Foundation, have supported concerts in Greece

and Turkey, with the aim of encouraging cultural dialogue between young people as a model for peace and understanding.

Günel, Murat *(b. 1976, Turgutlu, Manisa),* educator and director. He has served as general director of the Koç School(*) since 2018.

After graduating from industrial vocational high school, Günel studied physics at Balıkesir University Necatibey Faculty of Education. While working as a science teacher in Istanbul, he was granted a Ministry of Education scholarship for postgraduate study in the USA. He studied at Iowa State University, receiving a master's (2003) and doctorate (2006) in science education. After his return to Turkey, he taught at Atatürk and Ahi Evran Universities, becoming an associate professor in 2008 and professor in 2014. He was appointed general director of the Koç School in 2018.

In addition to contributing numerous articles to books and journals, Prof. Günel also manages national and international educational projects and serves on the publications board of several international science education journals.

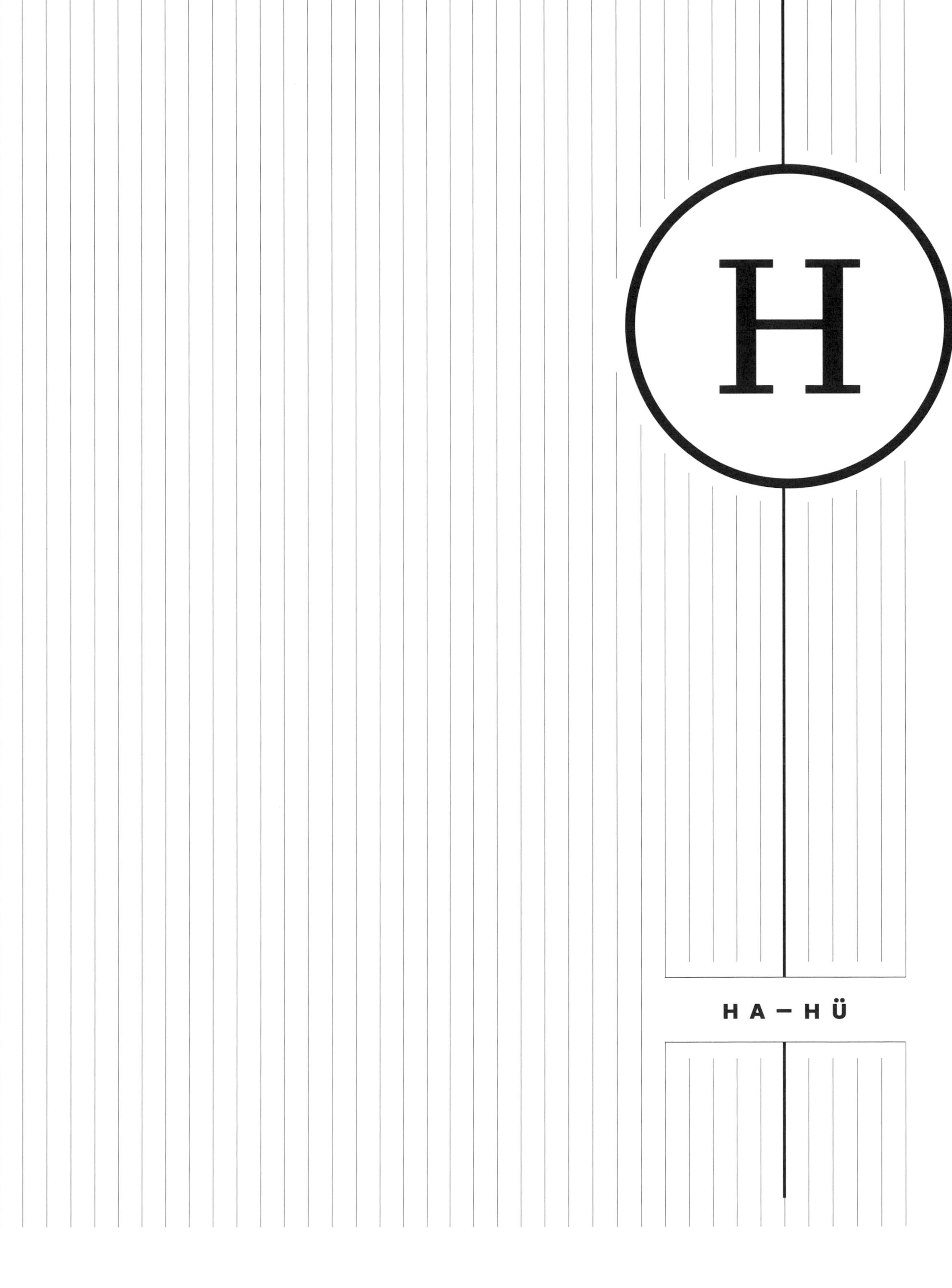
H
HA–HÜ

Hadrian Award *see* **World Monuments Fund Hadrian Award**

Hand in Hand for Development *see* **17 Schools Project**

Harvard University Vehbi Koç Chair of Turkish Studies, the chair established in 1997, with contributions from the government of Republic of Turkey and Vehbi Koç Foundation(*), with the aim of supporting international research and learning about the history, culture, civilization, and social and economic development of Turkey.

In 1995, the agreement on the foundation of the Chair of Turkish Studies was signed by Harvard University and the government of Turkey, who donated 750,000 dollars to the university for the purpose. Vehbi Koç Foundation undertook the project, donating 1,750,000 dollars to Harvard to ensure that the professorship began as soon as possible. The professorship was created at the Harvard University Faculty of Arts and Sciences, on November 7, 1997, under the chairmanship of Professor Cemal Kafadar(*). Harvard's Ottoman and Turkish Studies website was also established within the remit of the professorship.

Harvard University Vehbi Koç Chair of Turkish Studies opening ceremony, 1997

Haydarpaşa Numune Education and Research Hospital Vehbi Koç Emergency Medical Center, medical institution operating in the Üsküdar district of Istanbul. It is one of the main projects in the health sector to receive regular financial support from the Vehbi Koç Foundation(*) (VKV), which helps with building construction and repairs, purchasing medical equipment and other matters.

In 1983, at the request of Vehbi Koç(*), the VKV took action to establish a permanent facility to provide health services in the event of traffic accidents. A committee from Houston Methodist Hospital in the USA compiled an analysis report on the issue and the decision was taken to collaborate with Haydarpaşa Numune Hospital. VKV covered the construction costs for the center, which opened in 1985 with the name Haydarpaşa Numune Hospital Vehbi Koç Foundation Traffic Accident and Primary Care Treatment Facility. In 1993, the center was renovated and extended by VKV. In 2001, the center was renovated once again with the help of a large investment from VKV and, in 2002, it reopened as Haydarpaşa Numune Education and Research Hospital Vehbi Koç Emergency Medical Center. In 2006, the Haydarpaşa Numune Hospital Emergency Medical Clinic began operating from here. In 2015, extensive alteration works were carried out to increase capacity at the center.

The clinic, which is open 24 hours a day, seven days a week, deals with 500 people every day, and is also an education and research center.

HEAD *see* **Journal of Education and Research in Nursing (HEAD)**

HeCe Education, Culture and Mutual Aid Foundation, non-governmental organization founded in 2017 to lead education, culture and cooperation initiatives for the benefit of individuals and the public. The foundation aims to establish schools at every level, provide scholarships for students, develop and implement civil responsibility projects and operate as a think tank. The İncek Uğur Private Pre-School, affiliated with the foundation, was opened in the Gölbaşı district of Ankara in time for the academic year 2017-18. The Vehbi Koç Foundation(*), which shares common aims in education, has contributed towards founding costs and student scholarships for the HeCe Foundation.

Hierapolis Excavations, excavation works in the ancient city of Hierapolis, close to Pamukkale, 20 kilometers north of the city center of Denizli. One of the biggest ancient cities in Turkey, the site joined the UNESCO World Heritage list in 1988. Excavation works and reconstruction of the ancient theater in Hierapolis have been supported by Tofaş, a Koç Holding(*) company, since 2005 and the Vehbi Koç Foundation(*) since 2013.

Thought to have been founded in the early second century BCE by Eumenes II of Pergamon, Hierapolis is said to take its name from Hiera, wife of Telephus, the legendary founder of Pergamon. Hierapolis is known as a "holy city" due to its many places of worship. Throughout history, the city was an important center of healing due to its proximity to the therapeutic underground springs of Pamukkale. Its original Hellenistic fabric remained until the great earthquake during the reign of the Roman emperor Nero (60 BCE), following which the city was completely rebuilt in the style of a typical Roman city. A martyrium was erected for the Christian Apostle Saint Philip after he was crucified in Hierapolis in 80 AD, making the city an important center of religious visits. It became a center for the episcopacy during the Byzantine era from the fourth century AD onwards. Towards the end of the twelfth century, the city came under the control of the Anatolian Seljuks.

The excavation and restoration work, which was started by Italian archaeologists in the 1950s, is now in the hands of a team led by Professor Francesco d'Andria of Salento University (Lecce, Italy). The team includes nearly 100 experts from a number of different countries, primarily Italy and Turkey. Among the most significant discoveries so far unearthed in Hierapolis are the ancient theater, the Necropolis, the hot springs, the Great Church, the St. Philip Martyrium, the Frontinus Gate, the Gymnasium, the Temple of Apollo and the Plutonium. Built almost 1,800 years ago, the amphitheater is one of the finest examples of Roman theaters. With renovation work now completed, it can be used for cultural events and has a seating capacity of 12,000 spectators.

Hoover, Alden R(obbins) *(b. January 6, 1877, Muscatine, Iowa, USA – d. May 10, 1940, Elizabeth, New Jersey, USA)*, first chief physician of the American Hospital(*).

Hoover completed his undergraduate education at Iowa State University in 1902 and became a physician in 1905 after completing medical studies at the same university. After he married in 1906, the American Board of Commissioners for Foreign Missions (ABCFM) assigned him and his wife to the American Hospitals in Merzifon and Talas respectively. He took leave between July 1914 and May 1915 to study at the Mayo Brothers Hospital in Rochester, Minnesota, USA. In May 1915, he went to Istanbul to tackle the typhus epidemic, remaining there until December 10 when he returned to the USA. He subsequently joined the American Military Medical Corps and rose to the rank of major. In 1918, he left the ABCFM and returned to Istanbul with the American Red Cross and Near East Aid Committee. He worked in the establishment of the American Hospital, becoming chief physician in 1920.

As chief physician at the American Hospital from 1920 to 1924, Dr. Hoover dedicated his years in management to ensuring the development of

Dr. Alden R. Hoover's ABCFM registration card
http://www.dlir.org/archive/orc-exhibit/items/show/collection/8/id/13057

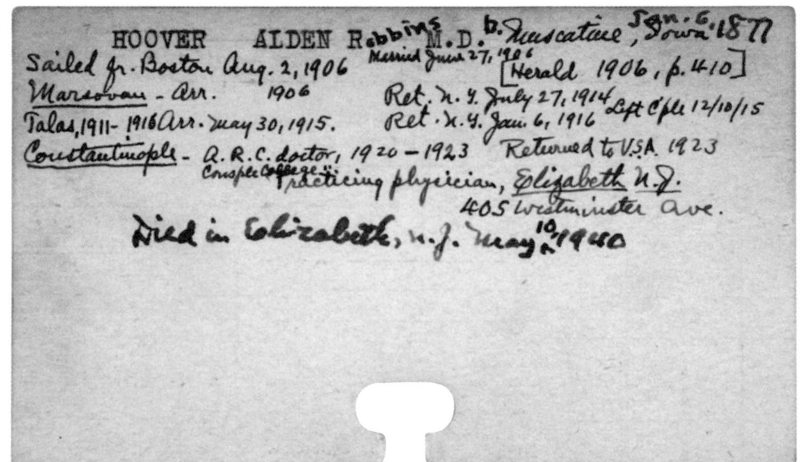

HOOVER ALDEN Robbins M.D. b. Muscatine, Iowa Jan. 6, 1877
Sailed fr. Boston Aug. 2, 1906 Married June 27, 1906 [Herald 1906, p. 410]
Marsovan - Arr. 1906 Ret. N. Y. July 27, 1914 Left Cple 12/10/15
Talas, 1911-1916 Arr. May 30, 1915. Ret. N. Y. Jan. 6, 1916
Constantinople - A.R.C. doctor, 1920-1923 Returned to U.S.A. 1923
practicing physician, Elizabeth N.J.
405 Westminster Ave.
Died in Elizabeth, N.J. May 10, 1940

the American Hospital by raising money to fund and equip the hospital in order to keep it afloat. In addition to the first hospital building in Çarşıkapı, a mother and baby health clinic was also opened in a commercial complex close to the Blue Mosque. During this time, the American Hospital also moved into the building of the old German Hospital in Sıraselviler, Taksim, which was occupied by the British during the war.

Dr. Hoover left this role for personal reasons in 1924, returning to the USA, where he opened a private clinic in Elizabeth, New Jersey. He died there in May 1940.

In her book, *A Bosporus Adventure (1871-1924)* published in 1934, Mary Mills Patrick, headmaster at the American College for Girls in Üsküdar and later American College for Girls in Arnavutköy, refers to the major role Dr. Hoover played in initiating medical and health education at the school. She also describes his fame as a doctor in the Near East, revealing that in the early 1920s he was summoned by telegraph to Greece to treat a member of a royal family: he successfully performed a difficult operation to save a princess's life.

Hotamışlıgil, Gökhan S. *(b. June 24, 1962, Rize)*, physician and scientist who received the Vehbi Koç Award(*) for health in 2013. Dr. Hotamışlıgil researches the genetic mechanisms of widespread and complex conditions such as diabetes, obesity and atherosclerosis and new methods of treatment.

After graduating from Ankara University School of Medicine in 1986, Hotamışlıgil completed a doctorate in biochemistry and molecular pharmacology at Harvard University in 1994. He became professor in 2003 and is currently James S. Simmons Professor of Genetics and Metabolism at Harvard T. H. Chan School of Public Health (HSPH) and head of the Department of Genetics and Complex Diseases. He is also engaged in studies at the Harvard-MIT Broad Institute, Harvard Stem Cell Institute and Joslin Diabetes Center. He has written hundreds of papers, which have been referenced more than 40,000 times, resulted in over 10 patents and formed the basis of a large number of drug development programs. The studies carried out at the Hotamışlıgil Laboratory at HSPH focus on using simple chemical process to treat and prevent Type 1 and Type 2 diabetes, which affect nearly 350 million people across the world and are currently incurable. As part of these studies, Hotamışlıgil and his team discovered a hormone, known as lipokine, which is capable of stopping illnesses such as diabetes and hepatic lipidosis. In 2014, the Sabri Ülker Center for Nutrient, Genetic and Metabolic Research was founded at HSPH, under the management of Dr. Hotamışlıgil, with a 24 million-dollar donation from Yıldız Holding. In 2017, studies carried out at the center, which aims to support the work of the Hotamışlıgil Laboratory, led to the discovery of the Nrf1 molecule, known as the "metabolic protector", which ensures that cholesterol levels inside a cell remain within safe levels.

Hotamışlıgil was made a principal member of the Turkish Academy of Sciences (TÜBA) in 2004, and in 2007 he received the American Diabetes Association's Award for Outstanding Scientific Achievement. In 2013, he received the Vehbi Koç Award for "pioneering work in health and science". Explaining why he had been chosen, the selection board described Gökhan Hotamışlıgil as "a Turkish scientist serving all of humanity as a global actor in the universal field of science," who had "made many of his scientific discoveries with other Turkish scientists he had invited from Turkey to his laboratory" and was "one of our successful people, leading Turkish society in health and science". In his speech at the award ceremony, Professor Hotamışlıgil stressed that intellectual and scientific transformation was of vital importance for Turkey, saying, "Science, art and education are the main focus of this prize and also at the heart of the Vehbi Koç Foundation's mission; they are also the most important building blocks for the movement for intellectual transformation that we seek. For me, it is a great privilege, joy and source of pride to be a part of this and for our work to be lauded in my own country in this way."

Hotamışlıgil has received science awards from a number of institutions, including the National

Institutes of Health, the International Association for the Study of Obesity, Columbia University, and TÜBİTAK. He has served as editor of a large number of international medical and research journals and been a member and consultant of various academic and research bodies. He also received the HSPH Mentoring Award for his success as a member of the teaching staff. In 2018, he was awarded the Diabetes Prize for Excellence by the European Association for the Study of Diabetes and Novo Nordisk Foundation.

Hüseyin Kocabaş Collection, an Anatolian civilizations collection comprising nearly 30 different types of artifact, primarily coins and archaeological pieces. In 1983, the collection of nearly 7,000 pieces was bought by the Vehbi Koç Foundation(*) (VKV) and brought to the Sadberk Hanım Museum(*) for exhibition.

Hüseyin Kocabaş (1909-81) was a businessman from Bursa, who began collecting antiquities at the

age of 10, over the years amassing a large collection. Once a week, he used to open up a floor of his apartment building in Nişantaşı, in order to exhibit the items to interested persons and scholars. Following the death of Kocabaş, the collection, composed of coins and archaeological pieces, which was the second greatest of it kind in the world, was put up for sale by his heirs. It was bought by the VKV with donations from members of the Koç family(*) and companies in Koç Holding(*). The disused waterside residence next to the Azaryan Mansion(*), which hosts the Sadberk Hanım Museum, was bought and renovated as a venue for the collection. It opened in 1988 and was named the "Sevgi Gönül Building".

The Hüseyin Kocabaş Collection reflects the cultural treasures of the civilizations living in Anatolia between the sixth millennium BCE and the end of the Byzantine era, including a variety of terracotta and metal pots, figurines, early cutting tools, glasswork, beads, early examples of seals, coins, decorative items, early musical instruments, grave stelae, tablets, lamps and various metal pieces. These pieces are exhibited in the museum in chronological order according to their period of origin: Prehistoric, Protohistoric, Neolithic, Phrygian, Mycenaean, Geometric, Archaic, Classical, Hellenistic, Roman and Byzantine.

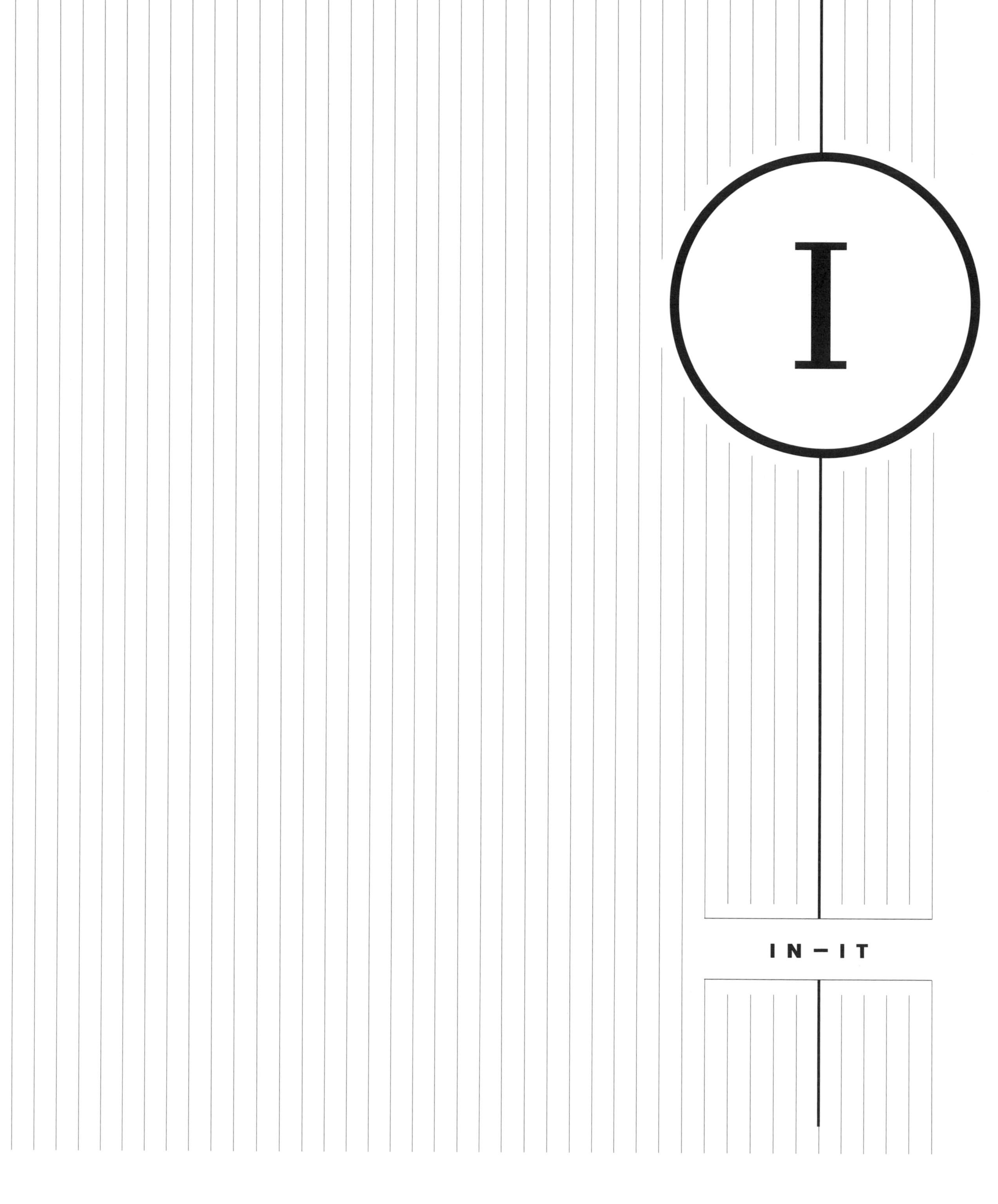

I

IN–IT

International Baccalaureate *see* **Koç School**

International Istanbul Biennial *see* **Istanbul Biennial**

International Sevgi Gönül Byzantine Studies Symposium, a series of conferences organized every three years with the aim of sharing Turkish and international research on the Byzantine era on a global platform. It is held in memory of Sevgi Gönül(*), who was a life-long supporter of efforts to promote research on the Byzantine era in Turkey and encourage society to embrace their cultural heritage. The first two symposiums were held by the Vehbi Koç Foundation(*) (VKV) at the Istanbul Archeology Museums in 2007 and 2010. The third was organized by ANAMED(*) in its own auditorium with support from the VKV, and the fourth symposium was arranged by GABAM(*) and held at ANAMED, once again with support from the VKV.

The theme of the first symposium, held from June 25-28, 2007, was "Change in the Byzantine World in the 12th-13th Centuries"; the theme of the second symposium, held from June 21-23, 2010, was "The Byzantine Court: Source of Power and Culture". An exhibition was held in parallel with the first symposium, and titled, "The Remnants: 12th and 13th Centuries Byzantine Objects in Turkey". An exhibition held together with the second symposium was titled "Byzantine Palaces in Istanbul". The theme of the third symposium, held from June 24-27, 2013, was "Trade in Byzantium" and it was accompanied by an exhibition of the Istanbul Yenikapı Excavations; the exhibition was held in collaboration with the Istanbul Archeology Museums and titled "Stories from the Hidden Harbor: Shipwrecks of Yenikapı". The fourth symposium was given the theme "Byzantine Identity and the Other in Geographical and Ethnic Imagination" and was held from June 23-25, 2016. It was accompanied by an exhibition titled "Byzantium's Other Empire: Trebizond" and was held at ANAMED. In addition to the exhibition catalogs, the following books, consisting of the symposium proceedings, were also published: *I. Uluslararası Sevgi Gönül Bizans Araştırmaları Sempozyumu: Bildiriler/First International Sevgi Gönül Symposium: Proceedings* (Ödekan, Ayla et al. [ed.], 2010) and *The Byzantine Court: Source of Power and Culture, Papers from the Second International Sevgi Gönül Byzantine Studies Symposium* (Ödekan, Ayla et al. [ed.], 2013) and *Trade in Byzantium: Papers from the Third International Seville Gödel Byzantine Studies Symposium* (Paul Magdalino and Nevra Necipoğlu [ed.], 2016).

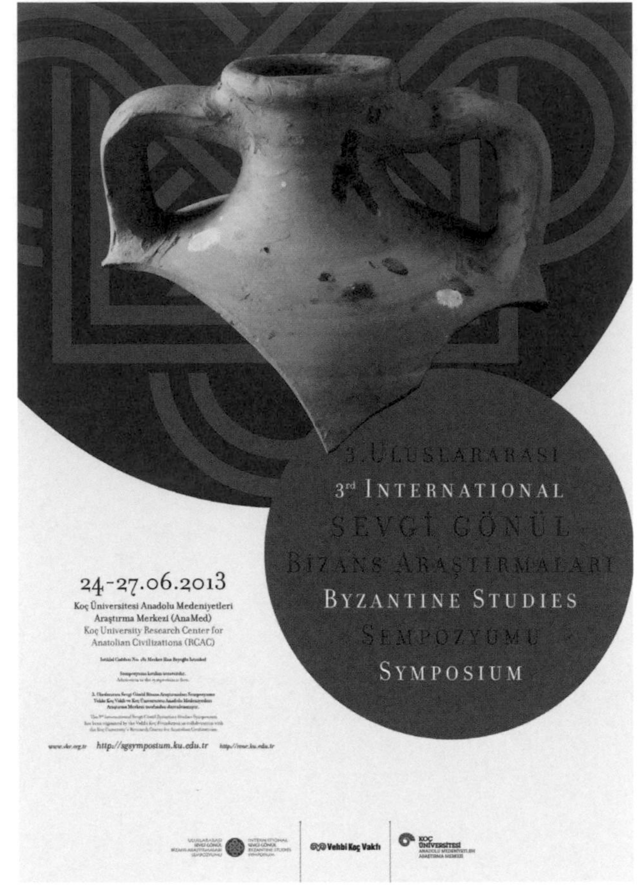

Iris Foundation Award for Outstanding Contribution to the Decorative Arts, granted since 1997 by the New York based Iris Foundation, which spreads awareness of world cultures and supports education in decorative arts, design history and material culture. These annual awards are granted to academicians, businesspeople and professionals who have made an outstanding contribution to the advancement of decorative arts. In 2012, the Koç family(*) received the award in recognition of their support for arts and culture, in particular the opening of the Koç Family Galleries of Ottoman Art at the Metropolitan Museum(*).

Istanbul Biennial, full name INTERNATIONAL ISTANBUL BIENNIAL, contemporary art event organized every two years by the Istanbul Foundation for Culture and Arts (İKSV). Plastic arts exhibitions previously held as part of the Istanbul International Festival were launched as a separate event, named the Istanbul Biennial, in 1987. The five biennials between 2006 and 2016 were funded by the Vehbi Koç Foundation(*) (VKV) with Koç Holding(*) as the main sponsor. The aim of this support was to widen engagement in contemporary art in Turkey, especially among young people, attract new audiences and stimulate greater overall interest. In 2015, it was decided to continue this support to include the next five biennials over the 2016-26 period.

Showcasing hundreds of local and international artists and art groups who represent the latest trends in contemporary art, the Istanbul Biennial aims to create a meeting point for visual artists and audiences from different cultures and build an international cultural network for artists, curators, arts circles and critics from Turkey and across the globe. Launched just before the 1990s, which saw a rapid increase in city biennials across the world, the Istanbul Biennial has become the most popular and internationally recognized arts event organized in Turkey. The tradition it has established, together with the city's geographical and cultural position, have earned it an important place among international contemporary art biennials.

Rather than an exhibition approach based on national representation, the Biennial adopts a model using the exhibits to facilitate a dialogue among the artists and between them and their audience. The curator, who is selected through an international advisory board, invites contributions from artists and projects that fit the conceptual framework devised for each biennial.

Rapidly growing in popularity, the event now attracts hundreds of thousands of visitors and includes the publication of a biennial book containing exhibition photographs and articles relating to the conceptual framework of the exhibition. In addition to guided tours around the exhibits, the Biennial hosts panels, conferences and workshops allowing both visitors and art students to follow the latest discussions and developments in the art world. There are also tours and activity programs aimed at children and young people.

Entry to the 13th Istanbul Biennial in 2013 was free of charge for the first time, due to the support of VKV and Koç Holding. As part of the event, a children's book, *A Colorful Journey in a Time Machine: Istanbul Biennials for Children* was published narrating the journey of the Istanbul biennials for over almost a quarter of a century and aiming to stimulate interest in contemporary art among young audiences.

INTERNATIONAL ISTANBUL BIENNIALS 1987-2017

- **1. 1987: "Contemporary Art in Traditional Spaces"**
  General Coordinator: Beral Madra (Turkey)
- **2. 1989: "Contemporary Art in Traditional Spaces"**
  General Coordinator: Beral Madra (Turkey)
- **3. 1992: "Production of Cultural Difference"**
  Director: Vasıf Kortun (Turkey)
- **4. 1995: "ORIENT/ATION-The Image of Art in a Paradoxical World"**
  Curator: Réne Block (Germany)
- **5. 1997: "On Life, Beauty, Translations and Other Difficulties"**
  Curator: Rosa Martínez (Spain)
- **6. 1999: "The Passion and the Wave"**
  Curator: Paolo Colombo (Italy)
- **7. 2001: "Egofugal - Fugue from Ego for the Next Emergence"**
  Curator: Yuko Hasegawa (Japonya)
- **8. 2003: "Poetic Justice"**
  Curator: Dan Cameron (USA)
- **9. 2005: "İstanbul"**
  Curators: Charles Esche (England) and Vasıf Kortun (Turkey)
- **10. 2007: "Not Only Possible, But Also Necessary: Optimism in the Age of Global War"**
  Curator: Hou Hanru (China)
- **11. 2009: "What Keeps Mankind Alive?"**
  Curators: Ivet Ćurlin, Ana Dević, Nataša Ilić and Sabina Sabolović (What, How & for Whom-WHW curator collective) (Croatia)
- **12. 2011: "Untitled (12th Istanbul Biennial), 2011"**
  Curators: Adriano Pedrosa (Brazil) and Jens Hoffmann (Costa Rica)
- **13. 2013: "Mom, am I barbarian?"**
  Curator: Fulya Erdemci (Turkey)
- **14. 2015: "Saltwater: A Theory of Thought Forms"**
  Curator: Carolyn Christov-Bakargiev (USA)
- **15. 2017: "a good neighbor"**
  Curators: Michael Elmgreen (Denmark) and Ingar Dragset (Norway)

Istanbul Jazz Festival, annual festival with an emphasis on jazz, organized by the Istanbul Foundation for Culture and Arts (İKSV) every July since 1994. The festival gives Turkey's music lovers the opportunity to watch world-famous jazz artists, and also includes the presentation of a Lifetime Achievement Award for artists who have made a major contribution to the development of jazz in Turkey. At the 23rd Istanbul Jazz Festival in 2016, the Vehbi Koç Foundation(*) funded almost 200 Syrian refugees living in Turkey to watch Damon Albarn and the Orchestra of Syrian Musicians. Similarly, at the following year's festival, almost 300 Syrian refugees were sponsored to attend a concert given by the Syrian Women's Choir, which is made up of Syrian female migrants living in Turkey. In 2018, 200 refugees living in Istanbul were given the opportunity to watch Robert Plant & The Sensational Space Shifters at the closing concert of the 25th Istanbul Jazz Festival.

Istanbul Rahmi M. Koç Museum, museum of industry, transport and communication affiliated with the Rahmi M. Koç Museology and Culture Foundation(*). Located in Hasköy, Istanbul on the left bank of the Golden Horn, the museum consists of the historical Lengerhane building, the old Hasköy Shipyard and adjacent open-air exhibition area immediately opposite. When it opened in the Lengerhane building in December 1994, it was Turkey's first museum of industry, and grew to its current size later after the shipyard and other annexes were purchased and transformed into exhibition spaces.

The Lengerhane building is thought to have been built during the era of Sultan Ahmed III (early eighteenth century) over the remnants of twelfth century Byzantine foundations. The building, which was used as a foundry for producing anchors and rodes, is known to have been renovated during the era of Selim III (late eighteenth century). In the Republican Era, it was used by the Cibali Tobacco Factory as a tobacco warehouse for many years, but left to its own fate after extensive fire damage in 1984. Subsequently, the Tekel (Turkish State Monopoly of Alcohol and Tobacco Products) began to use the garden as an alcohol depot. Along with the historical Lengerhane building, the site also includes an adjacent, small wooden roof-enclosed outbuilding and an inner courtyard surrounded by stone walls, which were bought by the Rahmi M. Koç Museology and Culture Foundation in 1991. After two and a half years of restoration work, the museum opened to the public in 1994.

Covering a total area of 11,250 square meters, the Hasköy Shipyard is as significant as the Lengerhane from the point of view of industrial archaeology. It was established in 1861 for the maintenance and repair of vessels from the Bosphorous transport company, Şirket-i Hayriye, starting out as several workshop buildings. Over time it expanded, and a 45-meter timber slipway with a steam traction winch was added. In 1910, the winch was converted to electrical power. The Istanbul city line steamers, named "Kocataş" and "Sarıyer", funnel numbers 75 and 76, were built here in 1938. Due to changes in sea transport regulations, the Hasköy Shipyard changed hands frequently until the 1980s. By the time it was bought by the Rahmi M. Koç Museology and Culture Foundation in 1996, it had fallen into

disuse. The shipyard, along with the 14 buildings enclosing it in a U-shape, were restored in keeping with their original style and opened in 2001 as an extension of the museum's exhibition area.

Last to be added was the area next to the shipyard, reaching from the street, Hasköy Caddesi, to the Golden Horn, which also became an open air exhibition area.

A large number of the items in the museum are compiled from the personal collection of Rahmi M. Koç(*). Other museum exhibits are donated or borrowed from various organizations and individuals. The core of the collection is made up of original pieces, together with their models and scientific and mechanical objects. The museum's collections are exhibited under the headings, Atatürk, Road Transport, Rail Transport, Navigation, Aviation, Living History, Machinery, Communication, Models and Toys, Scientific Devices and Letterpress Printing. The exhibits, which predominantly relate to the nineteenth and twentieth centuries include land, air, sea and rail vehicles, models and engines, clocks and their mechanisms, astronomical instruments, binoculars, microscopes, abacuses, calculators, printing presses, telephones, gramophones, radios, phonographs, cine cameras, cameras, televisions, bicycles, motorbikes and pushchairs. The open-air exhibition space contains classic cars, a huge Turgut Alp winch, the "B-24 Liberator" and other aircraft, the anchored "Fenerbahçe" ferry and the "TCG Uluçalireis" submarine.

SOME EXHIBITIONS AT THE ISTANBUL RAHMİ M. KOÇ MUSEUM

- **İhap Hulusi Görey Private** *(February-March 2002)*
- **Blue Exhibition** *(September-November 2002)*
- **Halfdan Was Here** *(November 2002-January 2003)*
- **Dream Machines** *(May-June 2003)*
- **The Probability of Harmony** *(December 2004-February 2005)*
- **The Genius of Leonardo** *(November-December 2006)*
- **Air, Land and Marine Vehicles Painting** *(February-March 2007)*
- **Vehbi Koç - The Story of a Century 1901-1996** *(February-March 2008)*
- **The Brain: Mysterious Journey** *(April-June 2008)*
- **From Dolmabahçe to Anıtkabir 1938-1953** *(December 2008-March 2009)*
- **Henry Kupjack Miniature Rooms** *(December 2008-September 2009)*
- **Yalvaç Ural Tin Toys** *(April-September 2009)*
- **Circumnavigation with Nazenin IV** *(June 2009-June 2010)*
- **Ships and the Sea** *(14 November 2009)*
- **Mysteries of the Deep Blue** *(December 2009-March 2010)*
- **Zeugma–Bridge: Jale Kutadgobilik** *(April-May 2010)*
- **Istanbul Piers and Ferries** *(September-November 2010)*
- **Sea and Istanbul** *(February-November 2011)*
- **Invisible Musicians** *(February-June 2011)*
- **Daniel Buren Voiles Toiles** *(September 2011-January 2012)*
- **Magic Realism – Rugs and Kilims** *(December 2011-March 2012)*
- **The Legacy of Byzantine Ships** *(April-September 2012)*
- **Motoring Legends in Istanbul** *(October 2012-March 2013)*
- **Ontraxs! 2012 Winner** *(November 2012-June 2013)*
- **Here Comes the Sun** *(November 2012-July 2013)*
- **Medieval Ports from the Aegean to the Black Sea** *(April-October 2013)*
- **Piri Reis at Tersane-i Amire After Five Centuries** *(July-October 2013)*
- **Models Exhibition** *(December 2013-June 2014)*
- **Bridging Two Continents – Bosphorus** *(October 2013-June 2014)*
- **Yersiz Yurtsuz** *(July-October 2014)*
- **Hector of Troy** *(November 2014-March 2015)*
- **Dolls House** *(November 2014–June 2015)*
- **Naval Battles in the Dardanelles Campaign** *(March–December 2015)*
- **Then & Now Gallipoli Campaign** *(March–December 2015)*
- **Lighthouses** *(April–May 2016)*
- **On the Ground and in the Sky** *(June–October 2016)*
- **In the Wake of Ships** *(December 2017–February 2018)*
- **Miraculous** *(February–March 2018)*
- **God Speed** *(April–June 2018)*
- **Distant Seas** *(June–November 2018)*

In addition to weekend workshops, the museum organizes a number of different educational programs aimed at the school curriculum. There is also a peripatetic museum project, called "Müzebüs" (Museumbus), for students who are too far away to visit the museum.

In 1996, the Istanbul Rahmi M. Koç Museum received the European Museum Forum (EMF) European Museum of the Year Award, followed in 2001 by the Arts and Culture Grand Prize awarded by the Turkish Ministry of Culture and Tourism.

THE STORY OF THE ISTANBUL RAHMİ M. KOÇ MUSEUM IN THE WORDS OF ITS FOUNDER

When I was a child—I forget how old—my father, Mr. Vehbi Koç, returned from a trip to Germany and presented me with my first electrical toy train. This was the start of my passion for collecting mechanical and industrial objects. Over the years the collection expanded so much that my homes, offices and warehouses were overflowing.

When the Koç Group entered into a closer relationship with large, worldwide, industrial concerns in the 1950s, I noticed that some of the companies had museums where they displayed their products from the very first model. I was much impressed by this practice and considered doing the same with our own products. However, I thought that such a museum in Turkey would be of little interest except to industrialists. The idea remained with me and, whenever I went abroad, I would make a point of visiting scientific and industrial museums. I remember in particular the "Deutsches Museum" in Munich and the "Science Museum" in London. But it was when I saw the "Henry Ford Museum" in Detroit that I immediately decided to gather all my collection under one roof. After receiving positive views and much encouragement from my colleagues, my mind was made up.

I started looking for a suitable location and simultaneously increased my collecting activities. I bought anything I found agreeable, pleasing, or which attracted my interest. Not every piece was in good condition, so a workshop had to be established for their restoration. Meanwhile the search for a suitable site in Istanbul continued.

Eventually Dr. Bülent Bulgurlu, who was been of great assistance to me in these matters, told me of an alcohol storage building belonging to Tekel at Hasköy on the Golden Horn. We went together to see the building and it left a lasting impression on us. With foundations dating back to the twelfth century, the "Lengerhane" building had been used in the 1730s as a foundry for making anchors and other castings for the navy. It was now a total ruin, having been destroyed by a fire in 1984 while it was being used for tobacco storage by Tekel. Only the garden was still in use as an alcohol depot. We bought the building in 1991 and had it restored to its original state by 1993. From the colorful appearance of its brickwork, it could easily be mistaken for a mosque, or a Byzantine church.

The Rahmi M. Koç Museum was opened to visitors in 1994. In 1996 it was honored to receive a special award from the Council of Europe's "European Museum of the Year Award".

In accordance with our expansion plans, in 1996 we purchased the Hasköy Shipyard, which was being privatized. The shipyard was founded in 1880 and is just across the road from the present museum. This proximity and its water frontage made it an ideal site. Like the Lengerhane, it is a Grade II listed historical building. It opened in July 2001, and exhibits mostly full-size objects that, we believe, will be of great interest to both Turkish and foreign visitors.

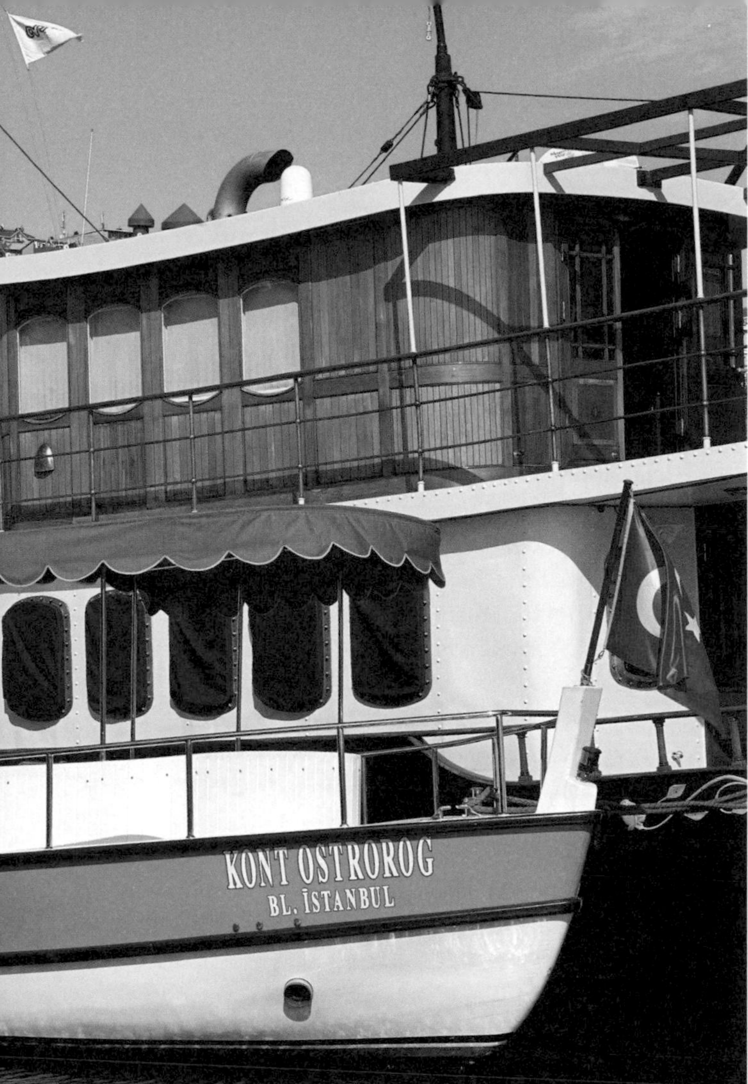

Much effort has been expended by many of my colleagues, technical staff, academicians and professors to bring the museum to its present state. Also universities, schools and the armed forces have given great support and assistance in many ways including supplying exhibition pieces. Many valuable items have been donated or loaned by museum visitors, sometimes by our acquaintances and sometimes by others. I would like to thank them all for their generosity. I would particularly like to express my thanks and deep gratitude to the Boğaziçi University and the Kandilli Observatory and Earthquake Research Institute for playing such a leading role in all this. It is true that a lot of time, effort and cost have been expended, but this is amply repaid by the appreciation of the visitors and increase in their numbers over time.

Rahmi M. Koç

http://www.rmk-museum.org.tr/en/rmk_chairmans_message.htm

Istanbul Research Institute, research body that, "aims to unearth Istanbul's history, cultural structure and human profile through the Byzantine, Ottoman and Republican periods by following the traces of civilization which spread from the city's center to its surroundings. The institute develops and supports projects that feed this purpose and works to share the results of these efforts through national and international events with related institutions and the public, and through a rich publication series." It began its activities on March 1, 2007, as part of the Suna and İnan Kıraç Foundation, and was the second major phase of a wide-ranging arts and cultural project that began with the opening of the Pera Museum(*) in 2005.

The institute is located in Tepebaşı in the old Rosolimo Apartment built by the Italian architect Guglielmo Semprini towards the end of the nineteenth century. The ground floor is used as a gallery for exhibitions highlighting the institute's projects. The Atatürk and the Republican Studies section includes the institute's main library, containing relevant academic publications, as well as the Istanbul Library and a reference section for the general reader. The Ottoman Studies Section contains a library of modern Ottoman research, as

well as the Şevket Rado Manuscript Library, which is made up of almost 1,000 manuscripts from the Şevket Rado collection. The manuscripts have been transferred to a digital format to prevent deterioration and facilitate access for researchers. The Byzantine Studies Section holds a library of contemporary Byzantine research, as well as the Semavi Eyice Library, where researchers have access to rare editions and over 30,000 periodicals, offprints, numerous archive materials belonging to Professor Semavi Eyice. In addition to books on Byzantine art and history, the Semavi Eyice Library also holds travelogues and archaeological/art publications relating to various periods of Islamic, Turkish and Ottoman history, art, architecture and literature.

The Suna and İnan Kıraç Foundation Photograph Collection, collated by Suna Kıraç(*) and İnan Kıraç(*) over many years, contains over 120,000 old photographs of Istanbul from before and after the establishment of the Republic. One of most valuable parts of the institute's archive, this collection also includes engravings, maps, musical scores and numerous newspaper clippings relating to Istanbul's cultural heritage.

Since 2012, the institute has published the *Annual of Istanbul Studies*, which features unique studies on different aspects of the city's historical, archaeological and cultural identity. Other books are also published as part of the Symposium Series, Classical Works Series, Special Series and Istanbul Studies Series, which focuses on doctoral theses about Istanbul.

ISTANBUL RESEARCH INSTITUTE PUBLICATIONS

- **Ağır, Aygül, *İstanbul'un Eski Venedik Yerleşimi ve Dönüşümü* (The Old Venetian Settlement of Istanbul and its Transformation),** *2009*
- **Arslan, Murat and Kaçar, Turhan (ed.) *Byzantion'dan Constantinopolis'e İstanbul Kuşatmaları* (Sieges of Istanbul from Byzantium to Constantinople),** *2017*
- **Cheynet, Jean-Claude, Gökyıldırım, Turan and Bulgurlu, Vera (ed.), *Les sceaux byzantins du Musée archéologique d'Istanbul* (The Byzantine Seals of the Archaeological Museum of Istanbul),** *2012*
- **Çokuğraş, Işıl, *Bekâr Odaları ve Meyhaneler. Osmanlı İstanbulu'nda Marjinalite ve Mekân (1789-1839)* (Bachelor Rooms and Taverns: Marginality and Space in Ottoman Istanbul),** *2016*
- **Genim, Sinan (ed.), *Konstantiniyye'den İstanbul'a. XIX. Yüzyıl Ortalarından XX. Yüzyıla Boğaziçi'nin Anadolu Yakası Fotoğrafları* (From Konstantiniyye to Istanbul. Photographs of the Anatolian shore of the Bosphorus from the mid 19th to the 20th Century),** *2012*
- ***İstanbul Araştırmaları Enstitüsü Yazmalar Kataloğu*, 3 vol. (Istanbul Research Institute Catalog of Manuscripts),** *2014*
- **Kaynar, Hakan, *Projesiz Modernleşme. Cumhuriyet İstanbulu'ndan Gündelik Fragmanlar* (Modernization without Blueprints: Daily Fragments from Republican Istanbul),** *2012*
- **Kılıç, Filiz (ed.), *Âşık Çelebi, Meşâ'irü'ş-Şu'arâ* (Senses of Poets),** *2010*
- **Mabeyinci Pavlos, *Ayasofya'nın Betimi* (The Depiction of Hagia Sophia),** *2010*
- **Mazlum, Deniz, *1766 İstanbul Depremi. Belgeler Işığında Yapı Onarımları* (Istanbul Earthquake of 1766: Structure Repairs in the Light of Documents),** *2011*
- **Ousterhout, Robert, Klein, Holger and Pitarakis, Brigitte (ed.), *Kariye Camii Yeniden/The Kariye Camii Reconsidered*,** *2011*
- **Özkaya, Gökçen, *18. Yüzyılda Istanbul Evleri. Mimarlık, Rant, Konfor, Mahremiyet* (18th-Century Istanbul Houses: Architecture, Property Income, Comfort, Privacy),** *2016*
- **Pitarakis, Brigitte and Tanman, Gülru (ed.), *Life Is Short, Art Long: Healing in Byzantium-New Perspectives*,** *2018*
- **Yavuz, Mehmet Fatih, *Byzantion. Byzas'tan Constantinus'a Antik İstanbul, Antik Edebi Kaynaklar* (Byzantion: Ancient Istanbul, Ancient Literary Sources from Byzas to Constantine),** *2014*

Since its opening, the institute has hosted conferences, international symposiums and a series of talks known as "Chamber Talks". Among symposiums organized by the institute are: Theodoros Metokhites, the Chora Monastery and Constantinopolis in the Palaiologos Era (2007), 12th International Symposium on Boat and Ship Archaeology (2009), Cultural Life of Caves, From Paleolithic Shamans to the Seven Sleepers (2012), Views from Byzantium (2012), "Meclis" as a Cultural Circle (2013), 11th International Symposium of Byzantine Sigillography (2014), Imagining the City: Representations of Istanbul from Art to Life (2014) and Discovering Byzantium in Istanbul: Scholars, Institutions and Challenges, 1800–1955 (2017).

Suna and İnan Kıraç received the Istanbul Tourism Honorary Award for the contribution they made to Istanbul by opening the Pera Museum and Istanbul Research Institute.

EXHIBITIONS ORGANIZED BY ISTANBUL RESEARCH INSTITUTE

- **"Ottoman Architect" D'Aronco** *(September 18–December 15, 2006)*

- **Ali Emîrî Efendi and His World: Fermans, Berats, Calligraphies, Books** *(January 24–July 1, 2007)*
- **The Dervishes of Sovereignty, The Sovereignty of Dervishes: The Mevlevi Order in Istanbul** *(November 15, 2007–March 30, 2008)*
- **Long Stories: Istanbul in the Panoramas of Melling and Dunn** *(May 29–July 23, 2008)*
- **Cities of the Three Books: Jerusalem and the Holy Land in 19th Century Photographs** *(September 9–October 19, 2008)*
- **Wooden Istanbul: Examples from Housing Architecture** *(October 30, 2008–April 26, 2009)*
- **The Logbook of the Ottoman Navy: Ships, Legends, Sailors** *(May 15–October 04, 2009)*
- **Ankara: City of the Black Calpac, 1923-1938** *(October 29, 2009–March 28, 2010)*
- **From the Capital of the Empire to the Modern City of the Republic: Henri Prost's Istanbul Plans 1936-1951** *(May 3–July 18, 2010)*
- **The Crescent and the Sun, Three Japanese in İstanbul: Yamada Torajiro, Ito Chuta, Otani Kozui** *(October 16, 2010–February 13, 2011)*
- **Impressions from Afar: 18th-Century Istanbul in the Paintings of Clara and Luigi Mayer** *(March 23–September 15, 2011)*
- **1283: Atatürk in Photographs from the Suna and İnan Kıraç Foundation Collection** *(November 10–November 24, 2011)*
- **From the Shores of the Nile to the Bosphorus: Traces of the Kavalalı Mehmed Ali Pasha Dynasty in Istanbul** *(December 7, 2011–March 31, 2012)*
- **Mindful Seed Speaking Soil: Village Institutes of the Republic 1940-1954** *(April 18–October 27, 2012)*
- **Atatürk: More than Just a Man... Suna and İnan Kıraç Foundation Atatürk Photograph Collection** *(November 10–November 30, 2012)*
- **The Architect of Changing Times: Edoardo De Nari 1874-1954** *(December 18, 2012–April 20, 2013)*
- **The Anatomy of a Tradition: 150 Years of Robert College 1863-2013** *(June 15–August 31, 2013)*
- **Republic: New Individual, New Life** *(December 11, 2013–May 17, 2014)*
- **Taksim: The Heart of Istanbul** *(June 5–October 07, 2014)*
- **Ekrem Hakkı Ayverdi (1899–1984): Architectural Historian, Restorer, Collector** *(November 5, 2014–April 11, 2015)*
- **Journey to the Center of the East 1850-1950: 100 Years of Travelers in Istanbul from Pierre de Gigord Collection** *(June 4–October 17, 2015)*
- **The Republic in Istanbul: Scenes from a Celebration** *(October 27, 2015–January 30, 2016)*
- **The Şişli Mosque: An Ottoman Building in the Early Republican Era** *(February 16–September 18, 2016)*
- **The Four-Legged Municipality: Street Dogs of Istanbul** *(October 27, 2016–September 16, 2017)*
- **Imaginary World of a Paper Architect: Nazimî Yaver Yenal** *(October 4, 2017–March 3, 2018)*
- **A Window to the West: 150 Years of the Galatasaray Lycée, 1868-2018** *(September 14, 2018–February 23, 2019)*

Istanbul Tanpınar Literature Festival (ITLF), international literary festival organized in Istanbul every year since 2009. Named after the writer Ahmet Hamdi Tanpınar, it has the distinction of being Turkey's first international literary festival. The event is organized by the Kalem Cultural Association in partnership with Kalem Rights Agency and with support from a number of official bodies and civil society groups. The Vehbi Koç Foundation(*) was the festival's main sponsor in 2012, 2013 and 2014.

The ITLF aims to provide a collaboration platform for writers and publishers from Turkey and foreign publishers, editors, writers, translators, translation fund providers and literary festival organizers, while at the same time enabling foreign writers to meet Turkish readers and authors.

Every year has a nominated theme, which provides a focal point for free readings and debates, discussions and workshops. The festival also organizes meetings for state school pupils, children's workshops, signing days and literary gatherings. The festival activities are held across a number of Anatolian cities and previous themes have included "City and Time", "City and Humans", "City and Food", "City and Fear", "City and Games", "City and Journeys", "City and Borders", "City and Voices", "City and Imagination" and "We Follow Literature".

Italian Hospital, a historic hospital situated on Defterdar (İtalyan) Yokuşu, a steep street stretching from Tophane to Cihangir in the Beyoğlu district of Istanbul. In 1998, it was taken over by the American Hospital(*), affiliated with the Vehbi Koç Foundation(*) (VKV), who intended to run it as a hospital specializing in oncology and rehabilitation. However, due to various issues, it was not officially opened until July 1, 2005, only to close again on August 15, 2006 after continued financial loss.

The Italian Hospital can be traced back to a small dispensary founded in the 1820s to serve Genoese sailors in Istanbul's Galata district. Initially staffed by one physician and a few nuns, it was originally known as the Sardinia Hospital, but renamed the Royal Italian Hospital in 1861, following the unification of Italy. The hospital grew over time and in 1876 moved to its current location in a building constructed by King Victor Emmanuel II of Sardinia. A new pavilion was added in 1898. The nuns fled the hospital when it was occupied by German forces during World War I but returned once the war was over. In 1936, the hospital was expanded with the addition of a two-story surgery building and was by now serving all Istanbul residents, not simply the Italian community.

In 1997, talks began between the VKV and the Italian Consulate with a view to providing certain medical programs and services which were not available at the American Hospital. As a result of the agreement signed by the two parties in March 1998, the Italian Hospital was leased by the American Hospital for 20 years. The agreement included the provision that the name of the institution, now under the management

of the American Hospital, would be protected. It was also stipulated that ownership would remain with the state of Italy, that a certain number of beds would be reserved for Italian citizens and that the hospital would undergo renovation works to a value of nearly nine million dollars. Plans for pain management programs and home healthcare medical services were included within the founding of an extensive cancer screening, diagnosis and treatment center and long-term care and rehabilitation unit.

It was planned that the renovation work would be completed in nine months and that the hospital would open in 1999, but the renovation period was extended as a result of an objection lodged by someone living next to the hospital. In the meantime, due to the need for the latest medical equipment, the renovation budget rose to 11,5 million dollars. Three million dollars of this sum were covered by the Fiat Fund of the Vehbi Koç Foundation. In a ceremony attended by the Italian foreign minister on November 18, 1999, the building, renovated by the restoration project of Architect Fahrettin Ayanlar(*), was renamed after the grandson of the Fiat founder, Giovanni Alberto Agnelli, who died from cancer many years ago. The new 50-bed hospital covered a site of nearly 8,250 square meters, but due to various obstacles it did not officially open for service until July 1, 2005. On August 15, 2006 the hospital closed, and later it was managed by the Universal Hospitals Groups, although it closed once more in 2013.

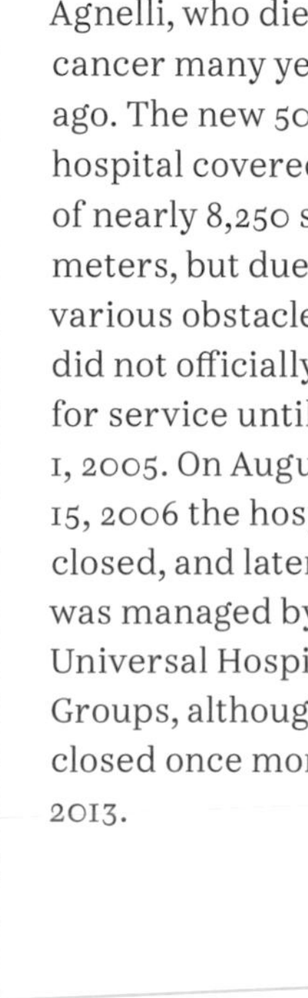

"Agnelli's donation was considered too generous for our cancer patients"

In the Agnelli family, there were only two male heirs to carry on the name. One was Gianni (Giovanni) Agnelli's son, Edoardo Agnelli, but sadly he suffered from drug addiction and committed suicide. The family's only hope was Giovanni Alberto Agnelli, son of Umberto Agnelli, Gianni's brother, but he died at an early age from cancer. The Agnelli family donated millions of dollars to fund cancer treatment at the Italian Hospital in memory of the young man. The hospital had once been funded by the Italian government and the nursing care provided by nuns. However, over time it found itself both in financial trouble, without any nuns to provide care and falling into a state of neglect. The Italian government later transferred the hospital to the Vehbi Koç Foundation. With additional support from the Agnelli family, the hospital was transformed into a cancer center with state-of-the-art radiotherapy equipment. The building was exceptionally stylish and attractive, but unfortunately was closed down on the grounds that it was an "illegal construction", following a campaign by certain ill-meaning people living nearby. It is still closed today (2003). As a cancer patient myself, I find this situation exceptionally upsetting and leave those who placed obstacles in the path of the hospital to the mercy of God.

Sevgi Gönül, *Sevgi'nin Diviti* (From Sevgi's Pen), Vehbi Koç Foundation Publications, Istanbul, 2003, p. 215; *Hürriyet*, February 2, 2003

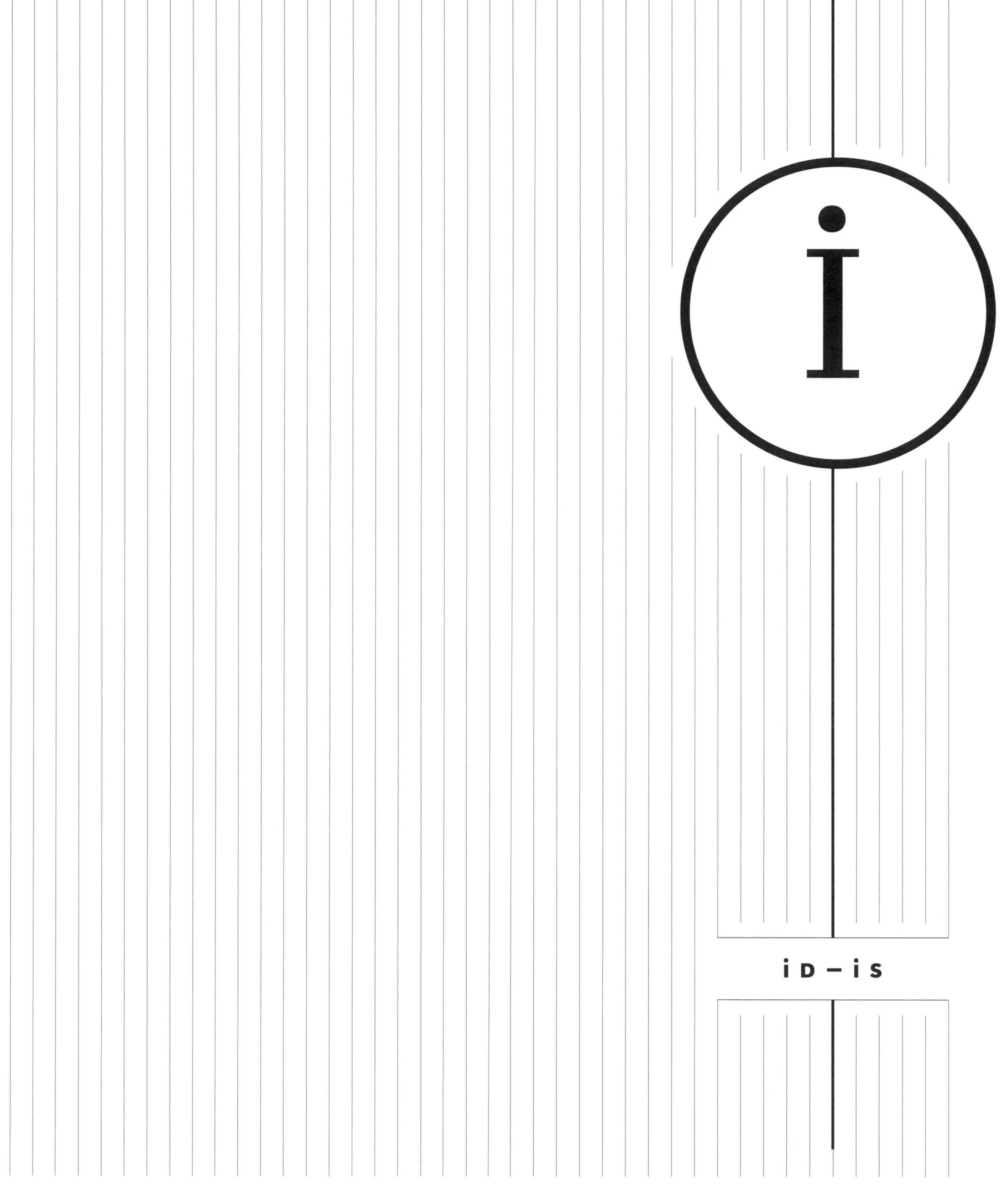

i

iD – iS

İdil Biret Documentary, documentary made with sponsorship from the Vehbi Koç Foundation(*) about the life and career of famous pianist İdil Beret.

Production of the 56-minute documentary, *İdil Biret: Portrait of a Child Prodigy*, began in 2008 and was directed by Eytan İpeker. Together with İdil Biret's personal archives, material was also researched from other personal and corporate archives in Australia, England, France and Turkey. The documentary included numerous previously unseen archive documents, images and recordings, as well as interviews with famous artists giving an insight into Biret's artistic life. The documentary was first shown on April 8, 2016 at the Pera Museum(*) as part of the 34th Istanbul Film Festival.

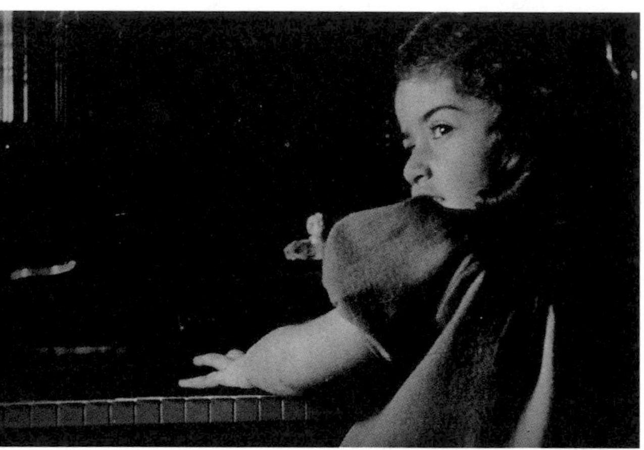

İlkel, M(ehmet) Fahir *(b. 1925?, Edirne – d. September 8, 1993, Istanbul)*, senior manager who served at Koç Holding(*) companies for many years. He was also a member of the Vehbi Koç Foundation(*) (VKV) Board of Directors between 1985 and 1993.

He completed his engineering education at Robert College(*) undergraduate department (now Boğaziçi University) in 1944. He received a master's degree in mechanical engineering from the Michigan University, USA, in 1946. İlkel stayed in the USA, working for the company, Allis Chalmers, but returned to Turkey in 1949. After 12 years at the General Directorate of Highways and one year at Ereğli Demir Çelik İşletmeleri, he moved to Koç Holding in 1962, followed by Demir Export and Arçelik respectively. In 1973, he joined the Koç Holding Executive Committee, under the chairmanship of Rahmi M. Koç(*), but was appointed Minister of Energy and Natural Resources in the government of Bülent Ulusu, established after the military coup on September 12, 1980. After holding the position from December 23, 1981 to December 13, 1983, he returned to Koç Holding and was appointed chair of the managing committee. He became vice chair of the Koç Holding Board of Directors in 1987 and chair of the Arçelik Board of Directors in 1991, when it was vacated by Vehbi Koç(*).

One of the founders of the Turkish Education Foundation(*), İlkel also played a prominent role in the establishment of Koç University(*). He was appointed chair of the university's executive committee in March 1990 and joined the Board of Trustees in March 1992. At the time of his death on September 8, 1993, he was serving on the VKV Board of Directors and was also on the boards of directors of several Koç Holding companies.

FAHİR İLKEL'S MINISTRY STORY IN THE WORDS OF VEHBİ KOÇ

On December 15, 1981, Prime Minister Bülent Ulusu called me at home in Yeniköy to ask how I was. Then he said, "I want to know how you feel about something—I 'd like to know your wishes and if you'll agree. I want to go into collaboration with one of your managers, Fahir İlkel. What do you think?" I replied, "He's a valuable and earnest friend. We've been working together for 12 years, I think. He's still in Germany. He'll be back in a couple of days. I'm ready to accept any orders from you that are for the good of the country. I just want to express this one concern: I started working at the time of Atatürk and I've lived through various periods. I and my company were never exposed to the tiniest bit of gossip. The [current] atmosphere is really bad. I'm worried that people will accuse me of influencing the army. They'll say one of Koç's managers is a minister and he made sure this and that was done. The matter concerns both me and you. Besides, whether Fahir İlkel will accept the job you've allocated, is completely up to him."

The prime minister replied, "The President said he didn't have any objection to it. You people have a lot of experience in the private sector, and can be of great service. The President is coming to my office at 12 pm today for a meeting. I'll pass on your views on all this. But regardless of whether Mr. İlkel

accepts or not, he should come to Ankara when he gets back from Europe. I want to talk to him."

When Mr. İlkel came back from Germany, I wrote to him saying, "If you accept the offer they make you when you go to Ankara, it's going to last until the army restores civilian power. According to my estimation, that will be at most one and a half years."

Mr. İlkel went to Ankara. He accepted the job of Minister of Energy and Natural Resources and began working there. Following that, we held a meeting at the Holding on December 21, 1981 and proposed that Yüksel Pulat took over Fahir İlkel's duties. Mr. Pulat accepted and set to work. A circular was sent round the organization informing everyone of the situation.

Mr. İlkel resigned from our board of directors due to his new position.

On November 6, 1983, there was a general election and the Ulusu Government stepped down. Fahir İlkel returned to his duties.

Vehbi Koç, *Hatıralarım Görüşlerim Öğütlerim (Recollections, Observations, Counsel)*, Vehbi Koç Foundation Publications, İstanbul, 1987, p. 63-64

İnan, Umran (Savaş) *(b. December 28, 1950, Erzincan)*, scientist who has served as president of Koç University(*) (KU) since 2009.

İnan graduated from the Middle East Technical University Department of Electrical Engineering in 1972 and was awarded an MSc from there in 1973. In 1977, he received a PhD from Stanford University (SU) Department of Electrical Engineering in geophysics and very low frequency radio science. After working at the same university as a researcher and part-time lecturer, in 1982 he became a full-time member of the academic staff. He became an associate professor in 1985 and professor in 1992. Until his appointment as president of KU in 2009, he was a faculty member at SU, where he carried out research in geophysics, near-space, ionospheric and atmospheric physics, radiation belts, electromagnetic wave-particle interaction, and very low frequency radio science. From 1997 to 2010, Professor İnan was director of the Space, Telecommunications and Radio Science Laboratory (STAR Lab) of the Stanford University.

Professor İnan is vice president of the International Union of Radio Science (IURS) and also a member of numerous scientific bodies, including the American Geophysical Union, Electromagnetics Academy, Turkish Academy of Sciences (TÜBA) and the Science Academy. Among the awards he has received are: the Tau Beta Pi Award for Excellence in Undergraduate Teaching from Stanford University, 1998; NASA Group Achievement Award in 1983, 1998 and 2004; Allan Cox Medal for Faculty Excellence in Fostering Undergraduate Research from Stanford University, 2007; Appleton Prize from the IURS and Royal Society of London, 2008 and the Special Award from the Scientific and Technological Research Council of Turkey (TÜBİTAK). In 1993, he received the US Antarctic Service Medal, and an Antarctic peak was named "İnan Peak" in recognition of his work in the area.

The following books were written by Professor İnan: *Engineering Electromagnetics* (with Aziz İnan; 1998), *Electromagnetic Waves* (with Aziz İnan; 1999), *Principles of Plasma Physics for Scientists and Engineers* (with Marek Gołkowski; 2011), *Numerical Electromagnetics* (with Robert A. Marshall; 2011). Over 300 of his articles have been published in peer-reviewed journals.

İnegöl Vehbi Koç Elementary School
see **17 Schools Project**

İnönü Foundation, a foundation set up in honor of İsmet İnönü (1884-1973), second president of the Republic of Turkey and close colleague of Atatürk. From its headquarters in Ankara, the organization aims to ensure İnönü's memory is passed on to future generations and is one of the civil society organizations supported by the Vehbi Koç Foundation(*).

Established by the İnönü family on February 22, 1983, on the suggestion of Erdal İnönü (1926-2007), the foundation's first president was Mevhibe İnönü

(1897-1992), the wife of İsmet İnönü. After her death, the role was taken over by their daughter, Özden İnönü Toker (b. 1930).

The İnönü Archive compiled by the foundation contains over 5,000 books, almost 7,000 documents and more than 3,000 photographs. Several venues have been turned into museum houses for the foundation: the Orchard House (Pembe Köşk) in the Çankaya district of Ankara, bought by İsmet İnönü in 1924; the İsmet İnönü House on the Istanbul island of Heybeliada and the house in Izmir where he was born in 1884. The houses are open to visitors during certain periods and also used to host conferences and exhibitions.

Among the activities of the foundation are the publication of books and brochures, particularly with regard to İsmet İnönü and the Treaty of Lausanne, organizing conferences, exhibitions and story, essay and caricature competitions. It also holds a commemorative concert for İsmet İnönü every year in December.

İnönü Vehbi Koç Middle School

see **17 Schools Project**

İstinye Campus *see* **Koç University**

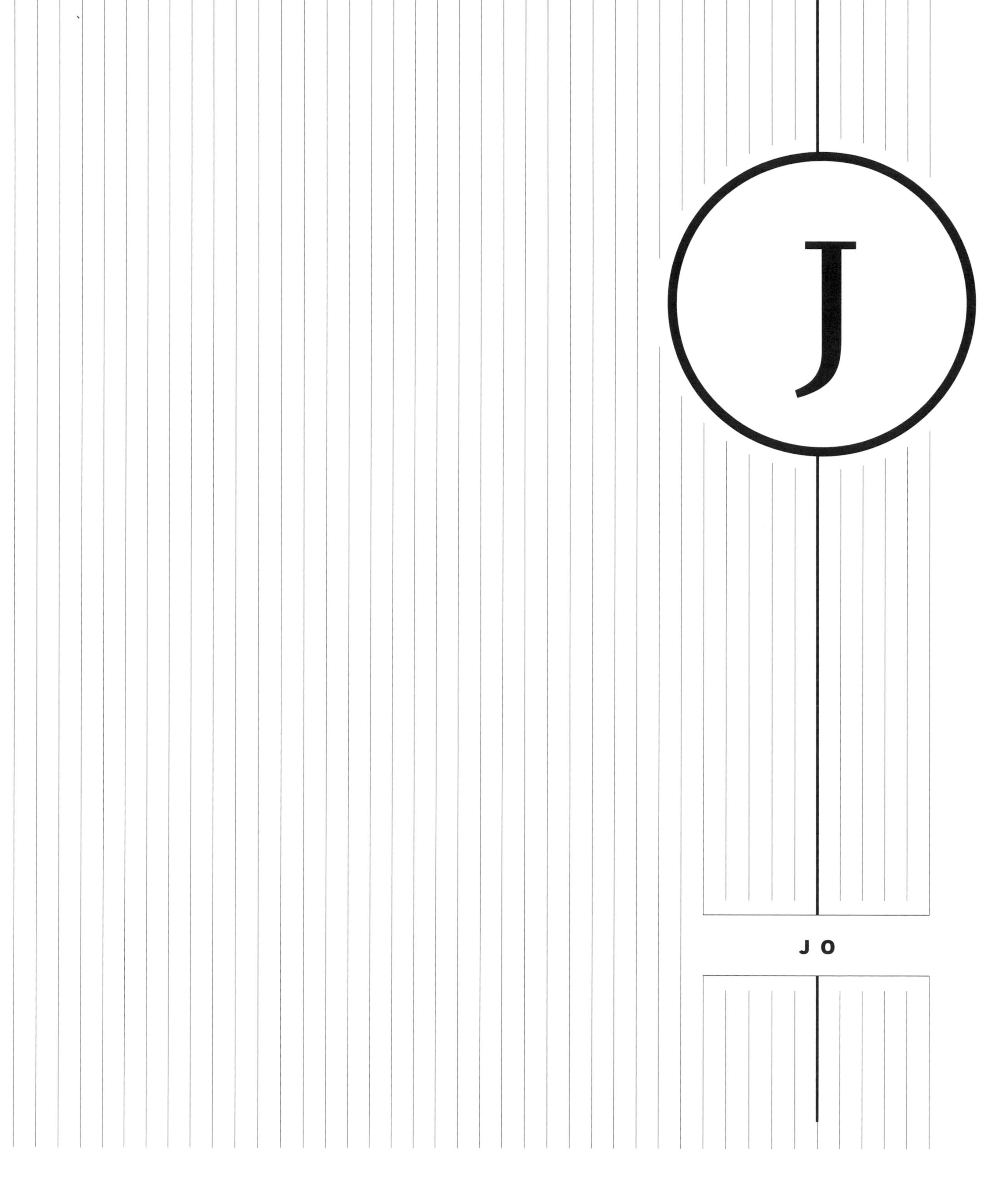

JO

Josephine Powell Collection, a collection of objects, photographs and documents related to the culture and lifestyle of Anatolian villages and nomads, assembled by the US photographer, collector and traveler, Josephine Powell(*) (1919-2007). The weaving tools and hand-woven items, such as rugs, bags and tents, were donated to the Vehbi Koç Foundation(*) (VKV) in 2006 and are kept in the Sadberk Hanım Museum(*); another portion of the collection, containing around 35,000 field notes, slides, photographs and books, can be found at ANAMED(*). Powell's archive contains nearly 28,000 slides, which have been digitalized, cataloged and made available to the public by the Suna Kıraç Library(*).

Between September 1 and 14, 2003, an exhibition was held by the History Foundation in the historical Darphane-i Amire building in Istanbul, introducing parts of the collection to the public for the first time. Forty rugs and hand-woven items repaired with funds from JP Morgan Bank were included in the exhibits, alongside three tents from Central and East Anatolia, which were unique examples of their kind. From April 30 to May 2, 2007, as part of the 11th International Conference on Oriental Carpets (ICOC), an exhibition titled, "Giving Back the Colors: Anatolian Rugs and Weaving Tools from the Josephine Powell Collection", was hosted at the Yıldız Sarayı Silahhane in Istanbul with support from the VKV. Items from the kilim collection Powell donated to the VKV were put on permanent exhibition at the Vehbi Koç Büyükdere Mansion in July 2018. A selection of Powell's photographs were exhibited to the public, between June 11 and October 21, 2012, as part of the opening exhibition of the ANAMED gallery, titled "What Josephine Saw: 20th Century Photographic Visions of Rural Anatolia"; a book was also published bearing the same title.

Journal of Ankara Studies, bi-annual journal published by VEKAM(*) since 2013. Interdisciplinary peer-reviewed journal containing original articles and opinion pieces in Turkish and English on the cultural, political and economic development of Ankara, its geological transformation and contemporary urban issues. The journal aims to collate original academic work that sheds new light on Ankara and the surrounding area, support related studies and help bring them to public attention.

Journal of Education and Research in Nursing (HEAD), scientific journal which has been published in Turkish and English by SANERC(*) since 2004. The peer-reviewed journal was published biannually from 2004 to 2009, triennially from 2010 to 2017, and has appeared quarterly since 2017. The magazine features review papers and research on new findings and developments in all areas of nursing and healthcare, as well as case reports and translations.

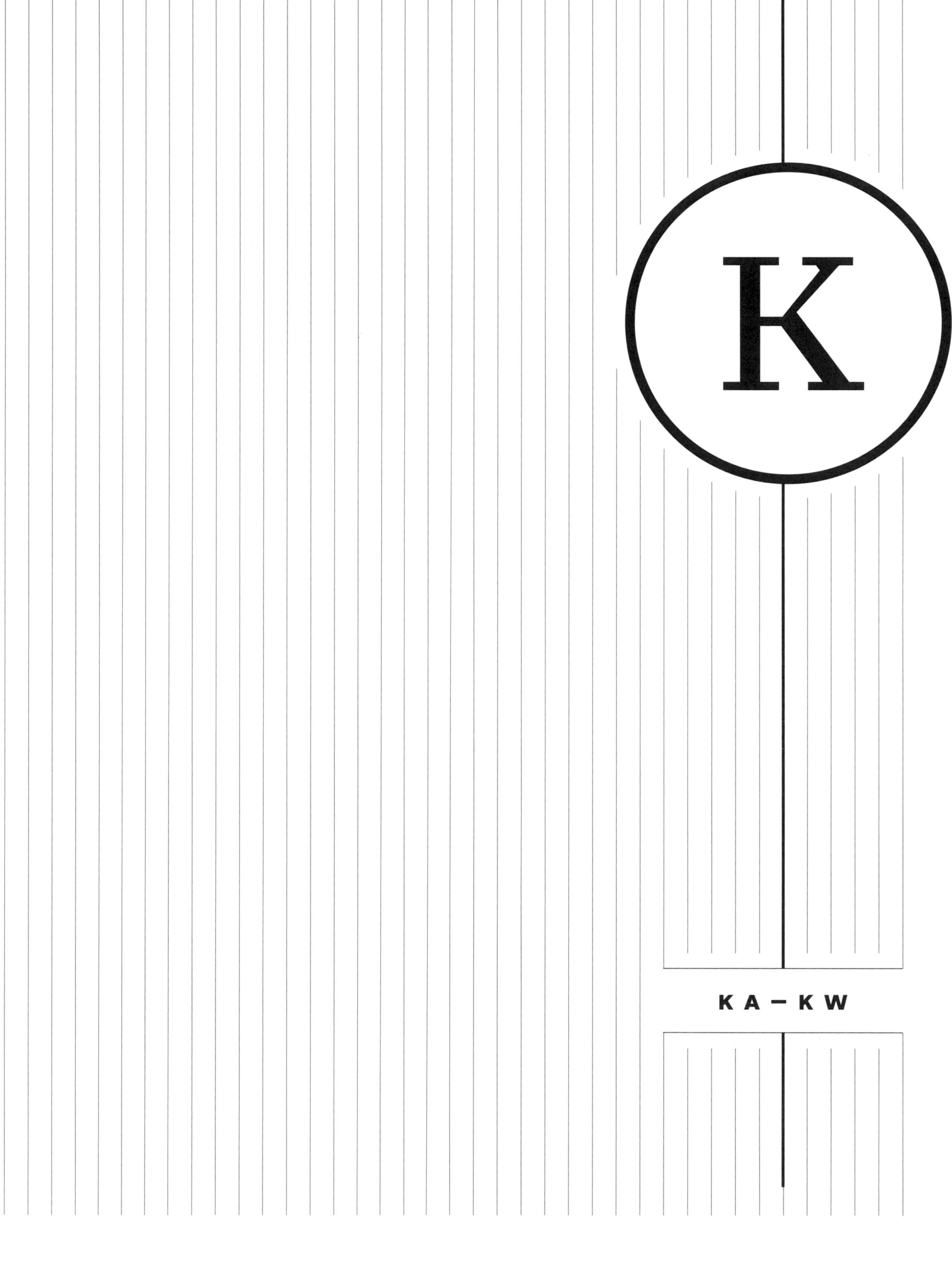
K
KA – KW

Kafadar, Cemal *(b. August 15 1954, Istanbul),* historian. He has been the Harvard University Vehbi Koç Chair of Turkish Studies(*) since the position was established in 1997.

After completing his secondary education at Istanbul High School for Boys (1965-69) and Robert College(*) (1969-73), he studied at Hamilton College in the USA, graduating in 1977. He received a master's degree in Ottoman history at the Islamic Research Institute at McGill University in Canada (1977-81), staying on to study for a doctorate (1981-1986). Professor Kafadar was a member of the academic staff at Princeton University Department of Near Eastern Studies (1985-89), transferring to Harvard University Department of History in 1990. In 1997, he was made Vehbi Koç Chair of Turkish Studies. He served as director of the Harvard University Center for Middle Eastern Studies (1999-2004 and 2009-10) and still lectures in the university's Department of History, teaching archival research, popular culture and Ottoman historiography. Professor Kadafar was a guest lecturer at EHESS (École des Hautes Études en Sciences Sociales) in Paris from 1997 to 1998 and at Boğaziçi University in 2005 and 2009. His areas of interest are the social and cultural history of the Middle East and Southeast Europe at the beginning of the modern era.

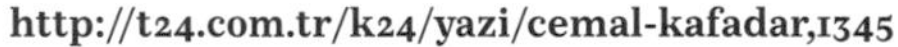

http://t24.com.tr/k24/yazi/cemal-kafadar,1345

Professor Kafadar has published numerous books, including *Suleiman the Second and His Time* (with Halil İnalcık, 1993), *Between Two Worlds: The Construction of the Ottoman State* (1995), *Kim Var İmiş Biz BuradaYoğ İken – Dört Osmanlı:Yeniçeri, Tüccar, Derviş ve Hatun* (Who Was Here While We Were Not – Four Ottomans: a Janissary, a Merchant, a Dervish and a Lady; 2009) and *Kendine Ait Bir Roma: Diyar-ı Rum'da Kültürel Coğrafya ve Kimlik* (A Rome of One's Own: Reflections on Cultural Geography and Identity in the Lands of Rum; 2017). He received the Presidential Office Grand Culture and Arts Prize in 2010.

Kaleiçi Museum, full name THE SUNA & İNAN KIRAÇ KALEİÇİ MUSEUM, a museum affiliated with AKMED(*), which is part of the Vehbi Koç Foundation(*). It is situated in Kaleiçi, Antalya in the Traditional Antalya House and the Church of St. George, both registered as protected cultural assets. The museum, which opened to visitors as a private museum in 2000, aims to document traditional Turkish folk cultural artifacts and introduce them to new generations.

After it was acquired by Suna Kıraç(*) and İnan Kıraç(*) in a state of disrepair, the Traditional Antalya House was restored between 1993 and 1995. A classic example of nineteenth century Antalya houses with exterior anterooms, the house entrance is covered in traditional mosaics featuring botanical and geometric designs fashioned from pebbles set into a special mortar. On the top floor, there are three rooms opening onto a type of open hall known as

"hayat". The decoration of hand-carved ornaments and wooden strip ceilings was inspired by the Tekelioğlu Mansion, one of the most significant examples of civil architecture in Kaleiçi, Antalya. The rooms are made up to reflect a household during a wedding in nineteenth century Antalya, using special effects to show wedding traditions such as hosting guests for coffee, the groom's traditional shave and the henna night.

The second building in the museum garden is a Greek Orthodox church built in honor of Hagios Georgios. Although the construction date is unknown, an inscription on the church itself states that it underwent extensive renovation in 1863. Following the population exchanges in the 1920s, the church's congregation became extinct and for a long time the building was used just for storage. During this time it fell into disrepair, losing its original wooden features, but has now been faithfully restored. The church is rectangular with a single nave and a vaulted ceiling, representing heaven, which is decorated in shades of blue with simple hand-painted and stucco motifs. Since its restoration, the church has been used as an exhibition space, presenting a range of art works from the Suna and İnan Kıraç collection, particularly Çanakkale ceramics. It is also used for concerts and other cultural activities.

Karşıyaka Elementary School Library, a library built by the Vehbi Koç Foundation(*) (VKV) at Karşıyaka Elementary School in the Bahçelievler neighborhood of Çorum. The school, with an intake of almost 1,800 pupils, had no library until a campaign started by one of its Turkish teachers on social media in 2012, during which 10,000 books were donated. The library was built through the initiative of Mustafa Kemal Ulusu, son of Nuri Ulusu, librarian to Atatürk. The construction was financed by VKV and the opening took place in late 2013.

Keleş, (Güven) Evren *(b. March 9, 1964, Ankara),* physician and director. He served as general director (2007-14) and chief physician (2008-10) at the American Hospital(*).

Keleş completed his secondary education at Saint-Joseph Private French High School in 1978 and graduated from Hacettepe University Faculty of Medicine in 1987. From 1988 to 1990, he undertook a residency in brain and nerve surgery at Marmara University School of Medicine. He completed postgraduate studies in neuro-oncology at Washington University Department of Neurosurgery in Seattle, USA, from 1991 to 1992, and in the following year began serving as chief intern in the Department of Brain and Nerve Surgery at Marmara University School of Medicine. He worked in the Department of Neurosurgery at the American Hospital from 1995 to 1998. From 1997 to 2006, he was a member of the teaching staff at California University, San Francisco, specializing in the surgical treatment of brain tumors. Dr. Keleş began working at the American Hospital in 2006 and served as general director from 2007 to 2014. He served as responsible director for a while in 2008, when he became chief physician until 2010.

Prof. Keleş was appointed associate dean at Koç University(*) School of Medicine in 2010 and became a professor in 2014. He taught neurological surgery until 2018, while also performing his duties as dean. Prof. Keleş has published around 30 book chapters and more than 40 scientific papers, and has also served on the editorial board of *Neuro-Oncology* and the *Journal of Neuro-Oncology.*

Kıraç, Can *(b. May 22, 1927, Ankara),* director and businessman. In addition to serving in other roles at Koç Holding(*) he was a member of the Vehbi Koç Foundation(*) (VKV) Board of Directors between 1987 and 1993.

Kıraç spent his childhood in Eskişehir, graduating from the Galatasaray High School in 1946 and the Agriculture Faculty of Ankara University in 1950. From 1949 to 1950, he was the president of the Turkish National Student Federation. On August 29, 1950, he began working with Bernar Nahum at the Automobile Branch of Koç Ticaret AŞ in Ankara. In 1957, he was appointed vice manager of the Egemak company in Izmir, where Vehbi Koç(*) was a partner; in 1958 he became company manager. Kıraç became one of the founding partners of Koç Holding in 1963, and in 1968 he returned to Istanbul to work at the holding's Automotive Group.

Kıraç was appointed to the Koç Holding Executive Committee in 1973, and in 1982 was made the head of the Automotive Group. In 1984, he became a member of the holding's managing committee, becoming chair in 1987. Kıraç served on the Koç University(*) Executive Committee and Board of Trustees, which was formed by the VKV on the foundation of Koç University. At the end of 1991, he retired by his own request, ending his 41-year career with the Koç Group(*).

Kıraç, who published books titled *Anılarımla Patronum Vehbi Koç* (Memories of My Boss, Vehbi Koç; 1995), *Anılar Olaylar* (Memories and Happenings; 2004) and *Kolajlı Taşlamalar* (A Collage of Satire; 2004), was in 2006 elected as an honorary member of the Turkish Society of Journalists. In 2013, Eskişehir Osmangazi University gave him an honorary doctorate. Mehmet Gündem published two books on Kıraç—*Can Kıraç Antika Adam* (Can Kıraç the Old Boy) and *Can Kıraç Eldivensiz Adam* (Can Kıraç Bare-Knuckled)—in 2017.

Kıraç, İnan *(b. 1937, Eskişehir)*, director and businessman who spent many years as a senior director at Koç Holding(*) companies. Between 1993 and 1997, he was also a member of the Vehbi Koç Foundation(*) (VKV) Board of Directors. He is the husband of Suna Kıraç(*), the youngest daughter of Vehbi Koç(*) and Sadberk Koç(*), and the father of İpek Kıraç(*), member of the boards of directors at Koç Holding and VKV.

After graduating from Galatasaray High School, İnan Kıraç studied economics at the City College of Business in London. In 1961, he began his professional life at Ormak AŞ, a Koç Holding company. In 1966, he was made general manager of Otoyol, a Fiat trucks manufacturer.

İNAN KIRAÇ, STARTING WORK AT THE KOÇ GROUP...

After my brother İnan Kıraç graduated from Galatasaray High School, he completed his military service and began searching for a career start... İnan was nine years younger than me. When we lost our mother in 1946, he was still an elementary school student of ten years old. Our father's death at the age of 57 was also a cause of great "domestic pain" for us at an early age...

From then on, İnan and I had to rely on each other to overcome the difficulties of life... When I was married in 1954, İnan felt like he had been "left alone"...

He seemed to withdraw into himself, and began working as a translator at the Kemer Dam building site... I wished that he would do some more serious work and be able to test his self-confidence at a more advanced level...

While I was living in Izmir, I shared my thoughts with Bernar Nahum in 1961. "You raised me, and now it is İnan's turn. As you know, we are not a big family, and

İnan is a youth of character and merit. If you take him under your wing and make him your apprentice, this country will benefit from a successful person," I said, and opened the first door to Koç for İnan...

Monsieur Bernar took note of my proposal and promised to talk to Vehbi Koç and let me know his decision. However, I was really surprised by the idea that Bernar Nahum, who had partner and manager status, would need to get the permission of Mr. Koç to employ a young person... But my surprise turned into great astonishment fifteen days after I talked to Mr. Nahum. Monsieur Bernar told me on the telephone, "I talked to Mr. Koç about İnan. He had an objection I had not anticipated; he said that it was not right for two brothers to work at the same group!" While I was searching for an answer, he explained Mr. Koç's objection. "Can is successful in İzmir and could in future take on important roles. An unexpected problem with his brother could prevent that. That is why I don't think it's right for him to work with his brother." I had nothing left to say... Bernar said, "If you like, talk to Mr. Koç yourself, maybe you can convince him," leaving the door open just a hopeful crack...

The first time I visited Istanbul following this disappointing conversation, I decided to visit Mr. Koç at Merkez Han, which was the Koç headquarters in the 1960s. My aim was to introduce him to İnan... I began the discussion by putting the emphasis on me: "As you can see, I work with spirit and I feel that you like me! My brother İnan is made of the same stuff. I believe he would work with total loyalty. Allow İnan a three-month trial period with Monsieur Bernard, just like you allowed me, and if he's no good, you can throw him out!" After I said all these things one after the other, I made a comparison that I still smile to remember: "We are fish without bones, you will not be disappointed! Please accept İnan and meet him." Mr. Koç said, "What do you mean by fish without bones?" and I answered, "We are two brothers in life! We have no-one else to support us but each other!" which gave the conversation a dramatic air... Interestingly, Mr. Koç's answer to my emotional approach was to say, "Do you not consider yourself as bones?"

Despite all this, the conversation ended on a positive note. Vehbi Koç said, "Your brother should come to me at eleven o'clock on Tuesday next week. As you know, Tuesdays are my lucky days!" I felt on top of the world. I don't want to go into detail here about how I prepared İnan before sending him to Istanbul. I will leave that for when I write the story of his life! But the truth is that Vehbi Koç, in hiring İnan for Koç, once again, showed that he was a great judge of character. With this decision, he chose not only today's successful Chair of the Koç Holding Executive Committee, but at the same time his future son-in-law.

On December 29, 1967, when Istanbul Mayor Haşim İşcan solemnized the marriage among all the family members in the magnificent salons of Çankaya Apartment, the long-time residence of the Koç family, Vehbi Koç, reveling in the joy of seeing his children grown up and married, said, "All my children are now in their nests! I hope that their husbands too will be successful!" In doing so, he sought to conceal the true depths of his hopes and joys, as if he was frightened of letting it show.

Can Kıraç, *Anılarımla Patronum Vehbi Koç* (Memories of My Boss, Vehbi Koç), Milliyet Publications, Istanbul, 1995, pp. 173-74

In 1970, he became the general manager of Tofaş Oto Ticaret, the marketing and distribution company for Fiat automobiles produced in Turkey. In 1973, he became the coordinator of Tofaş Group within Koç Holding, and in 1980, he became the vice president responsible for Tofaş. After carrying out this role until 1987, he became a member of the Koç Holding Managing Committee and president of the Automotive Group. From 1993 to 1994, he was simultaneously president of the Automotive Group, a member of the Koç Holding Board of Directors and the chair of the Managing Committee. In 1994, Kıraç became the chair of the board of directors, the highest position in Koç Holding. In March 1998, after his retirement, he established the Kıraça Group of Companies together with close colleagues.

In 1996, together with his wife, Suna Kıraç, İnan Kıraç set up one of the Antalya region's most active cultural bodies, AKMED(*), and the Kaleiçi Museum(*). One of the founders of TEGV(*), he also undertook the founding of the Suna-İnan Kıraç Education Park(*) in Antalya (2001) and the TEGV Ali Numan Kıraç Activity Center in Eskişehir (2006).

The Suna and İnan Kıraç Foundation(*), which carries out activities related to arts, culture, education and health, was established in 2003 by İnan and Suna Kıraç together with their daughter, İpek Kıraç(*). The Pera Museum(*), also affiliated with the foundation, was opened in 2005. In the same year, the Neurodegeneration Research Laboratory was established in partnership with the Boğaziçi University Foundation(*), later becoming affiliated to Koç University(*). The Istanbul Research Institute(*) was established in 2007 to undertake research relating to Istanbul in the Byzantine, Ottoman and Republican eras.

In 2008, Suna and İnan Kıraç received the Skalite Award for their exceptional contribution to the protection of cultural assets. In 2009, they received the Istanbul Tourism Honorary Award for their contributions to Istanbul through opening the Pera Museum and the Istanbul Research Institute. In the same year, they also received the Mimar Sinan Fine Arts University Special Academy Award in recognition for the Pera Museum.

İnan Kıraç played a leading role in the establishment of the Galatasaray Education Foundation in 1981 and also served as its president. Mustering the support of Galatasaray High School graduates and advocates, he ensured that the institution gained its most modern structure in the history of the republic. Through his political, financial, diplomatic and managerial efforts, he also played a pivotal role in the establishment of Galatasaray University and Galatasaray Elementary School. İnan Kıraç was bestowed with the rank "Officier" of the Légion d'honneur on December 14, 1997, by the President of France in recognition for his role in Turkish-French relations; subsequently, on December 2, 2011, his rank was raised to that of "Commandeur". He has also been awarded honorary doctorates from Istanbul University, Galatasaray University and Süleyman Demirel University.

İnan Kıraç, who also served in the management of various foundations and societies involved in education, health and sports, built an elementary school in Istanbul, named after his mother Semiha Kıraç. Together with his brother Can Kıraç(*), he restored the family house and his father Ali Numan Kıraç's offices in Eskişehir, designating it to Osmangazi University Faculty of Agriculture for use as a museum and library.

Kıraç, İpek *(b. November 29, 1984, Istanbul),* director and businesswoman. In addition to her other roles, she is chair of the Koç School(*) Board of Directors and a member of the board of directors at the Koç Holding(*), the Vehbi Koç Foundation(*) (VKV), and the Suna and İnan Kıraç Foundation(*). Since 2012, she has been serving as a board member and CEO of Sirena Marine AŞ, which is one of the affiliates of Kıraça Holding.

İpek Kıraç, who is the daughter of Suna Kıraç(*) and İnan Kıraç(*) and the fourth grandchild of Vehbi Koç(*) and Sadberk Koç(*), completed İstek Foundation Elementary School and graduated from VKV Koç Private High School (*see* Koç School) in 2002. She chose to study biology at university as her mother Suna Kıraç had amyotrophic lateral sclerosis (ALS). She continued her education in biology at Brown University in the USA and completed it in 2007. Following this, she spent a month learning about ALS with Dr. Robert Brown, who runs one of the world's most respected ALS research centers at Harvard University. Kıraç received a master's degree in Public Health from Brown University in 2011.

İPEK KIRAÇ'S DECISION TO STUDY BIOLOGY

Studying biology was the only way I could physically hope to help my mother; there was nothing else I could have done other than to sit and watch. It felt like the only way I could contribute was through biology. But of course, I also liked biology very much. My biggest lifelong dream was to work in a lab, which I also felt was a contribution to my mother. I mean, that was what I tried to do. It feels like I haven't tried enough. My ideal is to have a laboratory of my own in Turkey. I want to work in that laboratory. I want it to be a globally-recognized laboratory and I want to do what I love there. I am like my mother: I will definitely not do anything I do not like. I like biology and I will not do anything other than biology, because it is what I love to do. Many people ask me "why don't you study economics, or business?" I'm already going to carry the names of Suna and İnan Kıraç to the end. I will embrace what my parents leave to me. But that does not mean that I will do anything that I don't want to do. I will not work at Koç Holding: I can't. I want to establish my own life. I want to establish my own family.

Suna Kıraç, *Ömrümden Uzun İdeallerim Var* (My Ideals, Longer Than My Lifetime), *Suna and İnan Kıraç Foundation Publications,* Istanbul, 2006, p. 276

In 2003, İpek Kıraç established the Suna and İnan

Kıraç Foundation(*) together with her mother Suna Kıraç and her father İnan Kıraç. In 2005, the foundation pioneered the establishment of the Neurodegeneration Research Laboratory (NDAL) as part of the Boğaziçi University Molecular Biology and Genetics Department. The laboratory, which was the first model of academic cooperation between a state university and a private foundation in Turkey, is today affiliated to Koç University(*). It is considered to be a center of expertise in the molecular diagnosis of genetic and complex diseases not just in Turkey, but on an international level as well.

İpek Kıraç began her professional career in 2012, becoming the CEO of Sirena Marine Denizcilik ve Ticaret AŞ, a subsidiary of Kıraça Holding, which had been established in 1998 by her father İnan Kıraç and Claude Nahum. Sirena Marine, which was the first Turkish company to manufacture yachts on a production line, has built over 300 yachts from 2006 to the present day, at the same time becoming a global brand by blending the skills of well-known yacht designers with local expertise.

"My mother taught me to fight"

My mother taught me to fight, both while she was working and when she was ill. If there are two people I have taken as role models in life, one is my mother and the other is my father. I grew up seeing how resolutely they worked. I took their determination, resoluteness, hard-working attitudes, and ways of thinking as examples for myself. As Suna and İnan Kıraç's daughter, the more I could resemble them in my working life, the better it would be for both me and for the company.

http://www.ensonhaber.com/inan-kiracin-kizi-ipek-kirac-is-hayatina-basladi-2012-02-27.html

İpek Kıraç, who is a member of the board of trustees of TEGV(*) and the Galatasaray Educational Foundation as well as being on the board of directors of the Suna and İnan Kıraç Foundation and VKV, is also a member of the board of directors of Koç Holding, Sirena Marine AŞ, Karsan Sanayi AŞ, Temel Ticaret ve Yatırım AŞ, Zer Merkezi Hizmetler AŞ and Moment Eğitim Araştırma Sağlık Hizmetleri ve Ticaret AŞ.

An education unit which TEGV opened in 2004 at Beykoz Anadoluhisarı was named after İpek Kıraç.

Kıraç, Suna *(b. June 3, 1941, Ankara)*, née KOÇ, a businesswoman and philanthropist. In addition to her other roles, she has served as Koç Holding(*) Board of Directors vice chair, Vehbi Koç Foundation(*) (VKV) Executive Committee chair and board of directors member, Suna and İnan Kıraç Foundation(*) founding member and chair of the board of directors, member of the boards of trustees at Koç University(*) (KU), Turkish Education Foundation(*) and Robert College, chair of the board of directors of the Koç School(*), a founding member and honorary president of TEGV(*), and a member of the board of trustees of the Turkish Family Health and Planning Foundation(*).

Suna (LEFT) **and Sevgi Koç sisters**

As the fourth and youngest child of Vehbi Koç(*) and Sadberk Koç(*) after Semahat Arsel(*), Rahmi M. Koç(*) and Sevgi Gönül(*), she was born in the family's Ankara orchard house in Keçiören (today's VEKAM[*] operational center). She completed her elementary schooling at the Turkish Education Association (TED) Elementary School. In 1952, she entered the Istanbul Arnavutköy American College for Girls (*see* Robert College). During her last year at the college she decided to go to the USA to study business and finance and was accepted at Pennsylvania University Wharton School of Finance. However, her father Vehbi Koç said "My shop counter is the best university. I'll train you," and she stayed in Istanbul. Not wanting to solely go to "Vehbi Koç University", she registered to study banking and finance at the undergraduate department of Robert College (today's Boğaziçi

University). She chose her lessons for the benefit of her business experience, focusing on topics such as business administration, balance sheets and financial statements.

In October 1960, she began working alongside her father at the Istanbul branch of Koç Ticaret AŞ in the Beyoğlu Merkez Han(*). Her first duty was to look after the documents coming in and out. She joined her father at the administrative meetings of the Koç companies, did internships at different departments, and came to know the group and Vehbi Koç's working style intimately.

SUNA KIRAÇ, IN THE WORDS OF CAN KIRAÇ

Vehbi Koç's working relationship with Suna Kıraç began in the 1960s, and after Sadberk Koç passed away in 1973 they became much closer. They both had much in common: their talent for taking responsibility was similar and their working styles were very compatible. Their determination to get to the bottom of issues and problems and even their habits of keeping notes were the same. They both had the same feelings of suspicion or trust for the same people. Even in their thoughts on finance they had completely parallel thinking.

[...]

What is true is that being both Vehbi Koç's child and his colleague was one of the rare opportunities a person gets in life. At the same time, it was a "tough" kind of life! It was an opportunity, because there are very few true "fathers" left in present day Turkey from the Vehbi Koç school and with his experience. The tough part was living with it, because as long as Mr. Koç was around, there was no question of his children living independent lives and being their own selves. This situation resembled a champion sportsman being always under his coach's control to keep him in shape.

Can Kıraç, *Anılarımla Patronum Vehbi Koç* (Memories of My Boss, Vehbi Koç), Milliyet Publications, Istanbul, 1995, pp. 378-79

In 1963, after Koç Holding was founded, she was one of the first five members of the board of directors of the holding along with Vehbi Koç, Rahmi M. Koç, Bernar Nahum and Hulki Alisbah(*). In 1965, she was made the general secretary of the holding and fulfilled the role for five years. In December 1967, she married İnan Kıraç(*), the general manager of Otoyol, a Koç Holding company and in 1970 was appointed to the Koç Holding Executive Committee alongside İsak de Eskinazis(*), Bernar Nahum and Ziya Bengü under Rahmi M. Koç's presidency. Also in 1970, she took on the role of assistant director of the Koç Holding Personnel and Administrative Affairs Department. In 1974, after becoming the holding's director responsible for human resources, she focused on promotion and competence standards throughout the group's companies and on strengthening the group's corporate identity.

VEHBİ KOÇ'S "RIGHT HAND"

Suna Kıraç began to shine after the management of Koç Holding moved to Fındıklı. For years, many predictions were made about who Vehbi Koç's "right hand" was. Even if Mr. Koç had many very close colleagues, none of them had entirely earned the label of "right hand", because Vehbi Koç was by nature his own "right hand man"! However,

if we insist on finding a "right hand" for him, only Suna Kıraç could be given this title, because she had taken on the role of communicating between her siblings and her father.

Bernar Nahum, *Koç'ta 44 Yılım* (My 44 Years at Koç), Milliyet Publications, Istanbul, 1988, pp. 98-99

Kıraç was made vice chair of the Koç Holding Board of Directors in 1980 and signed off some important decisions in the transition of the company from assembly to main manufacturing. In 1994, she became the chair of the Arçelik AŞ Board of Directors, one of Koç Holding's leading companies. The technological investments, capacity increases and work on improving quality carried out under her direction prepared the groundwork for the Koç Holding brands Arçelik and Beko to become producers on a global scale.

During the 40 years of active working life in which Suna Kıraç worked to develop, grow, and especially institutionalize and perpetuate Koç Holding, she also carried out some important developments in the areas of education, culture, art and healthcare. Arguing that the philanthropic enterprises and investments made by Vehbi Koç and VKV should be directly looked after by VKV, she worked to establish a "management foundation" approach. This policy adopted by VKV came to fruition in 1988 with the founding of the Koç Private High School (*see* Koç School) and in 1993 with Koç University. Kıraç played a vital role in the determining and shaping of the vision of both educational establishments.

Kıraç also took on social responsibility in the educational arena, which she saw as the country's biggest structural problem. In 1995, she laid the groundwork for TEGV, which would become one of Turkey's most important civil society organizations working in this area. She contributed both her money and time to the development of the foundation. VKV set up the Suna-İnan Kıraç Educational Facilities Support Fund which sponsored the TEGV education park in Kepez, Antalya. It was established in 2001 and named the Suna-İnan Kıraç Education Park(*).

SUNA KIRAÇ'S VISION FOR EDUCATION

I want to re-emphasize this, that education means broad horizons, vision, self-confidence, efficiency and quality. So, keeping up or catching up with the times can only be achieved with well-educated clear heads. A modern national education policy, which is well laid-out and where every precaution has been taken is, necessary. It is the only way that Turkey's young generations can be raised well, and that Atatürk's principles and reforms can be maintained.

It is said that America will have three important sectors in the twenty-first century: education, health, and communication and the media. If we look at it from this perspective, both the state and the private sector must set aside funds for education. Expecting education from the state is not the right approach. Within the education policy drawn up by the state, education must be privatized as far as possible and become monetized. It is impossible for serious educational institutions to be for-profit. Education and health are systems that develop every moment, and like an endless well they swallow up every penny in order to keep up with the times. The cost of education is very high: I believe—and I cannot think otherwise—that this cost should be taken from those who can afford it and those who cannot should be given scholarships for the opportunity of a quality education.

Suna Kıraç, *Ömrümden Uzun İdeallerim Var* (My Ideals, Longer Than My Lifetime), Suna and İnan Kıraç Foundation Publications, Istanbul, 2006, p. 203

Kıraç also carried out many personal art and culture projects. Together with her husband İnan Kıraç, she pioneered the VKV's establishment of AKMED(*) in Kaleiçi, Antalya in 1996 and the Kaleiçi Museum(*) in 2000. In 2003, she established the Suna and İnan Kıraç Foundation, together with her husband İnan Kıraç and her daughter İpek Kıraç(*). As chair of the foundation's board of directors, she continued to contribute to art and culture with the opening of the Pera Museum(*) in Tepebaşı, Istanbul in 2005 and the Istanbul Research Institute(*) in 2007. Within the foundation's healthcare work, she led the opening of the Neurodegeneration Research Laboratory (NDAL) as part of the Boğaziçi University Molecular Biology and Genetics Department.

In addition to her active business life, Suna Kıraç was recognized for her contribution to society in the fields of education, health and social services, receiving the State Outstanding Service Medal, awarded by the Turkish cabinet on October 23, 1997. In 1995, she received the Galatasaray Educational Foundation Medal of Honor for her contribution to the Galatasaray University Suna Kıraç Library(*). In 1999, she was given an honorary fellowship from the London Business School for her exceptional management and leadership skills, and her contribution to Koç Holding, the business world and to the education of Turkish children. In 2001, she received the Foundation Associates Honorary

Award in the individual category from the General Directorate of Foundations and the Millennium Volunteers' Exceptional Service Award from the Voluntary Organizations National Women's Health Commission (KASAKOM) for her contribution to education. In the same year, she was chosen as Woman of the Year by the Antalya Branch of the University-Educated Turkish Women's Association for her contribution to the establishment of AKMED and TEGV's education park in Kepez, Antalya. Kıraç, who was awarded the title of honorary doctor by the Boğaziçi University Senate in 2008, won the Skalite Award in 2008, together with İnan Kıraç, for their contribution to protecting cultural assets. They received the Istanbul Tourism Honorary Award in 2009 for their contribution to Istanbul by opening the Pera Museum and the Istanbul Research Institute. In the same year they also received the Mimar Sinan Fine Arts University Special Academy Award for establishing the Pera Museum.

SUNA KIRAÇ FROM THE PERSPECTIVE OF TALAT HALMAN

Her most attractive side was her ability to make fun of herself and the world. On the one hand, she watched closely and knew well the worlds of economics, finance and commerce. On the other, she was interested in arts and culture. She had a great interest in theater. She used to watch plays. She had close relationships and friendships with thespians. She knew world theater very well, and whenever she went to New York she would go to the theatre regularly. She would go to the plays and cabarets and analyze them all very well.

Suna Kıraç, *Ömrümden Uzun İdeallerim Var*, p. 228

Several facilities to which VKV made significant contributions were named after her: a modern performance arts space (*see* Suna Kıraç Hall) established at Robert College in 1989, a library opened at Galatasaray University in 1993 for which she oversaw the founding, equipping and financing (*see* Galatasaray University Suna Kıraç Library) and a library at Koç University that opened in the same year (*see* Koç University Suna Kıraç Library). In 2008, the Suna Kıraç Inter-School Short Story Competition(*) was established by the Koç Private High School (*see* Koç School).

Suna Kıraç, who has fought with amyotrophic lateral sclerosis (ALS) since the year 2000, sold over 100,000 copies of her autobiographical book named *Ömrümden Uzun İdeallerim Var* (My Ideals, Longer Than My Lifetime). Published by the Suna and İnan Kıraç Foundation, it became one of the year's best-selling books and all income was donated to TEGV. In her book, she aimed to tell the story of "an Ankara family" as well as herself, detailing the mission she believes she has in life and the meaning of this mission for her country and her country's youth. She describes the fight with illness of a mother, wife and first-generation leading businesswoman who chose to live. The book went to a second edition in 2016, and a book aimed as a sequel to the first, *İdealler Gerçekleşirken... Suna Kıraç'ın İzinde 10 Yılın Öyküsü* (Bringing About the Ideals... 10 Years on Suna Kıraç's Path), was published by the Suna and İnan Kıraç Foundation in 2017.

Kocaeli University Vehbi Koç Foundation Ford Otosan İhsaniye Vocational College for Automotive Technologies, an educational institution which aims to train a qualified work force for the automotive sector. It applies a practical educational concept implemented in Turkish higher education for the first time. It was opened by the Vehbi Koç Foundation(*) (VKV) and Ford Otosan, a Koç Holding(*) company, as part of Kocaeli University (KOU).

The foundations of the school were laid in 2011 with a workshop attended by representatives of a wide range of sectors and arranged in partnership with KOU, Ford Otosan, VKV and Gölcük Municipality. Construction work was completed in August 2013 and teaching commenced in the 2013-14 academic year.

The school, which covers an area of 6,000 square meters, has 13 classrooms with a capacity for 400 students, a Ford Otosan studio with prototype vehicle production equipment and several laboratories. The school has departments for Motor Vehicle and Transportation Technologies, Machine Metal Technologies, and Business and Foreign Trade. Students spend the first two terms of their studies at the school and carry out an internship for most of their third term.

Koç, Ali Y(ıldırım) *(b. April 2, 1967)*, businessman. Alongside his other roles, he has been vice chair of the Koç Holding(*) Board of Directors and a member of the Vehbi Koç Foundation(*) Board of Directors since 2016.

Ali Koç is the third son of Rahmi M. Koç(*) and Çiğdem Koç (later Simavi) and the third grandson of Vehbi Koç(*) and Sadberk Koç(*). He completed his secondary education at Harrow School in London in 1985 and graduated with a business degree from Rice University, Houston, USA, in 1989. From 1990 to

1991, he attended the executive training program at the American Express Bank in New York. He served as a financial and organizational coordinator at Ramerica International Inc. in New York (1991-92) and an analyst for Morgan Stanley & Group (1992-94). He completed a master's degree at Harvard University (1995-97).

He began working as a coordinator for new business development at Koç Holding in 1997. In 2000, he became president of the Information Group Executive Committee and then chair of the Information Group in 2002. Between 2006 and 2010, he was president of the Corporate Communication and Information Group. In 2008, he became a member of the Koç Holding Board of Directors and was appointed vice chair in February 2016.

He is currently president of the board of directors at several Koç Holding companies, including Yapı Kredi Bank, Ford Otosan, Koçtaş, Koç Bilgi ve Savunma Teknolojileri AŞ, Koç Sistem, Otokar, Setur, and Otokoç, and vice chair of the board at TÜPRAŞ, Opet and other companies. He is vice president of the board of directors at Turkish Industry and Business Association (TÜSİAD), president of the National Competition Research Association, member of the Global Advisory Councils of Harvard University and Bank of America, and member of the board of directors at Foreign Economic Relations Board (DEİK) and Endeavor Active Entrepreneurship Support Association. Former president of the 1907 Fenerbahçe Association (2004-17), Koç was elected president of Fenerbahçe Sports Club in June 2018.

Ali Y. Koç married Nevbahar Demirağ (*see* Nevbahar Koç) on October 21, 2005; they have two children, Leyla Sadberk (b. 2006) and Kerim Rahmi (b. 2008) (*see* Koç Family).

Koç, Aylin E(lif) *see* Koç family

Koç, Caroline N(icole) *(b. September 12, 1971, Izmir)*, née GIRAUD, businesswoman. She has been a member of the Koç Holding(*) Board of Directors since 2016. Her husband is Mustafa V. Koç(*), the first son of Rahmi M. Koç (*) and Çiğdem Koç (later Simavi).

A member of the Giraud family, a family of Levantine heritage with roots in Izmir, she completed secondary education at St. George's School in Switzerland and undergraduate education in business at Babson College, USA. She married Mustafa V. Koç on July 14, 1992. The couple have two daughters, Esra (b. 1997) and Aylin Elif (b. 2001) (*see* Koç family).

Caroline Koç was director of Edwards of Hisar from 1992 to 1998. In 1998, she founded and managed the İlkadım Play and Education Center for Kids. She is the founder and current chair of the board of directors at Haremlique Istanbul (established in 2008) and Selamlique Istanbul (established in 2009).

She is also chair of the board of directors for the Turkish Family Health and Planning Foundation(*) (TAPV), a member of the board of directors for the Tohum Autism Foundation, and a founding member of the Turkish Foundation for Underwater Archeology (TINA) and the Contemporary Education Foundation of Turkey (ÇEV). She received the Women to Watch Award in 2015.

Koç, Esra *see* Koç family

Koç, Fatma *see* Koç Family

Koç, Kerim R(ahmi) *see* Koç family

Koç, Leyla S(adberk) *see* Koç family

Koç, Mustafa V(ehbi) *(b. October 29, 1960, Istanbul – d. January 21, 2016, Istanbul)*, businessman. In addition to other roles, he served as chair of the board of directors at Koç Holding(*) between April 2003 and January 2016, and was a member of the Vehbi Koç Foundation(*) Board of Directors between 2004 and 2016.

The eldest son of Rahmi M. Koç(*) and Çiğdem Koç (later Simavi) and the first grandchild of Vehbi Koç(*) and Sadberk Koç(*), Mustafa V. Koç attended Maçka Elementary School in Istanbul, followed by the Austrian High School's middle school and completed his secondary schooling at Lyceum Alpinum Zuoz in Switzerland. Between 1980 and 1984, he studied business administration at undergraduate level at George Washington University in the USA. In 1984, he returned to Turkey and began working as a consultant at Tofaş Oto AŞ.

A LETTER FROM VEHBİ KOÇ TO İNAN KIRAÇ

In a letter to İnan Kıraç, who was at that time the vice president of Koç Holding with responsibility for Tofaş, Vehbi Koç emphasized that Mustafa Koç should not be given a privileged position because he was from the family of the owner, and that quite the contrary, he would need to work in such a way as to gain mastery over all processes: "... If Mustafa is to be well-trained, he will begin everything from basics, he will forget he is a member of the owner's family, and he will investigate every task he begins down to the smallest details. In order to become successful, he will continue doing regular work, he will arrive before everyone and carry out instructions to the letter. If it is done in this way, it will be better for both himself and for his family. I thank you. Mustafa is entirely under your orders, in your safe-keeping. I wish you success."

Koç Holding, *Bizden Haberler* (News from Us), 2016, No. 434, p. 17

After serving as sales manager at the Kofisa Trading Company in Geneva (1986-89) and as sales manager and vice head of sales at Ram Foreign Trade Inc. (1989-92), in 1992 he moved to Koç Holding as vice president of the Industry and Trade Group. Mustafa V. Koç became president of the Construction and Mining Group in 1994 and in 2001 joined the Koç Holding Board of Directors, becoming chair in April 2003.

The path that Koç Holding would follow under Mustafa V. Koç's management was laid in 2005. The fundamental principles of a new strategic plan, that foresaw Turkey advancing through sustainable growth and stability, were defined as "focusing on sectors in which we are competitive, and which are close to the consumer", "achieving at least fifty percent of sales overseas", "leadership in the sectors we are part of" and "increasing the power of our brands and technology". The business interests of group companies were assessed from the perspective of various criteria, including growth potential, competitiveness, opportunities and threats, and the value reached in these areas; it was subsequently decided to focus on four main sectors: energy, durable consumer goods, the automotive sector and financial services. The largest business interests of Koç Holding were in these four sectors. According to 2006 data on Koç Holding, these four sectors accounted for 91% of profits, 82% of investment spending, 87% of turnover and 90% of overseas income.

During the tenure of Mustafa V. Koç as chair of the board, Koç Holding assets went from a total of $406 million in 2002 to $25.1 billion in 2015, while net profit rose from $20.6 million to $751.4 million. At the same time, it grew from around 20,000 employees to 52,000. Koç Holding, which was the only institution from Turkey in the Fortune 500, accounted for 8.5% of the Turkish economy at the end of 2015, 9% of exports, and 9.4% of total tax revenues. 18% of the total market value of companies on the Istanbul Stock Exchange was made up of Koç Holding companies. Under Mustafa V. Koç, Koç Holding purchased Turkey's biggest industrial establishment, TÜPRAŞ (2006) and one of the country's most important banks, Yapı Kredi (2005).

Mustafa V. Koç was a member of the Young Presidents' Organization, EastWest Institute, JP Morgan International Council, Rolls-Royce International Advisory Board, Bilderberg Meetings Executive Committee and Council on Foreign Affairs International Advisory Board, as well as vice chair of the Turkish Industry and Business Association (TÜSİAD) Board of Directors (1999-2004) and the chair of its High Advisory Council (2005-10), the president of the Foreign Economic Relations Board's (DEİK) Turkey-US Business Council (1993-2000) and Finland's honorary consul-general in Istanbul (2006-13).

The Italian government awarded Mustafa V. Koç the Cavaliere d'Industria medal in 2005 and the Leonardo International Award in 2012.

Mustafa V. Koç, who took an active interest in sports including golf, horse riding, aviation and diving, was the president of the Istanbul Golf Club from 1998 to 2004 and from 2010 to 2015.

His interest in wildlife photography began in 2006, and his work was exhibited between May 25 and August 20, 2010 in the Istanbul Rahmi M. Koç Museum(*) under the title "Karşılaşmalar/ Wild Encounters"; he also published a book of the photographs with the same title. He donated the income from the sales of the book to the Turkish Family Health and Planning Foundation(*).

Mustafa V. Koç married Caroline Giraud (*see* Caroline Koç), a member of the long-established Levantine Giraud family of Izmir, on July 14, 1992, and the couple had two daughters: Esra (b. 1997) and Aylin Elif (b. 2001) (*see* Koç family).

After Mustafa V. Koç suffered a fatal heart attack on January 21, 2016, the Mustafa V. Koç Scholarship Fund, worth 10 million Turkish lira, was formed by the Turkish Education Foundation(*) (TEV) out of donations to TEV and contributions by Koç Group(*) companies (2017). It is envisaged that in the first 10 years the fund will give scholarships to 3,000 girls who are being educated at vocational high schools. If they continue their education at state universities, they will continue to receive the scholarships.

Due to his enthusiasm for sports and his contributions to different areas of sporting activity, in 2017 the Turkish National Olympics Committee in collaboration with Koç Holding began the Mustafa V. Koç Sports Award(*) program. Individuals and institutions who represent Olympic principles and values such as "friendship, excellence, respect, solidarity, equality, and a humanitarian and universal approach" may be nominated for the award, set up with the intent of rewarding "contributions to Olympic values".

In 2017, a story and essay writing competition organized by the Koç School's Middle School Turkish Department is renamed the Mustafa V. Koç Story and Essay Writing Competition(*) in the memory of Mustafa V. Koç.

FAREWELL TO MUSTAFA V. KOÇ...

To the valued members of the Koç Group,

Every death is early. But Mustafa Koç has left us much too early. We, those who love him, have along with the country been deeply shaken. We are each in equal sorrow. It is hard to accept our loss, difficult to talk about it: there are no words.

For us, Mustafa V. Koç was much more than "Koç Holding Board of Directors Chair Mustafa Vehbi Koç". He was a wonderful father and husband, a dutiful child, a loving older brother, a true and faithful friend, a citizen in love with his country, a great philanthropist, an enlightened and visionary businessman, a passionate sportsman and sports-lover, and a leader who empowered and always supported his workers. But beyond this, he was a widely acclaimed and respected person, a modest man with a big heart and conscience. With his positive outlook and goodwill, he was an example to us all. The qualities that truly made him different were his humanistic values and uniting qualities. We can see that even as he leaves us, he has united those who knew him and those who did not, those here and abroad, all those who loved him, his friends, his followers and his colleagues; we are all united around the values that determined who he was, what he did, what he said and where he stood.

Mustafa Koç lived his life to the full with an energy that never seemed to end. In his work life, his social life and his hobbies, no matter what he did, he did the best. If you are a happy person, if you know how to embrace what life gives you and to share it with others, if you always keep your energy levels high, if you use

this energy to inspire those around you to action, if you know how to love life and create a wave of optimism around you, then you will be the sun around which your company, your friends and your family revolve: that is, you will be their Mustafa Koç. You will enlighten and warm them.

We will not forget Mustafa Koç's smiling eyes, his rubbing our shoulders, his winking from afar and his calming of troubled meetings. In fact, every day we will remember them more. He has left us with a huge hole. And it will not be possible to fill it.

Mustafa V. Koç, through his 32-year working life and his 13-year chairing of the board of directors, leaves us and our country with a huge, extremely successful and proud legacy. He last addressed us all together at the last Senior Directors' meeting. Most importantly, he discussed his own dreams. In this talk, Mustafa Koç said, "Vehbi Koç established our Group, our Holding, with his dreams. Rahmi Koç expanded our Group with his dreams and established new partnerships, beginning to open it up to the outside world. My dream was to make our group a globally-renowned company. With your leadership and the contribution of your teams, we have achieved all of these dreams one by one. With new acquisitions we have expanded our group. We have secured our domestic leadership. Today I want to share with you my dream for what happens next. My next dream: To become more important in the international arena and to carry out great successes, to take our long-standing domestic leadership overseas, to support our portfolio with companies and organizations that carry out their activities in the global arena."

Mustafa V. Koç shared his vision and his goals forcefully with us in this way. As a matter of fact, our last visit to America with him was carried out to this end, to evaluate potential investments. On this trip, I once again saw his determination in terms of his international vision. Now we will carry out these dreams and visions by keeping very close to one another.

Finally, I want to address Mustafa Koç on behalf of us all. Our dear Chair of the Board, my dear elder brother Mustafa, you have left us a flag for your vision and values, and you can be sure we will use our strength to work to carry it even further.

Our development in the economic, social and humanitarian fields will continue at the same pace. We will continue our valued projects that spread awareness of social responsibility across the country. In short, we will continue to serve our country in every area. In the international arena, we will bring our group up to the level you were aiming for, that you desired, and we will always work as best as we can for you. In the countries where we are active, your name will live forever through our company's history, sports clubs, associations, foundations and artistic ventures. But most importantly, your name will remain right here, engraved in our hearts. You have always trusted us. We too as Koç Group employees will work with all the strength we have to be worthy of your trust. Rest assured. Rest in peace and light. But we will always miss you.

You deserve much from us; if we deserve anything from you, in the name of our entire community allow us to give you our eternal blessing.

"Talk given by Koç Holding CEO Levent Çakıroğlu on Sunday, January 24, 2016 at Koç Holding headquarters at a ceremony held for Mustafa V. Koç", Koç Holding, *Bizden Haberler*, No. 434, 2016, p. 3

Koç, Nevbahar *(b. March 10, 1972, Istanbul)*, née DEMİRAĞ, daughter of Turgut Demirağ and Afet Demirağ (later Karacan), and wife of Ali Y. Koç(*), the third son of Rahmi M. Koç(*) and Çiğdem Koç (later Simavi).

Completing her elementary education in the USA, she continued her secondary education in Turkey, and received an undergraduate degree in fine arts from Loyola Marymount University in Los Angeles (1996). On October 21, 2005 she married Ali Y. Koç, and the couple had two children named Leyla Sadberk (b. 2006) and Kerim Rahmi (b. 2008) (*see* Koç family).

Nevbahar Koç is a current member of the board of directors of the Open Door Social Responsibility Association. She published a book in 2017, titled *Bosphorus Private*, written together with İrem Kınay and introducing 20 mansions on the Bosphorus.

Koç, Ömer M(ehmet) *(b. March 24, 1962, Ankara)*, businessman and collector. In addition to being chair and/or member in the board of directors of various Koç Group companies, he has served as chair of the Koç Holding(*) Board of Directors, as a member of the Vehbi Koç Foundation(*) Board of Directors, as the chair of the boards of trustees of Koç University(*) and the Turkish Education Foundation(*) (TEV), as the chair of the executive committee of the Sadberk Hanım Museum(*) and as the president of the Geyre Foundation(*).

Ömer M. Koç, who was the middle son of Rahmi M. Koç(*) and Çiğdem Koç (later Simavi) and the second grandson of Vehbi Koç(*) and Sadberk Koç(*), went to high school at Robert College(*). During his second year at high school, he went to Britain and spent two years at Millfield School. Later he went to the USA for higher education, first to Georgetown University and then to Columbia College, which is linked to Columbia University. In 1985, he completed his undergraduate education there in Ancient Greek Language and Culture. In 1989, he was awarded a masters from the Columbia University Business School.

Ömer M. Koç began his career as a sales personnel at the Kofisa Trading Company in Switzerland in 1985 and worked in the same role at the New York-based Ramerica International Inc. between 1989 and 1990. On returning to Turkey, he became a manager at Gazal AŞ, a Koç Holding company, between 1991 and 1992. From 1992 to 1996, he served as finance coordinator at Koç Holding and later as vice chair (1996-2000) and chair (2000-04) of the Holding's Energy Group. In 2004, he became a member of the Koç Holding Board of Directors. In May 2008, he was appointed vice chair of the board. The same year, he became the chair of the board of directors of TÜPRAŞ, Turkey's biggest industrial institution, which controls all the country's oil refineries. In 2016, when his older brother Mustafa V. Koç(*) passed away, he took on the role of chair of the Koç Holding Board of Directors.

He is currently chair of the board of directors of several Koç Holding companies including TÜPRAŞ and Tofaş and the vice chair of Aygaz and Arçelik.

An enthusiastic collector of the plastic arts and antique books, Koç has one of the most siginificant private libraries in Turkey. The library, which contains travelogues, memoirs, atlases, gravures and photographs of Istanbul, the Ottoman Empire, Turkey and the Middle East, is one of the most comprehensive of its kind. Ömer M. Koç's collection contains autographed original copies of books by renowned nineteenth and twentieth century authors. He also has other extensive collections including Iznik tiles, self-portraits, and the latest works of contemporary art.

Koç, Rahmi M(ustafa) *(b. October 9, 1930, Ankara)*, businessman, philanthropist and collector. Among other roles, he served as the honorary chair of the Koç Holding(*) Board of Directors, the vice president of the Vehbi Koç Foundation(*) Board of Directors, the founder and chair of the Rahmi M. Koç Museology and Culture Foundation(*) Board of Directors, the chair of the American Hospital(*) Board of Directors and the honorary chair of the Koç University(*) (KU) Board of Trustees.

He was born as the second child (*see also* Sevgi Gönül and Suna Kıraç) of Vehbi Koç(*) and Sadberk Koç(*) after Semahat Arsel(*) in the family's orchard house in Keçiören, Ankara (today's VEKAM[*] operations center). Together with his older sister, he grew up in the care of Austrian and German nannies. After completing the Turkish Education Association (TED) Elementary School in Ankara, he went to Istanbul and began at Robert College(*). After completing his high school studies in Britain, he went to the USA and studied business at Johns Hopkins University in Baltimore, Maryland. He carried out his military service as a reserve officer in the Military Academies. In September 1958, he began his career working at the Otokoç company in Ankara.

"Muster him for me, the company, and the nation"
VEHBİ KOÇ

In 1955, I met with Rahmi Koç in Washington. At that time, Rahmi Koç was studying at Johns Hopkins University in America. I invited him to lunch at La Salle du Bois, which was the biggest restaurant in Washington at that time. He found the lunch very expensive and said, "that's what I would spend in 15 days." I replied, "I'm sure you'll go to such restaurants yourself in the future." In those days, he had a fine Ford automobile.

After that trip, Vehbi Koç said that he hoped Rahmi would begin to work in the automobile business in Ankara. After Rahmi Koç completed Johns Hopkins University, he returned to Turkey and completed his military service as a reserve officer. When he came to Ankara, Vehbi Koç handed his son over to me and added "Muster him for me, the company, and the nation. That duty is much more important to me than all the money you have made and will make for us in future," he added.

Bernar Nahum, *Koç'ta 44 Yılım: Bir Otomotiv Sanayii Kuruluyor* (My 44 Years at Koç: An Automotive Industry is Established), Milliyet Publications, Istanbul, 1988, p. 80

In 1960, he moved to Koç Ticaret AŞ, which represented the Koç Group(*) in Ankara. Rahmi M. Koç moved to Istanbul when the Ankara headquarters of Koç Holding were moved there in 1964, a year after its founding. In December 1969, he took over the role of general coordinator of Koç Holding from Hulki Alisbah(*). In 1970, he was made the chair of an executive committee formed of

Suna Kıraç(*), İsak de Eskinazis(*), Bernar Nahum and Ziya Bengü, which was established to carry out the principle decisions of the holding's board of directors, to follow the results and to manage relationships between the companies and the holding. In 1975, he began serving as vice president of the Koç Holding Board of Directors. In 1980, he became the chair of the managing committee set up to coordinate relations between the Automotive Group and the Industrial and Trade Group and ensure intra-group communication between high-level directors.

On March 30, 1984, Rahmi M. Koç was elected as chair of the board of directors of Koç Holding in place of his father, Vehbi Koç, who had stood down from the position and become honorary chair. In 1988, he became the chair of the newly-established Koç Holding Executive Committee. On April 4, 2003, he retired, handing his role on the board of directors over to his oldest son Mustafa V. Koç(*) and becoming the holding company's honorary chair.

THREE GENERATIONS, THREE ERAS: VEHBİ KOÇ WAS ASSEMBLY, I WAS PRODUCTION, THE CHILDREN ARE EXPANSION

Rahmi Koç divided up the Koç Group, which is only two years younger than the Republic, into three eras, saying, "My father Vehbi Koç's era was assembly, my era was production, and my children's era is imports, exports, and opening our brands up to the outside." He explained that he and his children found a ready-established institution with strong foundations. His words about his children's management, in fact, seem to answer questions that many wonder about these days: "I am not taking part in day-to-day work. They manage the work day-by-day. Beneath them are professionals. We told them to use the professionals well. You need do nothing else and they will run things very well. Each of them looks after a group. I am happy. They get on well with one another, that's the most important thing."

Rahmi Koç described how one of the biggest problems in the global world of family businesses,

internal family clashes, has not happened at Koç: "As you know, big fortunes, big companies, big groups have disappeared due to fights between family members. Or they have crumbled and shrunk. We don't have that. The children have so far carried it very well. I hope they will continue doing it after we are gone." Rahmi Koç said that his father Vehbi Koç had taken important steps on the road to corporatization, but that there were still important differences:

"Corporatization is important. We give authority to professionals, but within our defined budgets. They don't go outside the budget; if they do, they need permission."

Rahmi Koç continued in response to my question about where the Koç Group saw itself in the upcoming years: "In order for the Koç Group to continue like this, it needs to open up to the world. From now on, our investments will be abroad, but life is not easy there. We have a reputation here: we need to very gradually establish ourselves, make investments, be successful. All of our children have that philosophy, because in their youth they worked at our companies abroad."

News by Jale Özgentürk, *Hürriyet*, January 31, 2016

Rahmi M. Koç with his sons:
(FROM LEFT TO RIGHT) **Ali Y., Mustafa V. and Ömer M. Koç**

Rahmi M. Koç took on important roles at national and international institutions representing the business world. In 1961, he joined the Administrative Council of the Turkish National Committee of the International Chamber of Commerce (ICC), becoming a member of the board of directors and chair of the executive committee in 1987. The same year, he was elected member of the Business Advisory Council, newly set up by the International Finance Corporation (IFC). At a meeting in Paris in November 1994, Koç was elected president of the ICC, where he served for two years.

Koç was one of the Turkish Industry and Business Association's (TÜSİAD) honorary presidents, and between 1990 and 1994 he was chair of the Supreme Consultative Council. He has also been president of the Turkish-Greek Business Council, the co-chair of the Business Advisory Council for South Eastern Europe (BAC SEE) and a member of the International Advisory Board of the Council on Foreign Relations. Rahmi Koç is the founder and the honorary president of the Global Relations Forum (GRF).

Under his mother's influence, Rahmi M. Koç became interested in collecting from his childhood onwards and over many years has amassed a large personal collection of objects. In 1991, he began to work towards the establishment of Turkey's first industrial museum, aiming to protect, promote and nurture industrial culture. Construction began in 1992 in a historical building known as the Lengerhane in Hasköy on the Golden Horn. Rahmi M. Koç became lifetime president of the Rahmi M. Koç Museology and Culture Foundation(*) established in 1993 and the Istanbul Rahmi M. Koç Museum(*) opened the following year in 1994. This was followed by the foundation of the Ankara Rahmi M. Koç Museum(*) (2005), Sevim and Necdet Kent Library in Ayvalık (2007) and the Ayvalık Rahmi M. Koç Museum(*) (2014) under the auspices of the Rahmi M. Koç Museology and Culture Foundation.

COLLECTING ACCORDING TO RAHMİ M. KOÇ

What is the philosophy of collecting?

In essence, collecting is a passion and at the same time a discipline. It demands sacrifice and persistence. It is a labor of patience. Things of all sorts can be collected. Not only is collecting a pleasant pastime, it also develops a person and adds a lot to his life. Over time a strong bond develops between the collector and his collection. At the same time collecting is also a matter of budgeting. There is no rule that says a person with a lot of money will have a great collection.

How did you get started? Did your family circle have an influence on you?

My interest in collecting started when I was very small. During the summer holidays when all the other kids were swimming in the Bosphorus, my mother would take me with her to the Grand Bazaar so she could keep an eye on me. During that period I overheard how the sales of antiques and collections were negotiated. The spark that was lit in me then later turned into a flame. In time I was collecting antiques of all kinds. When I became more conscious of what I was doing, I got interested in archaeological artifacts. And I began to collect them for the museum as a licensed collector.

How did the idea for a museum of industry come about?

First I thought of collecting the products manufactured by the Koç Group in a museum, but friends I consulted warned me that such a museum would not attract interest, so I broadened the base. When I was setting up the Rahmi M. Koç Museum we wanted it to have things that would interest everybody from seven to seventy.

How did you get interested in cars?

I got a lot more interested in cars when I went to the U.S., to Johns Hopkins University. I was awed by Henry Ford, who was nothing less than a genius. Later when I made a business trip to Detroit in 1956, I toured the Henry Ford Museum at Dearborn and was extremely impressed. It was there, with those feelings, that I said to myself: God willing, I too will found a museum like this in Turkey one day. In time, houses, offices, warehouses, literally every place I had filled up with collections of all sorts. In the end I decided to found a museum and share my collections with the public. That in short is the story of the birth of our museum.

Skylife, June 2011
https://www.skylife.com/en/2011-06/rahmi-koc-pioneer-of-private-museology-in-turkey

Rahmi M. Koç, who is known for his passion for the sea, was a leading figure in the establishment of the DenizTemiz Association/TURMEPA(*) in 1994 and its first president. The organization was founded to "make the protection of (Turkey's) beaches and shores a national priority and to ensure a more habitable Turkey with clean seas is left for future generations". In 2001, he passed on the presidency and became the honorary president.

Between 2004 and 2006, Rahmi M. Koç fulfilled his childhood ambition of traveling around the world in a sailing boat. During the 657-day tour made on the Nazenin IV sailboat, he covered 28,250 nautical miles and visited five continents. A compilation of his travel memoirs and notes, titled *Sergüzeşttir Seyahatnamem* (My Travelogue is an Adventure) and *Nazenin IV ile Devr-i Âlem* (Around the World with the Nazenin IV) were published by American Hospital Publications in 2009. After his trip to Alaska in 2013, his memoirs were published in the book *Alaska* (2013).

RAHMİ M. KOÇ AND HIS PASSION FOR THE SEA

After the tour, all of our worldviews changed. We began to see the world differently. We understood better the importance of our lives and our health. We learned to live together. We learned about different cultures. When we compared them to our own homeland we saw that our country was incredible. I had been planning this trip since my childhood. But for various reasons we were a little late. After this type of trip, your way of looking at everything changes.

http://www.internethaber.com/koc-dunya-turunu-bitirdi-31036h.htm

I love the sea because it makes me forget everything else. When you are on the sea, all you do is concentrate—that is the thing, you have to. Problems, crew, things to buy and sell; that's what takes all your attention. The sea is very calming, it makes you healthy, and what is very interesting is that it's addictive: you throw yourself into big winds and storms and you say, "never again", but after you approach the harbor you forget everything, indeed soon afterwards that desire to go reappears...

Interview with Ayşe Arman, *Hürriyet*, June 29, 2008 http://www.hurriyet.com.tr/tek-erkek-evlat-olmanin-psikolojisiyle-buyudum-9298021

Rahmi M. Koç has been voted the year's most successful business person or industrialist on countless occasions by various institutions and groups, and he has received numerous taxpayer's awards, certificates of appreciation and plaques. His accolades include: the German Federal Republic Order of High Merit (1982), the Turkish Republic State Outstanding Service Medal (1997), the ICC Turkey National Committee and the Union of Chambers and Commodity Exchanges of Turkey (TOBB) International Success Award (2000), the Republic of Italy Order of High Merit (2001), the Republic of Austria Order of Major Service (2003), the Republic of Italy's Commendatore Medal (2006), the British Empire Order of Excellence (Commander's Medal) (2011) and French Officier dans l'Ordre National de la Legion D'Honneur.

In addition, Rahmi M. Koç has been awarded with honorary doctorates by Johns Hopkins University (1998), Eskişehir Anadolu University (1998), Izmir Ege University (1999), Ankara Bilkent University (2000), Constanta Ovidius University (2001) and Aydın Adnan Menderes University (2008).

He took a close interest in the American Hospital, joining the board of directors in 1966. A heart and vascular surgery intensive care unit opened in 1991 was named in his honor, as well as the Rahmi M. Koç Üçağız Elementary School in Kekova, which opened in 1987. In 2016, Koç University began the Rahmi M. Koç Medal of Science(*) award program to reward leading scientists with Turkish backgrounds who have contributed to universal knowledge either inside or outside the country.

Rahmi M. Koç was president of the Rotary Club in Turkey between 1976 and 1977, a Beşiktaş J.K. Congress member, and a member of the Istanbul/Turkey Open Seas Yacht Club and the yacht clubs in New York, Monaco and Biscayne Bay.

He married Çiğdem Meserretçioğlu (later Simavi) in 1960 and the couple had three sons—Mustafa V. Koç (b. 1960 – d. 2016), Ömer M. Koç(*) (b. 1962) and Ali Y. Koç(*) (b. 1967)—and four grandchildren (*see* Koç family).

Koç, Sadberk *(b. 1908, Ankara – d. November 23, 1973, Istanbul)*, née AKTAR, one of the founding partners of Koç Holding(*). She was married to Vehbi Koç(*), the founder of Koç Holding and Vehbi Koç Foundation(*) (VKV). They had four children: Semahat Arsel(*), Rahmi M. Koç(*), Sevgi Gönül(*) and Suna Kıraç(*).

Sadberk Koç was the second of four children born to Sadullah Efendi from the distinguished Aktarzade family from Ankara, and Nadire, who was from another established Ankara family, the Kütükçüzades. She spent her childhood years in Ankara. In May 1918, she moved with her mother and siblings to be with her father Sadullah Efendi,

Sadberk Koç, 1920s
Can Dündar, *Özel Arşivinden Belgeler ve Anılarıyla Vehbi Koç*, (Vehbi Koç through Documents and Memories from His Private Archive) 5th edition, Doğan Kitap, Istanbul, 2007, p. 55

who was involved in trade in Istanbul. Sadullah Efendi spent several years in the capital of the empire in order to send goods to a shop he had opened with his brothers in Ankara and to engage in the mohair (angora wool) trade, which they were also partners in. The family moved into a wooden mansion in the neighborhood of Yeldeğirmeni in Kadıköy, Istanbul.

Despite the concerns of her mother, who was a very traditional woman, Sadberk Koç and her younger sister Melahat (Çubukçu) were enrolled at the neighborhood's Sainte-Euphémie French Middle School for Girls (today's Kemal Atatürk Anatolian High School) at the request of their father, who identified with a western lifestyle. Her elder brother Emin (Aktar) was enrolled at the French Saint-Joseph School in Şifa, Kadıköy (today's Istanbul Saint-Joseph Private French High School).

In 1925, a short time after her elder sister Adile (Mermerci) married, she was engaged to Vehbi Koç in accordance with the wishes of his parents, her aunt Fatma from the Kütükçüzade family and her uncle-in-law Mustafa Rahmi Efendi (Koç) of the Koçzades (*see* Koç family). The young couple got married at the start of 1926 and moved in to the house of Vehbi Koç's parents in Ulus, Ankara. Sadberk's mother, who had lost her husband a short time before, also moved to Ankara with her son and youngest daughter.

VEHBİ KOÇ TELLS OF HIS MARRIAGE...

The last days of 1925... I was 24 years old. As I had started work at 16 years old, an age when I could be called a child, my mind was only focused on working, making money, getting my name known among those doing the same work, and finding new areas of business. I had never thought of marrying.

I understood that as my age was approaching 25, my mother and father had decided to marry me off. At that time in Anatolia, there was a tradition: it was desirable for girls to marry aged 18-20 at the latest and for men to marry at 25 years old, as soon as they had finished their military service. The reason for this was to establish a household, so that men and women not go astray and could have children in their youth. They would want their children to be boys and four children were expected. "One for the mother, one for the father, one for security and one spare," they used to say. They knew from the start that one of the male children would die at war, so that was why they counted one as security.

One day my mother said, "We're going to marry you off". I asked, "With whom?" and she replied, "With your aunt's daughter." They had decided to marry me to my mother's younger sister's daughter.

In Anatolia there was a tradition, that may not be necessarily good, to marry off young people to their relatives so that the family fortune would not be divided, so the couple would know each other well and get on well. Sometimes the continuation of these family lines caused the reappearance of diseases suffered by family ancestors.

I did not oppose the match at all. At that time it wasn't like it is now, when the betrothed can get together, eat and drink and go wherever they choose. In those days, the engaged couple would avoid each other. A young person would only see their betrothed at the engagement and after the wedding.

They got me engaged. The tradition was to put on rings, and we did. It was clear that my father had decided to give me a good wedding because he

Sadberk Hanım with her children Semahat and Rahmi (1945)

had not given me a circumcision ceremony. I too was earning money. Our house in the Karaoğlan Market in Ankara was demolished due to a compulsory purchase order, and we had a three-story wooden house built opposite the Finance Ministry. Later Celal Sahir and after him Atıf Benderlioğlu lived there. There were storks' nests on top of it. Later, the municipality purchased that house too and demolished it. After I got married we moved there as a family.

It was decided to hold our wedding in the first week of 1926. The marriage was solemnized by my father-in-law, Sadullah Efendi, in his house in Ulucanlar and the wedding was in our house. At the wedding, friends old and young, male and female, were invited to lunch. In the evening, we gave a dinner with alcohol, which in those days they called an *alla franga* feast. The week began on Fridays. Our wedding also began on Friday, and it continued day and night for a week. Over that week, my father, my mother and I got very tired, we were worn out.

Sadberk Hanım with her daughters Sevgi (LEFT) and Suna

At that time the distinguished people of Ankara were the president and members of the İstiklal (Independence) Court: Ali Çetinkaya, Kılıç Ali, Necip Ali and Dr. Reşit Galip. They all came to the wedding. Münir Nurettin was on the Presidential Music Board, and he came and sang beautiful songs. On Thursday afternoon, the bride would go from her house to the man's house and the groom would uncover her face in a ceremony.

I was so tired that I forgot to open up the bride's face. But they reminded me, and we uncovered her face. I saw the face of the woman I had married, Sadberk Hanım, my aunt's daughter, from close quarters for the first time. She played a huge role in the success of our married life and our family harmony as well as my business life.

At that time, there was no tradition of couples going on honeymoon. The bride would come to the house, and the next day she would set to work. In the first weeks, guest after guest would come, the mother-in-law and father-in-law would get up early and the bride would serve them. At that time, working hard in the house was the tradition. Women both served and raised the children, nevertheless they were healthy and hearty.

While on the subject of marriage, I want to fulfill an important obligation.

I married in 1926. Right up until today, Mrs. Koç has had a huge influence on my success; there were seemingly endless and irresolvable problems in business life. It is very important for a man who starts work early, and comes home in the evening with a frowning face, to be met by his appeasing wife saying, "Are you upset, are you tired?" and that she adapts to her man's life devoid of enjoyment or entertainment. Children reflect the example of their parents as sensitively as a camera. That's why when raising children, great sacrifices are required. Mrs. Koç, for all these years, has paid maximum attention to these issues and as I have been very busy, she has taken on her shoulders the biggest weight of raising our children. I am grateful to her.

Can Dündar, *Özel Arşivinden Belgeler ve Anılarıyla Vehbi Koç* (Vehbi Koç through Documents and Memories from his Private Archive), 5th Edition, Doğan Kitap, Istanbul, 2007, pp. 64-68

Sadberk Koç gave birth to her daughter Semahat in 1928 and her son Rahmi Mustafa in 1930 in the family's orchard house in Keçiören, Ankara (today's VEKAM[*] operational center). As she wanted her children to learn a foreign language, she raised them with the support of foreign nannies. In 1938, she bore her third child, Sevgi, and in 1941 her youngest daughter, Suna. Sadberk Koç was a traditional, affectionate mother; she took full responsibility for all domestic affairs, and most of all raising the children, allowing Vehbi Koç to devote all his strength and concentration to his work. In 1951, the family moved to their Çankaya Apartment at Halaskârgazi Avenue in Şişli, Istanbul, both for the sake of the children's education and because Vehbi Koç wanted to pursue his business there.

Sadberk Koç's biggest passions were handicrafts, gardening and medicinal herbs. Her interests in Turkish-Ottoman fabrics, embroidery and garment manufacture led her over time to become a collector. Her pieces, collected with the rent from a piece of Koçtaş land allocated to her, were placed in suitcases and chests at the top floor of her house. At one stage, she had hoped to display the works, which had become an outstanding collection, in a museum of her name. But at that time Vehbi Koç did not agree with the idea, and as Sadberk Koç's personal income was not enough to carry through, she did not fulfil this dream in her lifetime. In a will prepared after a bout of illness in 1967, Sadberk Koç must have presumed that no museum would be opened in her own name, but asked that "the few things she had collected" be displayed in a pavilion attached to a museum in Ankara or Istanbul and that this pavilion be given her name.

In 1971, Sadberk Koç was diagnosed with cancer, and despite two operations in London she could not be saved. She died on November 23, 1973 and was buried in the family plot at Zincirlikuyu.

After his wife's death, Vehbi Koç made her wish come true. As a result of the family's campaigning, the law prohibiting individuals from establishing museums was changed, and in 1977 Vehbi Koç donated the Azaryan Residence he owned at Büyükdere to the VKV to be turned into a museum in his wife's honor. The building was renovated and opened in 1980 as the Sadberk Hanım Museum(*), Turkey's first private museum, displaying objects from the Sadberk Koç collection.

"I miss you, mom..."
SEVGİ GÖNÜL

For as long as I can remember, I wandered the flea markets and curiosity shops with my late mother, who was interested in old knick-knacks.

In these types of shops—and you'd need a thousand witnesses to say they were shops—all the things thought to be old and things that really were old were piled up in a heap, displayed in dust and grime.

In order to find something genuinely old among them, you needed to look very carefully and spend a good deal of time. Rare as it was, it was possible to find some interesting and old pieces, and for reasonable prices.

At those times, the knowledgeable antiques dealers you see today were rare in Istanbul, and

Sadberk and Vehbi Koç with their children:
(FROM LEFT TO RIGHT) **Sevgi Gönül, Rahmi M. Koç, Semahat Arsel and Suna Kıraç (1973)**
VEKAM Archive

there were no scholars at the flea market. I enjoyed this type of shop very much. To find something that no-one else had spotted, even if it was hard, gave me and my mother a thrill. (p. 84)

Sevgi Gönül, *Sevgi'nin Diviti* (From Sevgi's Pen), Vehbi Koç Foundation Publications, Istanbul, 2003, p. 84; *Hürriyet*, December 16, 2001

***

My mother was an extremely conservative and traditional person.

She was religious, I don't know whether that was because of my older sister who kept getting ill or something else, but she was a person who trusted God and always carried out her worship, but she also had many non-Muslim friends. Although she had a very soft voice and a very good temper, she raised us all with a lot of discipline. She would give each of us individual attention and was never sparing with compassion.

Throughout her life, she lived with her mother-in-law and was very respectful of my father. Whenever he left or arrived at the house, she would always meet him and accompany him in.

Throughout the days we lived together, I only saw them fight once, and I didn't know what to do. My father was a workaholic and he didn't have the time to cater to his wife's wishes, but as he was an extremely tidy person, he had no tolerance for the slightest bit of mess. He was a difficult man.

My mother took all these difficulties in her stride and said nothing. If it were me I wouldn't have tolerated it, but it was evident she loved my father very much. On top of that, there was no question of courting in that era and as my father was her aunt's son she had only seen him once before they got married.

She was very neat and tidy and a great housewife. She knew home economics very well. As she didn't know how to cook, she was continually watching the chef, trying to overcome her complex over her lack of knowledge, and she would beg us, "Whatever you do, go to the kitchen and learn some things from the cook." It must have backfired, because none of us ever learned to cook. Supposedly, the way to the heart is through the stomach...

She never related our problems to our father, she always tried to solve them herself. When we got married she put a large amount of money in our pockets. It turned out that her own mother had not given her money, and that at that time as my mother was a newly-wed she was too embarrassed to ask for money, so she had suffered for days without any. And when we were married, she gave us advice: "If you fight with your husbands, don't come telling me; you will kiss and make up, but I won't forget it." She always took the side of her bride and grooms. She was extremely respectful of them, just so we girls and her bride would be happy. She would come to the door to welcome them, just as she did for her husband. She was a good housekeeper and never bragged about it.

She made very beautiful knitting and lacework. She was very hard working and never wasted time. She followed politics very closely, and she would host all the Anatolian traders' wives with the same grace as the politicians' wives she met through her husband.

She was very interested in the garden and flowers, and especially in folk remedies made from herbs. She would try them all on us. She forced us all to drink donkey's milk, because she believed it was very close to mother's milk. She was very generous, whenever she went anywhere on a trip, whatever she bought she would buy five of it—one for her own home, and one each for her four children. She never made any distinction between us. Every child had to have everything. She loved beauty. She chose to buy beautiful things.

Sometimes I think I'm glad I don't have a child, because I could never have been a mother of her quality, so compassionate and selfless. God knows well what he will give to each person.

I don't know if your short life merited so much sacrifice, but it is this that makes me remember you with such joy.

Mom, I miss you.

Sevgi Gönül, *Sevgi'nin Diviti*, Vehbi Koç Foundation Publications, Istanbul, 2003, pp. 128-29; *Hürriyet*, May 12, 2002

"I can still recall my mom's scent after 30 years"

My mother lived almost all of her life with her mother-in-law. She had a hard-working husband who had no other joys in his life but work. He was a man who made a lot of money, always invested his money in his business and avoided luxury. To such an extent that he was a husband who could comfortably say, "I'm very tired, let's not go tonight" at the last minute to a woman who had dressed herself up, got a hairdresser to come to the house and spent all day preparing for the Republic Ball, which at that time everyone was desperate to go

to. My mother was very helpful to my father, who provided emotional support to his little sister, who had lost her husband at a young age. In short, my mother was a long-suffering woman, and if Vehbi Koç managed to succeed in building a giant business empire, he is fifty percent in his wife's debt, no-one should be fooled about that.

My father was a very neat man, he would regularly open the drawers, take the bottom handkerchief and ask for the cupboards to be reordered. I will never forget, he had an operation and on his first day out of bed, he tidied all the files; I was surprised at his neatness. My mother tolerated this difficult man. I always wonder if she was in love with this man, whom she had married without seeing or meeting. I never understood. As you know, that is the Anatolian upbringing; feelings should not be made clear, or it would be rude. My mother revered my father. She arranged the whole house according to my father's way of living. Meal times, bed times, times for listening to the news —she arranged everything, absolutely everything according to him. Even if we girls were not as self-sacrificing as she was, we have tried to apply what we saw from our mother for our own husbands.

My mother raised four children. Each of us had health problems and school problems and my mother dealt with all of them; she tried not to let my father see our problems so he had a clear head for work.

Sevgi Gönül, *Sevgi'nin Diviti*, p. 262; *Hürriyet*, May 11, 2003

SADBERK KOÇ IN HER DAUGHTER SUNA KIRAÇ'S MEMOIRS

She was a good mother and a perfect housewife. She was passionate about fine handicrafts and she loved flowers. Her life and surroundings were filled with beautiful things. She even saw the value of a tiny strip of cloth. Until the final years of her life, she would raise cows in order that we children and her relatives could drink pure milk; it made her happy. The only thing she would complain about was if we didn't give back the milk pails.

She was the first person to introduce beauty, history and art to the Koç family. She took care to live an ordered life like my father. My mother never stayed to the end of a wedding to see the cake being cut, because she used to say, "If you sleep late, you get up late and your energy for the next day is lost". She was not the boss of the Koç Group, but she was the boss of the Koç kitchen.

My mother was an extraordinary woman. On the one hand she obeyed tradition and custom, and on the other, she was for the times an extremely modern woman. She was of the type that wore a scarf to the market and a hat to a marriage. Like my father, she talked little and listened a lot. She was a content person, and she had a personality that stayed modest after my father became rich. Thinking about it, she had no idea how to cook, but she could give good directions. There was always a chef. She thought long-term. Even when we were little, she would buy bridal fabric, thinking about her "three girls". She loved shopping.

She was a neat woman. She never used anything other than white sheets and towels. She would sew her own sheets. Whatever she bought, she would buy for 24 or 36 people. She was generous. She loved giving gifts. My dad used the word "hanım" (madame) to call to my mother, but others used the even more formal address of "hanımefendi". This epithet was well suited to my mother and although the main reason for people using it might have been her unusual name, many people used it out of respect. When the museum she had hankered after was set up, it was called "Sadberk Hanım" (Madame Sadberk) rather than Sadberk Koç because of the name she was more commonly identified with. (pp. 20-21)

In Ankara, male children were more important. Female children were in the background. My mother's real insistence on this issue influenced several decisions that were made. She was very influential in ensuring we had a good education, were raised well and in later years came to have equal shares in the company. She said that the biggest problems in families came from inequalities between siblings. On this issue, she put a lot of pressure on my father. Our introduction to working life was actually my father's decision. My mother supported it. (p. 91)

Suna Kıraç, *Ömrümden Uzun İdeallerim Var* (My Ideals, Longer Than My Lifetime), Suna and İnan Kıraç Foundation Publications, Istanbul, 2006

Koç, (Ahmet) Vehbi *(b. July? 20, 1901, Ankara – d. February 25, 1996, Antalya)*, businessman and philanthropist. The first big private entrepreneur of the Republican era and the founder of Turkey's first holding company, Koç Holding(*). He was an industrial pioneer, founded the Vehbi Koç Foundation(*) (VKV), and played a leading role in the establishment of several civil society organizations including the Turkish Education Foundation(*) (TEV), the Turkish Family Health and Planning Foundation(*) (TAPV) and TEMA(*).

CHILDHOOD

Vehbi Koç was born in a summer house in the neighborhood of Çoraklık in Keçiören, Ankara, in 1901 as the only male child of Koçzade Hacı Mustafa (1874-1928), who was from the line of Hacı Bayram Veli, and Kütükçüzade Fatma Hanım (d. October 28, 1963). His sisters Zehra (Kütükçüoğlu) and Hüsniye (Aktar) came after his birth.

AT THE TIME THE GRAPES BECOME MOTTLED...

I don't know which day I was born. In the old days, they didn't think of birthdays as important. Some families wrote their children's birthdays in the back of a Quran. I couldn't find out my own birthday, so I asked my mother. She said, "You were born at the time when the grapes become mottled." When my business developed I began travelling to Europe. At the hotels I went to they would ask, "What's your date of birth?" I would give whatever day came to mind. One day I went to Zurich. I had stayed in the Carlton Elite hotel in Zurich a few times before. In those big hotels, they keep cards on their regular customers, so they don't bother them with the same questions every time...

The hotel reception clerk asked me, "I looked at your card, and every time you come you have said a different date of birth, which one is correct?" and I laughed.

When I returned to Turkey I explained the situation at home, and I added what my mother had said. I and the children thought about it. We calculated that the month the grapes became mottled in Ankara was July, and we decided my birthday was July 20. Since that day, I have said that my birthday is July 20, and that was how it was sorted out. The children began to celebrate my birthday on July 20.

Vehbi Koç, *Hayat Hikâyem (My Life Story)*, 4th Edition, Vehbi Koç Foundation Publications, Istanbul, 1983, p. 7

Aged five, Vehbi Koç began studying at the neighborhood school known as Topal Hoca's school near the family's winter house on the street, Karaoğlan Caddesi (Today's Anafartalar Caddesi). Between 1908 and 1913, he attended another elementary school in the locality. In 1914, he was enrolled at the Ankara High School (today's Ankara Atatürk High School), which was located in Hacettepe and known as the Taş Mektep. However, he wanted to start his career as soon as possible, and with this in mind, in 1916 while in the last year of middle school, his grandfather Kütükçüzade Hacı Rıfat lodged a request for his withdrawal from school on the grounds of "income difficulties".

The orchard house in Keçiören, today used as the VEKAM operational center

Can Dündar, *Özel Arşivinden Belgeler ve Anılarıyla Vehbi Koç*, 5th Edition, Doğan Kitap, Istanbul, 2007, p. 23

Vehbi Koç at the first Grand National Assembly
(SECOND ROW, SIXTH FROM THE LEFT)
VEKAM Archive

ENTRY TO THE BUSINESS WORLD

When Vehbi Koç was still in school, he regularly visited a wheat trading shop his father opened with three friends in Atpazarı. His uncle Aktarzade Sadullah was a partner in a drapery in Çengelhan(*) and one summer holiday, he worked there for five months. In 1917, he began working in a corner shop he opened together with his father under their houses in Karaoğlan Caddesi. A while later, his father sent him to Istanbul to buy goods. There he met a few businessmen and established relations that would help him later in life. Although his father opposed the idea, Vehbi Koç expanded the shop to sell ironmongery, leather goods and construction materials in addition to groceries, herbs and spices.

When 1920 came, Vehbi Koç came of military service age. He started working as an assistant proofreader at the Grand National Assembly printing press, which had opened that year, and this work was counted as his military service. Later he did military service of around a year at the Guardsmen Troop Command in Ankara.

After military service he again began to work at his father's shop. During the Sakarya War, his family went to Çankırı. When the war ended, his father returned to run the shop, but Vehbi Koç stayed for three more months with other family members in Çankırı and sent various goods he collected there to Ankara. After he returned to Ankara he continued to go to Istanbul from time to time to purchase goods. In this period, he met "Istanbul's grand traders". In his own words, "his mind was only on working, making money, having his name known by others doing the same work, and finding new areas of business."

As 1925 ended, his mother and father thought that the time had come and revealed their decision for him to marry Aunt Nadire's daughter Sadberk (Aktar). The couple's wedding ceremony took place in the first week of 1926. Semahat (Koç) Arsel(*), the first child of Vehbi and Sadberk Koç(*), was born in 1928 at the orchard house in Keçiören, where VEKAM(*) is now based. Following this, their children Rahmi M. Koç(*) (1930), Sevgi (Koç) Gönül(*) (1938) and Suna (Koç) Kıraç(*) (1941) were born.

After their marriage, his father's business, "Hacı Mustafa Rahmi", was transferred to him

Sadberk Koç
VEKAM Archive

Vehbi Koç (1917)
VEKAM Archive

and he registered it on May 31, 1926 at the Ankara Chamber of Commerce (ATO) under the name "Koçzade Ahmet Vehbi". This laid the foundations for the Koç Group(*). Later Vehbi Koç would enter the board of directors of ATO, and in 1928 he was selected as chair, a role he would continue to fulfil until 1951, except 1937.

In 1928, Vehbi Koç opened the Ankara agencies for Ford and Standard Oil (today's ExxonMobil). These were his first steps into the automobile and gas-benzine business. In the same year, his father Hacı Mustafa Efendi died.

In 1931, he set off on a tour of Europe with three friends, traveling to Budapest, Vienna and Paris. Influenced by what he had seen, when he returned he built the Koç Han on Çankırı Avenue in Ulus and moved his businesses there.

HIS YEARS AS A BUILDING CONTRACTOR

Vehbi Koç, who entered the building contracting business through his buying and selling of construction materials, undertook the construction of Ankara Numune Hospital as his first big contracting venture. The construction began in 1932 and was completed in 1933 for the 10th anniversary of the Republic. Later he would build the Cebeci Pediatric and Maternity Hospital, the Ankara Hospital, and the State Railroads Hospital, as well as partnering with the Haymil company to build the Elazığ-Palu railroad. However, he liquidated his construction business due to the low rate of profit from contracting work.

In 1934, the iron pipe factory, Koç Demir Boru, was established in partnership with the Hovagimyan Brothers on Istanbul's Golden Horn, but was liquidated when it failed to compete with imported alternatives. This was Vehbi Koç's first attempt to enter the manufacturing business.

In 1935, he went on another journey through Europe with two friends. Suffering from work-related exhaustion and ill-health, he sought treatment from Prof. Hans Eppinger in Vienna. It was on the doctor's recommendation that he decided to get more exercise and, after returning to Turkey, he tried several different activities before taking up riding as a member of the Ankara Equestrian Sports Club. He continued this sport until 1967, when he broke his shoulder and arm in a riding accident.

A LONDON ADVENTURE...

When Vehbi Koç fell from his horse, breaking his shoulder, his daughters Semahat and Suna immediately took him to London. He needed to stay in London for three weeks. His daughters were worried that this accident would turn Vehbi Koç off horse riding. They gave their father a suggestion: that they would all go together and get Vehbi Koç some jodhpurs.

"He was willing. We took him to a famous British shop called Horse and Ride. We sat my father in the changing rooms. As his arm was wrapped in a cast, we took off his trousers ready to put him into the jodhpurs. Suna and I were on the floor, with one leg of the jodhpurs in her hand and one in mine, trying to put them on our father. But jodhpurs are much tighter and narrower. While we were struggling, the trousers got completely stuck—we couldn't pull them up or down any further. My father began to shout, "Who asked you for jodhpurs? Why on earth did you bring me here? I don't want them, my arm hurts!" The shop assistant didn't know what was happening behind the curtain, but came running in fear at the sound of Turkish shouts. "What are you doing? Why are you shouting?" he asked. And I and Suna were laughing so much we couldn't get the trousers off. At this point, my father was complaining about us in Turkish to the shop assistant: "They forced me to come here, to make me buy jodhpurs, and I don't want them!"

Semahat Arsel remembers the day with laughter even now. Under the surprised looks of the shop staff, the father and two daughters got themselves together and left the shop.

Suna Kıraç, *Ömrümden Uzun İdeallerim Var* (My Ideals, Longer Than My Lifetime), Suna and İnan Kıraç Foundation Publications, Istanbul, 2006, pp. 152-53

OPENING THE FIRST STORE IN ISTANBUL

Vehbi Koç, who in Ankara had "left behind shopkeeping and joined the merchant class", opened a shop in Galata in order to expand his business in Istanbul. The main function of the shop, run by İsrail Anastasyan, was to procure goods necessary for the firm in Ankara and send them there. In 1937, the Koçzade Ahmet Vehbi firm established its Istanbul Branch at Fermeneciler, Galata in the name of Vehbi Koç ve Ortakları Kollektif Şirketi. The other partners in the company were İsrail Anastasyan and Emin Güraç. Later İsak Altabev (Altabef) would join, bringing the company's partners up to four. This organization in Istanbul would be remembered by Vehbi Koç as "Our Galata Group". In order to continue as an agent for Standard Oil, a concession first obtained in 1928, he also established the Vehbi Koç ve Ortağı Petrol İşleri Kollektif Şirketi in 1937.

Due to the diversification and development of the Koçzade Ahmet Vehbi firm's business, Vehbi Koç decided to form a corporation. Koç Ticaret AŞ was established on June 29, 1938 with 300,000 lira of capital. In doing so, he chose corporatization to avoid the problems of sole proprietorship companies. The company had two stores, one dealing with construction and the other with automobiles, and Fazıl Öziş was made general director.

A private partnership named Koç ve Ortağı Kalorifer Havagazı İşleri which was to deal with coal gas plants was established in 1940 in Ankara. In 1942, the Koç Ticaret Galata Branch opened in Istanbul and the affairs of the Vehbi Koç ve Ortakları Kollektif Şirketi were transferred to this branch. The Beyoğlu Branch opened in 1944. The same year, Bernar Nahum, who would work for Koç Group companies for around 40 years, began to work as the manager of the automobile branch of Koç Ticaret AŞ. In 1950, Hulki Alisbah(*), who would take on various roles at Koç Group until he passed away in 1975, was made general director of Koç Ticaret AŞ.

Vehbi Koç with construction workers at the Numune Hospital site
VEKAM Archive

Vehbi Koç in his office at Koç Ticaret AŞ (1938)
VEKAM Archive

FROM TRADING TO INDUSTRY

Vehbi Koç continued various business relationships with a variety of German, British and American companies throughout World War II. On April 25, 1945, he established his first company abroad, the Ram Commercial Corporation in New York. Its aim was to sell goods and provide consulting services to official delegations who came to America to buy goods, but the company was closed down in 1954 when it failed to meet expectations. However, through this company, franchises were obtained from several companies, including General Electric, USA Rubber (today Uniroyal, Inc.), Oliver, Burroughs, York, and Sheaffer.

Vehbi Koç's 52-day visit to the USA in 1946 marked the beginning of his move towards industry. Although he was able to persuade General Electric to establish a joint enterprise in Turkey, similar talks with US Rubber ended unsuccessfully. In 1947, as his first industrial enterprise, he established the Ankara Oksijen Fabrikası, which continued operating until 1955. The General Elektrik TAO, which he established in 1948 together with General Electric to produce lightbulbs, was the first joint investment made in Turkey with a foreign company.

Vehbi Koç entered the council of the Republican People's Party (RPP) in 1946 at the request of İsmet İnönü. The council was known as the Parliament of Forty. This duty, which he carried out for around two years, led him to become known as a RPP supporter, and in 1951 he fell out with the Democratic Party government and left his role as chair of Ankara Chamber of Commerce. In the same year, Vehbi Koç and his family moved to Istanbul. Arçelik AŞ, which he established in 1955 in order to produce steel office equipment, later entered into the production of durable consumer goods and white goods, particularly fridges and washing machines. He also established companies such as Türk Demir Döküm, Aygaz, Bozkurt Mensucat, and Türkay in this period. The group's first investment in tourism, the Divan Hotel, opened in 1955.

At the start of 1956, Vehbi Koç went to the USA with Bernar Nahum and Kenan İnal to meet with Ford Company President Henry Ford II. However, when plans to establish a joint truck assembly factory in Turkey failed to get off the ground, Vehbi Koç established Otosan Otomobil Sanayii AŞ in 1959. On November 20, 1963, with the

Vehbi Koç (1976)
VEKAM Archive

establishment of Turkey's first holding company, Koç Holding AŞ, the Koç Group reached a crucial point in its process of corporatization.

In 1964, at the initiative of the Koç Group, Uniroyal tires began production in Turkey. Türk Siemens, a partnership with the German firm Siemens, opened a Turkish cable factory in 1966. Also in 1966, Otosan began the production of Turkey's first local automobile, the "Anadol", made with fiberglass bodies using Ford technology. A longstanding canned goods and fruit juice production project came to fruition with the establishment of Tat Konserve Sanayii (Tat Canned Foods Industry) in 1967.

The Koç Group continued to grow throughout the 1970s. In 1970, Ram Foreign Trade Inc. was established as the first central exporting organization in Turkey. In 1971, the Tofaş factory, established after an agreement reached with the Italian Fiat company in 1968, was opened for production. It produced the automobile "Murat 124", with sheet-metal bodies, which entered the Turkish market. In 1962, Aygaz went public, beginning with 10% of its shares being offered for purchase by company employees, and in 1973, 56% of the shares in Koç Yatırım ve Sanayi Mamulleri Pazarlama AŞ were sold to the public. In 1974, the holding company, which included numerous companies active in different areas, bought the control stock of Turkey's first supermarket chain, Migros-Türk Ticaret AŞ. The group's third enterprise in the tourism sector after the Divan Hotel and the travel agency Setur (established in 1964) was the Divan Talya Hotel in Antalya, which opened in 1975.

In 1984, Vehbi Koç passed over his role as chair of the Koç Holding Board of Directors to his son Rahmi M. Koç, but continued working as the holding's honorary president. He subsequently spent a large proportion of his time involved in foundation and philanthropic work. On February 25, 1996, he died of a heart attack suffered at the Divan Talya Hotel in Antalya.

SOCIAL CONTRIBUTIONS AND CHARITABLE WORK

Vehbi Koç began his social contributions and charitable work in culture, education and health with the construction of the Ankara University Vehbi Koç Student Dormitory(*), which opened in 1951. This type of work gained pace in the 1960s, and among his other philanthropic activities in this era were: Ankara University School of Medicine Vehbi Koç Eye Bank (1963, today the Ankara University School of Medicine Vehbi Koç Eye Hospital[*]), Istanbul University School of Medicine Cardiology Institute (1964), Admiral Bristol Hospital Vehbi Koç Cancer Pavilion (1967), the Eskişehir Academy of Economic and Commercial Sciences Vehbi Koç Library and Research Center Building(*) (1968) and the Middle East Technical University Vehbi Koç Student Dormitory(*) (1968).

The VKV, which was established in 1969, marked a significant step in the direction of corporatizing this social contribution and charitable work. The Turkish Education Foundation was established in 1967 by 205 philanthropists under Vehbi Koç's leadership and made a major contribution to education through sponsoring schools and giving scholarships. The Atatürk Library(*) was constructed in Taksim, Istanbul, for the 50th anniversary of the Republic; it was completed in 1976 and donated to the Istanbul Metropolitan Municipality.

This philanthropic work also continued after 1980. The Sadberk Hanım Museum(*) in Istanbul was established to fulfil the last wishes of Vehbi Koç's wife Sadberk and when it opened in 1980 it was Turkey's first private museum. The Haydarpaşa Numune Hospital Vehbi Koç Foundation Traffic Accidents and Primary Care Treatment Facility (today the Haydarpaşa Numune Education and Research Hospital Vehbi Koç Emergency Medical Center[*]) was a VKV initiative which opened in 1985. TUGEV(*)

Vehbi Koç with President of Turkey, Süleyman Demirel, at the opening of Koç University
Koç Holding Archive

(1984; the Tourism Development and Education Foundation) and the Turkish Family Health and Planning Foundation (1985) were established under Vehbi Koç's leadership in the same era.

One important development in the educational field was the establishment of the Koç Private High School (*see* Koç School) in 1988. This was followed in 1993 with the establishment of the Koç University(*). In the cultural arena, in 1994 the Vehbi Koç Ankara Studies Research Center (*see* VEKAM) was founded in the orchard house belonging to the family in Keçiören, Ankara.

AWARDS AND MEDALS

The most important accolade received by Vehbi Koç throughout his lifetime came when he was chosen as "Businessperson of the Year" by the International Chamber of Commerce (ICC) in 1987. He received the award from Prime Minister Rajiv Gandhi in a large ceremony held in New Delhi, India.

Vehbi Koç received the Lifetime Achievement Award from the US Population Institute in 1991 in

Vehbi Koç with Rajiv Gandhi greeting attendees at the ceremony where he received the ICC Global Businessperson of the Year Award, New Delhi, February 11, 1987
VEKAM Archive

Vehbi Koç at the ceremony in Geneva, receiving the World Population Award from UN Secretary General Boutros Boutros Ghali
VEKAM Archive

recognition for his work in the Turkish Family Health and Planning Foundation (TAPV): he led the way for its foundation and served as president until 1996. In 1994, the United Nations granted their World Population Award, given for initiatives to prevent world population growth, to Vehbi Koç in recognition of the TAPV.

Some of the other awards and medals given to Vehbi Koç include the Federal German Republic Medal of Merit (1974), The Italian Grande Ufficiale Medal of Merit (1975), the Gold Mercury International Award (1983), an honorary doctorate from Anadolu University (1984) and an honorary doctorate from Middle East Technical University (1991).

BOOKS WRITTEN BY AND ABOUT HIM

Vehbi Koç wrote two books: *Hayat Hikâyem* (1973; English translation, *My Life Story: The Autobiography of a Turkish Businessman,* is published in 1977) and *Hatıralarım Görüşlerim Öğütlerim* (1987; English translation, *Recollections, Observations, Counsel, 1973-1987,* is published in 1991). An anthology based on these books, titled *Vehbi Koç Anlatıyor - Bir Derleme* (Vehbi Koç Tells - A Compilation), was published in 2018. The most significant books written about him are: Bernar Nahum's *Koç'ta 44 Yılım: Bir Otomotiv Sanayii Kuruluyor* (1988; My 44 Years at Koç: Establishment of an Automotive Industry), Can Kıraç's *Anılarımla Patronum Vehbi* Koç (1995; Memories of My Boss, Vehbi Koç), Salih Sayar's *Bir Bayilik Öyküsü: Vehbi Koç ile 40 Yıl* (1999; A Story of a Dealership: 40 Years with Vehbi Koç), Fazlı Ayverdi's *Vehbi Koç ile 30 Yıl* (2001; 30 Years with Vehbi Koç), Can Dündar's *Özel Arşivinden Belgeler ve Anılarıyla Vehbi Koç* (2006; Vehbi Koç through Documents and Memories from his Private Archive) and *Özel Arşivinden Belgeler ve Anılarıyla Vehbi Koç, 1961-76* (2008; Vehbi Koç through Documents and Memories from his Private Archive). The catalog of an exhibition held in 2012 by VEKAM to commemorate the 16th anniversary of Vehbi Koç's death was also published with the title *A Son and the Pioneer of the Republic... Vehbi Koç (1901-1996).*

VEHBİ KOÇ THROUGH THE EYES OF HIS CHILDREN

"He remained committed to his life and work until the day he died."
SEMAHAT ARSEL

One of the most important personality traits of Vehbi Koç was that he adapted very quickly to change. Other than that, he had an ability for analysis that surprised everyone. As soon as he saw a person, he would be able to make an extremely accurate evaluation of her or him.

On the other hand, he placed a lot of importance on his relationships with people, and used to say that he had always learned a lot from the people he valued.

If Vehbi Koç ever had a question stuck in his head, he would go over it and do whatever it took to find the answer to it. He made it a principle throughout his life to examine everything he was going to do in detail before doing it.

I don't think it would be wrong to divide up my father's life into before and after my mother's death. When my mother was alive we avoided arguing with him. On her death, my father's emotional side came out. He became softer, more tolerant, and had a more compassionate side. Now we could more comfortably tell him what we thought. After my mother's death, I began joining him on his overseas travels. I believe we both enjoyed this travel companionship a great deal. My father would pay a lot of attention to the people, the way of life, and the workplaces in the countries we went to, taking lessons for our own companies and our own country.

My father worked throughout his life for the values he cared about without abandoning them for a moment. He remained committed to his life and work until the day he died."

Koç Holding, *Bizden Haberler* (News from Us), February 2015, No. 422, p. 6

"His life was an example."
RAHMİ M. KOÇ

Vehbi Koç gave much importance to family unity. He put a democratic form of governance into place for us children as well, never making a distinction between us. Indeed, even our births took place in the same room of our orchard house in Keçiören, Ankara with the same midwife. We got the same education.

In all his actions, our father was selfless in order to be an example to us. He lived a very orderly life. On every issue he was incredibly well-disciplined, from his smoking to his bedtimes; from his walking to his savings... He had no tolerance for unnecessary costs. The reason was that he had seen many rich families reduced to nothing. He stayed well within his means.

If we are to summarize his life's philosophy, he used to emphasize this: "I could have lived the most luxurious life, I could have lived in the

most luxurious places, I could have driven the most luxurious cars. I did none of these things. I didn't want to be a bad example to my children and colleagues. I have never regretted my actions. If I re-live my life, I would repeat and continue what I have already done."

His business philosophy, too, was, "I may not get all that I am owed, but I must pay my debts down to the last *kuruş*."

His foresight, compliance with the law, prudence and circumspection have led our family and the Koç Group to where we are today and made the Koç name our most valuable asset. Now, when I turn and look back, I see again how correct my father's advice was.

Bizden Haberler, No. 422, p. 7

"Vehbi Koç was very principled."
SEVGİ GÖNÜL

In Can Kıraç's book *Anılarımla Patronum Vehbi Koç* (1995), Sevgi Gönül explains her father Vehbi Koç in these words: "He was very principled, very organized, very patient, adored Rahmi and worshipped Suna, but despite this he was a very different type of father who never made it clear whom he loved and was afraid of becoming dependent on anyone. For years, we were afraid of our father being in the house. Our mother gave us clear conditions. When father was at home we could not talk loudly, could not make noise, could not talk to our friends on the telephone. One day, by coincidence, I was left alone at home with my father. But that day I learned that he was no-one to fear. There were never any problems between us. Our father wrote his death before our mother's in his own life scenario. When mother died first, my father had to change some of the scenes he had written in his head. The Sadberk Hanım Museum is the result of some of these scene changes. My father wanted one room of the museum to be set aside for him."

Bizden Haberler, No. 422, p. 8

"My shop counter is the best university."
SUNA KIRAÇ

When I got to the last year of high school I decided to go to America to study business. I was a successful student, I was ambitious, and my family had no financial difficulties. So all the conditions were favorable. But my father played on my heartstrings. The year was 1960, my father was only 59 years old and he said, "I've grown old. I don't want to pass away without you." My family wouldn't allow me to go. I was very sad, and I cried. My father told me, "My shop counter is the best university. I will train you." And that is what happened. We worked together for 35 years. I am a graduate of "Vehbi Koç University". I am the first and only student at this unique school. I also signed up for what is now known as Boğaziçi University. I did not want to make do with just "Vehbi Koç University", I wanted to get an academic education. While I was continuing my studies there, I began an internship at the Koç Group. I was entrusted to Filiz Ofluoğlu. I was not treated any differently as Vehbi Koç's daughter, and I was expected to do everything that was expected of the other interns. I liked learning. I was disciplined. I made sure to do my best at whatever was asked of me and it never occurred to me to loaf around. I knew that even if you were Vehbi Koç's daughter, compliments were based on merit. I tried to be worthy of such compliments.

On October 1, 1960, I began working at the Istanbul branch of Koç Ticaret AŞ and I worked together with my father until he passed away, that was on February 25, 1996. I never managed to graduate from his university.

Bizden Haberler, No. 422, p. 9

Koç family, a family of entrepreneurs and philanthropists who played a large role in the development of trade and industry in Turkey from the first quarter of the twentieth century onwards.

The family's heritage goes back to the established Ankara families of the Koçzades, Kütükçüzades, Aktarzades and Müderriszades. The Koç family began with Vehbi Koç(*), who established his first firm in 1926. Vehbi Koç and Sadberk Koç's(*) children Semahat Arsel(*), Rahmi M. Koç(*), Sevgi Gönül(*) and Suna Kıraç(*) maintained their father's entrepreneurial and philanthropic approach. The family's third generation, grandchildren Mustafa V. Koç(*), Ömer M. Koç(*), Ali Y. Koç(*) and İpek Kıraç(*), have continued the same traditions of entrepreneurialism and philanthropy during their time as directors of Koç Group(*) organizations.

Koç Family (1991)

FROM LEFT TO RIGHT (STANDING) **İnan Kıraç, Caroline Koç, Rahmi M. Koç, Dr. Nusret Arsel, Ömer M. Koç, Erdoğan Gönül;** (SEATED) **Mustafa V. Koç, Suna Kıraç, Sevgi Gönül, İpek Kıraç, Vehbi Koç, Semahat Arsel, Ali Y. Koç**

Koç Holding Archive

KOÇZADES, AKTARZADES, KÜTÜKÇÜZADES, MÜDERRİSZADES...

Koçzade Mehmet married Necibe, the granddaughter of Mustafa bin Salih, who was head of the İnayetler branch of the Hacı Bayram ancestral line. Mehmet and Necibe's son [Hacı] Mustafa Efendi, was Vehbi Koç's father. Attarbaşızade Sadullah, the father of Vehbi Koç's wife Aktarzade Sadberk Hanım, was the son of Attarbaşızade Emin, who married Necide, daughter of Sadullah İzzet of the Müderriszades, who were also from the Hacı Bayram line.

The three Aktarzade siblings were Sadullah, Hacı Kerim and Rasim. Sadullah married Nadire, the daughter of Hacı Rıfat of the Kütükçüzades; Hacı Kerim married Halime, the daughter of Mustafa Kazım of the Çubukçuzades... Aktarzade Sadullah's son Emin married Koçzade Mustafa's daughter Hüsniye and his daughter Sadberk married Vehbi (Koç): in other words, two siblings married two siblings who were their aunt's children. Fatma (Koç), the sister of Sadullah's wife Nadire, is the mother of Koçzade Hüsniye and Vehbi.

Suavi Aydın et al., *Küçük Asya'nın Bir Yüzü: Ankara* (A Face of Asia Minor: Ankara), Dost Bookstore Publishing, Ankara, 2005, p. 299

Vehbi Koç's father, Koçzade Hacı Mustafa Rahmi Efendi, and mother, Kütükçüzade Fatma Hanım

Sadberk Koç's father, Sadullah Aktar, and mother, Nadire Aktar

THE FAMILY'S FOURTH GENERATION

Koç, Aylin E(lif) *(b. April 25, 2001, Istanbul)*, the second child of Mustafa V. Koç(*) and Caroline Koç(*). Aylin Koç completed her elementary education at the Koç School(*) in 2013. Pursuing her secondary education at Marlborough College in England, she worked at TEGV(*) and Koç Holding(*) during the summer of 2018.

Koç, Esra *(b. March 19, 1997, Istanbul)*, full name ESRA MARIANNE ÇİĞDEM KOÇ, the first child of Mustafa V. Koç and Caroline Koç. Esra Koç completed her secondary education at the Koç School (2015) and is currently studying history and the history of art at Brown University in the USA.

Koç, Kerim R(ahmi) *(b. May 12, 2008, Istanbul)*, the second child of Ali Y. Koç(*) and Nevbahar Koç(*). He is currently (2019) receiving secondary education at the Koç School.

Koç, Leyla S(adberk) *(b. May 15, 2006, Istanbul)*, the first child of Ali Y. Koç and Nevbahar Koç. She is currently (2019) continuing secondary education at the Koç School.

Koç Family (2012)

FROM LEFT TO RIGHT (SEATED) **Dr. Nusret Arsel, Semahat Arsel, Leyla S. Koç, Rahmi M. Koç, Kerim R. Koç, İnan Kıraç;** (STANDING) **Aylin E. Koç, Ali Y. Koç, Mustafa V. Koç, İpek Kıraç, Ömer M. Koç, Caroline Koç, Esra Koç, Nevbahar Koç**

Koçzade Hacı Mustafa Rahmi Efendi
(1874-1928)

Kütükçüzade Fatma Hanım
(*d.* 1963)

Zehra Kütükçüoğlu
(*d.* 1988)

Halim Kütükçüoğlu
(*d.* 1935)

Hüsniye Aktar
(*d.* 1963)

Vehbi Koç
(1901–1996)

Dr. Nusret Arsel
(1922-2014)

Semahat (Koç) Arsel
(*b.* 1928)

Çiğdem (Meserretçioğlu) Simavi

Rahmi M. Koç
(*b.* 1930)

Caroline (Giraud) Koç
(*b.* 1971)

Mustafa V. Koç
(1960-2016)

Ömer M.Koç
(*b.* 1962)

Esra Koç
(*b.* 1997)

Aylin E. Koç
(*b.* 2001)

Kütükçüzade Nadire (*d.* 1957) — **Sadullah Aktar** (1880-1925)

Emin Aktar (1905-1989)

Melahat Çubukçu (1912-1989)

Adile Mermerci (*d.* 1995)

Sadberk Koç (1908—1973)

Sevgi (Koç) Gönül (1938—2003) — **Erdoğan Gönül** (1933—2003)

Suna (Koç) Kıraç (*b.* 1941) — **İnan Kıraç** (*b.* 1937)

Ali Y. Koç (*b.* 1967) — **Nevbahar (Demirağ) Koç** (*b.* 1972)

İpek Kıraç (*b.* 1984)

Leyla S. Koç (*b.* 2006)

Kerim R. Koç (*b.* 2008)

Koç Family Galleries of Ottoman Art at the Metropolitan Museum, two galleries in the Metropolitan Museum Islamic Arts Section in New York, established in 2009 with the support of the Vehbi Koç Foundation(*) (VKV) and named after the Koç family(*). For its 40th anniversary, the VKV donated 10 million dollars to expand, redesign,

Metropolitan Museum, Gallery 459
http://www.artnet.com/magazineus/features/saltz/metropolitan-museum-islamic-art-11-4-11_detail.asp?picnum=7

and renovate the galleries. Koç family members attended the opening ceremony in the Metropolitan Museum on November 1, 2011. The first exhibitions were "Carpets, Textiles, and the Greater Ottoman World" in Gallery 459 and "Ottoman Palace Arts (14th-20th centuries)" in Gallery 460. The gallery, which reflects the multi-layered society and art of the Ottoman era, will carry the Koç name for 75 years.

Koç Group, a term referring to companies in Koç Holding(*) as well as institutions such as the Vehbi Koç Foundation(*), Koç University(*), and Koç School(*). It is also used to describe companies in the Koç Group which existed prior to the foundation of Koç Holding in 1963.

Koç Holding, full name KOÇ HOLDİNG ANONİM ŞİRKETİ, the first holding and the largest group of private companies in Turkey. Founded by Vehbi Koç(*) in 1963, it has been a pioneering force in Turkey. Its headquarters are in Nakkaştepe, Üsküdar district, Istanbul (*see* Koç Holding AŞ Headquarters at Nakkaştepe).

HISTORY

In 1916, Vehbi Koç began working in a corner store belonging to his father, Hacı Mustafa Rahmi Efendi. In 1926, his father, transferred the Koçzade Hacı Mustafa Rahmi company to him and on May

31, 1926, it was registered with the Ankara Chamber of Commerce under the name Koçzade Ahmet Vehbi. The history of Koç Holding can be traced back to the founding of this company, which over time expanded its lines of business. Influenced by the development works in Ankara at the time, the company turned its attention towards construction materials and hardware. In 1928, it entered into a distributorship agreement with Ford and began trading in automobiles. In the same year, it became a franchise for Standard Oil and began dealing in gas and petroleum. As business developed in

Ankara, another branch was opened in Istanbul. An important development during this time was the dawn of contracting work, which began with the construction of Numune Hospital in Ankara. In 1937, the Istanbul branch was transformed into the Vehbi Koç ve Ortakları Kolektif Şirketi later known as the Galata Group. Turkey's first joint stock company, Koç Ticaret AŞ, was founded in Ankara in 1938 and the Galata Group became the company's Istanbul branch in 1942. Koç Ticaret was unique in being the first Turkish company to allow its workers to have a share in its profits.

After World War II, the Koç Group(*) began to focus on manufacturing. As well as expanding his business horizons, Vehbi Koç's travels in Europe and America marked the beginning of efforts to meet Turkey's science and technology deficit through licensing agreements. The first Turkish company based in the USA, Ram Commercial Corporation, was founded in 1945 in order to establish ties with American companies by purchasing franchises. Following Vehbi Koç's trip to the USA in 1946, Turkey's first light bulb factory was founded in partnership with General Electric in 1948.

In the 1950s, the Koç Group ventured into import substitution manufacturing investment. It began establishing production companies to secure foreign exchange savings and create a network of distributors nationwide. Turkey's first radiator manufacturer, Türk Demir Döküm, and first refrigerator manufacturer, Arçelik, were established during this period. This was followed in the early 1960s by the foundation of Gazal and Aygaz, liquid petroleum production and distribution companies, and the tire manufacturer Uniroyal. The group's first investment in tourism was the Divan Hotel, which opened in 1956.

As the number of Koç Group companies operating in a number of sectors increased, the need arose for a new organization that suited its diversity and rate of growth. In response to this need, Koç Holding AŞ was founded in 1963 to act as a decision-making body for the group and lead efforts to strategize, supervise, coordinate and provide guidance. The board of directors was chaired by Vehbi Koç. This was a significant step towards developing the Koç Group into a corporate entity. The Vehbi Koç Foundation(*) (VKV), which Vehbi Koç hoped to make into a shareholder and found together with the holding, was not established until 1969, following the new law on foundations in 1967.

VEHBİ KOÇ'S OPENING REMARKS ON THE FIRST GENERAL MEETING OF KOÇ HOLDING

(February 24, 1964, Merkez Han, Beyoğlu, Istanbul)

Dear shareholders,

It is 3 p.m. on Monday, February 24th. We gathered here for a meeting of the general board of Koç Holding, which was announced in the Commercial Registry Gazette on December 11, 1963: a company with a history of twenty days as of New Year. I would like to take this occasion to share some words with you.

This is the most important moment of my commercial career.

In the autumn of 1916, we set to work on my father's behalf as Koçzade Hacı Mustafa Rahmi with a 120 lira fund, selling groceries at Karaoğlan Bazaar. As the years passed, the shop changed its line of business and in 1926, it was transferred to me by my late father who believed I could do the job. It was registered with the Chamber of Commerce and I began working as Koçzade Ahmet Vehbi.

My business progressed year by year and so I decided to make it a joint stock company. After consulting some expert friends, eleven years after taking the company on, I founded Koç Ticaret A.Ş. in July 1937. Our company continued to grow a little more every year with the support of valued colleagues and we established joint stock and limited companies with the profits.

On the one hand I was working and on the other, I was scrutinizing the state of companies that had been established before mine, both at home and abroad. A large number of companies founded in Turkey before

and during my lifetime, organizations such as Abdurrahman Naci Demirağ, Bekir Kara, Avunduk and Ali Albayrak, fell apart following the deaths of their founders.

I observed how large European companies had managed to stay on their feet for many years. I came to the conclusion that the best thing to do would be to ensure that the business could exist without me. From 1948 onwards, I had our financial and judicial laws analyzed.

As the establishment of a foundation that contained the holding didn't comply with our civil law, we tried for years to get a special law passed rather than setting up a holding liable to double corporation tax, but to no avail. Eventually, in 1961, the situation was resolved, we accelerated our attempts to establish a holding and finally succeeded.

We will only be able to establish the foundation we envisage if a special law is introduced. Until that time, philanthropic work will continue with the revenue from stocks worth five million lira, which are from my own shares in the holding.

Our most important intentions in founding the holding are:

- To ensure that after my death, this organization, which so much work has gone into, will continue.

- Binding those who work in the company today, and who will work in the company in the future, to the organization by selling them shares.

- Providing for the futures of those who leave the company by recognizing the value of social issues within the holding.

Personally, I am very happy to be establishing the holding. Today, the board consists of 48 founding partners in this building, in the future there will be thousands. Koç Holding will continue to grow and be the largest private sector organization in Turkey. The public and the government will see how beneficial it is to the country and keep hold of it. But what matters more than all of this is that it will be an example for those who come after us, many more holdings will be established, and this country will continue to progress.

Take the balance sheet from global company Siemens for its first year of operations. Like us, it began with a fund that was small by the standards of the day. We also began with a small fund and we, too, are progressing.

When the holding was founded, with the exception of a few acquaintances, I received support from a large number of people. I would like to thank them.

People are mortal. One day, I will leave the business for some reason or another. Up to ten years after the founding of the holding, many important duties will fall to my wife, my children, my sons-in-law and the incumbent administrative colleagues.

From the age of 17, I worked day and night for 46 years, and this is where I have arrived. Now I am handing it over to you. If you want me to rest in peace, you must carry this organization on. It must not fall apart due to petty whims.

Don't bring in talentless, incapable men who are slaves to their personal opinions and caprices. The success of all companies is carried on the shoulders of capable people. Companies we work with today, such as Ford, Siemens and General Electric, are the best examples of this.

Follow the same path as these companies.

It has taken me 10 years to achieve the ideas that came to me during the Yalova meeting in 1954. And I am very grateful. There's still plenty of work to do within the company. And it's our duty to effect this as soon as we can.

I'd like to end by offering you all my respect and affection.

Vehbi Koç, *Hayat Hikâyem* (*My Life Story*), 4th Edition, Vehbi Koç Foundation Publications, Istanbul, 1983, pp. 94-101

A portion of Aygaz and Koç Holding shares were sold to those working in the Koç Group so that public savings could be invested and contribute to capital accumulation. In one sense, this was the first instance of public offering in Turkey. In late 1973, 56% of Koç Yatırım ve Sanayi Mamulleri Pazarlama AŞ was offered to the public.

In the 1960s, the Koç Group founded various industrial plants through collaboration or partnership with foreign companies. Companies established in this period were (Ford) Otosan, which would later become a partnership with Ford; Tofaş, founded in partnership with Fiat; Türk Siemens founded in partnership with Siemens, and Mako, founded in partnership with Magneti Marelli. The first automobile to be produced locally, the Anadol, was manufactured during this period. The group entered the food industry with Tat Konserve. On the other hand, enhancing its companies' technology, know-how and experience through various license agreements, the group was later able to create its own technology.

In the 1970s, Koç Holding's fields of operation expanded significantly. The group was able to operate in a wide range of areas, from automotive to white goods, agricultural equipment to textiles, liquid petroleum gas to heating equipment, from the food industry and retail to tourism, finance and insurance services. The automotive companies Otokar and Karsan also joined the group during this period. From 1970 onwards, taking economic necessities and competition with the Common Market into consideration, the group moved towards exporting and founded Turkey's first foreign trading company, Ram Foreign Trade.

During the 1980s, the holding developed its banking operations. Koç American Bank was founded in partnership with the American Express Company in 1986 and later became a wholly-owned subsidiary, renamed Koçbank in 1993.

Believing in corporatization, in 1984 Vehbi Koç transferred the chair of the holding's board of directors to his son, Rahmi M. Koç(*), but continued to serve as honorary chair.

In 1990, Ram Foreign Trade became the first Turkish exporting company to exceed 500 million US dollars, while Arçelik became one of the largest manufacturers of white goods in Europe. The 2000s began with the vision of "becoming one of the world's leading companies". This vision relied on a focus on the energy, consumer durables, automotive and financial services sectors. It was in this context that Koç Finansal Hizmetler was founded in 2001, in partnership with one of Europe's leading banks, UniCredito Italiano.

Rahmi M. Koç passed the role of chair of the board on to Mustafa V. Koç(*) in April 2003, but continued to serve as honorary chair and remained a member of the board of directors. One of the most significant developments in this new era was the entry of two new companies to the holding in 2005: TÜPRAŞ, the largest industrial enterprise in Turkey, and Yapı Kredi Bank. The merger between Yapı Kredi and Koçbank in 2006 led to Yapı Kredi Bank becoming the fourth largest bank in Turkey. Ömer M. Koç became chair of the board of directors following the death of Mustafa V. Koç on January 21, 2016.

KOÇ HOLDING TODAY

Koç Holding operates across a number of fields, including energy, automotive, consumer durables, finance, food, retail, construction, tourism, transportation, defense and information technology. Foreign companies in partnership with holding companies are: Ford Motor Co. (US), LG Electronics (South Korea), UniCredit Group (Italy), Fiat Auto SPA (Italy), Fuchs Petrolub AG (Germany), B&Q (England), CNH Industrial NV (Italy) and Voltas (India). CEO of Koç Holding Levent Çakıroğlu(*) described the cornerstones of the group's current strategy for 2018 as: "expanding our global presence, increasing competitiveness, developing our technology and innovative capabilities and creating powerful brands".

KOÇ HOLDING COMPANIES (2018)

Consumer Durables Group
Arçelik AŞ
Arçelik LG Klima San. Tic. AŞ
Beko A and NZ Pty Ltd. (Australia)
Beko Deutschland GMBH
Beko Egypt Trading LLC (Egypt)
Beko Electrical Appliances Co. Ltd. (China)
Beko Electronics Espana SL
Beko France SAS
Beko Italy SRL
Beko LLC (Russia)
Beko PLC (United Kingdom)
Beko SA (Poland)
Beko SA Cesko (Czech Republic)
Beko Shanghai Trading Co. (China)
Beko Slovakia SRO
Beko Ukraine LLC
Defy Appliances (Pty) Ltd.
Elektra Bregenz AG
Grundig Intermedia GmbH
SC Arctic SA

Energy Group
Akpa AŞ
Aygaz AŞ
Aygaz Doğal Gaz Toptan Satış AŞ
Demir Export AŞ
Ditaş Deniz İşletmeciliği ve Tankerciliği AŞ
Entek Elektrik Üretimi AŞ
Opet Fuchs Madeni Yağ AŞ
Opet International London Ltd.
Opet Petrolcülük AŞ
Opet Trade (Singapore) Pte. Ltd.
THY-Opet Havacılık Yakıtları AŞ
TÜPRAŞ-Türkiye Petrol Rafinerileri AŞ

Finance Group
Koç Finansman AŞ
Yapı Kredi Bank Azerbaijan
Yapı Kredi Bank Moscow
Yapı Kredi Bank Nederland NV
Yapı Kredi Faktoring AŞ
Yapı Kredi Finansal Kiralama AO

Yapı Kredi Portföy Yönetimi AŞ
Yapı Kredi Yatırım Menkul Değerler AŞ
Yapı Kredi-Koray Gayrimenkul Yatırım Ortaklığı AŞ
Yapı ve Kredi Bankası AŞ

Automotive Group
Ford Otomotiv Sanayii AŞ
Koç Fiat Kredi Finansman AŞ
Otokar Otomotiv ve Savunma Sanayii AŞ
Otokoç Otomotiv Tic. ve San. AŞ
Otokoç Sigorta Aracılık Hizmetleri AŞ
Tofaş Türk Otomobil Fabrikası AŞ
Türk Traktör ve Ziraat Makinaları AŞ

Other Sector Companies
Ark İnşaat AŞ
Bilkom AŞ
Divan Turizm İşletmeleri AŞ
Düzey Tüketim Malları Sanayi Pazarlama ve Ticaret AŞ
Inventram AŞ
Koç Bilgi ve Savunma Teknolojileri AŞ
Koç Sistem Bilgi ve İletişim Hizmetleri AŞ
Koçtaş Yapı Malzemeleri AŞ
Marmaris Altınyunus AŞ
Ram Foreign Trade Inc.
RMK Marine Gemi Yapım Sanayii ve Deniz Taşımacılığı İşletmesi AŞ
Setair Hava Taşımacılığı ve Hizmetleri AŞ
Setur Servis Turistik AŞ
Tanı Pazarlama ve İletişim Hizmetleri AŞ
Tat Gıda Sanayi
Tek-Art Kalamış ve Fenerbahçe Turizm Tesisleri AŞ
Yapı Kredi Kültür ve Sanat Yayıncılık Ticaret ve Sanayi AŞ
Zer Merkezi Hizmetler AŞ

In 1995, Koç Holding appeared for the first time on *Fortune* magazine's list of the 500 largest global companies; the holding has featured on the list every year, except for the 1998-2004 period, and is today the only company in Turkey on the list. Among the first five entries on the Istanbul Chamber of Industry's (İSO) list of the largest industrial enterprises in Turkey in 2017, four were companies affiliated with Koç Holding (TÜPRAŞ, Ford Otosan, Tofaş, Arçelik). On the 2017 list prepared by the Turkish Exporters Assembly, the 10 largest exporting houses included four companies associated with the holding. With over 11,000 distributors and service points nationwide, the number of people working for the holding reached almost 94,000 and total assets climbed to 27.6 billion US dollars. Total turnover for 2017 was 7% of GDP and exports constituted 10% of Turkey's total exports. The market value of the holding companies on the Istanbul Stock Exchange amounted to nearly 19% of the total value. The holding's total foreign income for the same year was around 17.9 billion US dollars.

As part of the Turkish Transparency and Disclosure Research carried out between 2005 and 2008 by Sabancı University Corporate Governance Forum and Standard and Poor's, Koç Holding was found to be among the top five most transparent companies in Turkey every year. The holding featured alongside three group companies on the European Commission's list of the top 2,500 companies investing in research and development, making up 10% of total research and development investments in the Turkish private sector.

After signing the United Nations Global Compact Agreement in 2006, the concept of responsible citizenship embraced by Koç Holding took on an international dimension as official policy. The For My Country project, which began in the same year, reflects the holding's understanding of social responsibility and aims to popularize the approach among Koç Group companies, workers, distributors and suppliers. As part of the project, the holding chose "Societal Gender Equality" as its theme for the 2015-17 period, earning a place on the list of "10 Influential Leaders" compiled by UN Women. The Vocational Education: A Crucial Matter for the Nation(*) project, run from 2006 to 2013, was a collaboration between Koç Holding and the Ministry of Education, supported by the VKV. It received numerous national and international awards for corporate social responsibility.

Koç Holding AŞ Headquarters at Nakkaştepe, a group of buildings housing the central administration of Koç Holding(*) and the Vehbi Koç Foundation(*) (VKV). The site is in the İcadiye neighborhood of Nakkaştepe on the edge of Kuzguncuk district in Üsküdar, Istanbul.

The current location of the facility was once the site of a mansion, thought to have been built in the early twentieth century and given as a wedding present by Sultan Abdulaziz (r. 1861-76) in 1901 to his youngest daughter, Emine Sultan (1873-1920) when she married Mehmed Şerif Pasha (Çavdaroğlu) (1873-1958), the governor of Istanbul. The mansion, known during that time as the Emine Sultan Mansion or Palace, had a large,

beautiful pool and was surrounded by high walls with doors opening onto all the surrounding streets from the grove-style garden. The main door was on the side of Nakkaştepe Elementary School, its outbuildings and stables overlooked the street, Aziz Bey Sokağı. The mansion was used by Emine Sultan and her husband as a summer house until her death in 1920. It was inherited by Mehmed Şerif Pasha after Emine Sultan's death. It was used as a school for a time after Mehmed Şerif Pasha was exiled together with other members of the Ottoman dynasty in 1924. It was severely damaged by a fire in 1935.

Known as the Mehmed Şerif Pasha Mansion, the building and its 23,219 square meters of grounds were acquired by the Koç Group(*) in 1978. The architect Sedad Hakkı Eldem(*) drew up a restoration project (1978-1987) to enable the site to be used as the headquarters of Koç Holding. Between 1986 and 1988, it was faithfully restored by Garanti İnşaat AŞ based on Eldem's project. It was recreated referencing information taken from old photographs and archives, and using remnants of the stables, head coachman's building, the *ağa dairesi* (agha's quarters), the *selamlık* (men's quarters) and harem.

Koç Holding and VKV moved into the new facilities in September 1988, having previously operated from a building in Fındıklı, Kabataş since 1967. The facility, which covers a total area of 11,500 square meters, comprises six main buildings: the Old Selamlık Building, housing the CEO, CFO, and chief offices of the Tourism, Food, Retail, Automotive, Defense Industry, Other Automotive and Information Group, Energy, Consumer Durables, Banking and Insurance, and Audit Group, together with the directorates of Corporate Communication, External Affairs and Human Resources; the Old Harem Building, housing the offices of the late Vehbi Koç(*), of Rahmi M. Koç(*), honorary chair of the Koç Holding Board of Directors and of the late Mustafa V. Koç(*), former chair of the board of directors, as well as the offices of the late Sevgi Gönül(*) and Suna Kıraç(*), and the Legal Consultancy Department; the Ağa Dairesi, housing the Koç Holding cafeteria and a venue for various social events and meetings; the Old Hammam Building, housing the office of the Strategic Planning Coordination and the Nakkaştepe branch of Yapı Kredi Bank; the Stables, housing the office of Ömer M. Koç, chair of the Koç Holding Board of Directors, the Accounting Directorate, and the office of the Information Services Coordination and Audit Group; and the former Head Coachman's Building, housing the Office Management staff.

The Nakkaştepe facilities received the Europa Nostra Award in 1990 for "faithful restoration and renovation" (*see* Europa Nostra Awards).

THE STORY OF KOÇ HOLDING AND THE VKV'S MOVE TO THE NAKKAŞTEPE FACILITY IN THE WORDS OF CAN KIRAÇ

On the morning of September 13, 1988, after performing the morning prayer, Vehbi Koç was praying that Nakkaştepe would bring good fortune to the Koç family and the Koç group...

That same morning, at 9:30 a.m., members of the Koç family, including Vehbi Koç, and Koç Holding employees were on a marble terrace, participating in a "sacrifice ceremony" and "prayers" to celebrate the opening of the Nakkaştepe facility.

Koç Holding became a legal entity on November 20, 1963; from November 20, 1963 to December 24, 1967 (four years and one month) it was based at Merkez Han in Galatasaray, it was then based in a building in Fındıklı, Kabataş, from December 15, 1967 to August 20, 1988 (twenty years and eight months).

The Koç Holding Nakkaştepe facility, from start to finish, owes its existence to the vision, stubborn persistence and perseverance of Rahmi Koç... Uğur Ekşioğlu worked hard to purchase the land and Tezcan Yaramancı put a lot of effort into the construction work...

The workforce at Koç Holding, which directs the operations of the Koç Group companies and determines its new developments, now has a calm, classic and contemporary working environment.

During the 28-month construction period on the Nakkaştepe facility, Vehbi Koç remained in the background, closely following the developments, criticizing the Family Committee and Managing Committee by occasionally saying, "Rahmi's gone over the limit!"... He thought much of it was unnecessary, especially the swimming pool, the relaxation rooms allocated to the chair and vice chair, and the sumptuous Ottoman-style lounges in the main buildings... World famous architect Professor Sedat Hakkı Eldem, who was in charge of the project to renovate the Mehmet Şerif Pasha mansions, was determined not to cut any corners on the project. Professor Eldem sadly died two months before the Nakkaştepe facility opened for business and never got to see the work completed in accordance with his project. Another issue that bothered Vehbi Koç was what the Koç Holding staff, who had previously been accustomed to working in an office measuring 5,000 square meters, would make of the office at the Nakkaştepe facility, which covered 13,000 square meters!

In fact, he wanted to restrict Koç Holding's operations to just 5,000 square meters of the new space and settle a few other Koç companies on the empty floors! In Vehbi Koç's view, it was time to end the "era of the sultanate" and begin the "age of austerity"! So much so that, before Koç Holding moved from Fındıklı to Nakkaştepe, when it was uncertain which bridge would be best for the staff to travel over from various areas of the European side of Istanbul, he researched it himself, considering it his duty to determine the time differences between the first bridge and the Fatih Sultan Mehmet bridge, together with the petroleum expenses, and informed the relevant colleagues with a circular!

Ultimately, Vehbi Bey agreed for the Nakkaştepe facility, which would go on to win the 1990 Europa Nostra award, to be wholly used by Koç Holding, but he did not grant permission for use of the swimming pool, gymnasium or tennis courts until late 1991...

Can Kıraç, *Anılarımla Patronum Vehbi Koç* (Memories of My Boss, Vehbi Koç), Milliyet Publications, Istanbul, 1995, pp. 327-28

KOÇ-KAM, full name KOÇ UNIVERSITY GENDER STUDIES CENTER, is a multidisciplinary research and implementation center operating from Koç University(*) (KU). It was founded in 2010 through the efforts of Semahat Arsel(*), chair of the Vehbi Koç Foundation(*) Board of Directors. Covering a wide range of disciplines including sociology, social psychology, law, philosophy, political science, history and visual arts, the center aims to help teaching staff and researchers carry out research, lead national and international research projects, and engage in scientific and educational activities on the issues of gender and women both inside and outside the university.

The center's principal areas of research include the family, gender, personal development and human development; women's human rights; gender, law and politics; feminism, feminist theory and philosophy; gender in the visual arts; women's health, body politics and care; women's movements, participation and democracy. KOÇ-KAM, which serves as a center for gender studies, supports high quality research projects in the field by offering the Research Awards program and the Gender Certificate program—aimed at the students of KU. In addition, the Abadan Awards were created by KOÇ-KAM in 2015 with the aim of encouraging students and/or postdoctoral researchers studying at home and abroad. The program

Prof. Çiğdem Kağıtçıbaşı (MIDDLE) **together with the "Human Development Award" winners, Dr. Şebnem Özdemir and Dr. Burak Altıntaş, at the ceremony (December 26, 2016)**

includes two awards offered in alternate years: the Professor Yavuz Abadan Constitutional Law Award is granted "for studies relating to constitutional law, with an emphasis on political theory, legislative, executive and judicial studies and human rights"; and the Professor Nermin Abadan Unat Social Sciences Award granted for "research relating to the social sciences with a focus on women's studies".

Prof. Çiğdem Kağıtçıbaşı at the Semahat Arsel Distinguished Fellow Award ceremony (January 7, 2015)

Working in partnership with UNESCO, the center has designed and implemented a gender equality education program aimed at those working in the private sector. KOÇ-KAM organizes numerous panels, symposiums, seminars, workshops and other events every year, and in 2012 it became an institutional member of the European Association for Gender, Research, Education and Documentation (ATGENDER). In 2015, KOÇ-KAM inaugurated the Semahat Arsel Honorary Distinguished Fellow Award for "women of high international standing and those working in gender and women's studies". The first prize was awarded to the first female director general of UNESCO, Irina Bokova(*).

In May 2016, the UNESCO Chair in Gender Equality and Sustainable Development was established at KU in honor of the KOÇ-KAM director, Professor Çiğdem Kağıtçıbaşı. The Human Development Research Award was also created to be granted by the chair. Following Professor Kağıtçıbaşı's death, the role of director was assumed by Professor Bertil Emrah Oder, dean of KU School of Law.

Koç Model School, a project designed to create a new perspective on education, run in partnership by the Vehbi Koç Foundation(*) (VKV), the international architectural design company Cannon Design and the Ministry of Education. It is envisaged that the physical space at the Koç Model School will help to change attitudes to education and learning. The project's key aims are: to implement a model for an exemplary middle school, taking into account the educational environment, approach, management model and the school's relationship to its surroundings; to use the model school approach and the experience gleaned during the project as a guide; to act as a pilot project for adopting a different schooling system in Turkey and to precipitate the building of a future educational institution.

The project, which began in 2010 with the aim of building a new and innovative elementary school, was adjusted following the implementation of 12-year compulsory education (known as the 4+4+4 system) in 2010. As a result of this new law, the decision was taken to demolish Ziya Ünsel Middle School in Beykoz and build a new middle school in its place. Built by the VKV from a turnkey project drawn up by Cannon Design, the Koç Model School is expected to serve over 500 middle school students and on completion, ownership will be transferred to the Provincial Special Administration and rights of use will be transferred to the Ministry of Education.

The project aims to be a participatory and exemplary model, even in its implementation phase, with Turkish experts and institutions in the field contributing to the design and operation of the school. These include ERG(*), TEMA(*), Koç School(*) and TED University, as well as several architectural and engineering companies, and educational consultants.

In February 2014, work began on the school's culture of teaching and learning. Consequently, between February and September 2014, numerous workshops were organized to develop theories, objectives and aims for a new learning environment. Attended by the representatives of teachers, students and parents, and educational consultants, the groups discussed questions such as "What is the ideal learning environment?" and "What makes the ideal teacher?". They also examined special practices for in-class management and an orientation program for 5th grade classes. In September, a "Learner's Agenda", put together based on the views of teachers and students, was distributed to all students and teachers with the aim of accelerating the adoption of the model school culture.

The educational research carried out with teachers and parents was repeated in 2015, when the AÇEV(*) "Support for Mothers Program" was implemented. The program supports mothers and children by helping with child development and education. Two educational programs aimed at teachers were run in 2016; the first focused on learning with different materials and in different environments, while the second focused on game-based learning principles and using brain teasers together with class materials. In 2017, two educational programs were organized for teachers, one on project writing and management, another on communicating with teenagers. Construction started in June 2018 and in-school trainings and workshops still continue. The school is scheduled to open in September 2019.

A PROTOTYPE FOR INNOVATIVE APPROACHES TO EDUCATION: KOÇ MODEL SCHOOL

...Let's take a closer look at Koç Model School... It's a four-story building; on the lower two floors are spaces dedicated to community. The dining space has the ability to turn into a space where the community can gather, and it can also turn into a place of performance. It has a really nice gymnasium that also serves as a shelter in earthquakes. As you move upward there are clusters of different disciplines on each floor, and each hall has a shared center space. That was done consciously because we believe that this center space will help advocate interdisciplinary learning. Just the design of the space allows for serendipitous connections, running into other disciplines on that floor. We call these learning clusters "learning hubs". There are three learning hubs dedicated to each of the disciplines and at the center of these is a project studio that they open out to and share. The project studio is meant to have the agility to really curate a project over a long period of time, it is a shared space.

Learning hubs for the arts and sciences are located on the same floor and are linked by a community space in the center which connects not only horizontally but also vertically. There is a mathematics hub, a science and technology hub, there is an art learning hub, there are studios dedicated to artwork, including 3-D artwork, there is a design and technology hub, learning hubs dedicated to languages, to music, a dance studio. The school is filled with this sense of twenty-first century skills, allowing a collision of the arts and the sciences that is really critical. We are also advocating for very agile furniture that allows the changing of these learning spaces from instruction to collaboration without much effort. We are also advocating for technology to become completely embedded, so to take away the need.to plug and unplug in the environment. We have also brought some green space into the building itself.

Everything we build now has to be regenerative, has to use less energy, has to celebrate the core values and essence of us as human beings, meaning having access to daylight, access to view, access to green space, access to fresh air, access to our ability to adjust our own environment. This is why we need

to understand properly who we are designing for and how they would like to interact with each other. That is the core of learning: interaction, how we treat each other, how we want to be treated. In fact, insight we have today about how the brain works is telling us that learning is most effective when we do things, make things, when we actually have the ability to create something physical. Learning is no longer just thinking about facts and theories, about acquiring knowledge, but about how we activate this knowledge.

"Conversation with Trung Le, Head Designer at Cannon Design Educational Group", *VKV 2012 Annual Report*, pp. 9-11

Koç Private Primary, Middle and High School *see* **Koç School**

Koç School, full name VEHBİ KOÇ FOUNDATION KOÇ PRIVATE PRIMARY, MIDDLE AND HIGH SCHOOL, a private school founded by the Vehbi Koç Foundation(*) (VKV). It is located on the Eski Ankara Road, in Tuzla, Istanbul's Tepeören neighborhood. It is composed of Koç High School, established in 1988, and Koç Primary School, which was opened in 1998 in order to adapt to the K12 mandatory education system from kindergarten to high school. The 4+4+4 regulation introduced in 2012 stipulated that education must include kindergarten, elementary school, middle school and high school. With a multicultural teaching staff, innovative educational methods and an integrated bilingual education program from kindergarten to 12th grade, the Koç School has a global vision, which aims to "raise well-rounded, confident individuals who are respectful of difference, who can think independently and creatively, are sensitive to social issues and the environment and possess the qualities to be good citizens".

HISTORY

Koç Private School, the foundations of which were laid on the 60th anniversary of the Koç Group(*) in 1986, began by teaching 224 students at pre-high school and pre-middle school levels in the 1988-89 academic year. John C. Chalfant(*), who was made director of the project in 1987, was also appointed director of the school that same year and continued in this role until the high school produced its first graduates in 1992. Atakan Demirseren(*), who was an educational consultant during the foundation of the school, served as chief deputy director from 1988 to 1998. From 1992 to 1996, Gerald Shields(*) was director of the school, which had now reached an intake of 753 students. In 1994, the International Baccalaureate (IB) was introduced in Turkey for the first time at Koç Private High School. In 1995, the school produced its first batch of graduates, who had joined at middle school level. During the tenure of John R. Chandler(*), who became the school's third director in 1996, the eight-year compulsory education system was introduced, precipitating the establishment of Koç Private Primary School in 1998. Chandler's title changed and he became the school's first general director that same year.

In 2005, when J. Anthony Paulus(*) began serving as the school's second general director, a 12th grade was added to the High School, taking the school's total attendees up to 2,000. In 2012, during the time of the school's third general director, Robert Lennox(*) (2008-13), the 4+4+4 national compulsory education system was introduced. The school could continue within the K12 system by splitting into three entities: primary, middle and high school.

Sevgi Gönül (LEFT) **and Suna Kıraç at the Koç School**

Koray Özsaraç(*) took over from Lennox in 2013, becoming the Koç School's fourth general director. In 2016, it was renamed as the Koç School. After the departure of Özsaraç in 2018, Prof. Murat Günel(*) was appointed as director.

"Individuals who can work anywhere in the world, but never forget where they came from..."
SEMAHAT ARSEL

My sister, Suna Kıraç, worked extremely hard on the foundation of this school and was deeply committed to this project. She was the one who made it successful. Suna worked very closely with my father because someone in the family was needed to keep track of matters such as acquiring the necessary permissions and forging ties with the teachers. Suna thought that education was so important, a civilizing force in people's lives. My father also wanted to ensure that everyone received an education, whether they were rich or poor. This made him a wonderful person in my eyes. My father attached as much importance to Turkey as he did to his own work. He tried to solve the country's problems. Education was one of these. When he realized that our fellow citizens were not receiving a proper education, he began providing scholarships. He later realized that the scholarships were not enough. We established Koç Private High School because he wanted to found his own school. The core aim was to create students who embraced Turkish traditions and customs, and subsequently Turkish culture, and whose education earned them a place as citizens of the world. In other words, we wanted to raise individuals who could work anywhere in the world, but would never forget where they came from.

İzzeddin Çalışlar (ed.), *VKV Koç Özel İlköğretim Okulu ve Lisesi 1988-2008* (VKV Koç Private Primary and High School 1988-2008), Istanbul, 2008, pp. 19-23

"Our belief in education..."
SUNA KIRAÇ

Throughout his career, my father, Vehbi Koç, believed that the most valuable part of any organization was well-educated staff and maintained that good staff only arose from good education. It was for this reason that our first significant social facility was established in a place where it could contribute to education and in 1951, Maltepe Koç Student Dormitory was established for Ankara University students. In the speech he gave at the dormitory's opening ceremony in April 15, 1951, Vehbi Koç said: "I believe that any endeavor that helps to better nurture the young people in whose hands Atatürk entrusted the country and Republic is the greatest form of benevolence in the revolution we are living through. This facility arose from that belief." Nearly 40 years have passed since that day. During this time, along with our father, our belief in education has persisted, growing ever stronger, and we have continued in our efforts to develop numerous educational facilities for Turkey. Our belief in education guided us to found the Vehbi Koç Foundation Koç Private High School project in Kurtköy, Pendik. This project introduced an important innovation: assuming responsibility for the running of the facility... When founding the school, we used the most contemporary education possible as our model. We adopted English-language education at this Turkish private school, though naturally classes on Turkish language and culture are taught in Turkish.

Çalışlar, *VKV Koç Özel İlköğretim Okulu ve Lisesi 1988-2008*, p. 25

EDUCATION

The Koç School curriculum provides a comprehensive, consistent education from kindergarten through to the 12th grade. The school's student-centered curriculum allows for active learning in a multicultural environment, as well as placing emphasis on training students to respond to the needs of the age with interdisciplinary studies, projects and research supported by the use of information technologies. This program

aims to develop fundamental knowledge and skills at all levels, familiarize students with cultural and conceptual perspectives, inform and raise student awareness of matters affecting the world and the influence of these on Turkey, lead problem-solving and conflict resolution processes using positive approaches, develop creativity and awareness, and teach students about the importance of being responsible citizens by means of internal and external activities.

"Nothing is as it used to be..."
KORAY ÖZSARAÇ

Nothing is as it used to be, and the kids are quite aware of this fact. Production and consumption models have evolved at an incredible pace and created an environment of deep uncertainty for us educators... The first thing that we do at the Koç School is to accept this environment of uncertainty. Take a look at the prevalent school model: there are boxes that consist of classrooms on the one hand, and classes and recesses on the other, with the assumption that learning takes place inside these spatial and temporal boxes. But when you look at the nature of learning, this is obviously wrong. The things we truly learn, we learn differently. What differentiates us is that we try to break with this idea of learning, and this is something our students connect to. We don't limit our expectations of our students to exams and essays, but want to ensure that learning connects to the real world.

We need to be a school for teachers also. We need to engage them in further study, training and projects to help expand horizons and liberate thinking. Let me give you an example. Recently, some teachers asked for a classroom which did not locate the teacher at the head of the class. So, we found a special paint that turns the walls into a writing surface and painted the whole class room. Now, teachers and students are free to write anywhere they like. The teacher is no longer at the center of the class and there is no hierarchy. Some may find this totally unacceptable, and of course this doesn't make them bad teachers. We try to give our teachers as much freedom as possible. They enjoy full autonomy as long as they can justify their methods and be held accountable. In fact, we regard autonomy and accountability as the two most important principles to govern all employees and students. We are already seeing some positive results. Recently, for instance, some students and teachers resolved an issue involving classroom allocation among themselves without consulting anyone else. We, as the school administration, were not informed and did not need to be. I cannot say that everything in the school functions like this, but I can say that everyone at school takes these values into consideration. Just like in every community and in each change process, there will always be some front runners, while some will prefer to wait and see, and some will perhaps never want to change.

"Conversation with Koray Özsaraç, General Director of Koç School", *VKV 2015 Annual Report*, pp. 81-87

Every year, Koç School accepts 40 female and 40 male students into its kindergarten according to a lottery drawn before a notary. These numbers vary from year to year, and students are accepted to the 3rd and 5th grade according to available places. Students who complete their eight years of elementary education can continue on to the High School, which also accepts students following assessment and evaluation exams. English-language education begins in kindergarten and gradually becomes more intensive. Teaching at the school is bilingual; social science classes are taught primarily in Turkish, science classes are taught primarily in English. From 6th grade onwards, students begin learning a second foreign language of their choice (German, French or Spanish) and they continue with it at high school. The aim is for graduates to be able to effectively use their second foreign language.

The school has been a leading institution, reforming education in Turkey, since it was founded. Koç High School, where the IB program was implemented in Turkey for the first time in 1996, also ran the implementation process in other schools in the country. It developed a multidisciplinary social studies program to include history, geography and sociology, ensuring that the program could be delivered in Turkish. Turkey's first national and international university advice offices were also established at Koç School.

INTERNATIONAL BACCALAUREATE: IB

The IB program aims to provide an education of sufficient quality and standards to be accepted by universities worldwide. Students who complete the IB program receive a diploma which ensures they can access university at an international level. The program makes a point of helping students to develop critical thinking and encourages personal development and social integration, linking the knowledge that students have developed at school with their skills in the outside world. Its aims include instilling students with common principles and values, encouraging awareness of societies and cultures, and enriching the Ministry of Education's program of education with international standards.

Club-based and extra-curricular pursuits, which aim to encourage students to complement their progress with social activities relating to their interests and abilities, are an important part of the educational practice at Koç School. These take place during and outside lesson times at elementary school, after school at middle school, and in accordance with students' timetables at high school. Extra-curricular activities include archeology, astronomy, the European Youth Parliament(*), biology, drama, philosophy, photography, Model UN, model planes, nanotechnology, origami, psychology and chess, in addition to team sports such as basketball, table tennis, volleyball and swimming, etc. At middle and high school levels, extracurricular activities can be initiated and managed by students. Following an introduction to the activities at the beginning of the academic year, students can choose to participate in existing activities or begin others if they wish. Events such as the Suna Kıraç Inter-School Short Story Competition(*), Sevgi Gönül Art Night, Vehbi Koç Memorial Day, Model UN Development Program (MUNDP) Conference, Atakan Demirseren Mathematics Competition, Koç Mathematics Week, Careers Day, Ramfest Jr, Portfolio Presentation Day, and the Talent Show have become time-honored traditions. In 2017, the story and essay writing competition organized by the Koç Middle School Turkish Department was renamed the Mustafa V. Koç Story and Essay Writing Competition(*) in memory of the late Mustafa V. Koç.

STUDENT MAGAZINES

- BOYUT: **High school literary magazine. A magazine distributed to and prepared by students, comprising essays and writings on literary matters.**
- EDGE JR – MATH: **Co-edited by the middle school's mathematics, science, IT and arts departments. An English-language magazine compiled by students on mathematics studies. The magazine is distributed to middle school students.**
- EPIC AUTHORS: **Middle School English-language magazine. A magazine featuring essays, writings and other work in English. It is distributed to middle school students.**
- ERA: **History magazine, first published in 2014. Comprises essays, interviews and miscellanea written by students in relation to history.**
- FELSEFE: **High school philosophy magazine. Magazine distributed to students, featuring essays and writings on philosophical issues produced by students.**
- KOÇİ: **Koçi, first published in 2014, is a magazine distributed to elementary school students, which**

shows the work of elementary school students in both Turkish and English.

- LUMINOUS PANDEMONIUM (LP): **English-language magazine produced by pre-high school students, distributed to preparatory year students.**
- PLUTO: **High school science magazine. English-language magazine featuring students' scientific studies.**
- TOHUM: **Middle school literary magazine comprising student essays and writings, and distributed to students.**

SOME OF THE KOÇ SCHOOL'S TRADITIONAL ACTIVITIES

- **Vehbi Koç Memorial Day**
- **Model United Nations Development Program Conference (MUNDP)**
- **Careers Day**
- **Koç Mathematics Week**
- **Suna Kıraç Inter-School Short Story Competition**
- **Mustafa Koç Story and Essay Writing Competition**
- **Sevgi Gönül Art Night**
- **Atakan Demirseren Mathematics Competition**
- **Portfolio Presentation Day**
- **Ramfest Jr**
- **Talent Show**

Koç School employs over 300 teachers, one in five of whom are foreign. The school provides teachers with constant support in developing their teaching skills. Throughout the year, teachers participate in a number of in-house training programs, seminars, symposiums and conferences both inside and outside of the school and share the best examples from their experiences with their colleagues. The school also supports teachers in continuing their academic development by improving their language skills, and pursuing educational attainments such as master's degrees and doctorates.

THE CAMPUS

Koç School has a world-class campus, offering students a living space in the heart of nature. The campus covers an area of nearly 650,000 square meters, 620,000 of which is open-air. Seventeen percent of the grounds are landscaped. As well as the high, middle and elementary school buildings on campus, there is also a science building, with a separate branch of the sciences (physics, chemistry and biology) on each floor, dormitories, lodgings for the director and students, a social area for residents, a covered semi-Olympic sized swimming pool (also a covered teaching pool and open-air swimming pool) and open-air sports areas. The buildings cover an area of approximately 30,000 square meters, and have a total usage area of 54,000 square meters. There is an athletics track with an artificial turf football field in the center, which is the largest track belonging to any school or university.

In addition to the classrooms, the school buildings also contain laboratories, handicraft and ceramics studios, events rooms, art and music rooms, a covered sports center with adjustable stands which can host two basketball matches at once, a conference hall seating approximately 1,100 people, three separate medical rooms with full-time doctors and nurses (the high school medical room is open 24/7 and an ambulance is available for emergencies), a dining hall serving onsite home-cooked meals, a cafeteria (Sevgi Gönül Student Center) and numerous libraries. The middle school and the primary school have their own individual libraries, in addition to the Suna Kıraç Library and the Atatürk Library which contain over 60,000 books. In 2017, Koç School set up a renewable energy plant using solar energy and began producing its own electricity.

SOCIAL OPPORTUNITIES

Today, Koç School has over 2,000 students, with almost half attending the primary and middle schools and half attending the high school; one in five of the high school students (approximately 120 students) are boarders. A large proportion of these students board at the school for seven days a week and the rest for five days—these include students from numerous different Turkish provinces.

VKV scholarships are granted to high- achieving students from across Turkey, providing them with the opportunity to study at the school. Approximately 40% of Koç School students receive scholarships of various proportions. Nearly 20% of those given scholarships receive 100% off their fees.

Aiming to give students a solid cultural ground, the school corridors feature exhibitions of works from prestigious museums such as the Sadberk Hanım Museum(*), the Istanbul Rahmi M. Koç Museum(*) and Pera Museum(*). In addition, exhibitions of the students' own works are a different educational mechanism, enabling students to see concrete examples of what they are studying, establishing links between concrete and abstract terms and stimulating creative thought.

Koç School was one of the first establishments in Turkey to introduce The Duke of Edinburgh's International Award (The International Youth Award until 2013), which aims to support personal development. At the time of writing, over 200 Koç

School students have received awards on the program, which is composed of four sections: public service, adventure and discovery, skills development and physical development.

A large proportion of Koç School graduates continue their higher education abroad. In 2017, approximately 60% of graduates went abroad, while 51% of those choosing to continue their studies in Turkey took up scholarship places at foundation universities. Koç School, which is a member of the European Council of International Schools and the National Association for College Admission Counseling, features on the Guide to Excellence, compiled by Cambridge University Student Union to promote the best schools worldwide.

Koç University, a private higher education institution in Istanbul founded by the Vehbi Koç Foundation(*) (VKV). It opened on a temporary campus in İstinye in 1993 and moved to a permanent campus in Rumelifeneri in 1999. Its mission as an exemplary educational and research institution is to bring together highly talented young people and skilled educational staff to support the development of creative, world-class graduates who can think critically and contribute to science on a global scale.

HISTORY

The management of the VKV, including Vehbi Koç(*) and members of the Koç family(*), began working on the idea of founding a university after establishing Koç Private High School (*see* Koç School) in 1988. At a meeting of the VKV Board of Directors in September 1988, the decision was taken to set up a University Executive Committee and compile a feasibility report. The report was

Ömer M. Koç, chair of the Koç University Board of Trustees, at the graduation ceremony, Rumelifeneri Campus, 2017

prepared by Professors Bülent Gültekin, Özer Ertuna, Işık İnselbağ and Seha Tiniç(*). As a result of the committee's investigation, it was concluded that the university should start as a small-scale but high-standard facility. It would be independently run, selecting its own students, and provide the most talented young people with an education of the highest quality that would enable them to contribute to the country as soon as possible; it would aim to be a "perfect" learning institution and a "center of excellence". For the first stage, the report proposed a structure comprising three units: College of Arts and Sciences, the College of Administrative Sciences and Economics and the Graduate School of Business.

At the meeting of the VKV Board of Directors on December 20, 1989, the decision was taken to "found a university providing English-language education under the name Koç University"; the University Executive Committee was placed in charge of planning the investment, design and preparations for the official application. It was envisaged that the project would be financed by an investment fund composed of donations made by Koç Holding(*) companies to the VKV over a five year period and that a working fund would also be established inside the VKV.

During the process of setting up the university,

a number of unexpected bureaucratic and administrative difficulties were encountered regarding the legal procedure for establishing a foundation university, allocating land to the university, modifying construction plans, and managing the construction process. Tamer Şahinbaş(*) was made director of Koç University (KU) in February 1990, after the foundation management took the decision to appoint an executive manager to solve these and other issues.

Following three years of work, KU's establishment was legally completed on March 5, 1992, when the law relating to the establishment of the university was passed by the Turkish Grand National Assembly. The VKV Board of Directors designated the KU Board of Trustees on March 9, 1992. Rahmi M. Koç(*) was chair of the board, which included Suna Kıraç(*), Ömer M. Koç(*), Can Kıraç(*), M. Fahir İlkel(*), Yavuz Alangoya, Bülent Gültekin and Tamer Şahinbaş. On March 16, 1992, Tamer Şahinbaş was appointed founding president of KU.

On April 26, 1992, a ministerial cabinet granted a plot measuring 160 hectares, known as Mavromoloz State Forest, inside the borders of Rumelifeneri village to KU for a period of 49 years. However, when it emerged that construction work could not begin immediately, the search began for a temporary campus so that teaching could start sooner. Ultimately, the decision was taken to transform the old Türkay match factory in İstinye into a campus; the factory was already owned by the VKV and being used as a warehouse. The necessary arrangements were made over a short period of about nine months and by September 1993, the KU İstinye Campus was made serviceable, with classrooms, laboratories, a library, a gymnasium, cafe and canteen.

The university's academic structure was also formed during this period. Following recruitment work carried out by a research committee, composed of Suna Kıraç, Bülent Gültekin and Tamer Şahinbaş, decisions were taken to appoint Professor Seha Tiniç as president, Professor Seymour Smidt as dean of the College of Administrative Sciences and Economics, and Professor Attila Aşkar(*) as dean of the College of Arts and Sciences.

KU began teaching 189 undergraduate and 42 postgraduate students at its İstinye Campus on October 4, 1993. Vehbi Koç taught the university's first class on the same day, summarizing his expectations for the university, while referencing his own experiences. KU was formally declared open on October 12, 1993, and produced its first graduates in 1995, when a group of students completed MBAs. The undergraduate degree programs produced their first graduates in 1997.

Koç University graduation ceremony, Rumelifeneri Campus, 2017

VEHBİ KOÇ'S FIRST LESSON, OCTOBER 4, 1993

Today, in the West, the university and the business world work in nested fashion. Especially in the United States, managers from business and industry frequently hold lessons and conferences in universities, and participate in debates. I hope that this habit takes hold in our country and in our universities as well. My speaking here today and your first lesson is symbolic. As the founder of this university, I would like to convey some issues I have found useful from the "University of Life," where I have been studying for the past 70 years. People learn something every day, yet the education and the learning of people who are open to novelty takes a lifetime and never ends.

First, I would like to tell you how the idea of opening a university came about. I met many businesspeople during my travels to the West. I saw that large, institutionalized firms employed many well-educated, talented young people, who were fluent in languages. This had a major role in the progress of developed countries and the consolidation of their economies. Today the power that makes America, that makes Japan is largely economic. This in turn is made possible with talented people who run these institutions. In similar fashion, I believe that it is important to raise well-educated young people who are fluent in languages so that Turkey can also develop.

We spent considerable effort to establish a good university in Turkey. We have completed the planning, however because of formalities, it has not been possible to set up a university in the desired location and with the desired admission conditions. The Vehbi Koç Foundation Board of Directors decided to establish the university in this temporary location to prevent loss of time, to ensure that young people receive education and that faculty can be hired as soon as possible. Hence now, here, Koç University started education...

Here, we aim to take above average students and to bring them up to world class businesspeople. To this end, the Vehbi Koç Foundation will contribute five million dollars to the University every year. The aim of Koç University is to make it possible to provide good training and education to extraordinary young people. The future of our country will be secured because there are enough of them and because they will reach the leadership positions they deserve... the more qualified people we can train, the more we will be serving the country.

Geleceğe Açılan Bilim Kapısı: Koç Üniversitesi Kuruluş Tarihi (The Portal of Knowledge that Opens onto the Future: History of Koç University's Foundation), Koç University, İstanbul, 2002, pp. 18-19

The foundations for the permanent KU campus in Rumelifeneri were laid on May 31, 1996. The construction works began in September 1997 and were completed in November 1999. KU began the 2000-01 academic year at the Rumelifeneri Campus, which was officially opened in a ceremony in November 1999. The İstinye Campus was restructured as a modern education and meeting center where company managers could study for MBAs. In addition to its campuses at Rumelifeneri and İstinye, KU also operates from the Koç University(*) Health Sciences Campus in Topkapı.

"This university will remain and thrive in Turkey..."
VEHBİ KOÇ

I went to visit my father two weeks before he died. He felt suffocated by all the bureaucratic obstacles. He told me how he felt and I was sad that he was so upset. I said, "Father, forget all this business with the university. Let it stay in İstinye. Let's invest in some other way and forget about Rumelifeneri"... He replied—and it became my legacy. I'll never forget it. It was both a legacy and a guide: "I will die, you will die, the people causing all these problems will die... But this university will remain and thrive in Turkey..."

Semahat Arsel

Geleceğe Açılan Bilim Kapısı..., p. 126

THOUGHTS ON KU FROM THE KOÇ FAMILY

Since the day it was founded, the Vehbi Koç Foundation has served our country in three essential, fundamental matters which are necessary for the survival, welfare and happiness of individuals and society at large; they are education, culture and health. We work on the premise that expecting every effort and investment to come from the state is an outdated notion that needs to be abandoned. It's our objective to help the state and society by bringing together private, personal and corporate means in projects for the public good. Koç University, supported by ongoing contributions from our foundation, the Koç Group and the Koç family, is the newest and finest example of this belief in action.

Semahat Arsel

The world is globalizing rapidly and turning into one big marketplace. The big institutions want to work with the most talented managers, regardless of nationality, religion or race. For this reason, we need to support young people in such a way that they can work in every country, every field and every sector with all kinds of people, training them to be wise, skilled, open-minded and equipped with determination and scientific knowledge. The greatest source of wealth for this country is well-educated young people and it was this belief that drove us to found Koç University. It has already won our society more admiration and acceptance than many of the other initiatives we have taken for

the country. This institution is a source of pride for us and we foresee its students making significant, valuable contributions not just to their own sectors but to our country and the whole world.

Rahmi M. Koç

Education is too tough a job to be left entirely to the state. Economic crises can be overcome, political issues can be solved but it's impossible to fix a society that has wasted its young people. With this belief, we wanted to do our part; our country has beautiful people and a beautiful landscape, let's make sure its young people receive a great education too. We wanted to contribute towards raising highly skilled young people who will carry Turkey towards a strong and happy future. We wanted this modern educational institution to be an asset for Istanbul, Turkey and the world, not just with its educational and learning activities, but also with its architecture, its cultural environment and the human achievements it would stimulate... I hope that Koç University, born from this belief and longing, will be an example to everyone who shares similar values.

Suna Kıraç

Geleceğe Açılan Bilim Kapısı..., p. 15

ACADEMIC DEPARTMENTS AND TEACHING STAFF

The academic departments delivering English instruction at KU are: the College of Administrative Sciences and Economics, College of Engineering, College of Sciences, College of Social Sciences and Humanities, Law School, School of Nursing, School of Medicine, Graduate School of Business, Graduate School of Health Sciences, Graduate School of Sciences and Engineering and the Graduate School of Social Sciences.

COLLEGES

COLLEGE OF ADMINISTRATIVE SCIENCES AND ECONOMICS

This school is one of the first faculties founded at KU in 1993. It comprises Departments of Economics, Business Administration, and International Relations. In addition to the four-year degree course, the faculty also provides master's programs in economics and master's and doctoral programs in business and international relations.

COLLEGE OF ENGINEERING

The college, founded in 1999, offers four-year undergraduate programs, master's and doctoral programs in Computer Engineering, Electrical and Electronics Engineering, Industrial Engineering, Chemical and Biological Engineering, and Mechanical Engineering. It also runs interdisciplinary postgraduate programs in biomedical sciences and engineering (together with the College of Sciences and School of Medicine), computational science and engineering (together with the College of Sciences), materials science and engineering, industrial engineering and business management (together with the College of Administrative Sciences and Economics), molecular biology and genetics, and optoelectronics and photonic engineering.

COLLEGE OF SCIENCES

One of KU's first two faculties founded in 1993, the College of Arts and Sciences, was split into two in 2008 to create one College of Social Sciences and Humanities and one College of Sciences. The faculty gives four-year undergraduate programs in Departments of Mathematics, Physics, Chemistry, and Molecular Biology and Genetics. It offers master's and doctoral degrees in biomedical sciences and engineering (together with the College of Engineering and School of Medicine), physics, mathematics, molecular biology and genetics.

COLLEGE OF SOCIAL SCIENCES AND HUMANITIES

One of KU's first two colleges founded in 1993, the College of Arts and Sciences, was split into two in 2008 to create one College of Social Sciences and Humanities and one College of Sciences. The faculty teaches four-year degree courses on Archeology and Art History, English Language and Comparative Literature, History, Philosophy, Psychology, Sociology, and Media and Visual Arts. It also offers master's programs in psychology, archeology and art history, and design, technology and society. Doctoral programs are offered in sociology and history.

LAW SCHOOL

The Law School, which began began teaching in the 2003-04 academic year, provides four years of legal education, excluding the English preparatory year. Classes relating to the Turkish legal system are taught in Turkish; other law courses with comparative, theoretical and international aspects are taught in English. In 2007, a research center was established to work on the subject of international commercial law with donations from Semahat Arsel(*) and Dr. Nusret Arsel(*) (*see* NASAMER).

SCHOOL OF MEDICINE

The school was founded with support from the VKV, in partnership with the American Hospital(*), with the aim of contributing a new and different outlook to medical education in Turkey. It had its first intake of students in the 2010-11 academic year. The school offers six-year programs of medical education, excluding the preparatory year, and the first three of these take place at the KU Rumelifeneri Campus. Subsequent clinic-based study takes place at the Koç University Hospital(*), which opened in Topkapı, Istanbul, in 2014.

SCHOOL OF NURSING

The Koç University School of Nursing(*) was founded when the Admiral Bristol Nursing School affiliated with KU in 1999 and was turned into a college in 2016. The college, which is located in Koç University Hospital on the KU Health Sciences Campus in Topkapı, Istanbul, provides undergraduate teaching in nursing and also runs master's and doctoral programs in various branches of nursing at the KU Graduate School of Health Sciences.

As of 2018, 13,400 students have graduated from KU, which currently offers undergraduate and postgraduate courses, with 22 undergraduate, 29 master's and 26 doctoral programs. The university has a total of 194 research laboratories and operates 20 research centers, 5 research and education forums and 1 support center.

PRESIDENTS

- **Tamer Şahinbaş(*)** *(founding president; 1990-1992)*
- **Seha Tiniç(*)** *(1993-2001)*
- **Atilla Aşkar(*)** *(2001-2009)*
- **Umran İnan(*)** *(2009-)*

KOÇ UNIVERSITY RESEARCH CENTERS

- **AKMED(*)** *(Koç University Suna & İnan Kıraç Research Center for Mediterranean Civilizations)*
- **ANAMED(*)** *(Koç University Research Center for Anatolian Civilizations)*
- **GABAM(*)** *(Koç University Stavros Niarchos Foundation Center for Late Antique and Byzantine Studies)*
- **GLODEM(*)** *(Center for Research on Globalization, Peace, and Democratic Governance)*
- **IAM** *(Koç University Drug Research Center)*
- **KABAM** *(Koç University–AKKIM Boron-Based Materials & High-technology Chemicals Research & Application Center)*
- **KOÇ-KAM(*)** *(Koç University Gender Studies Center)*
- **KUAR** *(Koç University Arçelik Research Center for Creative Industries)*
- **KUASIA** *(Koç University Center for Asian Studies)*
- **KUSAM** *(Koç University Field Research Center)*
- **KUTTAM** *(Koç University Research Center for Translational Medicine)*
- **KUYTAM** *(Koç University Surface Technologies Research Center)*
- **KUREMER** *(Center for Global Public Law)*
- **KU-SPM** *(Koç University Social Policy Application and Research Center)*
- **KUTEM** *(Koç University Tüpraş Energy Center)*
- **KWORKS(*)** *(Koç University Entrepreneurship Research Center)*
- **MiReKoc(*)** *(Migration Research Center at Koç University)*
- **NASAMER(*)** *(Dr. Nusret–Semahat Arsel International Business Law Implementation and Research Center)*
- **SANERC(*)** *(Koç University Semahat Arsel Nursing Education and Research Center)*
- **VEKAM(*)** *(Koç University Vehbi Koç Ankara Studies Research Center)*

KOÇ UNIVERSITY RESEARCH AND EDUCATION FORUMS

- **CGF** *(Koç University Corporate Governance Forum)*
- **EAF** *(Koç University–TÜSİAD Economic Research Forum)*
- **KUDENFOR** *(Koç University Maritime Research Forum)*
- **KUSIF(*)** *(Koç University Social Impact Forum)*
- **KUMPEM** *(Koç University Migros Retailing Education Forum)*

KOÇ UNIVERSITY SUPPORT CENTERS

- **EÇADEM(*)** *(Koç University Support Center for Disabled Children and Their Families)*

KU employs approximately 473 full-time members of teaching staff, many of whom have received numerous awards, including TÜBİTAK and TÜBA awards. KU is one of the universities with the highest proportion of international academic publications per member of staff in Turkey.

25TH ANNIVERSARY OF KOÇ UNIVERSITY IN THE WORDS OF PRESIDENT PROF. UMRAN S. İNAN

Thanks to the extraordinary foresight and determination of the late Vehbi Koç, today we are celebrating the 25th anniversary of Koç University. Today, we share the pride of what has been achieved in its relatively short academic life since 1993; world class investments and nationally and internationally respected teaching staff have helped transform the university into a distinguished and venerated institution.

The speed with which we developed our academic research programs in this period has meant that the acquisition of new academic staff and doctoral students have gained rapid momentum. We have received more funds for academic research and development from Europe than any other university in Turkey and are among several universities to be granted the most project support from the Scientific and Technological Research Council of Turkey.

Also, in as little as 25 years, we have established international standard laboratories and research centers, which provide opportunities for research of global importance. For example, in 2014, we achieved the establishment of Koç University Hospital, a training and research facility. Our Research Center for Translational Medicine, which has received the most state funding in Turkey to date, is now open. Thanks to the Semahat and Dr. Nusret Arsel Science and Technology Building on our Rumelifeneri Campus, we have been able to provide new technological laboratories and classrooms and create study spaces for new postgraduate students and academic staff. I sincerely believe that these new facilities will put us in a much stronger position in our head-to-head competition with international universities.

STUDENT PROFILE AND SCHOLARSHIPS

As a non-profit foundation university, KU is one of Turkey's preferred universities among high-performing students, particularly for engineering, law and medicine studies. 51% of students who enrolled at the school in 2017 were selected from the top 20,000 students, and 74% were selected from the top 50,000. In the 2017-18 academic year, the number of undergraduate and postgraduate students amounts to nearly 7,000. KU has exchange program agreements with over 270 foreign universities from over 60 countries.

Out of KU's 2018 intake of students, 53% of places were allocated to scholarship students. Students are awarded scholarships of 100%, 50% and 25% based on the results of university entrance exams, and 38% of these are full scholarships. Students may also receive help in the form of subsistence grants. The university's Anatolian Scholarship Program(*) assists highly talented students who have performed well in the undergraduate placement exam but are unable to pursue an education at KU for economic reasons. Aiming to expand equal access to the best education, the program has been in place since 2011 and is sponsored by personal and corporate donors.

CAMPUS AND EXTRACURRICULAR ACTIVITIES

The Rumelifeneri Campus comprises three zones containing a series of three-story buildings: Koç Square, which includes the President's Office, Student Center, library (*see* Koç University Suna Kıraç Library), computer units, and dining, relaxation, shopping and meeting areas; the academic zone which contains faculty buildings interconnected by the Bosphorus Terrace, classrooms, an auditorium and laboratories; and the student dormitory zone which includes the secondary quads and the Koç Quadrangle, the cafeteria, health center and infirmary. The other buildings on campus are the gymnasium and energy center, the lodgings for teaching staff, a day care center and the president's lodgings. Aside from the Semahat Arsel Sports Center, which can seat 2,000 people, the campus also has open and closed swimming pools, an open tennis court, artificial turf football field and covered ice-rink. The university provides lodging for 2,871 students.

The Sevgi Gönül Cultural Center hosts a variety of cultural and artistic events. The recently opened Semahat and Dr. Nusret Arsel Science and Technology Building contains classrooms, laboratories and study spaces for academic staff and postgraduate students.

Over 80 student groups operate in the university's various social and cultural spaces. The Office of Activities and Volunteer Projects works with student groups to arrange short- and long-term projects and events.

Established in 2010, Koç University Press produces both academic and general publications on a broad range of subjects.

KU was admitted to the US Network of Excellence in 2004 and in 2012 it was ranked among the top 250 universities worldwide by Times Higher Education (THE). In 2017, it was listed between numbers 301-350 and was named the best university in Turkey for the third year in a row. KU came top in the THE 2018 listings for social sciences in Turkey, ranking between 151-175 worldwide and between 201-250 for engineering and technology.

In 2016, KU established the Rahmi M. Koç Medal of Science(*) to recognize leading scientists from Turkey who have contributed to science both at home and abroad.

Koç University College of Administrative Sciences and Economics *see* Koç University

Koç University College of Engineering *see* **Koç University**

Koç University College of Sciences *see* **Koç University**

Koç University College of Social Sciences and Humanities *see* **Koç University**

Koç University Entrepreneurship Research Center *see* **KWORKS**

Koç University First Aid Education Center (KUİYEM), an education center founded as part of Koç University School of Nursing(*) on April 7, 2010 to meet the need for first aid training, especially among the general workforce. The center aims to train people to deliver correct and informed first aid, leading courses such as "Basic First Aid Training", "First Aid Training Refresher", "First Aid Seminars" and "Preparing for Disasters". As well as providing first aid seminars to companies and institutions on request, it also arranges first aid awareness courses aimed at high schools and equivalent in partnership with Beylikdüzü Municipality.

KUİYEM has been based on the Koç University Health Sciences Campus(*) since 2016.

Koç University Gender Studies Center *see* **KOÇ-KAM**

Koç University Health Sciences Campus, location of the health-related units of Koç University(*) (KU) in Topkapı, Istanbul. Designed by the US architectural company Cannon Design, the campus covers an area of approximately 214,000 square meters. The design aims to create a campus environment with the flexibility to respond to the needs of the future and which promotes interdisciplinary integration and collaboration. The first stage of construction work was completed in September 2014 and the second stage in the final quarter of 2016.

The campus can provide teaching and assembly space for 2,500 people at any one time and houses the Koç University Hospital(*) general, pediatric and oncology hospital units, as well as KU Schools of Medicine and Nursing, SANERC(*) and the RMK Academy of Interventional Medicine, Education and Simulation (AIMES), lodgings, and dormitories for nursing students.

Koç University Hospital, a research and teaching hospital within Koç University(*) (KU) School of Medicine. The hospital opened in September 2014, and the second stage of construction, begun in November 2014, was completed in the final quarter of 2016.

Located on the Koç University Health Sciences Campus(*) in Topkapı, Istanbul, the hospital aims to "apply up-to-date medical approaches of the highest quality in the most transparent way". The campus includes general, pediatric and oncology hospital units, the KU Schools of Medicine and Nursing, SANERC(*), the RMK Academy of Interventional Medicine, Education and Simulation (AIMES) buildings, lodgings, and dormitories for student nurses. In 2016, the Medical Genetics, IVF and Bone Marrow centers began accepting patients; in 2017, the Gamma Knife, Cosmetic Dermatology, Undersea and Hyperbaric Oxygen Therapy Centers opened and the RMK AIMES began offering initial phase service.

The hospital contains teaching and research laboratories, 376 inpatient rooms, 12 operating rooms, an intensive care unit with 55 beds, 14 bone marrow transplant beds, 88 observation beds and 200 outpatient examination rooms. Students at KU School of Medicine complete their first three years at the Rumelifeneri Campus, and continue with clinic-based studies at Koç University Hospital from the fourth year onwards.

The architectural design of Koç University Hospital reflects its approach to patient care and treatment. In accordance with the hospital's principle of transparency, the design for the hospital's inner space has made extensive use of glass, but ensuring that patient privacy is protected. Due to the importance placed on research, the research laboratories are located in the center of

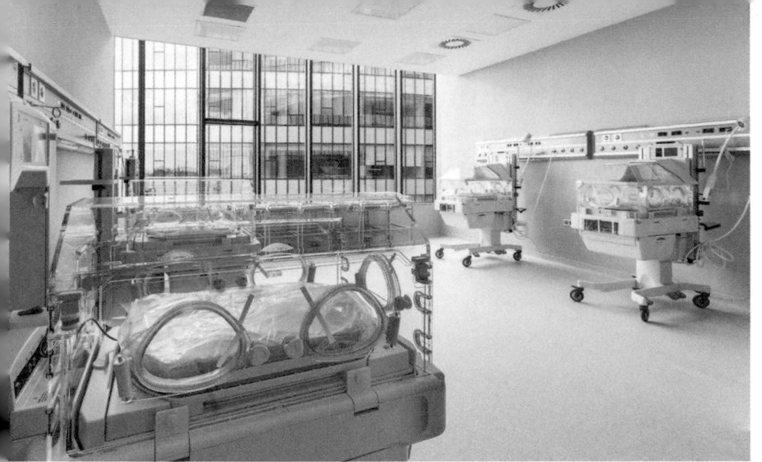

the hospital complex. Spatial divisions between disciplines and departments have also been avoided in order to encourage a holistic system which takes a complementary, interrogative approach to clinical applications and operates with a team spirit.

Koç University Law School
see **Koç University**

Koç University Press,
academic publisher based at Koç University(*) (KU). Established in 2010, the publishing house aims to fill the gaps in academic publishing in Turkey and the intellectual world at large.

Koç University Press (KUP) books are published as part of five different series. The "Burasının Bilgisi" (Knowledge From Here) series consists of books written about the geography of the Middle East, including Turkey, and/or by researchers from this area; these include works which contribute significantly to their field, question or change the paradigms, and adopt previously unused findings or methods of analysis which have yet to be applied. The series features research on history, art history, politics, sociology, archeology, gender studies and cultural studies. The "Uçbeyleri" ("Frontiers") series is aimed at the general reader, featuring interesting, pioneering and seminal studies on fields such as positive science, humanities, literary theory, art, law, medicine and ethics. The "Maddiyat" ("Materiality") series adopts the "Uçbeyleri" approach to finance, economics, business, innovation and entrepreneurship. The "Tuhaf Etki" (Strange Feeling) series began in 2017 and features local Turkish fiction, arousing a "strange feeling" when read; the series aims to bring together previously published, forgotten works, as well as eccentric texts published for the first time. In 2017, the press began a new series, "Tefrika Dizisi", publishing works of fiction serialized between 1831 and 1928 but not previously published in book form.

The revenue from sales of KUP books is used to fund scholarships for students at KU.

KUP books challenge approaches towards democracy, the problems of the modern art world, whether we can survive without property, the fundamental principles of a society shared by animals and human beings, how we can start from scratch if what we call "civilization" collapses, the supply equilibrium of global warming, how social justice should be established, the results of the obsession with youth, the history of pain, and what kind of a genetic future awaits humanity.

https://press.ku.edu.tr/en/content/those-who-question-world

Koç University Research Center for Anatolian Civilizations *see* ANAMED

Koç University School of Medicine
see **Koç University**

Koç University School of Nursing,
a nursing school which came into existence following the affiliation of the Admiral Bristol Nursing School(*) to Koç University(*) (KU) in 1999. It was founded in partnership with the Johns Hopkins University School of Nursing and runs undergraduate, master's and doctoral level degree programs which aim to "prepare students for a career in professional nursing and to cultivate individuals who combine critical thinking, universal values, academic excellence and an interest in research". The undergraduate program covers four years of education and two summer terms of English and practical clinical training.

Since the 2001-02 academic year, supported by donations from Semahat Arsel(*) and Dr. Nusret Arsel(*), KU School of Nursing and SANERC(*) (Semahat Arsel Nursing Education and Research Center) have been based in a building on the site of the old Güzelbahçe Hospital in Nişantaşı, Istanbul. The old School of Nursing on Büyük Çiftlik Sokak, Teşvikiye, was also transformed into a dormitory for nursing students. From July 2015 onwards, the school has been based on the Koç University Health Sciences Campus(*) in Topkapı, which is also the location of Koç University Hospital(*).

The school's classrooms and laboratories are equipped with audio-visual technology, providing students with easy access to scientific and technological developments; the library has a regularly updated collection of resources primarily in relation to nursing training. Since 2010, the school has arranged a two-day Nursing Students' Event every year.

Semahat Arsel, chair of the Vehbi Koç Foundation Board of Directors, at the Nurses Day, 1997

In March 2008, Johns Hopkins University, which has one of the best nursing schools in the world, evaluated the KU School of Nursing and gave it a grading of "superior".

In 2016, it gained college status, keeping its name as Koç University School of Nursing (*see* Koç University).

Koç University Semahat Arsel Nursing Education and Research Center

see **SANERC**

Koç University Social Impact Forum

see **KUSIF**

Koç University Suna Kıraç Library,

a library which began as part of Koç University(*) (KU) in 1993. It was opened at the KU campus in İstinye before moving to the Rumelifeneri Campus together with the university's other units in 2000. It is one of Istanbul's best-equipped academic libraries.

The Suna Kıraç Library is based in a four-story building of 8,300 square meters in the center of the KU campus. It can seat 900 people and offers individual and group study areas, as well as six four-person group-study booths and 15 study rooms for those who wish to work in small groups. There is also a reading room containing all current subscription magazines and daily newspapers, as well as a seminar room used to host events for showing users how to get the best out of the library resources. During the academic term, the library is open 24 hours a day, seven days a week. The area called the "24 Hour Reading Room" is always open throughout the year, independent of the library's inner spaces.

The library's collections include a broad range of print and digital resources with over 250,000 books and 170,000 e-books, largely in English and Turkish. It subscribes to over 63,000 magazines, including online publications, and 120 digital databases in various subject areas. The library also houses writings and rare artifacts relating to Ottoman and European history, literature and religion. As well as the KU Health Sciences Library in Topkapı, other libraries that provide services in connection with the KU Suna Kıraç Library are: ANAMED(*) library in Beyoğlu, Istanbul; AKMED(*) library in Kaleiçi, Antalya; and the VEKAM(*) library in Keçiören, Ankara.

The library digitizes different cultural objects and texts and makes them accessible online. Among those currently available are the Manuscripts Collection, the Josephine Powell Slides Collection, the Hatice Gonnet-Bağana Hittite Collection, The Soundscape of Istanbul, the Rahmi Koç Museum Echoes of Industrial Legacy and the VEKAM LoCloud Project.

The Suna Kıraç Library hosts annual gatherings of local and international library organizations and is a member of the IFLA (International Federation of Library Associations and Institution), IATUL (International Association of Scientific and Technological University Libraries), ALA (American Library Association), and LIBER (Ligue des Bibliothèques Européennes de Recherche).

Koç University Stavros Niarchos Foundation Center for Late Antique and Byzantine Studies *see* **GABAM**

Koç University Vehbi Koç Ankara Studies Research Center *see* **VEKAM**

Koçi *see* **Koç School**

Koçzade Hacı Mehmet Efendi *see* **Koç Family**

Koçzade Hacı Mustafa Rahmi *see* **Koç Family**

KODA *see* **Village Schools Exchange Network**

Korukçu, Ünal *(b. July 19, 1937, Ankara – d. September 25, 2009, Izmir)*, banker and manager. From 1985 to 1998, he was a member of the Vehbi Koç Foundation(*) Board of Directors representing Türkiye İş Bankası A.Ş.

After completing his secondary education at Karşıyaka High School in 1955, Korukçu studied at the Academy of Economics and Commercial Sciences, graduating in 1958. In 1960, he began working at the Central Bank of Turkey and from October 1964 to June 1965, he studied bank administration in Italy. He began working at Türkiye İş Bankası A.Ş. in January 1966. In July 1970, he resigned from his role at Türkiye İş Bankası A.Ş. after being appointed chair of the Supervisory Board for the Türk Dış Ticaret Bankası (later Dışbank), a partnership between the Bank of America and Türkiye İş Bankası A.Ş. In February 1974, he returned to Türkiye İş Bankası A.Ş. as deputy director of external affairs; he was made London representative for the bank one month later. In March 1976, he was made senior deputy director of the Izmir branch, becoming director in February 1978.

Korukçu was made deputy chief executive of Türkiye İş Bankası A.Ş. in October 1984 and was appointed CEO on May 26, 1988. He served as chair of the board of directors of the Banks Association of Turkey from November 1996 to October 1998. On October 28, 1998, he retired as the longest serving CEO of Türkiye İş Bankası A.Ş. During his retirement, he settled in Izmir and was chair of the Yaşar Holding Executive Committee from January 1999 to May 2001. He died in Izmir on May 25, 2009.

Kule, full name KOÇ UNIVERSITY KULE, Koç University(*) (KU) corporate communication publication. The magazine, which has been published since September 2002, is released every six months. Each issue of *Kule* takes a popular topic as its theme, featuring pieces on academic and other activities taking place at KU, as well as the latest innovations, and experiences and success stories from members of the community. The magazine was transferred to Koç University Alumni Association (KUMED) in 2018.

KURIOUS, Koç University(*) popular science website established in 2014. Based on its motto, "Science for all", the website at *kurious.ku.edu.tr* publishes in Turkish and English. Its objective is to contribute towards creating a "science-literate" society to help Turkey reach the same level as other scientifically and technologically advanced countries. The website tries to reach the broadest possible section of society, using plain language to communicate information about new discoveries, technological developments and studies in Turkey and abroad.

KUSIF, full name KOÇ UNIVERSITY SOCIAL IMPACT FORUM, is a research and practice center at Koç University(*) (KU) focusing on social impact.

KUSIF was founded in 2012 to support the activities of non-governmental organizations, funding bodies, social enterprises and private sector entities by assessing their social impact to help with planning, integrating social impact analysis into their working principles, and setting standards for measuring social impact.

The center also spearheaded the foundation of the Turkish Social Impact Group and publishes guide books and research reports on social impact analysis and social entrepreneurialism. It creates social impact classes for undergraduate students, implements the Community Engagement and Leadership Track Program at KU, facilitates collaborative ties between social entrepreneurs and the public, and works on transforming KU into a sustainable campus.

KUSIF runs a number of projects, including Social Impact Measurement Tools for Young Social Entrepreneurship ("Know Your Impact"), Social Impact Measurement for Funders, Improving the Social Impact of NGOs Targeting Women: A Common Approach to Measurement, and Social Impact Measurement For Civil Society Organizations. In May 2016, KUSIF set up the two-year Social Entrepreneurship Development Program, "Change with Business", in partnership with the Vehbi Koç Foundation(*) and UniCredit Foundation, with the aim of increasing social impact by supporting social entrepreneurs to ensure their own sustainability. The Management of Social Impact Program for Non-Governmental Organizations, set up in 2017, aims to raise the awareness of social impact management among NGOs and increase their understanding and skill levels.

Kütükçüoğlu, Zehra *see* **Koç Family**

KWORKS, officially known as KOÇ UNIVERSITY ENTREPRENEURSHIP RESEARCH CENTER, an organization founded by Koç University (KU) in 2014 to support technology-based business models in becoming sustainable and scalable technological enterprises. The center operates as an important meeting hub for entrepreneurs, investors and other members of the entrepreneurial ecosystem, supporting entrepreneurs through infrastructure and playing an acceleratory role in the process from business model stage to commercialization.

Based on KU's Şişli campus, KWORKS provides support to enterprises at all levels, from the business model stage to the investment process, designing enterprise programs especially for the needs of entrepreneurs.

For early-stage enterprises without a business model, the process begins with the Pre-Accelerator Program, and when this reaches the productization stage the client continues more intensely with product or service development as part of the Accelerator Program. The Accelerator Program ensures that enterprises have swift access to investment and make fast progress with product or service commercialization.

Together with KWORKS LAB, which was established in 2016 with support from the Ministry of Development and Istanbul Development Agency, the center also provides support throughout the product development process, from design to prototype, for entrepreneurs developing hardware. It ensures that entrepreneurs are able to present their products to clients with as little expense and as quickly as possible. KWORKS LAB provides entrepreneurs with access to a technological laboratory equipped with 3D scanners and printers, a laser cutting machine, CNC machine, drones, oscilloscope, and digital multimeter.

The KWORKS senior board is made up of over 50 mentors and leading figures in Turkish business, helping to provide entrepreneurs with invaluable experience. As of 2018, the program has received nearly 3,000 applications, supported 22 entrepreneurs on the Accelerator Program and 36 on the Pre-Accelerator Program.

KWORKS also supports the building of a sustainable innovation infrastructure, with programs aimed not just at the needs of technology entrepreneurs, but also of partner organizations. Corporate innovation programs are designed to create innovative solutions and support product development in companies' key technological fields or sectors.

Additionally, KWORKS hosts over 100 annual events and its program of seminars, training and workshops has quickly made it into a hub for the entrepreneurial ecosystem.

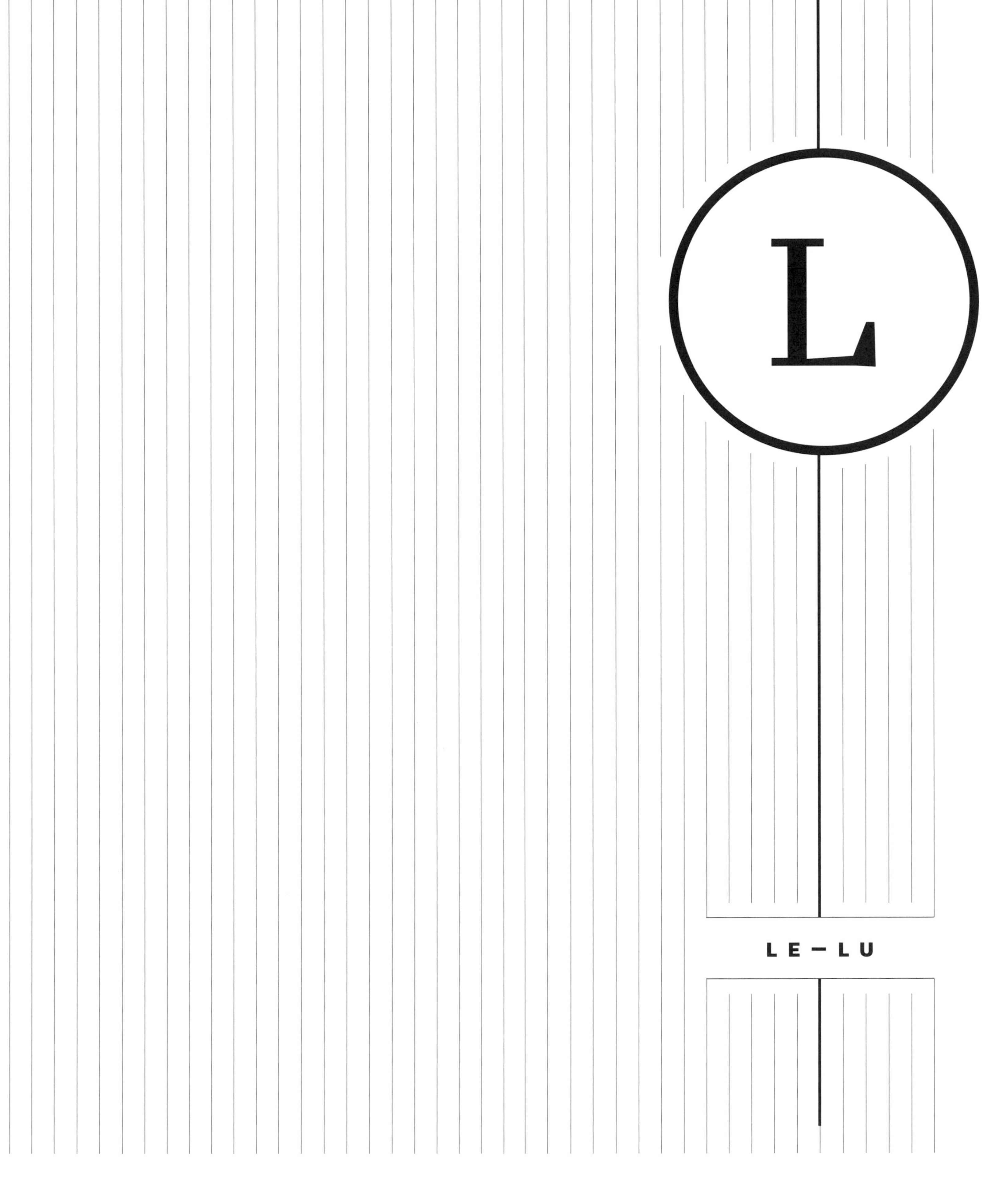

L
LE—LU

Lennox, Robert *(b. August 22, 1948, Belper, England)*, educational director. Lennox was the Koç Primary and High School (*see* Koç School) general director from 2008 to 2013.

After studying English and physical education at London University's Borough Road College (1966-69), he received a master's degree in education from Sheffield University (1981). From 1995 to 2008, Lennox worked in England and Bermuda as a middle school principal. In 2008, he became the Koç Primary and High School general director. During his tenure,

in 2012, Koç Primary and High School separated into Koç Primary, Middle and High Schools as part of the standardization of twelve-year mandatory education. Lennox retired from the school in 2013, but has continued serving as a consultant.

Lium, Rolf *(b. March 29, 1907, Minnesota?, USA – d. September 1986, Rye, New Hampshire, USA)*, physician and director. Lium served as chief physician at the American Hospital(*) from 1962 to 1966.

After completing a bachelor's degree at Carleton College in Northfield Minnesota and a medical degree at Harvard Medical School, Lium began working in Boston. In 1941, while working in Portsmouth Hospital in New Hampshire, he passed the American Board of Surgery exams to become a surgeon.

After coming to Istanbul in June 1962, Dr. Lium became the American Hospital's chief physician, developing new medical services and establishing cancer therapy and pediatric centers. During the same period, he also endeavored to increase the caliber of medical staff at the hospital. In July 1967, he resigned from his position and returned to the United States for "personal and family reasons".

Vehbi Koç(*) paid tribute to him with the following words, "Rolf Lium was a hard worker. He greatly expanded our hospital and found help from the United States to improve the administration and fix the finances."

Dr. Lium's three act play, *Kemal*, about the Ottoman palace and Atatürk's battles with the palace, was published in Switzerland in 1966.

Luminous Pandemonium
see **Koç School**

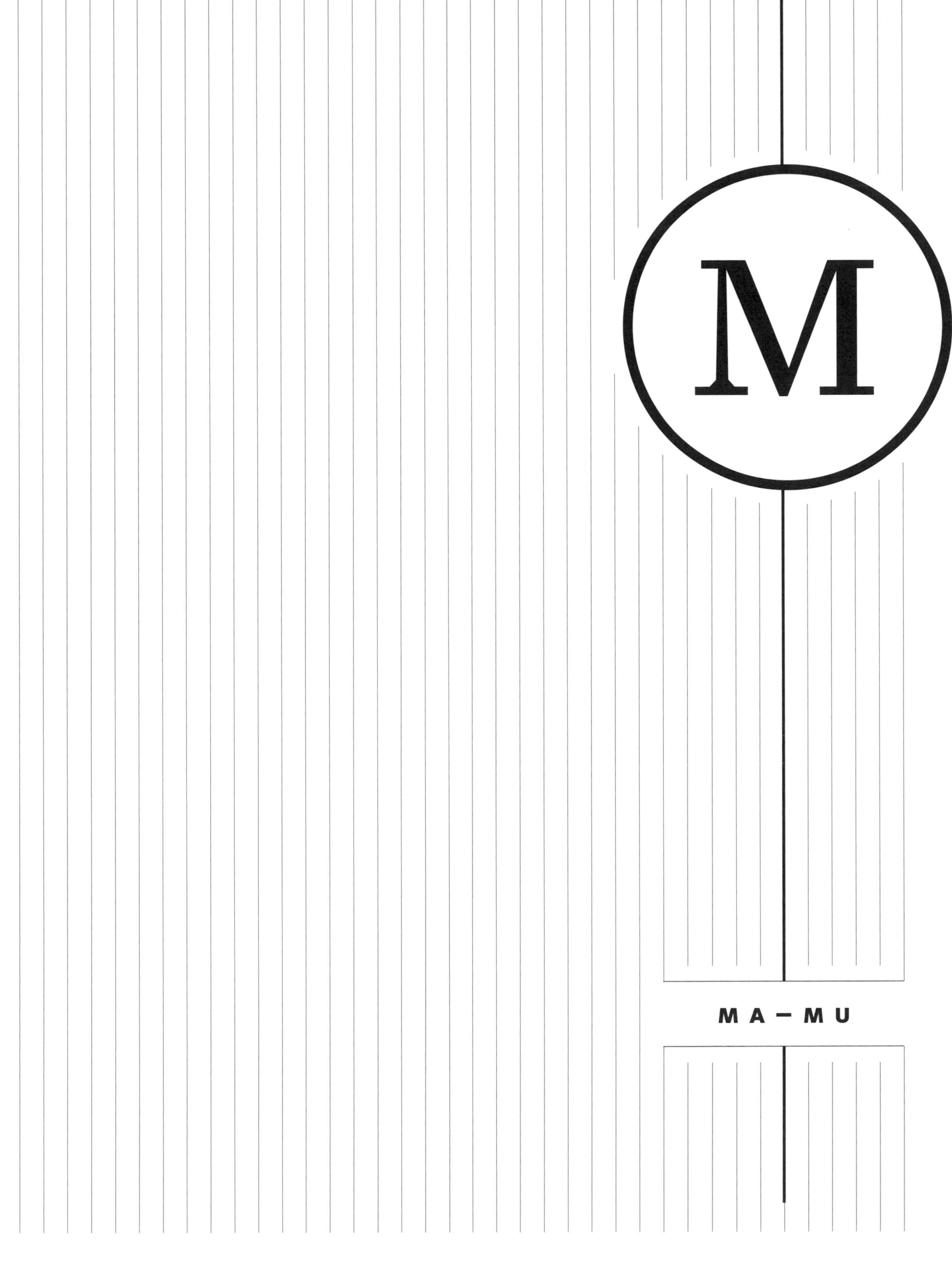
M
MA – MU

Mathematics Village *see* **Nesin Mathematics Village**

MedAmerican Medical Center, outpatient center serving the American Hospital(*) on Istanbul's Anatolian Side. Known as the MedAmerican Polyclinic, it opened in December 1997 in the Çiftehavuzlar area of Kadıköy. Although the polyclinic building is mid-sized at only 4,500 square meters, a full range of services is provided by doctors, who are exclusively from the American Hospital. The center has offered all basic outpatient services from the first day of its operations.

After a 10 million dollar investment, MedAmerican moved to a new building on Bağdat Street on June 11, 2015, becoming part of the Vehbi Koç Foundation(*) Healthcare Institutions. The center includes outpatient examination rooms for interventional and diagnostic treatments, as well as operating rooms equipped with digital systems and technology for operations that do not require hospitalization.

Megalli, Murad M(ichael) *(b. December 6, 1957, Egypt – d. February 4, 2011, Kurdistan Region of Iraq),* engineer, banker and collector.

Megalli emigrated to the United States as a teenager and studied civil engineering at George Washington University. After graduating in 1980, he worked as an engineer in the United States and Sudan for five years. In 1986, he received a master's degree from Yale University and began working at Citibank in New York. From 1987 to 1990, he worked in Citibank's Istanbul branch as an investment banker. Following this, he co-founded the consulting firm, Pangaea Partners Ltd. In 1997, he took over the Istanbul branch of Chase Manhattan Bank's investment banking operations for Central Asia, the Balkans and Turkey. In 1998, he was appointed as director of Chase's Russia and CIS operations. When Chase Manhattan merged with JP Morgan in 2001, becoming JP Morgan Chase, Poland was added to his area of operations. In the same year that Megalli moved to Turkey, he also took responsibility for operations in Turkey, Israel and Central Asia. In 2009, he became the CEO of operations in the Middle East, Northern Africa, Turkey and Central Asia. Megalli died in a plane crash while returning from a business meeting in the Kurdistan Region of Iraq in 2011.

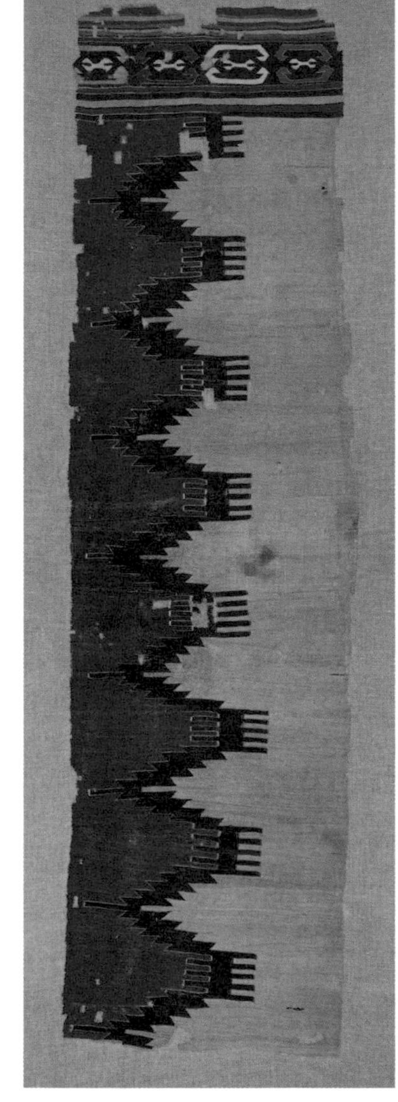

In addition to his work in the financial industry, Megalli amassed a collection of *ikat* textiles, unique to Central Asia, which were donated to the Textile Museum in Washington, DC, after his death. His collection of *kilims* was donated to the Sadberk Hanım Museum(*) in Istanbul.

Merkez Han, the current location of the ANAMED(*). It was the first building bought by Vehbi Koç(*) when he decided to move the headquarters of Koç Ticaret AŞ to Istanbul. Built in the early nineteenth century, the building is located on the street, İstiklal Caddesi.

Merkez Han is the oldest surviving building from before the Great Fire of 1831 in Pera, and is thought to have been the mansion of the Armenian Catholic Düzoğlu or Düzyan family. Today the building is partly used as ANAMED's cafeteria. In 1819, the building was seized from the family on the charge that it was a secret chapel, only to be returned in 1830. All that remains of the "secret" chapel is the carved stone "Lamb of God" panel on the building's third floor.

From 1881 onwards, the building housed the Club de Sport Oriental (which later became the Cercle d'Orient), a club for diplomats and high-ranking Ottoman officials. From 1883 to 1890, it was used as the Greek Consulate. Between 1898 and 1902, the Düzoğlu Mansion was renovated like other buildings on Cadde-i Kebir (now İstiklal Caddesi) as the street was widened. Due to this, turning the mansion into a five-story building subsequently needed structural reinforcement. Following these large-scale architectural changes, the Düzoğlu Mansion, still owned by the family, gained a function more in keeping with the socio-cultural developments of the late Ottoman Empire.

This multi-story, modern mansion then became a working building (*han*) in Beyoğlu, which was occupied by the US sewing machine manufacturer, Singer. It became known as Singer Han and the company continued to operate in the building after the foundation of the Turkish Republic.

When the building was bought by Vehbi Koç in 1960, it became known as "Merkez Han", and the following year it was occupied by one of the first Koç Group(*) companies, Gazsan Likid Gaz Ticaret ve Sanayi AŞ (Gazsan Liquid Gas Trade and Industry Inc.). Vehbi Koç's will stated that the building "will never be sold", and after housing various companies, in 2005, the building was transformed into a research center for Koç University(*). Academic activities began in the same year while Merkez Han underwent structural reinforcement and renovations. In 2008, these renovations and restorations, designed by the architect Fahrettin Ayanlar(*), were awarded with the Chamber of Architects 11th National Building Achievement Award. Renovations and structural reinforcements continued until the building's official opening in 2012.

SUNA KIRAÇ: MERKEZ HAN IN THE EARLY 1960S

On October 1, 1960, I started work at the Istanbul branch of Koç Ticaret AŞ working alongside my father until his death on February 25, 1996. I spent some interesting years at my workplace, which was in Merkez Han, a dilapidated building in the Beyoğlu district. This was a typical scene:

My father alone in one room; the meeting table was in his room. The late Hulki Alisbah in the room looking out onto the street. İsak de Eskinazis, who has also sadly passed away, sitting in the back room. My father's secretary, Zehra Tekbaş, typing with one finger as she sat in a windowless space that was more of a recess than a room. Haşim İşcan was in another room, while I sat in a recess opposite Zehra. There was a toilet as well. We constituted the entire cadre and the entire occupants of the floor. While we considered our premises to be perfectly clean and respectable, my mother, on one of her rare visits, pronounced it to be a dump, prompting the repair of the cracked marble stairs and toilet and the installation of a lift. Bless my late mother for showing her true self and meticulous attention to detail.

Suna Kıraç, *Ömrümden Uzun İdeallerim Var* (My Ideals, Longer than My Lifetime), Suna and İnan Kıraç Foundation Publications, Istanbul, 2006, p. 89

Middle East Technical University Vehbi Koç Student Dormitory, also known as THIRD DORMITORY, a B-type student residence in the Middle East Technical University (METU) campus in Ankara. It was built by Vehbi Koç(*) and donated to the university.

Construction began in 1967 and the building opened in the second semester of the 1967-68 academic year. Management of the building was handed over to the Vehbi Koç Foundation(*) in 1970. The dormitory, which consists of 101 four-bed rooms, has toilets and showers on every floor, a fully-equipped kitchen on alternate floors, two study lounges and an art room. The ground floor contains a canteen open to the students and accommodation is limited to female students.

In 1967, Vehbi Koç received the "Mala" Award from the METU Dormitories Building Contractor in recognition for providing the dormitory.

THE TALE OF BUILDING A STUDENT DORMITORY AT METU IN THE WORDS OF VEHBİ KOÇ...

I believe that for students to be successful, they must have comfortable living conditions and I loved seeing the benefits provided by the first student dormitory I built in Ankara. I had known the Middle East Technical University president, Kemal Kurdaş, for a long time. After he became president, he initiated numerous innovations and new works at the university. At the same time, he got involved with building student dormitories and sent a letter explaining the university's need for dormitories to a number of business people. This letter came to me on January 24, 1967 and summarized the work at METU as follows:

"It would be a great pleasure for all of us at the university to see you among us so you can witness the work here in person. Within four years, the university has achieved an intake of 4,600 students, increased the academic staff to over 500 and expanded the Middle East Technical University campus to include over 40 buildings and facilities with 13 million trees. Currently, our 1,150 male students live in two buildings built by the university and our 138 female students are being housed in rented apartments in the city. In order to meet the needs of the year ahead, we need to build a new dormitory for 1,000 students. Since we cannot meet this requirement from our own budget, we believe that the needs of our students can be met with donations and help from valued and benevolent citizens and institutions like yourselves: people who believe that higher education and technology is a vital part of our national life."

Vehbi Koç at the METU Campus together with the President Kemal Kurdaş (FAR LEFT) and the students

I was touched by this letter. I met with Kurdaş and he sent the project to me right away. It was beautifully planned. Once I had studied it, I agreed to build the dormitory. At that time, I was in London receiving treatment after I broke my shoulder falling off a horse. So I wrote to Hulki Alisbah asking him to inform Kemal Kurdaş of my decision on March 3, 1967:

"I'm getting old. On February 23, I could have died from my accident, God forbade. The Dormitory Act and Foundation Act, for some reason or other, is dragging on and on. While I still have the strength, I want to do a few things. I have no doubt you will do whatever you can do, and may God help you."

Hulki Alisbah and my son, Rahmi Koç, communicated my wishes to the Middle East Technical University. The Board of Trustees approved the decision, and on May 5, 1967, the dormitory's foundations were laid. The building was completed sooner than I expected, and so it was opened for students on February 12, 1968, in the second semester of the 1967-68 academic year. There were studies and lounges inside. Just as in the dormitory at Ankara University, a plaque was erected bearing my words:

"Helping to nurture young people is a debt owed to both humanity and the nation. For this reason, it was my happy duty to help with the student dormitory. I owe my gratitude to all those who sacrificed their labor and help, making my contribution even more valuable. What I expect from those who stay here is that, in return for the sacrifices that have been made for them, they study as mature and well-informed individuals. I believe that students from neighboring countries will remember the friendships and affection experienced here for as long as they live, and if they share it with their own countries and acquaintances, it will also be good for world peace.

Young people, this building was built for you, for you and future generations. I wish respect and success to all of you."

The building was named the "Vehbi Koç Student Dormitory." After anarchist movements gained hold in 1968, one student died in front of the building during clashes between students and security forces. In 1969, the "Vehbi Koç Student Dormitory" plaque was removed and replaced with the plaque, "Pirinçoğlu Dormitory," in memory of the dead student.

Vehbi Koç, *Hayat Hikâyem* (*My Life Story*), 4th Edition, Vehbi Koç Foundation Publications, Istanbul, 1983, pp. 118-19

Migration Research Center at Koç University *see* **MiReKoc**

MiReKoc, full name MIGRATION RESEARCH CENTER AT KOÇ UNIVERSITY(*), a research center established in 2004 to develop research and support collaboration between Koç University (KU) and the Foundation for Population, Migration and Environment (PME, Zurich). The center studies migration in Turkey and its surrounding areas and is the only academic program providing financial support for migration research in Turkey.

The aims of MiReKoc include: increasing the capacity of migration research in Turkey; creating new research fields and encouraging collaboration among those working in the field; evaluating migration research carried out in Turkey together with studies being conducted on a local and global scale; developing migration research in Turkey by correlating it with the "near abroad", which includes neighboring regions in Europe, Asia and Africa; bringing together scientists working in the migration field with non-governmental organizations (NGOs) and public sector players; and promoting dialogue between research and policy-making processes.

While bearing an undoubted significance as a sender, receiver and transit country in international migration systems, Turkey has also experienced heavy internal migration, particularly from rural to urban locations. The center primarily researches poorly documented periods of the country's migration history, as well as the study of strands and concepts of the migration phenomenon that have previously received scant attention. Facilitating the diffusion of an "original voice" for migration studies carried out in Turkey is another of the center's priorities, alongside the development of a migration studies interdisciplinary approach that incorporates economics, sociology, anthropology, political science, international relations, history, jurisprudence, demographics, urban studies, geography, psychology and pedagogy.

In addition to funding research projects and publishing project reports, MiReKoc organizes international conferences and multi-disciplinary workshops and seminars to discuss research agendas developed in different contexts. It creates international study and training programs, where scientific information can be shared across a broader academic spectrum including NGOs and local and national government officials.

PhD students and postdoctoral researchers working on migration issues can join the MiReKoc guest researcher program. Others wishing to gain experience in research are taken on as interns in the KU office and play an active role in migration research projects.

A support project to increase research, activities and coordination at MiReKoc was initiated by the Vehbi Koç Foundation(*) in 2016. Based in the Koç University Forced Migration Research Center (FMRC), it brings together all reliable sources relating to migration, particularly Syrian refugees, storing the information in an open access online database for all researchers and academic institutions.

THE MIREKOC BOOK SERIES

- **Balbo, Marcello, İçduygu, Ahmet and Serrano, Julio Pérez (ed.),** ***Countries of Migrants, Cities of Migrants,*** *Isis Press, Istanbul, 2013*
- **İçduygu, Ahmet (ed.),** ***Kentler ve Göç: Türkiye, İtalya ve İspanya Örnekleri*** **(Cities and Migration: Through the Examples of Turkey, Italy and Spain), Istanbul** *Bilgi University Press, Istanbul, 2012*
- **İçduygu, Ahmet and Kirişçi, Kemal (ed.),** ***Land of Diverse Migrations: Challenges of Emigration and Immigration in Turkey,*** *Bilgi University Press, Istanbul, 2009*
- **İçduygu, Ahmet and Sert, Deniz (ed.),** ***Borders Under Stress: The Cases of Turkey-EU and Mexico-USA Borders,*** *Isis Press, Istanbul, 2012*
- **İçduygu, Ahmet, Yükseker, Deniz and Aksel, Damla B. (ed.),** ***Migration around Turkey: Old Phenomena,*** *New Research, Isis Press, Istanbul, 2013*
- **İçduygu, Ahmet and Karaçay, Ayşem Biriz (ed.),** ***Critical Reflections in Migration Research: Views from the South and the North,*** *Koç University Press, Istanbul, 2015*
- **İçduygu, Ahmet and Göker, Gülru (ed.),** ***Rethinking Migration and Integration: Bottom-up Responses to Neoliberal Global Challenges,*** *Isis Press, Istanbul, 2015*
- **Karaçay, Ayşem Biriz and Üstübici, Ayşen (ed.),** ***Migration to and from Turkey: Changing Patterns and Shifting Policies,*** *Isis Press, Istanbul, 2014*
- **Karaçay, Ayşem Biriz, Sert, Deniz and Göker, Zeynep Gülru (ed.),** ***Waves of Diversity: Socio-Political Implications of International Migration in Turkey,*** *Isis Press, Istanbul, 2014*
- **Pitkänen, Pirkko, İçduygu, Ahmet and Sert, Deniz (ed.),** ***Migration and Transformation,*** *Springer, New York, 2012*
- **Sert, Deniz and Korfalı, Deniz Karcı (ed.),** ***Migration and Turkey: Changing Human Geography,*** *Isis Press, Istanbul, 2014*
- **Şimşek, Doğuş,** ***Ulusaşırı Kimlikler ve Londra'da yaşayan Kıbrıslı Türk, Kürt ve Türk Göçmen Çocukları*** **(Transnational Identities and Turkish, Kurdish, and Turkish Cypriot Immigrant Children Living in London),** *Istanbul Bilgi University Press, Istanbul, 2016*

SOME REPORTS FROM MIREKOC

- **İçduygu, Ahmet,** ***Turkey and International Migration. Report Prepared for the Annual Meeting of the OECD Expert Group on Migration,*** *November 2013*
- **İçduygu, Ahmet, Erder, Sema and Gençkaya, Ömer Faruk,** ***Türkiye'nin Uluslararası Göç Politikaları, 1923-2023: Ulus-devlet Oluşumundan Ulus-Ötesi Dönüşümlere*** **(Turkey's International Migration Policies, 1923-2023: From Nation-state Formation to Transnational Transformations),** *January 2014*
- **Korfalı, Deniz Karcı, Üstübici, Ayşen and Clerck, Helene de,** ***Turkey: Country and Research Areas Report,*** *January 2014*

SOME MIREKOC CONFERENCES

- **Past and Present Research Methods in Turkey,** *January 5, 2013*
- **The Metropolis-MiReKoc Academic Forum: Migration and Demographic Change: Causes and Consequences,** *March 18, 2013*
- **The Turkish-Greek Compulsory Population Exchange in its 90th Year: New Approaches, New Findings,** *November 16-17, 2013*
- **The MiReKoc 10th Year Symposium: Borders, Mobility and Diversity: Old Questions, New Challenges,** *November 20-21, 2014*

Mother Child Education Foundation

see **AÇEV**

Mustafa Koç Story and Essay Writing Competition,

a contest organized by the Koç School(*) Middle School Turkish Department and named after the late Mustafa V. Koç(*) in 2017. Students from the Koç School 8th grade class competed in the "essay" category and 8th grade students in other Istanbul schools competed in the "story" category. All short-listed entries were published in a booklet with illustrations created by Koç Middle School students.

Mustafa V. Koç Sports Award, an award in recognition of "contribution to Olympic values", created in 2017 by Koç Holding(*) in collaboration with the Turkish Olympic Committee. The award aims to support the vision of Mustafa V. Koç(*), who as well as being a business person, also made a major contribution to sports.

In 2017, the Olympic and world champion national wrestler, Taha Akgül(*), and the Paralympic Games and world champion national archer, Gizem Girişmen(*) were given the award for their "worldwide sporting success, achieved through the determination, discipline and commitment shown in their work and the embodiment of all the Olympic values in their personalities." In 2018, the European and World Champion national wrestler Yasemin Adar(*) received the award.

In her speech at the award ceremony in 2017, jury president Caroline Koç(*) stated the aim as: "to support young people with a passion and talent for sports" like Mustafa V. Koç and "encourage the values of sportsmanship and high ethics which were a major feature of his personality." She went on to describe the award's main objective as, "to spread Olympic values as a world view and a way of life, and to carry the message through exemplary people and organizations."

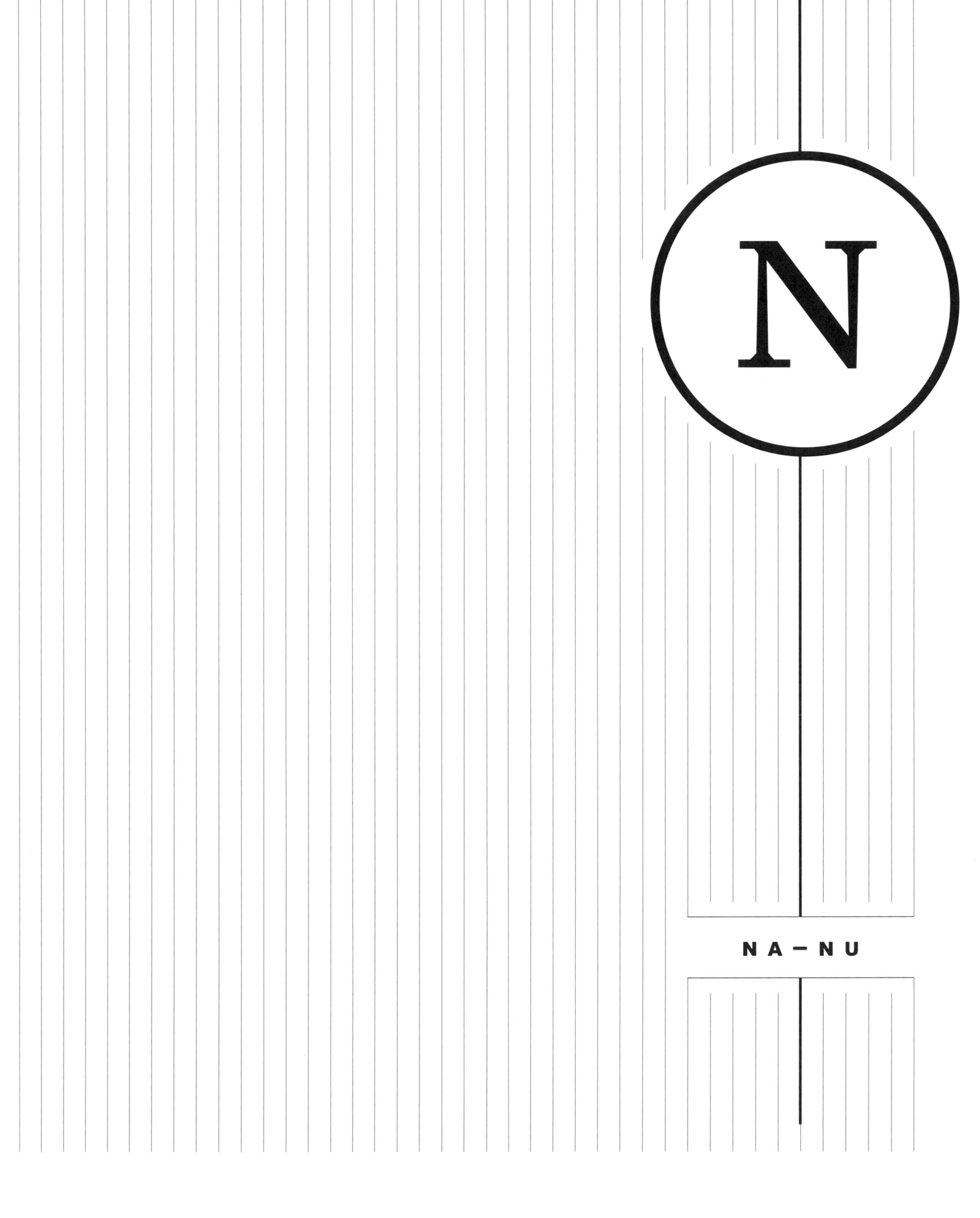
N
NA – NU

Nakkaştepe Facility *see* **Koç Holding AŞ Headquarters at Nakkaştepe**

NASAMER, full name DR. NUSRET-SEMAHAT ARSEL INTERNATIONAL BUSINESS LAW IMPLEMENTATION AND RESEARCH CENTER, an organization specializing in international trade law, founded in 2007 at the Koç University Law School(*) with contributions from Dr. Nusret Arsel(*) and Semahat Arsel(*). The center was created in response to the challenges of Turkish businesses competing in the globalized world market.

Its aims are to monitor developments in international trade, conduct and publish research, organize meetings and conferences, take part in educational and education-related events, and to collaborate with experts and organizations around the world. Since the center's foundation in 2008, it has organized and facilitated many international and domestic meetings. Papers presented at these conferences have been compiled in a book.

NASAMER'S FOUNDATION

For the past fifteen-twenty years, the international turn of Turkish businesses has made it extremely important to educate international trade lawyers in law systems of other countries and the sources of international trade law systems. From the beginning of the liberalization process in Turkey in the 1980s, when the country became attractive to foreign investors, developments in information technology also made conducting international business attractive to the Turkish business community. These are the reasons why we decided to establish a research center focused on international trade law at the Koç University Law School. Together with Semahat, we created a one million dollar fund and put together a board of directors from trusted individuals. The center was founded in 2007 to keep a close watch on all these developments, conduct and publish research, organize academic meetings and conferences, provide training seminars, and create collaborations with international scholars and organizations. The center is an important response to the challenges faced by Turkish businesses competing in a globalized world market.

Nusret Arsel, *Ana Duası* (A Mother's Blessing)
Yapı Kredi Publications, Istanbul, 2012, p. 137

Nesin, (Hüseyin) Ali *(b. November 18, 1957, Istanbul)*, a mathematician who established the Nesin Mathematics Village(*) and received the Vehbi Koç Award(*) in 2015 for his contribution to education with the Mathematics Village.

Ali Nesin completed his middle school education at Saint-Joseph French High School in Istanbul (1973) and high school education at Collège Champittet (1977) in Lausanne, Switzerland. He studied mathematics at Paris VII (Diderot) University (1977-81). After he received his doctorate in mathematics from Yale University (1985), he taught at the University of California, Berkeley (1985-86). In 1986, he returned to Turkey to complete his short-term military service. During this time, he was arrested and charged with "incitement to mutiny" after objecting to the same syringe being used to vaccinate numerous privates, but he was acquitted after the trial. After becoming professor in 1987, he taught at the Notre Dame University (1987-88) and University of California, Irvine (1990-96). In the 1993-94 academic year, he worked as a visiting lecturer at Bilkent University. Returning to Turkey in 1996, following the death of his father, Aziz Nesin, in 1995, Prof. Ali Nesin took on the management of the Nesin Foundation and also set up the Bilgi University Department of Mathematics, where he is still the chairperson. During the years 2001-02, Prof. Nesin worked as visiting lecturer at Lyon University, and he has been an elected member of the Science Academy(*) since 2013.

For ten years, Ali Nesin organized summer schools all over Turkey, driven by his belief that university mathematics education was inadequate. In 2007, with the support of Sevan Nişanyan, he established the Mathematics Village in Şirince, a village in the Selçuk district of Izmir. This non-profit institution, which is a global exemplar, opens its doors to over one thousand students every year. The school benefits from the voluntary support of respected academicians from Turkey and across the globe.

Prof. Ali Nesin at the award ceremony with Mustafa V. Koç

In 2015, Prof. Ali Nesin and the Mathematics Village received the Vehbi Koç Award for "breaking the mold of mathematics education in Turkey and for an exceptional achievement in the field of creative education." In his speech at the award ceremony, Prof. Nesin stated that mathematics, philosophy and art were not meant to bring money, but should be a way of life: "These things can't teach you what to think; they teach you how to think and to think about everything. They produce nothing, but are useful for everything. I give my students a problem to solve, and they think for two hours. The problem itself won't produce anything. But in order to persist in conjecture, conceptualize the problem correctly, explain the solution and solve the problem, you need to understand its challenges. This is useful for all things in life—in human relationships, in societal relationships and in your relationship with yourself." He also vowed that the award money would go to the construction of a Philosophy Village, also in Şirince.

Along with Prof. Nesin's various academic articles, he has also published the following popular books on mathematics: *Matematik ve Doğa* (Mathematics and Nature) (2007), *Matematik ve Sonsuz* (Mathematics and Infinity) (2007), *Matematik ve Oyun* (Mathematics and Games) (2007), *Matematik ve Korku* (Mathematics and Fear) (2008), *Matematik ve Develerle Eşekler* (Mathematics and Donkeys with Camels) (2008), *Matematik ve Gerçek* (Mathematics and Reality) (2009), *Matematik Canavarı* (Mathematics Monster) (2010) and *Matematik ve Sanat* (Mathematics and Art) (2012), as well as the following academic/scientific books: Önermeler Mantığı (Propositional Logic) (2009), *Sayma* (Counting) (2009) and *Sezgisel Kümeler Kuramı* (Intuitive Set Theory) (2009), *Analiz I* (Analysis I) (2011), *Analiz IV* (Analysis IV) (2011), *Analiz II* (Analysis II) (2015), *Temel Grup Teorisi* (Basic Group Theory) (2015), *Fen Liseleri İçin Matematik 1: Kümeler Kuramı* (Mathematics I for Science High Schools: Set Theory) (2017), and *Fen Liseleri İçin Matematik 2: Doğal SayılarYapısı* (Mathematics II for Science High Schools: The Structure of Natural Numbers) (2017). His correspondence with his father, Aziz Nesin, was first published in 1994 in four volumes as *Aziz Nesin-Ali Nesin Mektuplaşmaları* (Aziz Nesin and Ali Nesin: A Correspondence). In 2002, the book, *Canım Oğlum Canım Babacığım* (Dear Father, Dear Son) was printed in two volumes. From 2003 to 2013, Prof. Nesin was editor in chief of the Turkish Mathematics Association's magazine, *Matematik Dünyası* (Mathematics World). In 2016, a book created from biographical interviews with Aslıhan Lodi was published, *Matematik Köyünün Delisi Ali Nesin* (The Mathematics Village Idiot: Ali Nesin).

In addition to the major contribution he has made to the mathematics world over the last 20 years through numerous published articles, books, and research, Prof. Nesin has also changed the way many young people look at mathematics, making it more accessible and even a popular science. In 2018, Prof. Nesin was awarded the Leelavati Prize of the International Mathematical Union "for his outstanding contributions towards increasing public awareness of mathematics in Turkey, in particular for his tireless work in creating the Mathematical Village."

Nesin Foundation, a non-governmental organization (NGO) supported regularly by the Vehbi Koç Foundation(*) and established in 1973 to "ensure that children who grow up with few educational opportunities produce more than they consume, are constantly developing themselves, look internally and externally with a critical eye and grow up into productive individuals with social responsibility, self-confidence and altruistic values."

The Nesin Foundation's main site in Çatalca, Istanbul, accepts about forty pre-school or early-years elementary school children, who stay of their own volition until they feel they have enough education, skills and maturity to navigate society independently. The foundation has also established a farm covering 36,000 square meters not far from the site. The Nesin Publishing House is a subsidiary of the foundation.

The Nesin Mathematics Village(*), in Şirince in the Selçuk district of Izmir, is affiliated to the Nesin Foundation and won the Vehbi Koç Award(*) in 2015 together with its founder Ali Nesin(*). Work is underway to establish a Philosophy Village on land adjacent to the Mathematics Village.

Nesin Mathematics Village, a non-profit educational institution affiliated with the Nesin Foundation(*). It was established by Prof. Ali Nesin(*) to teach young people mathematics and encourage mathematics research. In 2015, the Mathematics Village and Ali Nesin received the Vehbi Koç Award(*) for education.

After his father, Aziz Nesin, died in 1995, Prof. Ali Nesin returned from lecturing in the USA and founded the Istanbul Bilgi University Department of Mathematics in 1996. Seeing that university students were insufficiently trained in mathematics, for ten years Prof. Nesin organized six to seven-week summer schools every summer. In 2007, based on these experiences, he established the Mathematics Village in Şirince in Izmir's Selçuk district with the support of Sevan Nişanyan. Through the Nesin Foundation, the Nesin Mathematics Village helps students at each level, from primary to higher education, entirely through donations from the public and

young people serving as volunteers. Every year more than a thousand students from Turkey and all over the world come to the Village, benefitting from working with the renowned academicians who volunteer there.

The Mathematics Village covers nearly 22,000 square meters of land, and includes accommodation for students, teachers, and staff, as well as indoor and outdoor classrooms, a conference salon, and a library. In addition to short programs scheduled during school holidays, there are also summer schools lasting from two weeks to three months, which are attended by about 150-250 high school and university students each day. In addition to their academic work, for one to two hours each day students are expected to work on a rotation basis to complete tasks such as laundry, cleaning, food preparation and watering the garden.

New Approaches in Civil Society Conference, International conference organized by TÜSEV(*) on the occasion of its twentieth anniversary. Supported by the Vehbi Koç Foundation(*) and the Sabancı Foundation, the conference, which took place on November 21-23, 2013 and was hosted by the Kadir Has University, had the theme "the next decade of non-governmental organizations". The principal purpose was to bring together TÜSEV members, non-governmental organizations and stakeholders in Turkey, enable them to share experiences with experts from various countries and build networks.

Nilüfer Koç Middle School
see **17 Schools Project**

Nursing Fund, a fund created under the auspices of the Vehbi Koç Foundation(*) (VKV) on December 15, 1974 with a provisory donation of five million Turkish lira from Vehbi Koç(*). The fund's purpose is to identify problems in nursing in Turkey and support the generation of viable and lasting solutions. In his letter to the VKV Board of Directors on December 3, 1974, Vehbi Koç explained the intentions behind the fund: "The five million lira donation I'm making is to enable the foundation to contribute to the national training of our nurses, so they can be knowledgeable, bound to their duty and possess the material and moral requisites of their vocation." A Nursing Committee, under the chairmanship of Semahat Arsel(*), was founded to manage the fund. It was composed of representatives of the Ministry of Health, the heads of nursing academies and representatives of the Turkish Nurses Association(*).

The following books, published with the proceeds of this fund, are used as core text books in nursing schools: *Hemşireliğin Temel İlkeleri* (The Fundamental Principles of Nursing), *Hemşirelikte Ana Psikiyatrik Kavramlar* (Key Psychiatric Concepts in Nursing), *Hemşirelik Teknikleri El Kitabı* (A Handbook to Nursing Techniques), *Hemşire Hasta İlişkilerinde Kişiler Arası Süreçler* (Interpersonal Procedures in Nurse-Patient Relations) and *İç Hastalıkları Hemşireliği* (Internal Medicine and Nursing). Every year since 1990, two nurses have been sent to Houston Methodist Hospital in the USA to be educated in intensive care nursing. From 1990 to 1992, courses in intensive care were organized with nurses working in intensive care units in a number of hospitals. On November 28-30, 1990, the "Views on Nursing Symposium" was held in Abant and attended by members of the Ministry of Health. At the time of writing, over 40 nursing research projects have been supported and more than 2,000 scholarships have been awarded to nursing students.

Today, the educational and vocational initiatives supported by the Nursing Fund are largely managed through SANERC(*) (Semahat Arsel Nursing Education and Research Center, founded in 1992) and Koç University School of Nursing(*), founded in 1999. The Nursing Fund has supported special vocational development projects led by nurses since 2003 as part of the "Vehbi Koç Foundation Nursing Fund Support Program".

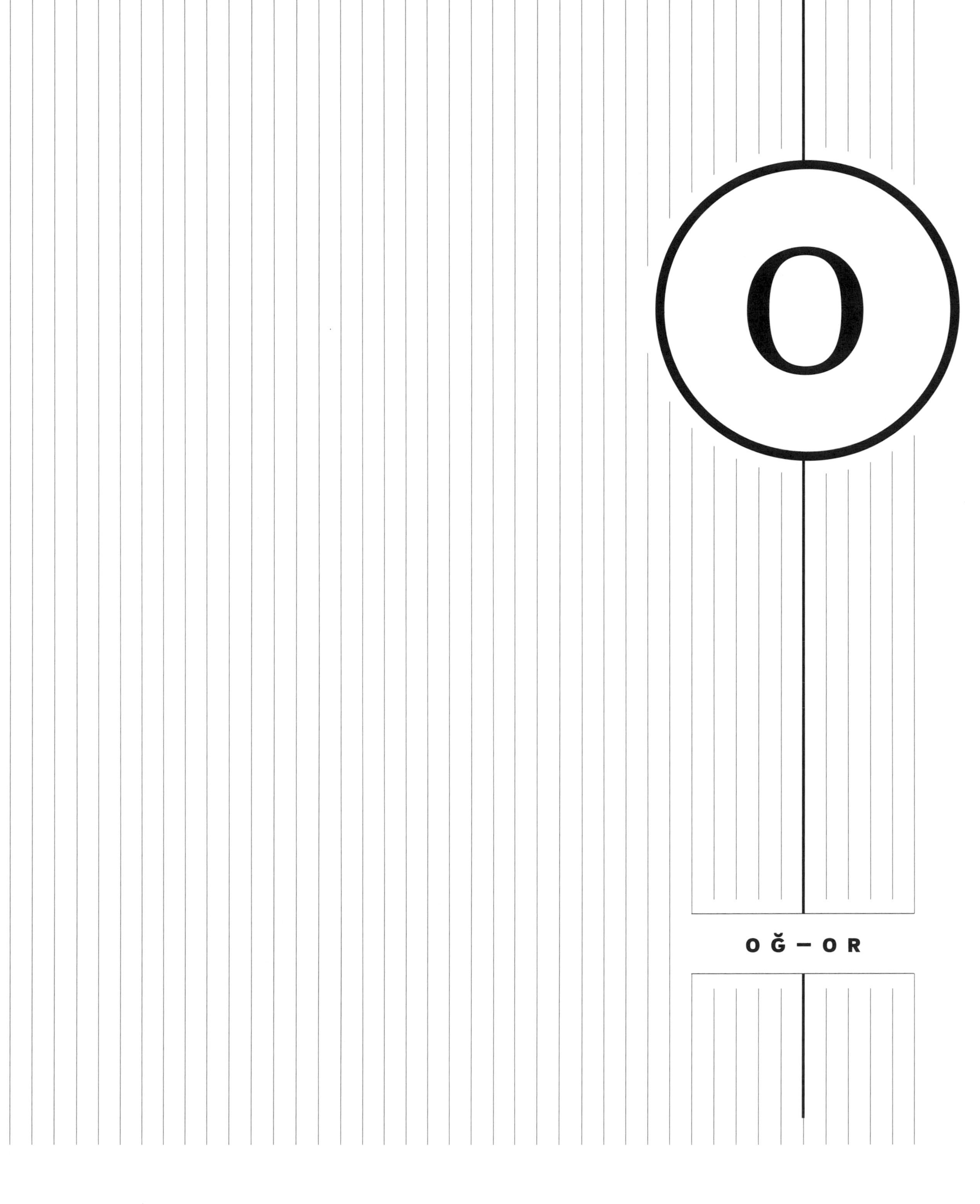

O

OĞ — OR

Oğuzman, Kemal *(b. December 15, 1927, Gümüşhacıköy, Amasya – d. June 30, 1995, Istanbul)*, lawyer and academician. Member of the Vehbi Koç Foundation(*) Board of Directors from its foundation in 1969 until his death in 1995. He also served for a long time as part of the management of Koç Holding(*) and as a consultant for companies affiliated with Koç Holding.

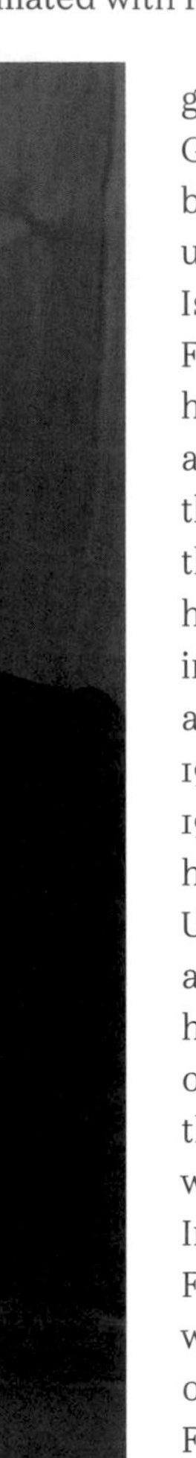

In 1946, Oğuzman graduated from Galatasaray High School, before completing undergraduate studies at Istanbul University (IU) Faculty of Law. Following his graduation, he was appointed assistant to the Civil Law Chair at the same faculty. In 1955, he received a doctorate in law, becoming an associate professor in 1957, and a professor in 1965. From 1973 to 1974, he served as Istanbul University's vice rector, and from 1970 to 1980 he was a representative of the Faculty of Law in the university senate. He was also a member of the Inter-university Council. From 1978 to 1980, he was a founding member of the Ege University Faculty of Law.

In addition to his expertise in civil law, Professor Oğuzman has written a number of works on labor and social security law. He was a member of the International Society for Labor and Social Security Law and served as president of the Turkish National Committee for Labor and Social Security Law. He represented both the government of Turkey and the Turkish Confederation of Employer Associations at International Labor Organization (ILO) annual meetings. He was involved in the commissions to create a new Civil Law Code in 1976 and 1981, serving as commission president from 1983 to 1984.

Following his retirement from the Istanbul University Faculty of Law due to reaching the mandatory retirement age, he served as dean of Galatasaray University Faculty of Law, where he had previously played a founding role and taught civil law in its early days. While working at Galatasaray, he fell suddenly ill and passed away on June 30, 1995.

Okutan, Nuri *(b. 1962, Eğirdir)*, statesman and winner of the Vehbi Koç Award(*) in 2006 for education.

He graduated from Ankara University Faculty of Political Science Department of Business Administration in 1986, before completing a master's degree at Uludağ University. Starting work in the same year, he served as district governor in various provinces and assumed the roles of branch manager, department head and deputy director in the Ministry of Interior. He served as the governor of Siirt (2000), Sakarya (2004), Trabzon (2007) and Şanlıurfa (2009). Okutan was appointed to Ankara in August 2011, retaining the rank as a non-commissioned governor, but resigned from the post in 2015 to become an Isparta MP.

While Okutan was governor of Siirt, he championed pre-school education and education for girls. As a result of work carried out during his governorship, pre-school education participation rates in Siirt rose from 4% to 64%, and Siirt rose to the top of pre-school education rankings in Turkey. During his governorship of Sakarya, he implemented several projects with the theme, "Let's Do It for Education, Sakarya"; these included developing pre-school education and encouraging reading habits among children. Okutan also placed great importance on cultural and architectural work. In recognition for his contribution to education, Okutan received the Vehbi Koç Award in 2006.

Nuri Okutan (MIDDLE) **at the award ceremony with Semahat Arsel and Mustafa V. Koç**

Onur, Jale *(b. February 10, 1952, Ankara)*, educator and director. She served as deputy general director of Koç School(*) from 2000 to 2012.

She completed her secondary education at the Üsküdar American Academy for Girls in 1970, graduating from the English Lanuage Teaching Department at Marmara University in 1974 and the German Philology Department at Istanbul University in 1979. In 1993, she received a master's degree in teaching a second language from the School for International Training in Vermont, USA. She began her doctorate in international education at Bath University in England in 2000, completing it in 2008.

From 1974 to 1978, Onur taught English at private schools in Istanbul and then worked as a translator and director of her own translation agency from 1979 to 1989. In 1989, she began teaching at Koç High School in the English preparatory department. After serving as deputy director of the middle school for two years (1996-98), she was appointed as deputy general director, a position she held until 2012. In 2013, she founded her own educational consulting company. She has been an associate professor in the Department of Foreign Languages of the Faculty of Education at Maltepe University since 2015 and published the book *Teaching in the Knowledge Age and International Baccalaureate* in 2016.

Operation Room Art Gallery *see* **American Hospital**

Orbis, international, non-profit organization dedicated to preventing blindness and treating eye diseases in developing countries. The Vehbi Koç Foundation(*) has provided periodic support to Orbis since 1982 by providing research and education scholarships to relevant health staff.

From its establishment in 1982 until the present day, Orbis has contributed to the treatment of 23.3 million patients with eye diseases and furthered the training of 325,000 medical professionals in 92 countries. Based in New York, its best known program, known as the Flying Eye Hospital, is located in a DC-10 jet plane. This traveling hospital accommodates a center for eye disease treatment and training, providing both education for medical professionals in the areas it visits and free treatments to patients.

In some countries, Orbis has created local treatment and education programs in specific hospitals. Its Cybersight program aims to establish an online communication network among health professionals treating eye diseases.

Orhangazi Koç Elementary and Middle School *see* **17 Schools Project**

Orhon, (Hüseyin) Talat *(b. September 24, 1924, Sürmene, Trabzon – d. December 5, 2006, Istanbul)*, banker and director. Represented Türkiye İş Bankası A.Ş. on the Vehbi Koç Foundation(*) Board of Directors from 1974 to 1980.

Orhon completed his secondary education at Trabzon High School and graduated in 1950 from Istanbul University Faculty of Economics. His career began at Türkiye İş Bankası A.Ş., where he served as assistant auditor, auditor and manager of the Şişli branch, before joining the bank's board of directors in 1967. He remained in this position until he was appointed as deputy chief executive in 1972. In October 1980, he became the general director of Türkiye Şişe ve Cam Fabrikaları AŞ (Turkish Glass Factories Inc.) and a member of its board of directors, retiring in 1989 when he reached the mandatory retirement age. He also served as deputy chair of the Türk Dış Ticaret Bankası (Dışbank) Board of Directors and chair of the Yatırım Finansman AŞ Board of Directors. In 1987, Orhon received an honorary doctorate from Istanbul Technical University.

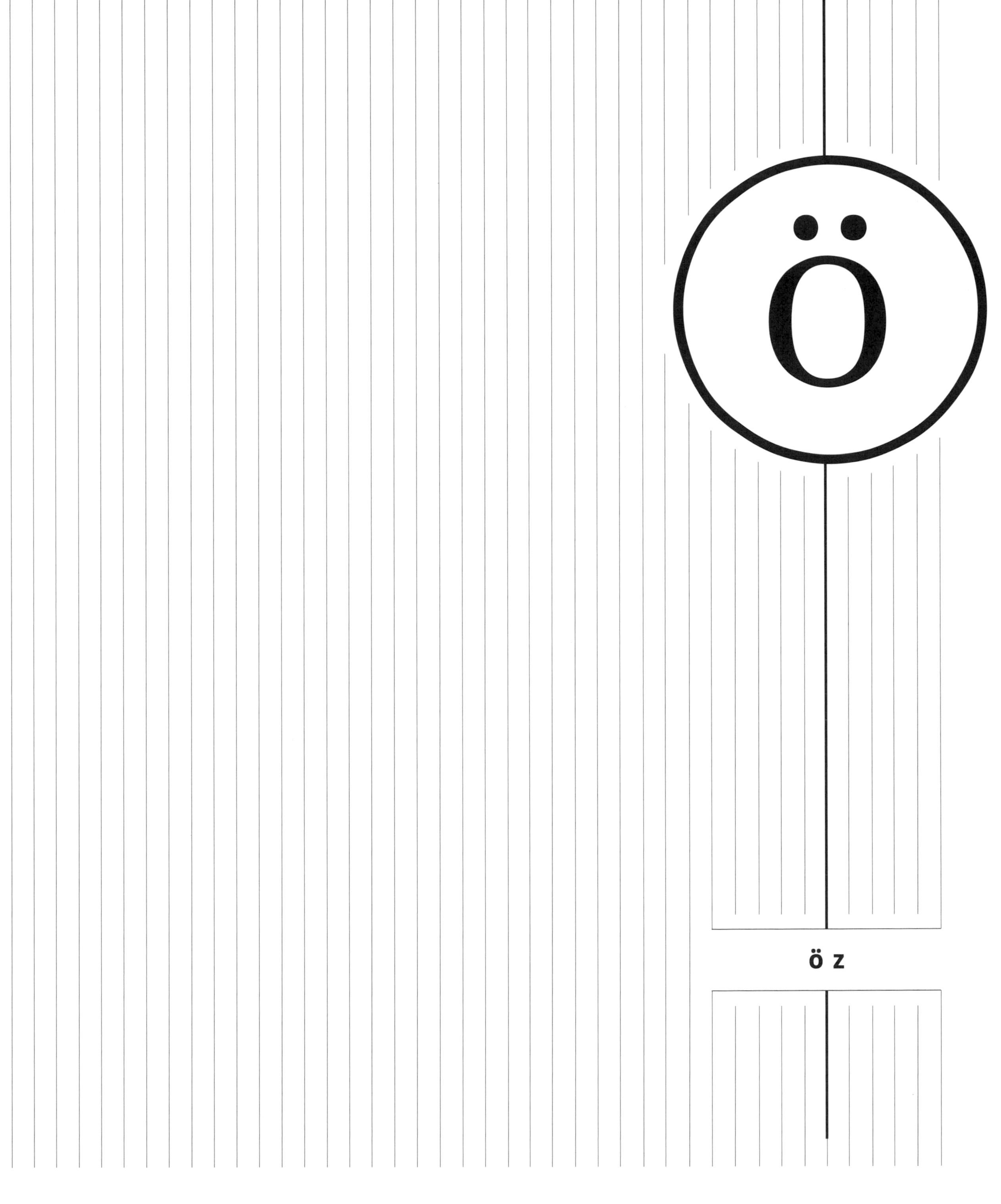

öz

Özaydınlı, Bülend *(b. 1949, Eskişehir)*, director and businessman. He represented Koç Holding(*) on the Vehbi Koç Foundation(*) Board of Directors from 2002 to 2006.

Özaydınlı graduated from Maarif College in Izmir in 1967 and received a bachelor's degree from the American University of Beirut in 1971. He began his career in 1972, serving in a variety of senior management roles at OYAK until 1987, when he became deputy general manager at one of the Koç Holding(*) companies, Maret AŞ. In 1990, he was appointed general manager of Migros. In 2000, he became the president of the Koç Holding Fiat (Tofaş) Group and alongside this position, he was appointed as the acting CEO in the following year and served as CEO from 2002 to 2007. On May 1, 2007, he resigned from Koç Holding and handed over to Bülent Bulgurlu(*).

When BC Partners bought Migros in 2008, Özaydınlı became a partner in Migros and assumed the chair of the Migros Board of Directors, stepping down in March 2016 to hand over to Tuncay Özilhan.

Özcan, Aydoğan *(b. 1978, Istanbul)*, scientist. In 2016, he received the Rahmi Koç Medal of Science(*) from Koç University(*) in recognition for his "outstanding fundamental scientific contribution to computational imaging, microscopy and photonics, and the development of innovative technologies for telemedicine, medical sensing and diagnostic applications."

Özcan graduated from Istanbul Atatürk High School of Science in 1996 and completed a bachelor's degree at Bilkent University Department of Electrical and Electronics Engineering in 2000. In 2005, he received a doctorate from the Department of Electrical Engineering at Stanford University, USA, staying on briefly as a postdoctoral fellow. In 2006, he became a researcher and lecturer at the Harvard Medical School Wellman Center for Photomedicine. In the following year, he was appointed assistant professor in the Department of Electrical Engineering at the University of California, Los Angeles, (UCLA) where he is still working at the Howard Hughes Medical Institute. He is also director of the Bio- and Nano-Photonic Laboratory connected to the School of Engineering and associate director at the California NanoSystems Institute at UCLA. Professor Özcan holds more than 30 patents in the fields of telemedicine, medical sensing, nanoscopy and wide-angle and lenseless imaging, along with 20 patent applications pending approval. In addition to publishing over 450 articles, he also published the book, *Non-destructive Optical Characterization Tools*, in 2008.

Professor Özcan's most popular invention is an application that transforms a mobile phone into a microscope that can be used for blood testing, enabling the results to be sent to a medical center with one click and providing a cheap and quick method of patient diagnosis. Due to this invention, in October 2012, the American magazine, *Popular Science*, named him "one of the ten most brilliant scientists in the world".

Professor Özcan is an elected member of several professional organizations, including the International Society for Optics and Photonics (SPIE), the Optical Society of America and the Biomedical Engineering Society. He is a founder and member of the board of Holomic/Cellmic LLC, which was named a "technology pioneer" by the World Economic Forum in 2015. He received the United States Presidential Early Career Award for Scientists and Engineers in 2011 and the Rahmi M. Koç Award for Science. His outstanding contribution to the fields of computational imaging, sensing and diagnosis earned him other awards from numerous prestigious organizations, including the Institute of Electrical and

Prof. Aydoğan Özcan (MIDDLE) **at the award ceremony with Koç University President Prof. Umran İnan** (LEFT) **and Rahmi M. Koç**

Electronics Engineers (IEEE) Photonics Society, the International Commission for Optics, the National Academy of Engineering Grainger Foundation, the Bill & Melinda Gates Foundation, the National Science Foundation, SPIE, the Massachusetts Institute of Technology (MIT) and the Okinawa Foundation.

Özdoğan, Mehmet (Celal) *(b. May 30, 1943, Istanbul)*, archaeologist known for his prehistorical archaeology work in the Marmara Region. He received the Vehbi Koç Award(*) in 2008.

Özdoğan graduated from Robert College(*) in 1963 and Istanbul University Faculty of Letters Department of Prehistory in 1969. Due to a lack of vacant staff positions in the department, he began to work as an "honorary assistant" in 1970 and completed his doctorate with a dissertation titled, "Fikirtepe" in 1979. In 1994, he became a professor of prehistory at the same faculty, and continued to teach there until his retirement in 2010.

At the beginning of his career, he worked on archaeological excavations at Çayönü (Batman) and Middle East Technical University's Keban and Lower Euphrates projects, where he developed a new model of surface investigation and explored the spread of the first farming communities from Anatolia to Southeast Europe. He played a role in the formation of the Turkish Academy of Sciences Cultural Sector and Cultural Inventory (TÜBA-TÜKSEK). His excavation work in the Marmara Region, especially at the Yarımburgaz Cave (Istanbul), Tilkiburnu and Taşlıcabayır (Kırklareli), and Pendik (Istanbul) Neolithic period, Toptepe (Tekirdağ) and Hocaçeşme (Edirne) shed light on the prehistoric cultures of the region. These excavations showed that cultural communication between Anatolian and Balkan cultures was not just limited to migration, but also included cultural adaptation and exchanges of knowledge.

Additionally, Professor Özdoğan focused on the historical development of archeology as a discipline, the establishment of archeological policies and the approach to "cultural heritage management" necessary to pass this on to society. During the course of this work, he initiated a new platform within international archaeological bodies and study groups, which facilitated discussion about the place of Turkish archaeology within world archaeology.

Prof. Özdoğan, who was an elected member of the Turkish Science Academy (TÜBA) (2002-11), the Science Academy(*) (2011) and the US National Academy of Sciences (2005), received the TÜBA Service Award in 2011. In 2008, he received the Vehbi Koç Award for culture in recognition of his "contribution to the field of prehistorical archaeology in the Marmara Region."

Professor Özdoğan's chief works include: *Aşağı Fırat Havzası 1977 Yüzey Araştırmaları* (1977; Lower Euphrates Basin 1977 Survey), *Neolithic in Turkey* (1999), *Türk Arkeolojisinin Sorunları ve Koruma Politikaları* (2001; Problems and Conservation Policies in Turkish Archaeology)

At the award ceremony (FROM LEFT TO RIGHT) **Mustafa V. Koç, Prof. Mehmet Özdoğan, Semahat Arsel, Minister of Culture Ertuğrul Günay, Rahmi M. Koç ve Governor of Istanbul Muammer Güler**

Güneydoğu Anadolu'nun Kültür Tarihindeki Yerine Farklı Bir Bakış (2003; A Different View on the Place of Southeastern Anatolia in Cultural History), *Arkeolojinin Politikası ve Politik Bir Araç Olarak Arkeoloji* (2006; Politics of Archaeology and Archaeology as a Political Tool), *Batı Düşünce Sistemi İçinde Arkeolojinin Yeri ve 21. Yüzyılda Yeni Arayışlar* (2008; The Place of Archaeology in the Western Thought Systems and New Quests of the 21st Century) and *Arkeolojik Kazılar: Bilimsel Çalışma mı? Toprak Hafriyatı mı?* (2011; Archaeological Excavations: Scientific Study or Earthworks?).

Özince, Ersin *(b. June 6, 1953, Havran, Balıkesir)*, banker and director. He was CEO of Türkiye İş Bankası A.Ş. and represented the company on the Vehbi Koç Foundation(*) Board of Directors from 1999 to 2011.

In 1970, he completed his secondary education at Izmir Private Turkish College and in 1975 graduated from the Middle East Technical University Faculty of Economics and Administrative Sciences Department of Business Administration. He began his career at Türkiye İş Bankası A.Ş. as an assistant inspector in January 1976. In 1986, he became assistant manager of the Accounting Department, followed by group manager in 1988. He was appointed the first director of Funds Managements when the department was founded and in 1992 became manager of the Yenişehir branch in Ankara. He became deputy chief executive in 1994 and the 15th chief executive officer of Türkiye İş Bankası A.Ş. on October 28, 1998. He was chair of the board of directors at the Türkiye Sınai Kalkınma Bankası (TSKB) from April 2009 to April 2011 and at the Banks Association of Turkey from November 1998 to May 2000 and June 2002 to April 2011. After leaving his position as CEO of Türkiye İş Bankası A.Ş. at the end of March 2011, Özince was elected as chair of the board of directors at Türkiye İş Bankası A.Ş. and Türkiye Şişe Cam Fabrikaları AŞ. He remained in the latter position until April 2017.

Özsaraç, Koray *(b. June 11, 1972, Karabük),* educator and director. From 2013 to 2018 he served as general director of the Koç School(*).

After completing his secondary education at Istanbul's Tarhan College in 1990, he graduated from Marmara University English Language Teaching Department in 1996. In 1998, he became a translator at Koç High School and was appointed as an English teacher at Koç Primary School in 2000. From 2004 to 2006, he studied for a master's degree on Teaching English to Speakers of Other Languages at Charles Sturt University, Australia. In 2008, he became the director of Koç High School, staying in the position for five years until he was appointed general director of the Koç School in August 2013. He remained there until 2018.

Öztuncay, Bahattin *(b. August 19, 1958),* writer, curator, arts and culture consultant and manager. He has been an arts and culture consultant at Koç Holding(*) Energy Group and Aygaz since 2002 and general coordinator of Arter(*) since 2009.

Öztuncay completed his secondary education at St George's Austrian High School in 1977 and graduated from Vienna University of Technology Faculty of Engineering with a master's degree in 1984. His interest in the photographic history of the Ottoman period and Istanbul began during his student days in Vienna. His first book on the subject, *James Robertson, Pioneer of Photography in the Ottoman Empire*, was published in 1992. In 1993, he was chosen as a corresponding member of the Royal Photographic Society of Great Britain in appreciation of his work on photographic history. His biographical study, *Vasilaki Kargopulo, Photographer to His Majesty the Sultan* was published in 1999, and his two volume book, *The Photographers of Constantinople*, featuring the biographies and selected photos of national and international photographic artists, was published in 2003. In 2004, he collated the book, *Hatıra-i Uhuvvet* (Memories of Friendship), which contained portraits of leading personalities of the Ottoman and Republican eras along with their signatures and dedications. In 2011, his book *Dynasty and Camera, Portraits from the Ottoman Court*, containing selected photos from the collections of Ömer M. Koç(*), was published. Öztuncay has curated and collated catalogs for several exhibitions at ANAMED(*) and the Sadberk Hanım Museum(*). He is also a member of the European Society for the History of Photography and sits on the board of directors of the Geyre Foundation(*).

PA—PR

Paulus, J(ohn) Anthony *(b. December 29, 1949, California, USA)*, educational institution director. Paulus served as the general director of Koç Primary and High School (*see* Koç School) from 2005 to 2008.

He studied in the Department of English Language and Literature at Stanford University (1968-72) and completed a master's degree in education at Boston University in 1979. From 1984 to 2005, he was director of various secondary education institutions in the USA. In 2005, he became general director of the Koç Primary and High School, remaining in the position until 2008.

Pekelman, Talat A. *(b. September 12, 1964, Istanbul)*, engineer and director. From 1999 to 2001, he served as general director of the American Hospital(*).

He completed his secondary school education in 1981 at Istanbul's Beşiktaş Anatolian High School and graduated from Istanbul Technical University as an electronics engineer in 1985. He received a master's degree in international business administration from Istanbul University in 1986 and in biomedical engineering from Boğaziçi University in 1989. After completing a management training program at Houston Methodist Hospital (1989-92), he became deputy general director of the American Hospital, followed by general director in 1999. He parted in 2001, becoming a director at PNB Consulting (2001-04) and Kürüm Holding (2005-17). He is currently serving as general director of Filokur.

Pera Museum, private museum founded by the Suna and İnan Kıraç Foundation(*). It aims to offer a diverse range of exceptional culture and arts services and has become one of Turkey's leading art institutions since it opened to the public on June 8, 2005.

Situated in Istanbul's Tepebaşı neighborhood, the Pera Museum is housed in the renovated former Bristol Hotel, designed by the Greek architect, Achilleas Manussos in 1893, and also includes an adjacent five-story building. The museum displays a selection of works from the Orientalist Paintings, Anatolian Weights and Measures, and Kütahya Tiles and Ceramics collections belonging to the Suna and İnan Kıraç Foundation. The Orientalist Paintings Collection, which is one of Turkey's richest collections in its field, consists of works created

The Anatolian Weights and Measures Collection, started by Suna and İnan Kıraç in the 1980s

between the seventeenth and twentieth centuries by European and Ottoman artists. Some of the most interesting items in the collection are those of Osman Hamdi Bey's, including his famous *Tortoise Trainer* painting. With almost 10,000 artifacts, the Anatolian Weights and Measures Collection is of global significance, mainly consisting of weights and measures instruments used in Anatolia from 2000 BCE to the present. The Kütahya Tiles and Ceramics Collection contains around 1,000 pieces reflecting a variety of periods and styles, which allow a detailed observation of the art form's development from the eighteenth to the twentieth century.

The museum has organized collaborative arts projects with leading museums, collections and foundations, including Tate Britain, the Victoria and Albert Museum, the St. Petersburg State Russian Museum, the JP Morgan Chase Collection, the New York School of Visual Arts, and The Maeght Foundation. In addition to the long-term thematic exhibitions at the Sevgi and Erdoğan Gönül Gallery, the museum has also introduced art lovers to the works of master artists like Jean Dubuffet, Henri Cartier-Bresson, Rembrandt, Niko Pirosmani, Josef Koudelka, Joan Miró, Akira Kurosawa, Marc Chagall, Pablo Picasso, Fernando Botero, Frida Kahlo, Diego Rivera, Goya, Alberto Giacometti, Grayson Perry, Cecil Beaton, and Giorgio de Chirico.

Pera Education is an informative program that introduces children, young people and adults to art. It also aims to increase overall awareness of museums by making art more accessible, enabling visitors to communicate with works on display and encouraging creativity. Pera Film has a wide-ranging program, run in parallel to the exhibitions, which gives museum visitors and cinema-fans a different experience through various activities, including screenings of classic and independent movies, animations, documentaries and shorts.

In 2009, Suna Kıraç(*) and İnan Kıraç(*) received the Istanbul Tourism Honorary Award for their contribution to the cultural fabric of Istanbul by opening the Pera Museum and the Istanbul Research Institute(*). In the same year they also received the Mimar Sinan Fine Arts University Special Academy Award for founding the Pera Musuem. This was followed in 2011, by the TÜYAP Art-Friendly Instititution Award in recognition for their work at the Pera Museum and later in 2014 by Turkey's Superbrands Award.

A SELECTION OF THE PERA MUSEUM'S TEMPORARY EXHIBITIONS

- **Young Expansion** *(June 8–September 30, 2005)*
- **Jean Dubuffet: An Impassioned Exploration** *(October 26, 2005–January 8, 2006)*
- **Around the World Under Glass** *(October 26, 2005–January 8, 2006)*
- **Henri-Cartier Bresson: Biography** *(January 31–April 9, 2006)*
- **Mehmed the Hunter: Paintings Commissioned by the 17th century Swedish Ambassador Claes Rålamb** *(June 1–October 1, 2006)*
- **Rembrandt: From the Collection of Museum Boijmans Van Beuningen in Rotterdam** *(September 20, 2006–January 7, 2007)*

- **From Konstantiniyye to Istanbul: Photographs of the Rumeli Shore of the Bosphorus from the Mid XIXth Century to XXth Century** *(October 20, 2006–January 7, 2007)*
- **Ali Emiri Efendi and His World: Fermans, Berats, Calligraphies, Books: A Selection from the Millet Manuscript Library** *(January 24–July 1, 2007)*
- **Pirosmani: A Legend in "Naïve" Art** *(August 2–October 7, 2007)*
- **Josef Koudelka** *(January 16–April 13, 2008)*
- **Miro: Prints, Paintings and Sculptures from the Maeght Collection** *(May 3–August 31, 2008)*
- **The Lure of the East: British Orientalist Painting** *(September 26, 2008–January 11, 2009)*
- **Picasso: Suite Vollard Engravings** *(February 16–April 18, 2010)*
- **Frida Kahlo And Diego Rivera From The Gelman Collection** *(December 23, 2010–March 27, 2011)*
- **Osman Hamdi Bey and the Americans: Archaeology, Diplomacy, Art** *(October 15, 2011–January 8, 2012)*
- **Sultans, Merchants, Painters: The Early Years of Turkish - Dutch Relations** *(January 21–April 1, 2012)*
- **Goya Witness of His Time: Engravings and Paintings** *(April 20–July 29, 2012)*
- **Manolo Valdés: Paintings and Sculptures** *(May 8–July 21, 2013)*
- **Dreams, Realities, Images: The Image of the Republic in Modern Turkish Painting** *(October 9–November 17, 2013)*
- **Andy Warhol: Pop Art for Everyone** *(May 7–July 20, 2014)*
- **Orientalism in Polish Art** *(October 24, 2014–January 18, 2015)*
- **Alberto Giacometti** *(February 11–April 26, 2015)*
- **Bare, Naked, Nude: A Story of Modernization in Turkish Painting** *(November 25, 2015–February 7, 2016)*
- **sea/see/saw: Commissioned Installation by Artists Caitlind r.c. Brown & Wayne Garrett** *(June 5, 2015–February 14, 2016)*
- **Mario Prassinos: In Pursuit of an Artist: Istanbul-Paris-Istanbul** *(May 25–August 14, 2016)*
- **Katherine Behar: Data's Entry** *(September 8–October 16, 2016)*
- **Félix Ziem: Wanderer on the Sea of Light** *(November 10, 2016–January 29, 2017)*
- **Cold Front from the Balkans** *(November 10, 2016–May 7, 2017)*
- **Mersad Berber: An Allegory of Bosnia** *(February 16–May 7, 2017)*
- **Doublethink Double vision** *(May 25–August 6, 2017)*
- **José Sancho: Erotic Nature** *(May 25–August 6, 2017)*
- **Look At Me!: Portraits and Other Fictions from the "la Caixa" Contemporary Art Collection** *(December 7, 2017–March 11, 2018)*

- **Re/Framing Louis Kahn: Photographs by Cemal Emden – Drawings and Paintings** *(December 7, 2017–March 11, 2018)*
- **Singapore Unseen** *(April 5–May 20, 2018)*
- **Istanbul's Seaside Leisure: Nostalgia from Sea Baths to Beaches** *(April 5–August 26, 2018)*
- **Shaken Image: Works from Hacettepe University Faculty of Fine Arts** *(April 5–August 26, 2018)*
- **School Square Galatasaray** *(September 14–November 25, 2018)*

philanthropy *see* charity

Pluto *see* Koç School

Post, Wilfred M(cIlvaine) *(b. October 25, 1876, Beirut, Lebanon – d. January 1, 1966, Williston Park, New York, USA)*, second chief physician of the American Hospital(*) (1924-26).

Post completed his undergraduate studies in the USA at Princeton University in 1897 and continued at Columbia University Medical School. After his

Dr. Wilfred Post's ABCFM registration card
http://www.dlir.org/archive/orc-exhibit/items/show/collection/8/id/15437

B. Beirut, Lebanon 1876, Oct 25
POST WILFRED MACILVAINE. M.D.
Princeton 1897 University
Sailed July, 1904 Columbia Univ.
[Herald 1904 p 456.]
Caesarea - arr Sept. 1904 Married Annie Stabb She died in 1925.
Konia, 1911 Ret. U.S.A. July 1911 – July 1912 Children
Arr. Konia Aug. 1912 Ret. U.S.A. June 2, 1914
Helen Read Post B 12/17/07 m 12/1/33
Arr. Cons'ple Aug. 1, 1921, to serve in Robert College 1 yr.
In Near East Relief work 1922–1923
Cons'ple College & American Hospital, 1923–1925
Wilfred M. Jr.
Sailed for U.S.A. May 12, 1925 Home, East Williston, L.I.
Married Nov. 6, 1927 to Ethel Hults,
Williston Park, Long Island
Died - New York, Jan. 19, 1966 Nassau Hospital
* Helen R Post Rosa

graduation, he was appointed to the American Hospital in Talas, Kayseri, by the American Board of Commissioners for Foreign Missions and remained there until returning to the USA for a year's leave in 1911. When he came back to Turkey in 1912, he was appointed to the American Hospital in Konya. At the end of 1914, Dr. Post once more returned to the USA. He was sent to Iran as the head of the American Near East Relief Committee at the end of World War I. In the 1921-22 academic year, he worked at Robert College(*) in Istanbul, before taking over from Dr. Alden R. Hoover(*) as the chief physician at the American Hospital from 1924 to 1926. During the same period, he also served as dean of the medical school at the Arnavutköy American College for Girls (*see* Robert College).

Admiral Mark L(ambert) Bristol(*) described him as, "a good man and a committed leader, but he has missionary tendencies. I see our hospital as a public service organization, and it shouldn't carry any religious connotations."

On his wife's death in 1925, Dr. Post returned to the USA, where for many years he worked as a surgeon at New York's Nassau Hospital and was also a medical consultant at the Near East Foundation.

Powell, Josephine *(b. May 15, 1919, New York, USA – d. January 18, 2007, Istanbul)*, American photographer, collector and traveler. Her collection of photographs, documents and objects relating to the life and culture of Anatolian villages and nomads of Anatolia were donated to the Vehbi Koç Foundation(*) (VKV).

Powell completed a bachelor's degree in art at Cornell University (1941) and received a master's degree from the New York School of Social Work at Columbia University in 1945. She left the United States in 1947 to work for the International Refugee and Resettlement Organization for Displaced Persons (IRRODP) in Tanganyika (now Tanzania) and later worked in Munich, Germany. In 1952, she moved to Rome where she earned a living as an architectural photographer.

Powell first visited Turkey in 1955 to photograph Byzantine mosaics and undertook her first extensive tour of the country in the same year. She was the first foreigner to gain permission to travel the entire country after the founding of the republic. Between 1952 and 1974, Powell traveled to many countries, including Afghanistan, India, Iran, Italy, Nepal, Pakistan, Russia and Yugoslavia, photographing historical monuments, architecture and ethnographic objects. The objects she gathered on these trips are today in the collections of the British Museum in London, the Tropenmuseum in Amsterdam and the Wereldmuseum in Rotterdam.

Powell, whose photographs appeared in hundreds of books and scientific publications, moved from Rome to Istanbul in 1974 to write a book about *kilims*. Discovering the paucity of previous work on the subject, she decided to travel around Anatolia to carry out further research. Powell developed an interest in flat weaving and tried to learn about handicrafts directly from Anatolian nomads. She tried to understand how the ethnographic objects were used, which materials they were made of and how they had been developed. She amassed a collection of Anatolian *kilims*, bags and similar handmade products that reflected the role and importance of weaving in rural Anatolia.

During her travels in the 1970s and 1980s, she photographed the daily life and handicrafts of Anatolian nomads and villagers, gradually developing an admiration for the lives and weaving arts of the village women. She built a rich archive, containing photographs of the nomadic, semi-nomadic and settled female weavers accompanied by notes on their flat weaving skills. Hoping to revive the natural dying techniques of villagers

in Western Turkey, she began the Natural Dye Research and Development Project (DOBAG) with her close friends, Harald and Renata Böhmer, in the mid 1980s. The project only marketed high quality *kilims* made by women, and these were sold through specific cooperatives of female entrepreneurs.

Powell also contributed to the founding of an ethnography department at the Turkish and Islamic Arts Museum in Istanbul. Her architectural photographic archive was donated to the Harvard University Fine Arts Library in 2002, and her collection of flat-woven rugs and ethnographic objects, field notes, and copies of all her photographs from Anatolia, together with her library of close to 1,400 books, were donated to VKV in October 2006. In the same year, Powell was awarded the George Hewitt Myers Award "for her outstanding contribution to the research and understanding of the weaving arts".

A selection of Powell's photographs were presented in an exhibition open to the public at ANAMED(*) from June 11 - October 21, 2012, titled "What Josephine Saw: 20th Century Photographic Visions of Rural Anatolia". A book was also published with the same title. Items from the kilim collection Powell donated to the VKV were put on permanent exhibition at the Vehbi Koç Büyükdere Mansion in July 2018. (*See also* Josephine Powell Collection)

Private American Marine Polyclinic *see* **American Marine Polyclinic**

Program for Developing School-Business Partnerships, a program dedicated to improving the quality of vocational education through collaboration between schools, the private sector and civil society groups. It is part of the Vocational Education: A Crucial Matter for the Nation Project(*) (MLMM), a partnership enterprise of the Vehbi Koç Foundation(*) (VKV), the Ministry of Education and Koç Holding(*) companies. From 2015 to 2017, the project was managed by the Ministry of National Education, the Turkish Enterprise and Business Federation (TÜRKONFED), the Turkish Confederation of Employer Associations (TİSK) and the Turkish Industry and Business Association (TÜSİAD), in partnership with the VKV, the Private Sector Volunteers Association (ÖSGD), the Education Reform Initiative (ERG)(*), the Teachers Academy Foundation, the Turkish Employers Association of Metal Industries (MESS) Education Foundation. This program aims to expand the School-Business Partnerships Model developed during the MLMM Project.

The MLMM Project provides scholarships, internships, and volunteer coaching support according to the needs and facilities of schools and businesses partnered through the scheme. The assistance extends to improving educational infrastructure and materials to meet current technological standards through wide-ranging support for materials, curricula and laboratories. The scholarships, curricula, laboratories, internships, personal and professional development, and employment opportunities have over time formed a bridge between the worlds of education and industry. This was achieved by improving sector-based collaborative relationships between the private sector and vocational schools, which lay at the core of the "School-Business Partnership Model".

The MLMM program aimed to increase both the number and quality of collaborations between business and vocational education institutions by setting up workshops and training sessions in different areas and regularly monitoring the subsequent collaborative partnerships. Participants in this work included chambers of industry and commerce, business associations, industrial parks, professional organizations, businesses, regional employment boards and vocational educational institutions. A pilot study involving about 70 representatives from businesses and vocational school institutions was carried out in Bandırma on November 27, 2014. Afterwards, school-business partnership workshops took place in the following locations: Eskişehir, hosted by the Eskişehir Industry and Business Association (ESİAD); Izmir, hosted by the Aegean Young Employers Association (EGİAD); and Bursa, hosted by the Bursa Industry and Business Association (BUSİAD). Each workshop was preceded by leadership training, facilitated by the MESS Education Foundation and given to the vocational and technical school administrators of these cities.

The MLMM School-Business Partnership Model was submitted to the International Labor Organization (ILO) and the United Nations Development Program (UNDP) as a successful "exemplary practice" for youth employment and vocational education across the world.

In 2018, School-Business Partnership workshops were organized as part of the Full Support for Vocational Education (METAD) Project with the collaboration of the Ministry of Education, MESS and the MESS Education Foundation.

R
RA – RU

Rahmi M. Koç Medal of Science, full name KOÇ UNIVERSITY RAHMİ M. KOÇ MEDAL OF SCIENCE, an award program initiated in 2016 by Koç University(*) to "encourage the development of science by rewarding successful, leading scientists of Turkish origin aged under fifty, who have contributed to the accumulation of universal knowledge in Turkey and abroad." The award is given for different categories in alternate years, with science, engineering and medicine in one year and administration, economics, social sciences, humanities and law in another. Medal nominations are determined by a committee of experts in the relevant fields, who are chosen by Koç University.

Ömer M. Koç, chair of the Koç University Board of Trustees, ath the award ceremony

In 2016, the inaugural medal was awarded to Professor Aydoğan Özcan(*) from the University of California (UCLA) and Howard Hughes Health Institute for his "outstanding fundamental scientific contribution to computational imaging, microscopy and photonics, and the development of innovative technologies for telemedicine, medical sensing and diagnostic applications."

In 2017, the medal for administration, economics, social sciences, humanities, and law was awarded to Professor Daron Acemoğlu(*) of the Massachusetts Institute of Technology (MIT) for his "trailblazing contribution to the fields of macro economic growth and development, labor economics and political economy".

The **Rahmi M. Koç Museology and Culture Foundation,** founded in 1993 by Rahmi M. Koç(*) to establish industrial and other museums, build up collections and develop museology and culture throughout Turkey. Rahmi M. Koç is the lifetime president of the foundation and Dr. Bülent Bulgurlu(*) is the lifetime vice president.

The following museums and organizations are part of the foundation: Istanbul Rahmi M. Koç Museum(*) (1994), Ankara Rahmi M. Koç Museum(*) (2005), Sevim and Necdet Kent Library(*) in Ayvalık (2007) and Ayvalık Rahmi M. Koç Museum(*) (2014).

Rahmi M. Koç Museums *see* **Ankara Rahmi M. Koç Museum, Ayvalık Rahmi M. Koç Museum, Istanbul Rahmi M. Koç Museum**

Read the Silence Project, founded by Boğaziçi University (BU) and maintained by Koç Holding(*) and the Vehbi Koç Foundation(*) to support the cognitive development and education of deaf people in Turkey.

The project was developed by BU academics expert in linguistics and education, who were convinced of the need for the deaf to access knowledge in order to fit into society. The project covers contributions to the linguistic acquisition and cognitive development of deaf children up to the age of six, and the production of educational materials in Turkish Sign Language and Turkish to improve the Turkish skill of adults over 15.

Redford, Scott

(b. November 1956, USA), art historian and director. Served as ANAMED(*) director from 2005 to 2015.

After receiving a doctorate in fine arts from Harvard University, USA, in 1989, Dr. Redford worked as an assistant professor at Georgetown University in both the School of Foreign Service and the Department of Fine Arts. Between 1997 and 2008, he lectured at the Culture and Politics Program of the School of Foreign Service. From 1990 to 2008, he was director of the university's McGhee Eastern Mediterranean Studies Center in Alanya. In the 2004-05 academic year, Professor Redford was a guest researcher at Bilkent University Department of Archaeology, and from 2005 to 2015 he served as the ANAMED director. Between 2008 and 2013, he also gave lectures at Koç University(*) on a range of subjects, including the Crusades, the Seljuks and Islamic architecture in Medieval Anatolia.

Professor Redford is currently the Nasser D. Khalili Professor of Islamic Art and Archaeology at the School of Oriental and African Studies, University of London (SOAS). He is also a member of the editorial boards for the following publications: *Adalya*(*), *Hacettepe University Social and Human Sciences Magazine*, and *Muqarnas*.

His chief published works are: *Landscape and the State in Medieval Anatolia: Seljuk Gardens and Pavilions of Alanya, Turkey* (2000); *Victory Inscribed: The Seljuk Fetihname on the Citadel Walls of Antalya, Turkey/TaşaYazılan Zafer: Antalya İçkale Surlarındaki Selçuklu Fetihnamesi* (with Gary Leiser, 2008), *The Archaeology of the Frontier in the Medieval Near East: Excavations at Gritille, Turkey* (2014) and *Legends of Authority: The 1215 Seljuk Inscriptions of Sinop Citadel, Turkey* (2014).

Research Center for Anatolian Civilizations *see* ANAMED

Robert College, officially known today as ROBERT COLLEGE OF ISTANBUL, the oldest American educational institution still operating outside of the USA. Vehbi Koç Foundation(*) (VKV) supported the school with donations.

Following the establishment of a boys' school in 1863, a school for girls, which later became known as the Arnavutköy American College for Girls, was opened in 1871. In 1971, the two schools merged into a co-educational institution under the name Robert College. According to the 1878-79 College Catalog, the school's aims were to "provide a comprehensive education like that of a first class American school, based on the same principles, and given to all students regardless of race or religion."

The original school, launched by the American missionary and educator, Cyrus Hamlin with financial support from the businessman and philanthropist Christopher R(hinelander) Robert, began with four male students in an old wooden building in Bebek on September 16, 1863. The school's first campus was built in 1869 on the outskirts of Bebek (currently Boğaziçi University's South Campus). In 1871, with the support of an American group, a school for girls opened at Gedikpaşa. In 1876, the school moved to a new campus in Üsküdar, moving again in 1914 to a more extensive campus in Arnavutköy.

When Christopher Robert died in 1878, he left a large portion of his fortune to Robert College. The school was later supported by donations from philanthropic individuals and organizations including the VKV and the Hisar Educational Foundation. (*See also* Suna Kıraç Hall)

For a long time, Robert College and the Arnavutköy American College for Girls were autonomous entities, but in 1932 they were brought under a single director, and in 1959 under the management of the same board of trustees. In 1957, Robert College was granted higher education status and began offering university-level education at its Bebek campus as Robert College Undergraduate Department. In 1971, Robert College and the American School for Girls in Arnavutköy merged into a co-educational entity on the Arnavutköy campus, retaining the name Robert College. That year, the Bebek campus was transferred to the government, and Robert College Undergraduate Department became a state university called Boğaziçi University.

With the introduction of eight-year mandatory primary education in 1997, Robert College closed its middle school but continued as a high school. Today's students have a bilingual high school education for five years, starting with their English preparatory first year.

Graduates of the 26-hectare campus in Arnavutköy include two Turkish prime ministers, four of Bulgaria's prime ministers, and many prominent business people, politicians, scientists and

artists. It is a member of the G20 School Group and holds a New York State Association of Independent Schools accreditation.

The school has an annual intake of around 200 pupils and runs over 100 activity clubs. The Student Council has organized an annual Fine Arts Festival every May since 1982, and the school hosts numerous other events, such as the International Istanbul Youth Forum, the International Model United Nations Conference, the Turkish Theater Festival and the Ethics Forum. The school also produces periodicals including the monthly *Bosphorous Chronicle*, the bi-monthly *Köprü* (Bridge) newspaper, the science journal *Kingdom Robertea*, the multilingual publication *Polyglot*, and three literary magazines: *Kaleidoscope*, *Martı* (Seagull) and *Oda* (Room).

Roosevelt, Christopher H. *(b. June 25, 1972, New York, USA)*, archaeologist, art historian and cultural institution manager. He has been a faculty member at Koç University(*) and director of ANAMED(*) since 2015.

He graduated in classics and geology from Colby College in the United States (1990-94) and completed a master's degree in archaeology at Cornell University (1997). He continued studying art history and archaeology at Cornell, receiving another master's degree (1998) and a doctorate (2003). He worked as an assistant professor at Boston University Department of Archaeology between 2003 and 2009 and was an associate professor there from 2009 to 2015. He joined the academic staff of Koç University Department of Archaeology and Art History in 2015 , becoming a professor in 2017. He has been the director of ANAMED since 2015, and has also been excavation leader for the Kaymakçı Archeology Project in the Gölmarmara town of Manisa since 2014.

Professor Roosevelt is an expert on Anatolian and Eastern Mediterranean Iron and Bronze Age archaeology and has written numerous academic articles and books on the subject, including *The Archaeology of Lydia, from Gyges to Alexander* (2009).

Rountree, George D(enton) *(b. March 14, 1937, Houston, Texas, USA)*, health institution manager. He joined the American Hospital(*) management staff in 1990, and was general director in the periods 1992-1999 and 2001-2006.

Rountree completed an undergraduate degree at Lamar University in Texas and a master's degree in hospital management at Washington University in Missouri. He undertook further training on health systems management at Harvard University Graduate School of Business Administration and Public Health. From 1969 to 1977, he served as assistant director at the Houston Methodist Hospital, later becoming president of the Multi-Care Health Corporation & Quadrus International in Houston (1979-90). In the same period, he also worked as a project manager for the establishment of the International Hospital in Istanbul (1987-90). In August 1990, Rountree joined the management team of the American Hospital, becoming general director in 1992 and remaining in post until 1999. From 1999 to 2000, he was CEO of the Medical Centers Management Company in Boston, but returned to his position as general director of the American Hospital in 2001. Under his management, the American Hospital showed significant quantitative, qualitative and financial improvement.

After he left the American Hospital in 2006, he provided consultancy services to healthcare establishments in Turkey, Greece, Sudan, Turkmenistan and the USA. He spent some time managing an olive farm near Erdek, Balıkesir, naming it Apostle Grove. Rountree has also taught at Istanbul University School of Business and at Washington University School of Medicine Healthcare Management Program.

Rumelifeneri Campus *see* **Koç University**

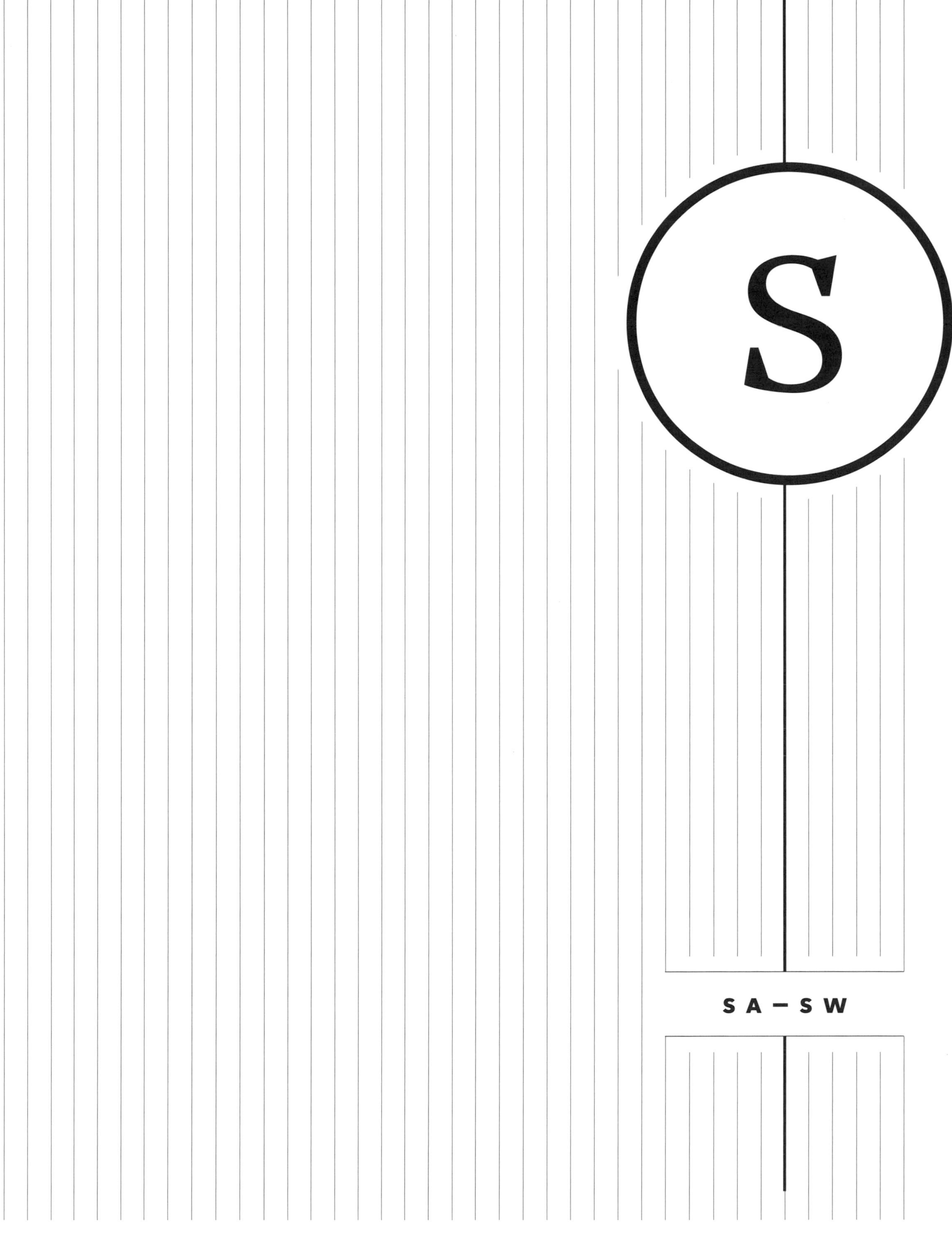
S
SA – SW

Sadberk Hanım Museum, full name THE VEHBI KOÇ FOUNDATION SADBERK HANIM MUSEUM, Turkey's first private museum opened on October 14, 1980 at the building known as the Azaryan Mansion(*) in Büyükdere, Sarıyer, Istanbul, to exhibit the private collection of, and in memory of Sadberk Koç(*), wife of Vehbi Koç(*). The museum is established through a fund formed in the Vehbi Koç Foundation(*) (VKV) in 1974.

Built at the end of the nineteenth century and purchased by Vehbi Koç in 1950, the Azaryan Mansion served as the Koç family's(*) summer retreat until 1977, when it was donated to the VKV for reassignment to a museum. It was converted into a museum following the restoration project during the years 1978-1980 by Sedad Hakkı Eldem(*).

Initially consisting of traditional costumes, embroideries, *tuğra*-stamped silverware and china acquired by Sadberk Koç, the museum's collection has grown in time through donations and purchases. The collection of Hüseyin Kocabaş, one of Turkey's leading collectors, joined the Sadberk Hanım Museum collection following his death in 1983. The mansion next door, believed to date from the turn of the twentieth century, was purchased to house the archaeological artifacts in the Hüseyin Kocabaş Collection(*). Once its façade was restored to its original form, this annex was opened on October 24, 1988 and named after Sevgi Gönül(*), whose dedication to the founding and development of the museum was considerable, and who served as president of the executive committee. The Sadberk Hanım Museum won the 1988 Europa Nostra award (*see* Europa Nostra Awards) for the "faithful restoration and renovation and opening up as an archaeological museum".

The original Sadberk Koç collection contained some 3,500 pieces; today the inventory exceeds 19,000. A key feature of the museum is its constant drive to enlarge its collection. Archaeological finds representing the material heritage of Anatolian civilizations from the sixth millennium BCE through to the end of the Byzantine period are displayed in the Sevgi Gönül Building. Predominantly Ottoman Islamic artifacts as well as goods produced for the Ottomans in Europe, the Near East and the Orient, Ottoman textiles, costumes and embroidery are exhibited at the Azaryan Mansion. The museum collections are constantly enlarged through donations and purchases at home and abroad.

The Sadberk Hanım Museum aims to gather archaeological and early Islamic pieces from the Seljuk, Ayyubi, Mamluk, Timurid and Safavid eras along with the finest examples of Ottoman art and preserve this cultural heritage for future generations under a controlled environment.

The Sadberk Hanım Museum today commands a distinguished position with its İznik ware, particularly tiles and ceramics from the fifteenth through to the seventeenth centuries, and Ottoman embroidery and women's costumes; this latter collection from the eighteenth and nineteenth centuries is the richest in the world. Constantly expanding through new acquisitions, the Ottoman textiles collection covering

the period from the sixteenth to the twentieth centuries also contains accessories such as embroideries, shoes, bags, hats and folding fans. The İznik ware collection is similarly expanded through purchases at domestic and foreign auctions.

The museum also displays Ottoman silver, *tombak* (gilded brass), brass and enamelware, Chinese celadon and porcelains, Kütahya tiles and ceramics, Çanakkale ceramics, European porcelain, Beykoz glassware, and examples of calligraphy and illumination.

A protocol signed with the George Washington University Textiles Museum in 2017 transferred to the Sadberk Hanım Museum 69 Anatolian carpets and textiles from the eighteenth through to the twentieth centuries that had been held in the Murat Megalli(*) collection.

In addition to the permanent exhibitions, temporary exhibitions on specific themes, scholarly publications and education programs aim to reach out to all sections of society; the museum serves as an education-cum-culture institution that uses contemporary museum practices to contribute to the artistic and scientific development of society, one that entertains as it informs. The Sadberk Hanım Museum also welcomes research and by lending items to exhibitions at home and abroad, contributes to the promotion of Turkey.

EXHIBITIONS HELD AT THE SADBERK HANIM MUSEUM*

- **A Heartfelt Passion, the Sevgi Gönül Calligraphy Collection** *(May 26–July 25, 2004)*
- **Reunited After Centuries: Works of Art Restored to Turkey by the Sadberk Hanım Museum** *(December 4, 2005–February 28, 2006)*
- **A Treasured Memory: Ecclesiastical Silver from Late Ottoman Istanbul in the Sevgi Gönül Collection** *(April 15–July 2, 2006)*
- **Prehistoric Figure Paintings** *(November 4–26, 2006)*
- **The 150th Anniversary of the Crimean War** *(December 9, 2006–February 25, 2007)*
- **Çatma and Kemha: Ottoman Silk Fabrics** *(April 15–June 10, 2007)*
- **Ancient Drinking and Libation Vessels** *(December 8, 2007–March 30, 2008)*
- **The Centenary of the Second Constitutional Monarchy** *(June 20–July 27, 2008)*
- **Tailors to the Court: M. Palma-D. Lena-P. Parma** *(November 27, 2008–January 11, 2009)*
- **Dance of Fire: İznik Tiles and Ceramics in the Sadberk Hanım Museum and Ömer M. Koç Collections** *(April 12–October 11, 2009)*
- **Women's Costumes from the Late Ottoman Era: The Sadberk Hanım Museum Collection** *(May 7–December 28, 2010)*
- **Dynasty and the Camera: Portraits from the Ottoman Court** *(January 8–May 29, 2011)*
- **Images in Clay: Ancient Terracotta Figurines in the Sadberk Hanım Museum Collection** *(November 18, 2011–May 20, 2012)*
- **Hand Skills Delight the Eye: Ottoman Embroideries in the Sadberk Hanım Museum Collection** *(December 7, 2012–August 4, 2013)*
- **Traces of Ancient Ages: Sadberk Hanım Museum Collection** *(December 6, 2013–May 25, 2014)*
- **Shoes, Sadberk Hanım Museum Collection** *(November 27, 2014–May 31, 2015)*
- **Jewel: Enamelled and Jewelled Objects in the Sadberk Hanım Museum Collection** *(December 3, 2015–May 31, 2016)*
- **Silver and Salt: Early Photographs from the Ömer M. Koç Collection: 1843-1860** *(May 25–October 31, 2017)*
- **Kütahya: The Sadberk Hanım Museum Kütahya Tile and Ceramics Collection** *(March 8, 2018–November25, 2018)*

* All exhibition catalogs have been published.

The Sadberk Hanım Museum Specialist Library is an authoritative institution among specialist libraries in Turkey, holding 8,700 printed books and 640 manuscripts. Of particular significance are the rare yearbooks called *sâlnâme*. Restoration and conservation of the pieces in the Sadberk Hanım Museum are conducted in the museum laboratory.

The museum's "Along to the Museum! Discover, Learn, Have Fun" project addresses children over eight years of age. A set of three educational books are published as part of this project. The two activity books entitled *Sanat Tarihi* (History of Art) ve *Arkeoloji* (Archaeology) were prepared to introduce young generations to Turkey's natural and cultural heritage as well as raise awareness of the importance of conservation. The third book designed to support active learning informs teachers about the pieces in the museum collections. Since spring 2016, the Sadberk Hanım Museum education projects have expanded beyond school groups; they now include activities on the last Saturday of each month to reach out to more children. These sessions are booked in advance. In 2017, over 7,500 pupils attended the museum's educational activities for children.

The Sadberk Hanım Museum is a member of the International Council of Museums (ICOM).

Preparations to move the museum to its new site at the Golden Horn Taşkızak Shipyard are currently under way.

MUSEUM PUBLICATIONS*

- Altun, Ara et al., ***Türk Çini ve Seramikleri/Turkish Tiles and Ceramics***, *1991*
- Anlağan, Çetin and Bilgi, Önder, ***Protohistorik Çağ Silahları/Weapons of the Protohistoric Age***, *1989*
- Anlağan, Çetin et al., ***Sadberk Hanım Müzesi/ Sadberk Hanım Museum***, *1995*
- Anlağan, Tanju, ***Sadberk Hanım Müzesi Kalıplı Kaseler ve Kabartmalı Kaplar/ Sadberk Hanım Museum Moldmade Bowls and Related Wares***, *2000*
- Bakar, İsmail, ***Sadberk Hanım Müzesi Yazma Eserler Kataloğu Hüseyin Kocabaş Koleksiyonu*** (Sadberk Hanım Museum Written Works Catalog Hüseyin Kocabaş Collection), *1997*
- Bakar, İsmail, ***Sadberk Hanım Müzesi Kütüphanesi Yıllıklar Sâlnâmeler, Nevsâller ve Takvîmle Hüseyin Kocabaş*** (Sadberk Hanım Museum Library, Hüseyin Kocabaş with Annuals, Yearbooks and Calendars), *2008*
- Carswell, John, ***Çin Seramikleri: Sadberk Hanım Müzesi Koleksiyonu /Chinese Ceramics in The Sadberk Hanım Museum***, *1995*
- Çağman, Filiz, ***Kat'ı-Cut Paper Works and Artists in the Ottoman World***, *2016*
- Donbaz, Veysel, ***Sadberk Hanım Müzesi'nde Bulunan Çiviyazılı Tabletler/Cuneiform Texts in the Sadberk Hanım Museum***, *1999*
- Hart, Kimberly (ed.), ***Giving Back the Colours: Josephine Powell Collection***, *2007*
- Hart, Kimberly (ed.), ***Kilim Örnekleri/Examples from Kilims, Josephine Powell Collection***, *2007*
- Öztuncay, Bahattin et al, ***İkinci Meşrutiyetin İlanının 100'üncü Yılı/100th Anniversary of the Restoration of the Constitution***, *2008*
- Tekin, Oğuz, ***Sivas Definesi: VI. Mithradates Dönemi Pontos ve Paphlagonia Kentlerinin Bronz Sikkeleri/ The Sivas Hoard: Bronze Coins of Pontos and Paphlagonia from the Reign of Mithradates VI***, *1999*
- Tekin, Oğuz, ***Sadberk Hanım Müzesi Antik Sikkeler Kataloğu/Catalog of the Ancient Coins in the Sadberk Hanım Museum***, *2003*
- Tezcan, Hülya, ***19. Yüzyıl Sonuna Ait Bir Terzi Defteri/A Late 19th Century Tailor's Order Book***, *1992*
- Üçok, Ayşe, ***Geçmişe Bir Yolculuk*** (Journey to the Past), *2004*

* The museum has also published the Sadberk Hanım Museum annual entitled *Palmet* between 1995 and 2004.

THE SADBERK HANIM MUSEUM AS TOLD BY VEHBİ KOÇ

My wife Sadberk Koç always welcomed my social projects and institutions I founded and encouraged me. "They will live on after you, and bring blessings on your memory," she used to say. When she was diagnosed with a terminal illness, and the prospect of death preyed on her mind, she frequently voiced a fear of "being forgotten." One day she said, "I don't want to be forgotten. I want those precious old objects I've collected all my life to be exhibited in a museum bearing my name. Please help me on this issue."

After she passed away, my children and I thought long and hard about her wish. I owned an old-style waterfront mansion in Sarıyer, known as the Azaryan Mansion, built at the turn of the twentieth century. Experts studied this four-story Ottoman-European mixture and declared it suitable for conversion to a museum. It had 1,200 square meters usable area. Restorations and alterations were carried out as needed. It was equipped with advanced fire prevention systems without compromising the timber character. These preparations took some four years. At long last, the Sadberk Hanım Museum was opened by the then Minister of Culture Cihat Baban on October 14, 1980. I was relieved to have carried out my wife's wish.

My second daughter Sevgi Gönül put her shoulder to it, and worked passionately during these preparations. The Sadberk Hanım Museum has changed and developed enormously in the intervening six or seven years. The acquisition of the Hüseyin Kocabaş Collection in 1983 enriched the museum with 9000-year-old Anatolian artifacts. The Sadberk Hanım Museum is already a major culture and arts center in Istanbul and Turkey. The rooms and halls of the country's first private museum open to the public display silver objects, jewelry and ornaments, examples of Turkish embroideries from the sixteenth through to the eighteenth centuries, Kütahya and İznik tiles from the same time and Turkish costumes, as well as Neolithic, Early Bronze Age, Hittite, Phrygian, Greek, Hellenistic, Roman, Seljuk, Byzantine and Ottoman objects. The museum also hosts cultural events like exhibitions, concerts, conferences, seminars and commemorations. It also participates in exhibitions and cultural events abroad. In no time at all, when the need to expand the display area arose, the building next door was purchased; construction started last year.

I believe my wife Sadberk Koç's soul will feel at peace now. This museum will live with her name, grow even richer in the future and convey our shared feelings to the future. The only thing that gives us peace here and in the afterlife is the knowledge that we have allocated our assets to benefit the generations after us.

Vehbi Koç, *Hatıralarım Görüşlerim Öğütlerim (Recollections, Observations, Counsel)*, Vehbi Koç Foundation Publications, Istanbul, 1987, pp. 159-160

THE STORY OF THE SADBERK HANIM MUSEUM AS TOLD BY SUNA KIRAÇ

Collecting Turkish and Ottoman objects began as an accidental hobby for Sadberk Hanım, but in time grew into a disciplined, exacting passion. She frequently visited the Grand Bazaar in search of new arrivals. And the merchants got to know and respect her. As her hobby developed into genuine expertise, Sadberk Hanım became a hawk-eyed collector. She not only knew about new works of art but also what they were worth. Occasionally the children would be taken along to these Grand Bazaar "expeditions"; Suna Kıraç recalls being bored out of their minds during the heated negotiations and exchanges. All the same, many years later she would write, "Mother must have passed on to all four of us her keen judgment; we all grew into collectors. So stuck was she on this vision of a museum that she didn't leave us a stitch!"

Sadberk Hanım now had a colossal collection kept in suitcases on the second floor. She dreamt of sharing this historic heritage with the Turkish public, yet hesitated to suggest this idea of opening a museum to her husband; on the one occasion when she had tried together with her friend, writer and fellow collector Nezihe Araz, Vehbi Koç had replied, "Why would you open a museum; if you're after charitable works, open a hospital or a school!" That was the year Vehbi Koç had secured the permit to form the Koç Foundation, so his priority was the investment in benevolent causes. Sadberk Hanım's personal income—the rent from the Koçtaş land—wouldn't stretch to establishing such a museum. The money sent from the Holding only covered household expenses, and Sadberk Hanım had used her personal money to collect historical objects.

Yet this vision of a museum had become a passion for her. In a will she drew up following an illness in January 1967, she had left her daughters one million liras each (with a note saying, "an extra 100,000 for Suna for her hope chest") and set her favorite jewel aside, "place it in my museum". She must have despaired that there ever would be a museum in her name in this will written six years prior to her death: she asked instead for "a few trinkets" she had collected to be displayed in an annex to a museum in Ankara or Istanbul, and this pavilion to be named after her. Sadberk Hanım's wish for her husband was that he remembers her.

When she was diagnosed with cancer six years later, she wrote a new will. This time she addresses Vehbi Koç as "my life, my husband" and

continues, "Our fifty years together might come to an end. God bless you and my children. Please be very happy. As for the children: they're the best we could have hoped for. Please forgive their faults for my sake. I give them my blessings." Her wish about the museum is as follows: "Build my museum, and leave it to Koç Holding." Sadberk Hanım had been fascinated by the Antonis Benakis Museum in Athens. Wouldn't it be wonderful to have her name and efforts to live on in a similar establishment!

Vehbi Koç acted after her death to carry out her wishes. Strangely, legislation proved to be an issue, and it took concerted effort by the family members for a new Act to allow private individuals to establish museums. Sadberk Hanım's will finally broke through the misfortune that had been hampering museums in Turkey, and threw open the gates of a brand new era.

The Sadberk Hanım Museum is located at the former Azaryan Mansion, the family's summer retreat. Following the restoration by Prof.Sedad Hakkı Eldem in the late nineteenth century mansion, which has a European vernacular style with three floors plus attic, the museum was opened on October 14, 1980, seven years after Sadberk Hanım's death.

Sadberk Hanım's dream had come true. The Koç family soon grew passionately fond of the museum. An additional building came into use to house the Kocabaş Collection purchased by the Koç Foundation in 1983, and it was renamed the Sevgi Gönül Building. This contribution by Sevgi Gönül was in effect fulfilling Vehbi Koç's wishes, from "an early will" just as her mother's, in his lifetime. The building and the restoration would later win the Europa Nostra Award in 1988.

Suna Kıraç, *Ömrümden Uzun İdeallerim Var* (My Ideals, Longer than My Life), Suna and İnan Kıraç Foundation Publications, Istanbul, pp. 222-26

Safranhan, also known as ZAFRAN HAN or ZAĞFİRAN HAN, historic caravansary in Ankara's district formerly called Atpazarı. Today it serves as an annex to the Ankara Rahmi M. Koç Museum(*) located in Çengelhan.

Built in 1511 by Hacı İbrahim bin Hacı Mehmed, the 42-room, two-story Safranhan with its arcaded courtyard is a fine example of classical Ottoman town caravansary. Restored on several occasions throughout its history, it has largely lost its original architectural characteristics. After the decline of the mohair trade in Ankara, it served first as a

prison and later as a warehouse in the final years of the Ottoman Empire and the early Republic era. The first film screening in Ankara was held at this site.

Acquired in 2012 by the Rahmi M. Koç Museology and Culture Foundation(*), Safranhan was restored to its original plan and opened as an annex to the Ankara Rahmi M. Koç Museum in 2016. The courtyard, glazed over during restoration, now serves as an exhibition space.

Sagalassos Excavations, a series of excavations carried out on the ancient city of Sagalassos, located on an incline at an altitude of 1,450-1,700 m, 7 km northeast of Ağlasun, Burdur, on the southern slopes of Mt Ağlasun in the Western Tauruses. The center of the ancient region of Pisidia, Sagalassos is one of the best preserved ancient cities in Turkey. As the longest-running pottery production center of the ancient world, it has been nominated for the UNESCO World Heritage List. The excavation and restoration work started in 2015 by the Global Heritage Fund is supported by the Vehbi Koç Foundation(*).

The city, where earliest traces of occupation go back 12,000 years, was conquered by Alexander the Great in 333 BCE. It developed rapidly after its incorporation into the Roman Empire in 25 BCE. Throughout antiquity, it was a center of pottery production and agricultural exports. The Roman Emperor Hadrian (r. 117-138) launched a major construction drive in the city. Earthquakes and an epidemic of plague in the year 600 signaled its decline.

After many years as an abandoned ancient settlement, Sagalassos was discovered by the French explorer Paul Lucas in 1706. The excavations led by the University of Leuven, Belgium, in 1990 have so far unearthed the city center, the world's highest ancient theater with seating for 9,000, two agorae, three nymphaeums, a Roman bath and several important statues including portrayals of Roman Emperors Hadrian and Marcus Aurelius (r. 161-180). The restoration project also covers the history of the settlement as well as the mutual impact of the local environment and the city, research into daily life and the economic, commercial and social orders. DNA tests on skeletons excavated in 1999 and the local population revealed kinship ties. Some of the priceless finds in the site are on display at the Burdur Museum. The excavation and restoration work carried out by the Global Heritage Fund at the Southeast Gate of the Upper Agora offers training opportunities to architecture, history of art and conservation students at Koç University(*), Middle East Technical University and Mardin Artuklu University.

Saint Euphemia Church Restorations, renovation work of an old Byzantine church in Sultanahmet, Istanbul, situated at the northeastern corner of the former courthouse, on land designated for today's Museum of Turkish and Islamic Arts Museum. Conservation/renovation work began on the church in 2013, following an agreement between the Vehbi Koç Foundation(*) and Istanbul Directorate of Surveying and Monuments, acting on behalf of the Turkish Ministry of Culture and Tourism. The work is managed by an academic board advised by

Professor Engin Akyürek from Koç University(*) Department of Archaeology and History of Art.

Euphemia was an eminent Byzantine Christian from Chalcedon, now a district of Istanbul called Kadıköy. She suffered extreme torture and eventually died as a result of her advocacy of local Christian rights against the Romans and her refusal to join a pagan festival organized in honor of the god Ares. She died in Chalcedon (Kadıköy) in 307 AD. After Euphemia was made a saint by the church, a church was built in her name in Chalcedon. Due to the Persian threat at the start of the seventh century, the sacred relics of Euphemia were moved to a church converted from an old palace in today's Sultanahmet district of Istanbul. The church, which was a popular pilgrimage place in the Byzantine period, was seriously damaged during the Latin occupation in 1204–61. After the occupation, it was restored and the frescoes were renovated. In 1939, the local prison (part of Ibrahim Pasha Palace) and some dwellings collapsed, revealing the western wall with its series of 14 frescoes depicting the life of Euphemia. The discovery prompted excavations by the German Archaeological Institute (DAI) in 1942. Construction of the Sultanahmet Courthouse, which began in 1950, caused considerable damage to both the Saint Euphemia Church and Ibrahim Pasha Palace. The only part of the museum visible today was saved from collapse by the dedicated efforts of Istanbul Archaeology Museums (IAM). The findings of archaeological excavations carried out by IAM and DAI from 1951 to 1952 and again in 1964 were published in a book.

Restoration work currently in progress at Saint Euphemia Church aims to repair the frescoes and architectural remains, build a modern roof over fragments dating back to the thirteenth century, landscape the area, and open the church up to the public as a museum.

Sancar, Aziz *(b. September 8, 1946, Savur, Mardin),* physician and scientist, who won Vehbi Koç Award(*) in 2007 for health sciences. In 2015, he was awarded the Nobel Prize in chemistry along with Tomas Lindahl and Paul Modrich for their studies in DNA repair.

Describing his parents as, "illiterate, yet who always placed great importance on education, and had full confidence that their children had the capacity to excel as long as they were educated", Prof. Sancar finished the Istanbul University Faculty of Medicine in 1969 and went to the

USA to carry out research in biochemistry in 1971. He completed his doctorate in molecular biology at the University of Texas in Dallas in 1977 and started working at the University of North Carolina School of Medicine in 1982. He currently serves as Sarah Graham Kenan Professor of Biochemistry and Biophysics at the University of North Carolina.

Author of over three hundred scientific papers, Prof. Sancar's work on DNA repair and regulation of the circadian clock has gained recognition worldwide. His study of the molecular mechanisms of DNA repair defined the "nucleotide excision repair" (NER) pathway used in the repair of all types of DNA damage. His work on the circadian clock demonstrated that mammals use a protein he named cryptochrome to regulate their daily cycles.

In 2007, he won the Vehbi Koç Award for "his extraordinary scientific qualities and outstanding contribution to human health". Prof. Sancar has also won several other awards, including the Presidential Young Investigator Award from the National Science Foundation, the American Society for Photobiology Research Award, and the Scientific and Technological Research Council of Turkey (TÜBİTAK) Science Award.

He has been selected as a fellow of the American Academy of Arts and Sciences (2004), and a member of the American Microbiology Academy (2005), US National Academy of Sciences (2005) and Turkish Academy of Sciences (TÜBA) (2006). In 2017, the Turkish Directorate of Health Institutes created the Aziz Sancar Science, Service and Incentive Awards.

Prof. Sancar (LEFT) **at the award ceremony with Mustafa V. Koç**

SANERC, full name, KOÇ UNIVERSITY SEMAHAT ARSEL NURSING EDUCATION AND RESEARCH CENTER, a center established as part of the American Hospital(*) in 1992, largely through the efforts of Semahat Arsel(*). It aims to contribute to the development and advancement of the nursing profession. On January 1, 2004, the center became affiliated to Koç University School of Nursing(*). The center's main objectives are to develop creative models in postgraduate nursing training, promote best practice, and carry out nursing research to develop ethical, evidence-based clinical practices.

SANERC began by offering just two training courses, but now delivers training in over 20 different areas. Training programs are developed following consultations on requirements and the course contents are updated annually. The center's work conforms to international standards and is based on the Johns Hopkins School of Nursing model. Ad hoc training is sometimes delivered to organizations that request it. To date, over ten thousand nurses and health professionals have participated in training seminars and programs organized by the center. SANERC also offers a consultation service for structuring nursing services in hospitals.

In 2010, SANERC's postgraduate nursing training was accredited by a subsidiary of the American Nursing Association, the American Nurses Credentialing Center (ANCC), which promotes excellence in nursing and healthcare through inspecting and awarding certification to training centers. SANERC is the only center in Turkey and the region to have received certification for its postgraduate continuing education programs.

The *Journal of Education and Research in Nursing(*) (HEAD)* was launched by SANERC in 2004 as a twice yearly publication. It has been published quarterly since 2017.

SANERC PUBLICATIONS

- **Akdemir, Nuran (ed.), *İç Hastalıkları Hemşireliği El Kitabı* (Internal Diseases Nursing Manual),** *1998*
- **Aksoy, Güler (ed.), *Cerrahi Hastalıkları Hemşireliği El Kitabı* (Surgical Diseases Nursing Manual),** *1998*
- **Atalay, Meliha (ed.), *Hemşirelik Esasları El Kitabı* (Rudiments of Nursing Manual),** *1997*
- **Badır, Aysel and Türkmen, Emine, *Elektrokardiyografi: EKG Analizi, Aritmilerin Tanı ve Tedavisi* (Electrocardiography: ECG Analysis, Diagnosis and Treatment of Arrythmias),** *2002*
- **Conk, Zeynep, *Çocuk Sağlığı ve Hastalıkları Hemşireliği El Kitabı* (Childhood Health and Diseases Nursing Manual),** *1997*
- **Coşkun, Anahit, *Doğum ve Kadın Hastalıkları Hemşireliği El Kitabı* (Birth and Women's Diseases Nursing Manual),** *1996*
- **Erefe, İnci (ed.), *Halk Sağlığı Hemşireliği El Kitabı* (Public Health Nursing Manual), 1998**
- **Kum, Nebahat (ed.), *Psikiyatri Hemşireliği El Kitabı* (Psychiatry Nursing Manual),** *1996*
- **Uyer, Gülten (ed.), *Hemşirelik Hizmetleri Yönetimi El Kitabı* (Nursing Services Management Manual),** *1996*

Sarıyer Vehbi Koç Foundation Hospitality and Tourism Vocational High School *see* Vehbi Koç Foundation Vocational and Technical Anatolian High School

Saylan, Türkan

Saylan, Türkan *(b. December 13, 1935, Istanbul – d. May 18, 2009, Istanbul)*, physician and civil society leader, who won the Vehbi Koç Award(*) in 2009 for education. Notable for her work in leprosy as well as her advocacy of the modernization of Turkish society and the principle of secularism.

Prof. Türkan Saylan (FOURTH FROM THE LEFT) **at the award ceremony with Semahat Arsel** (FAR LEFT), **Süleyman Demirel and Mustafa V. Koç** (SECOND FROM THE RIGHT)

Prof. Saylan finished the Kandilli Girls' High School in 1953 and the Istanbul University (IU) Faculty of Medicine in 1963. She completed her residency on dermatological and venereal diseases at the SSK Nişantaşı Hospital (1963-1965), and continued working there until 1968. Having joined the IU Faculty of Medicine as assistant lecturer in 1968, she rose to associate professor in 1972 and professor in 1977. She headed the IU Faculty of Medicine Department of Dermatology from 1982 to 1987. In February 2001, she was elected to the Higher Education Council (YÖK) as a council of universities member. Her tenure at YÖK ended in December 2002 on her retirement from the university position, but she was re-elected from the Cabinet quota in March 2003 and served until March 2007. In addition to her positions as lecturer at the IU Faculty of Medicine and director of the Lepra Center, Prof. Saylan also served as the voluntary medical director of Istanbul Lepra Hospital (1981-2002).

Prof. Saylan started work on leprosy in 1976 and founded the Battle Against Leprosy Association. She served the World Health Organization as a consultant on leprosy, the International Leprosy Union (ILU) as founding member and vice president, and was a member of the European Dermatological and Venereology Academy and the International Leprosy Association. In the meantime, she took a keen interest in the modernization of Turkish society. In 1989, she founded the Association for Supporting Contemporary Life (ÇYDD). She was a founding member and part of the management of the Lecturers Association and Istanbul University Women's Studies Application and Research Center (1990), the Kandilli Girls' High School Culture and Education Foundation (KANKEV) and the Foundation for the Support of Contemporary Life, Turkey (TÜRKÇAĞ) (1995). She received the International Gandhi Award in 1986, the IU Atatürk's Principles and Reforms Award in 1996, and the Rıfat Ilgaz Cultural Center Honorary Award in 2000. Her contribution to education merited the Vehbi Koç Award in 2009. Shortly before her death of cancer, on April 13, 2009, under the Ergenekon Operation, police searches took place at her home along with several offices of the ÇYDD, whose president she was at the time, causing widespread controversy.

Saylan, who was the author of numerous scientific articles and books on medicine, also contributed articles to the newspaper, *Cumhuriyet*. These are compiled into two titles: *Cumhuriyet'in*

Bireyi Olmak (An Individual in the Republic, 1998) and *Cumhuriyet'in Bireyi Olmak II* (An Individual in the Republic, 2003). Her childhood memories were published as *At Kız-BirYaşamdan Kesitler* (Horse Girl-Scenes from a Life, 2000). The 2004 title *Güneş Umuttan Şimdi Doğar, Türkan Saylan Kitabı* (The Sun is Born of Hope, the Book of Türkan Saylan), consists of biographical interviews. *Türkan, Tek ve Tek Başına* (Türkan, Alone and on Her Own, 2009), Ayşe Kulin's novel on Saylan's life, was later adapted to the screen and a TV series *Türkan* (2010-2011).

The **Science Academy,** non-governmental organization (NGO) that aims to pursue the principles of scientific merit, freedom and integrity, independent of government policies. The Vehbi Koç Foundation(*) supports the Science Academy Young Scientists Program (BAGEP) Scholarship Award(*), which began in 2013 and has funded 10 scholarships every year.

The Science Academy brings together Turkey's eminent scientists in order to maintain excellence in scientific methods, customs and practices as well as promote freedom and integrity in science. This work includes organizing summer schools, meetings and conferences to discuss scientific research results, new findings, science policy and education, ethics in science, developments of interest to the science community and also providing publications to inform the public and interested public and private bodies.

Following a statutory decree published in the *Resmî Gazete* (Official Gazette) on August 27, 2011, and which came into effect on the same day, the Turkish Academy of Sciences (TÜBA), which was established in 1973, ceased to be a de facto autonomous institution and was affiliated with the government. This led to the foundation of the Science Academy on November 25, 2011 by 17 former TÜBA members, who resigned from the TÜBA claiming that it no longer qualified as a science academy. The association, which selects its members exclusively on the grounds of scientific merit from among scientists who have made "important and valuable contributions to science", stipulates that all members must sign a Declaration of Academic Merit, Freedom and Integrity. Today, the Science Academy has 171 elected members and 32 honorary members, two of which are recipients of the Nobel Prize. The Academy is a member of the European federation of science academies known as the All European Academies (ALLEA).

The **Science Academy Young Scientists Program (BAGEP) Scholarship Award,** an award program created in 2013 by the Science Academy(*) with the aim of encouraging young scientists and rewarding exemplary practice. The Vehbi Koç Foundation(*) has supported the program by funding 10 scholarships every year since its foundation.

Established in 2013, the award program receives support from the public rather than government funds and seeks to identify the best young scientists under 40, rewarding and supporting them in new research. Young academics who win the award are provided with two years' funding of TRY 15,000 for each year to support their research. As part of the project, 20 awards were given in 2013, 43 in 2014, 42 in 2015, 48 in 2016, 42 in 2017, and 39 in 2018.

Semahat Arsel Honarary Award
see **KOÇ-KAM**

Semahat-Dr. Nusret Arsel Education Park, TEGV(*) education park founded in Etimesgut, Ankara, maintained by the Semahat-Nusret Arsel Education Facilities Support Foundation established by the Vehbi Koç Foundation(*) (VKV). VKV also meets the administrative costs of the park.

The park opened in June 2001, set on grounds of 10,652 square meters. Computer, technology, reading and activity rooms as well as drama, dreams and inventor's studios, library, offices and a multi-purpose hall are housed in the indoor space of 1,120 square meters. The outdoor area has basketball and football fields and an open-air chess board. Education programs cover mathematics, science, reading, art and information technology, while short-term activities include hygiene and oral and dental health alongside club and school support programs.

60,000 children have visited the park since its foundation.

Semahat-Nusret Arsel Ankara Orchard House *see* **Ankara Orchard House**

---

17 Schools Project, elementary-school building program that was launched as the Vehbi Koç Foundation(*) 13 Schools project in 1998. The schools, in various regions of Turkey, were later transferred to the Ministry of National Education through the "Build, Transfer, Maintain" model. Between 2006 and 2008, four more schools were added to the project, which was initiated to support eight years of core education and to mark the Republic of Turkey's 75th anniversary.

Designed to a uniform model by master architect Yıldırım Sağlıkova, every school was built to take about 500 students within 4,800 square meters of enclosed space containing 16 classrooms, a library, science-computer labs, and a 300-capacity multi-purpose hall.

Each school's maintenance costs and other similar requirements are covered by a Koç Holding(*) company in their area. Until the end of 2014, school administrators and teachers also received support from the Koç School(*)

Opening of Bursa Nilüfer Koç Elementary School, 1999

to raise teaching standards and the overall quality of education. This included regular seminars and development programs under the title of "Summer Seminars Hand in Hand with the 17 Schools".

Since 2000, the top three graduates from each school have been granted a scholarship, with a total of 51 students receiving support. From 2000 to 2016, the number of scholarships awarded to the graduates of these schools was 2,352.

A magazine, *Gelişim İçin El Ele* (Hand in Hand for Development), was published as part of the project. Every year, one school coordinates the publication from material produced by pupils

Construction of Bursa Nilüfer Koç Middle School, 1999

at schools involved in the project. Enough copies are printed so that every student in the 17 Schools project can receive a copy, promoting the project principle of supporting education through sharing.

Elementary and middle schools currently included in the project are: Ankara (Sincan Koç Elementary School), Bolu Koç Elementary and Middle School, Bursa (İnegöl Vehbi Koç Elementary School, Nilüfer Koç Middle School, Orhangazi Koç Elementary School and Middle School, Yenişehir Koç Middle School), Diyarbakır (Bağlar Vehbi Koç Elementary School, Kayapınar Vehbi Koç Elementary School), Elazığ Koç Elementary School, Eskişehir (İnönü Vehbi Koç Middle School), İstanbul (Beyazıt Ford Otosan Koç Elementary School, Beylikdüzü Koç Middle School), Kocaeli (Gebze Koç Middle School, Ford Otosan Koç Middle School), Şanlıurfa Koç Elementary and Middle School, Şırnak (Silopi Koç Elementary and Middle School), Van Koç Elementary and Middle School.

VKV PRESIDENT ERDAL YILDIRIM: THE EXCITEMENT ON OPENING DAY...

... I recall especially the children's excitement, the town people's excitement at the opening ceremonies of the 13 schools... There were also misunderstandings. For example, we were building a school in one of Orhangazi's relatively low-income neighbourhoods. "Why is Koç building a school here?", people were asking. In fact, just a few days before the school's opening, enrolment levels were still low. It turned out that families were thinking, "This must be a private school, we can't afford it". Of course, they were overjoyed to learn otherwise. It was very moving and very gratifying to witness all this...

Suna Dokur (ed.), *Forty Year Book*, Vehbi Koç Foundation Publications, Istanbul, 2009, p. 77

Sevgi-Erdoğan Gönül Education Park, TEGV(*) education park established in Şanlıurfa in line with Sevgi Gönül's(*) will and funded by the Vehbi Koç Foundation(*) (VKV).

Set on grounds totaling 8,119 square meters in the Eyyüp Nebi District allocated to the TEGV by the Şanlıurfa Municipality free of charge for 30 years, the education park opened in October 2010, although official inauguration took place on April 5, 2011. Each year, over 4,000 children benefit from the park that has an indoor space of 1,850 square meters. Built on two floors, it

houses drama, dreams and inventor's studios, activity, reading, computer and technology rooms, a library, a multi-purpose hall and offices. The outdoor area has basketball, volleyball and football fields, a children's play area, an open-air chess board, a mini amphitheater and walkways. Education programs cover mathematics, science, reading, art and information technology, while short-term activities include hygiene and oral and dental health alongside club and school support programs.

Approximately 25,000 children have visited the park since its foundation.

Sevim and Necdet Kent Library, founded by the Rahmi M. Koç Museology and Culture Foundation(*) and opened in Alibey (Cunda) Island of Ayvalık, Balıkesir in 2007.

The historic Agios Yannis chapel that today serves as the library and the adjacent big windmill comprise a section of a major monastery constructed in the fifteenth century. Abandoned after the 1920s population exchanges between

Turkey and Greece and fallen into disrepair, the ruins of the chapel and the windmill were restored after personal intervention by Rahmi M. Koç(*). The ancient chapel was reassigned as a library to house some 1,300 titles belonging to Ambassador Necdet Kent (1911-2002) and donated by his son Muhtar Kent. The library is named after Necdet Kent and his wife Sevim Kent (1918-2000), who was originally from Ayvalık.

Shepard, Lorrin A(ndrews) *(b. March 24, 1890, Antep - d. July 16, 1983, Haverhill, Massachusetts, USA)*, chief physician of the

American Hospital(*) from 1927 to 1957. Having dedicated his whole life to making the American Hospital the best health and treatment center in Istanbul, he was familiarly known as Mr. American Hospital.

His father Dr. Fred D. A. Shepard (1855-1915) was a surgeon at the Antep American Hospital. An 1881 medical graduate of the University of Michigan, Dr. Fred D. A. Shepard served at the Antep American Hospital from 1882 until his death from typhus in 1915.

Lorrin A. Shepard's mother Dr. Fanny Andrews A. Shepard (1856-1920) was also a physician, born to a missionary family in Hawaii. After obtaining her degree in medicine from the University of Michigan in 1882, she came to Turkey with her husband Dr. Fred D. A. Shepard. As a woman, however, she was not allowed to practice as a physician in the Ottoman Empire. She raised three children as she worked as a nurse, midwife and paediatric nurse at the Antep American Hospital and founded a lace and sewing workshop to help the widows and orphans of Antep.

Lorrin A. Shepard visited the USA every three or four years with his parents between 1890 and 1908 and started school in Antep. He later moved in with his paternal aunt to attend the New Jersey High School in Orange (1908-10) and finished as top of his year. He studied science at Yale University in New Haven, Connecticut (1910-14) and medicine at Columbia University (1914-18). He served at the Presbyterian Hospital of New York as general practitioner (1918-19). He got married in 1919, and at the wedding ceremony he and his wife were commissioned by the American Board of Commissioners for Foreign Missions. That same year he was appointed as physician to the Antep American Hospital in place of his father who had died in 1915. He was forced to leave in 1926 due to a dispute.

Dr. Shepard completed his surgical residency at the Bellevue Hospital, New York (1926-27) and was appointed as chief physician of the American Hospital in Istanbul in 1927. In 1934, he appealed to American donors to raise funds for the hospital's first building in Nişantaşı, whose planning, fundraising and construction he supervised in 1939. He contributed to the design of the Admiral Bristol Nursing School(*) in 1949 and oversaw its construction.

In 1957, Dr. Shepard retired from the American Hospital and returned to the USA, where he was appointed as director of the Yale University Office of International Students in the same year. He also prepared the library catalog of the Ottoman Manuscripts Collection of the university. In 1959, he moved to the family home in Boothbay, Maine, and died at the Union Mission Care Home in Haverhill, Massachusetts on July 16, 1983.

Shields, (Harvey) Gerald, *(b. November 27, 1937, Seaford, Virginia, USA)*, educator and administrator. Served as director of the Koç High School (*see* Koç School) from 1992 to 1996.

After obtaining a history degree

from Washington & Lee University in 1960, he completed a history master's at Tulane University, New Orleans in 1962 and a further master's in education at Harvard University (1967-69). Appointed as director of Koç High School in 1992, a post he would keep until 1996, Shields also served as a school counselor. It was in 1994, during his tenure as director, that the International Baccalaureate (IB) program was introduced in Turkey. The school's first batch of pupils that had studied in the Middle School from preparatory onwards graduated in 1995.

After leaving Koç High School, Shields served as headmaster in schools in Luxembourg, Germany, Venezuela, the USA and Indonesia.

Silopi Koç Elementary and Middle School *see* **17 Schools Project**

Sincan Koç Elementary School *see* **17 Schools Project**

Sivas Kangal Koç Anatolian High School, also known as the Koç Anatolian High School, founded in 2010 by the Vehbi Koç Foundation(*) in Kangal, Sivas.

Set on grounds of 12,300 square meters, and with an indoor space of 4,700 square meters, the school has 14 classrooms, three science laboratories, a 200-capacity sports hall and a library. The school had 320 pupils in 2018.

http://momentyapi.com.tr/Client/Projects/sivas-kangal-koc-anadolu-lisesi-nsaati175236.jpg

Social Entrepreneurship Development Program *see* **KUSIF**

Soma Underground Training Pit Project, Social responsibility project by Demir Export AŞ, a Koç Holding(*) company, the Celal Bayar University (CBU) and the Vehbi Koç Foundation(*).

The training pit project was developed in the wake of the mining disaster of May 13, 2014, when a fire followed by the flooding of the tunnel caused the death of 301 miners in Soma, Manisa. Aiming to train experienced and technically qualified miners, the training pit opened in the land allocated on the CBU Soma Vocational College grounds in 2015. Equipped with tools and materials used in working pits, its objective is to train students in the relevant departments of the college, novice miners and other workers who are about to take up jobs in mines.

Among the principal aims of the project are improving the knowledge and skill sets of mine workers on essential safety procedures in mines, best practice and an awareness of safety at work at all times.

Suna-İnan Kıraç Education Park, a TEGV(*) education park in the Kepez area of Antalya established with funds from the Vehbi Koç Foundation(*) (VKV). The park's running costs are also met by VKV.

The park is in the Yeşilyurt district on a plot of 14,700 square meters, which was allocated to TEGV by Kepez Municipality. It began operating in February 2001, but the official opening took place in October of the same year. The park, which since its opening has been visited by 60,000 children, also includes a 1,400 square meter undercover area containing drama, creative and "dream" workshops, together with a library, laboratory, multi-purpose hall, offices and activity, reading and IT rooms. The outdoor area includes basketball, volleyball and football fields, an outdoor chess facility and traffic education space. Education programs related to science, reading, art and technology are held in the park, along with club and school support activities and short term initiatives addressing hygiene, mouth and dental health.

THE MESSAGE FROM SUNA KIRAÇ READ AT THE PARK'S OFFICIAL OPENING CEREMONY

I'm sad that I can't be with you due to ill health. On the other hand, I'm overjoyed. My struggles are taking place inside a boundless ring of affection. I have ideals that are longer than my lifetime: resolving the educational inadequacies that lay behind all of our country's problems, the corporatization of the foundation and the Koç Group, and striving to achieve both. Enduring the worst economic crisis of the Republican Era has been exacerbated by the threats of terror and war that have become part of our world. In the midst of such a chaotic environment, my aims might seem utopian. However, economic crises can be overcome, political issues can be solved, but it's impossible to fix a society that has wasted its young people. I'm a lucky person. God showed me many beautiful things during my life. This education park gave me and İnan great happiness. I entrust this park to future generations and our daughter İpek Kıraç.

http://www.milliyet.com.tr/2001/10/21/yasam/ayas.html

Suna and İnan Kıraç Foundation, a civil society organization engaged in "educational, cultural, artistic and healthcare initiatives. The foundation contributes to the public good by giving material and moral support to people and organizations, aiming to raise public-spirited individuals that are of benefit to Turkish society." Established on October 27, 2003, by Suna Kıraç(*), İnan Kıraç(*) and İpek Kıraç(*), the foundation works in strategic partnership with other civil society bodies: the Vehbi Koç Foundation(*), TEGV(*) and Galatasaray Education Foundation.

The first large project of the Suna and İnan Kıraç Foundation was the Pera Museum(*) in Istanbul, a private museum that houses a number of valuable collections. The other large project, the Istanbul Research Institute(*), researches the city's history, cultural make-up and human profile, while at the same time developing and supporting projects in line with this objective. A third large project currently in the planning stage is the Suna Kıraç Cultural Center which will house large concert and theatre halls together with exhibition spaces.

The foundation provides scholarships to individuals and organizations in line with its educational objectives. As part of the individual scholarship program, scholarships are given directly to young pupils, at all stages of their education, who have achieved great academic success and have a wide range of extra-curricular interests. The other part of the scholarship program allocates annual scholarships to Turkey's top universities. Funds are presently designated to Koç University(*) and Galatasaray University. The universities award the scholarships themselves to successful students who meet the criteria. The foundation also provides an annual subsidy to the Galatasaray University Suna Kıraç Library(*).

The largest enterprise supported by the Suna and İnan Kıraç Foundation in the health field is the Neurodegeneration Research Laboratory (NDAL) opened as part of the Boğaziçi University (BU) Department of Molecular Biology and Genetics in 2005 and affiliated to Koç University today. The laboratory, which is the first academic partnership in Turkey between a state university and a private foundation, is recognized internationally as a center of expertise on the molecular diagnosis of genetic and complex diseases. Currently, the laboratory is affiliated with Koç University and specializes in research into motor neuron (especially ALS) and similar neurodegenerative diseases and the molecular mechanisms that cause them. The biannual Suna Kıraç Neurodegeneration Conference series has earned considerable recognition in the field of motor neuron development and neurodegeneration biology.

Additionally, the foundation's Molecular Biology Scholarship and Research Fund enables postgraduate BU students to continue their education at Brown University in the USA. The same fund also supports a biannual workshop, titled Model Organisms in Neurodegenerative Diseases. The Brain Sciences Fund gives financial support to research projects in the field as well as scholarships to postgraduate students.

In 2008, the Contemporary Art Foundation (ÇAĞSAV) awarded an honorary medal to "the Suna and İnan Kıraç Foundation for establishing the Pera Museum, one of the most important museums in Turkey, opening up its collections to visitors for the public benefit, supporting forward-looking projects with historical research and demonstrating an in depth understanding of traditional and contemporary art." Together with the Pera Museum and Istanbul Research Institute, the foundation has also received appreciation plaques from numerous organizations, including the Foundation of Educational volunteers (TEGV), the Union of Tourist Guides in Turkey (TUREB), the Anadolu University Faculty of Fine Arts, Marmara University Faculty of Fine Arts, Ali Emiri Efendi Library, Turkish Coffee Culture and Research Organization, Istanbul Rotary, WPO, YPO, JSI and ICP.

Suna-İnan Kıraç Kaleiçi Museum
see **Kaleiçi Museum**

Suna-İnan Kıraç Research Center for Mediterranean Civilizations
see **AKMED**

Suna Kıraç Hall, a multi-purpose hall at Robert College(*) built by the Vehbi Koç Foundation(*). It is one of two buildings (the other is an extra laboratory building) built by the VKV in 1989 on the Robert College Campus under the condition that "education would be provided free of charge to a minimum of two students in need of help". The 500-capacity hall, which has an expansive stage and state-of-the-art sound and lighting rig, is used by high school students for shows, concerts and other arts events.

Suna Kıraç Inter-School Short Story Competition, a short story challenge organized by the Koç School(*) in the name of Suna Kıraç(*) and held every year since 2008.

The competition aims to create an artistic and literary environment by bringing together students from different high schools and contributing to their literary leanings. It hopes to encourage students' creativity by publishing the competition entries in a book. Every year a different theme is announced and a three-person jury is established from among Turkey's leading literary figures. Cash prizes and a set of books are awarded to the winners in two categories: Koç School pupils and pupils at other schools. E-book collections of the stories written since 2008 by participants aged 14-17 can be accessed via the Pera Museum(*) website. (https://www.peramuzesi.org.tr/suna-kirac-oyku-yarismasi/).

Support Center for Disabled Children and Their Families
see **EÇADEM**

Swanker, Wilson A(bbs) *(b. March 29, 1909, Schenectady, New York, USA – d. September 9, 1991, Annapolis, Maryland, USA)*, served between 1957 and 1961 as the fourth chief physician of the American Hospital(*).

After graduating from Purdue University, he completed his medical education at the Jefferson Medical College in Philadelphia and opened a clinic in Shippensburg, Pennsylvania. During World War II, he served as a military doctor in Europe. After the war, he worked in the plastic surgery field in New York. In January 1957, he was appointed as chief physician of the American Hospital in Istanbul. After serving for four years, he resigned in January 1962 due to several reasons, including "private family circumstances, wanting to be involved in projects unrelated to the hospital, failing to secure the full support and trust of the hospital's board of directors and being unable to formulate his own vision for the future of the American Hospital."

He later returned to Washington and worked at the Defense Intelligence Agency. Following his retirement in 1972, Dr. Swanker took up voluntary work in the seashells section at the Smithsonian Institute Museum of Natural History.

His book *Anomalies of Infants and Children*, written together with David McCullagh Mayer, was published in 1958.

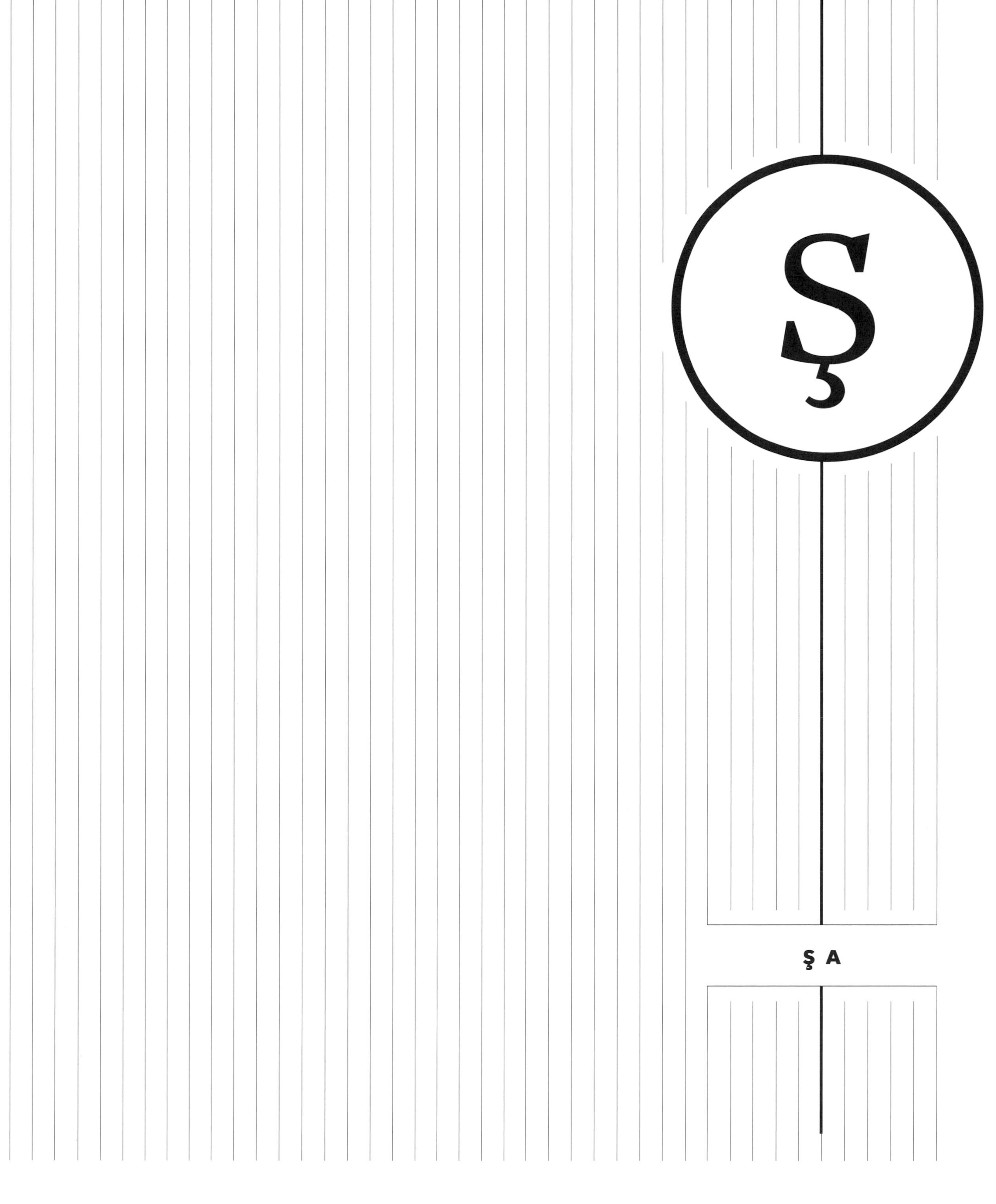

ŞA

Şahinbaş, Tamer *(b. June 25, 1940, Istanbul),* engineer and manager who represented Koç Holding(*) on the Vehbi Koç Foundation(*) Board of Directors from 1994 to 1996.

After completing his studies at Tarsus American College in 1958, Şahinbaş obtained a degree at the Middle East Technical University Department of Civil Engineering (1958-64). He received a master's degree from the same university in 1965. He served as a road bridge engineer in Denmark (1965-67), returned to Turkey in 1967 to complete his military service in 1969 and later worked at the State Planning Organization between 1970 and 1972.

In 1972, Şahinbaş took up a position as planning manager at Aygaz AŞ, a Koç Holding company, and moved to Koç Holding as planning coordinator in 1979. He was general manager of Koza İnşaat AŞ (1981-90) and founding president of Koç University(*) (KU) (1990-92). Şahinbaş was appointed in 1993 as president of human resources at Koç Holding and remained in this post until his retirement in 2000. At present, he continues to serve on the board of directors of Ramerica Inc.

Şanlıurfa Koç Elementary and Middle School *see* **17 Schools Project**

Şardağ, Necdet *see* **Vehbi Koç Foundation**

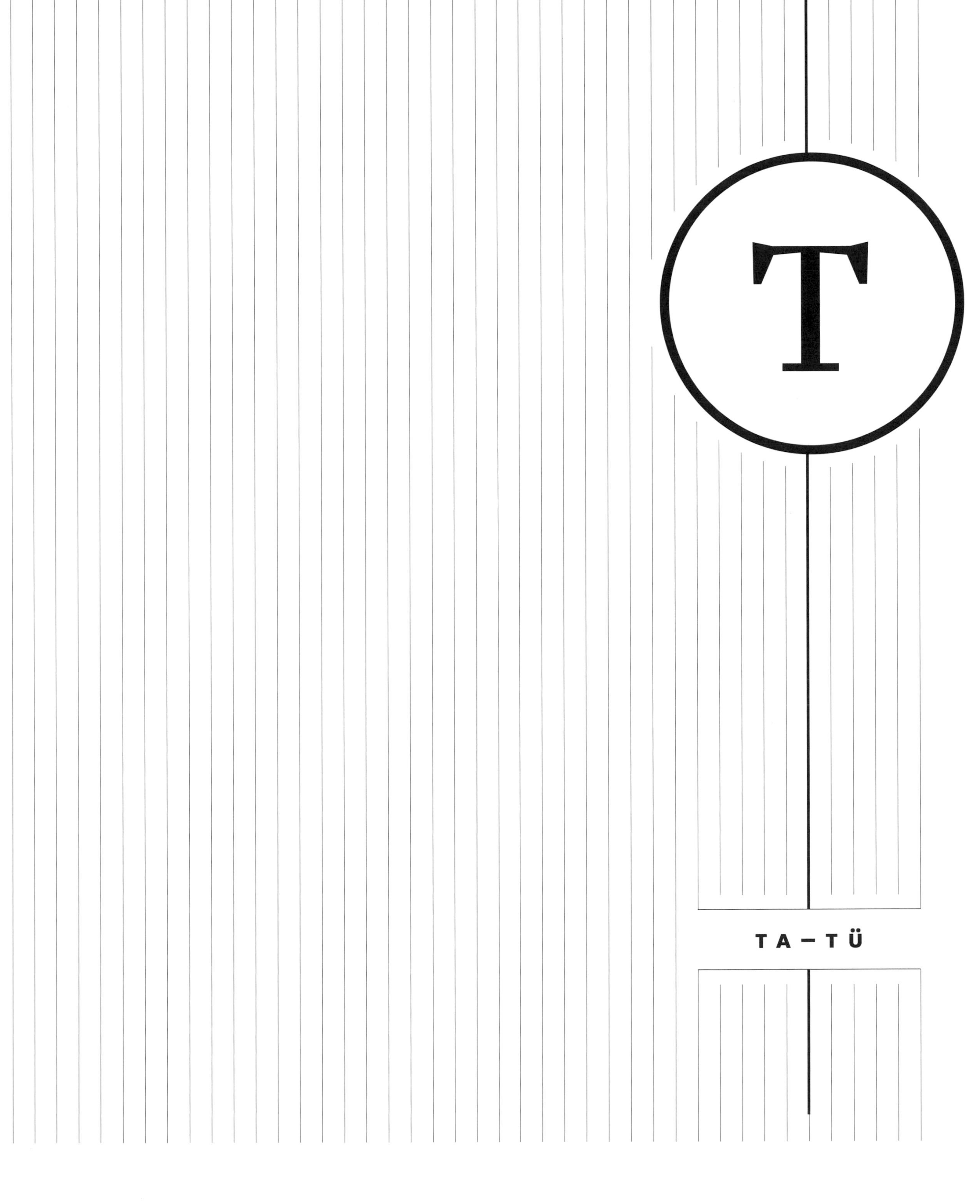

TA – TÜ

TANAS, non-profit art gallery in Berlin, entirely funded by the Vehbi Koç Foundation(*) (VKV). When written backwards it spells, SANAT, the Turkish word for art. The gallery tracked developments in contemporary art in Turkey and provided an international showcase for the work of relevant artists. Directed by René Block(*), TANAS opened in 2008 on Heide Street, in the area containing Berlin's contemporary arts centers. TANAS, which provided another important international platform for Turkey's artistic output, was seen as a means of ensuring ongoing communication and regular interaction between artists and curators from Turkey and German and international audiences.

Vahap Avşar, iBerlin exhibition, March 27-May 12, 2012
Photo: Uwe Walter

It was envisaged that TANAS would be in operation for five years as one of the important phases of the VKV's series of contemporary art projects. A total of 22 individual and group exhibitions were organized, predominantly featuring artists from Turkey. These were accompanied by artist talks, panels and special exhibition tours guided by different art professionals. With a focus on contemporary art in Turkey and bringing together artists, curators, writers and students, TANAS provided a diverse platform for producing and discussing art in Berlin's lively international art scene.

The gallery opened with Kutluğ Ataman's "Küba" exhibition on April 5, 2008 and its final exhibition, "The Unanswered Question. İskele2", took place between September 8 and November 3, 2013. Curated by René Block in partnership with Neuer Berliner Kunstverein, the exhibition brought the gallery's five years of activity to a close as planned from its inception.

TANAS EXHIBITIONS

- **Küba** *(April 5–June 1, 2008)*
  Kutluğ Ataman
- **Mahrem** *(June 15–August 10, 2008)*
  Curator: Emre Baykal
  Artists: Kutluğ Ataman, Samer Barkaoui, Samta Benyahia, Nezaket Ekiçi, Shahram Entekhabi, Bruna Esposito, Parastou Forouhar, Shadi Ghadirian, Mandana Moghaddam, Ebru Özseçen
- **Quartet – Graphic Prints from 4 Biennials**
  (September 6–November 09, 2008)
  Curator: René Block
- **Komunismus Sozialismus Kapietalismus (Communism, Socialism, Capitalism)**
  (January 3–March 14, 2009)
  Nasan Tur
- **Unemployed Employees – I found you a new job!**
  (April 4–May 30, 2009)
  Aydan Murtezaoğlu and Bülent Şangar
- **Red Thread – Entry to the 11th International İstanbul Biennial** *(June 16–August 8, 2009)*
  Curator: What, How & for Whom/WHW
- **Passengers** *(September 8–November 28, 2009)*
  Esra Ersen
- **Not Easy to Save the World in 90 Days – Turkey's Young Art Stage**
  (December 14, 2009–March 13, 2010)
  Curator: René Block
  Artists: Halil Altındere, Fikret Atay, Köken Ergun, Ali Kazma, Servet Koçyiğit, Ahmet Öğüt, Erkan Özgen, Şener Özmen, Cengiz Tekin, Nasan Tur
- **Things We Do – 8 Works from the Video Series Titled "Obstacles"** *(March 24–June 5, 2010)*
  Ali Kazma
- **Kısmet** *(June 12–August 7, 2010)*
  Ebru Özseçen
- **Tactics of Invisibility**
  (September 11, 2010–January 15, 2011)
- **TANAS/Berlin, Thyssen-Bornemisza Art Contemporary/Vienna and Arter/Istanbul collaborative exhibition project**
  Curators: Daniela Zyman and Emre Baykal
  Artists: Nevin Aladağ, Kutluğ Ataman, Cevdet Erek, Ayşe Erkmen, Esra Ersen, İnci Eviner, Nilbar Güreş, Hafriyat, Ahmet Öğüt, Füsun Onur, Sarkis, Hale Tenger, Nasan Tur, xurban_collective
- **Dim the Lights, 6:07 min** *(May 28–July 30, 2011)*
  Nevin Aladağ
- **The Speed of Colors** *(February 1–May 14, 2011)*
  Films, *1996-2010*
  Sarkis

- **To Multiply Is Human**
  (September 10–November 26, 2011)
  45 Years of Edition Block, *1966-2011*
- **Zwölf Im Zwölften (Twelve in Twelfth)**
  (December 10, 2011–March 10, 2012)
  Artists: Nevin Aladağ, Vahap Avşar, Ergin Çavuşoğlu, Nezaket Ekici, Şakir Gökçebağ, Nilbar Güreş, Servet Koçyiğit, Ahmet Öğüt, Ebru Özseçen, Anny-Sibel Öztürk, Canan Tolon, Nasan Tur
- **iBerlin** *(March 27–May 12, 2012)*
  Vahap Avşar
- **Turkish Art New and Superb** *(May 23–July 28, 2012)*
  Artists: Mehtap Baydu, Bashir Borlakov, Banu Cennetoğlu, Aslı Çavuşoğlu, Cevdet Erek, Ha Za Vu Zu, Nuri Kuzucan, Ali Miharbi, Yasemin Özcan, Serkan Özkaya, Güneş Terkol, Vahit Tuna, Shiri Zinn
- **Infinity Has No Accent**
  (September 8–November 24, 2012)
  Halil Altındere
- **Prefix & Suffix** *(December 8, 2012–March 2, 2013)*
  Şakir Gökçebağ
- **New Kids of the Block** *(March 16-May 11, 2013)*
  Artists: Ayşe Erkmen, Melanie Bisping, Bo Hee Choi, Sunah Choi, Dani Gal, Stephanie Gudra, Özlem Günyol-Mustafa Kunt, Jonas Hohnke, Sun-Hwa Lee, Michaela Meise, Esther Mittermeier, Nadia Pereira Benavente, Michael Pfrommer, Sascha Pohle, Stephanie Regenbrecht, Mandla Reuter, Jihun Song, Anne Staab, Dino Steinhof, Samuel Treindl, Nasan Tur, Birgit Wichern, Adrian Williams
- **Agoraphobia – Entry to the 13th Istanbul Biennial**
  (May 25–July 27, 2013)
  Curators: **Fulya Erdemci, Bige Örer and Kevser Güler**
  Artists: Jimmie Durham, Freee (Dave Beech, Andy Hewitt and Mel Jordan), LaToya Ruby Frazier, Amal Kanawy, Lux Lindner, José Antonio Vega Macotela, Cinthia Marcelle, Şener Özmen, Proyecto Secundario, Liliana Maresca (Liliana Maresca Ortaokulu Projesi), Christoph Schäfer, Mierle Laderman Ukeles
- **The Unanswered Question. İskele2**
  (September 8–November 3, 2013)
  Curator: René Block
  Artists: Adel Abidin, Johanna Adebäck-Merve Ertufan, Nevin Aladağ, Halil Altındere, Fikret Atay, Maja Bajević, Rosa Barba, Claus Böhmler, Candice Breitz, Jae Eun Choi, Sunah Choi, Braco Dimitrijević, Maria Eichhorn, Ayşe Erkmen, Andrea Faciu-Florin Bobu, Asta Gröting, Mona Hatoum, Pravdoliub Ivanov, Christian Jankowski, Annika Kahrs, Gülsün Karamustafa, Ali Kazma, Kimsooja Jarosław Kozłowski, Alicja Kwade, Jonas Mekas, Olaf Metzel, Bjørn Nørgaard, Ahmet Öğüt, Şener Özmen, Dan Perjovschi, Sonja Rentsch, Mario Rizzi, Michael Sailstorfer, Anri Sala, Sarkis, Superflex, Cengiz Tekin, Hale Tenger, Raša Todosijević, Endre Tót, Thu Van Tran, Rosemarie Trockel, Nasan Tur, Lawrence Weiner, Maaria Wirkkala

TAPV *see* **Turkish Family Health and Planning Foundation**

Teachers Network Project, a project aiming to increase the quality of education and student success rates in Turkey by creating an environment of constant interaction in which teachers can effect change and transformation. The network is based on the transformation theory developed by the "Teachers Research", which was carried out by the Vehbi Koç Foundation(*) (VKV) in collaboration with ATÖLYE and the Education Reform Initiative (ERG)(*). This work involved educational stakeholders, civil society groups as well as experts and institutions from different disciplines. The project was supported by VKV, together with the following six leading foundations in Turkey: AÇEV(*), Aydın Doğan Foundation, Enka Foundation, Mehmet Zorlu Foundation and the Sabancı Foundation. The project was planned with a seven-year lifespan and the first stage of the pilot finished in December 2017.

The basic approach of the Teachers Network is to empower teachers by giving support in an interactive environment able to meet their personal and professional needs. Rather than proposing solutions to teachers, first they are helped to identify their own problems, so that they can be resolved either by creating resources to meet their requirements or by ensuring that teachers have access to the resources available from stakeholders.

Content provided by civil society groups, universities and other bodies is collated in a resource pool called the Sustenance Web Menu, which contains materials to help teachers find solutions to the problems they encounter in their professional lives. It has been developed over time and now includes contributions, suggestions and feedback from teachers who are part of the network, making it an important tool for sharing success stories and solutions, both in and out of the school environment.

TEGV, full name TÜRKİYE EĞİTİM GÖNÜLLÜLERİ VAKFI (TURKISH FOUNDATION OF EDUCATION VOLUNTEERS), non-governmental organization (NGO) founded to support basic state education through the provision of extra-curricular education opportunities. It was formed on January 23, 1995 by 55 business persons, managers and academicians led by Suna Kıraç(*). One of the several NGOs regularly supported by the Vehbi Koç Foundation(*), TEGV won Cabinet approval in 2009 to "collect donations without need for further permits". Today TEGV's donors exceed 200,000.

TEGV's educational activities comprise child-centric education methods and programs appropriate to the developmental stages of children between 7 and 16 and designed to help them develop life skills. These activities intend to provide versatile education support in active learning environments to enable children of diverse skills to discover their own personalities and talents.

The original education programs created by TEGV are largely implemented by volunteers in various cities through its Education Parks, Learning Units and Mobile Firefly Learning Units. Over 2,7 million children have benefited since its foundation due to the work of over 82,000 TEGV volunteers.

Education Volunteers today operate a total of ten Education Parks: two in Istanbul, and one each in Ankara, Antalya, Eskişehir, Gaziantep, Izmir, Samsun, Şanlıurfa and Van. Built on expansive grounds allocated by local government, these parks possess all spatial and technological facilities essential for supporting multipurpose educational needs. Each Education Park has a yearly capacity of approximately 3,500 children on grounds of between ten and twenty thousand square meters, with fields for various sports including football and basketball. On average, the parks have 1,200 square meters of indoor space for computer rooms, libraries and studios.

Suna Kıraç at the opening ceremony of the TEGV Güzelcehisar Summer School with Prof. Yılmaz Büyükerşen (RIGHT)

Smaller Learning Units allocated to the TEGV in towns and cities with limited educational facilities today number 38, each of which has a yearly capacity of 700 children in indoor spaces varying between 250 and 300 square meters.

Twenty-four mobile learning units called Fireflies reach out to children in areas lacking Education Parks or Learning Units. Originally launched under the auspices of the Hope 2000 Project in the wake of the 1999 Marmara Earthquake to provide continuity in education to children in earthquake regions, the mobile learning units later developed into the Firefly Project covering every city. The Firefly units, which are housed in truck beds, each have a yearly capacity of 2,400 children and contain activity spaces, IT rooms and a living space.

To inform volunteers about its training activities, TEGV publishes *Düşler Atölyesi* (The Dreams Workshop), *Oyunlarla Spor* (Sport with Games) and *Okuyorum Oynuyorum* (I Read I Play), and for children it publishes *Eğlen Öğren Hijyen* (Have Fun, Learn, Hygiene) and *Kariyer Yolculuğuma Başlıyorum Ansiklopedisi* (Starting on My Career Journey Encyclopedia). It also produces a quarterly magazine, *eg, Eğitim Gönüllüleri* (ev, Education Volunteers). Supported by the Yapı Kredi Bank as part of the "I Read I Play" project, the TEGV website has also published several editions of *Renkli Kalemler* (Colorful Pens), which is a journal written by children coached by experienced writers and journalists in the following Education Parks: Istanbul (May 2014), Samsun (May 2014), Van (May 2014), Ankara (January 2015), Gaziantep (January 2015), Izmir (January 2015), Antalya (May 2015), Istanbul (May 2015), Eskişehir (June 2015) and Şanlıurfa (June 2015).

TEGV EDUCATION PARKS

- **ANKARA: Semahat-Dr. Nusret Arsel Education Park(*)**
- **ANTALYA: Suna-İnan Kıraç Education Park(*)**
- **ESKİŞEHİR: Atatürk Education Park Ali Numan Kıraç Activity Center**
- **GAZİANTEP: Gaziantep Metropolitan Municipality Education Park**
- **ISTANBUL: Sema and Aydın Doğan Education Park**
- **ISTANBUL: Ferit Aysan Education Park**
- **IZMİR: Çiğli Education Park**
- **SAMSUN: Samsun Metropolitan Municipality Education Park**
- **ŞANLIURFA: Sevgi-Erdoğan Gönül Education Park(*)**
- **VAN: Feyyaz Tokar Education Park**

TEGV'S OBJECTIVES IN THE WORDS OF SUNA KIRAÇ*

Our country faces an economic and political bottleneck. It has built up over the years and stems from the fact that not all members of the community have done their part.

Countries and people do not find themselves in such dire straits for no reason. It is mistakes and irresponsible acts that create this situation.

The real problem underlying all the problems our country faces is LACK OF EDUCATION.

The education level of our country lags behind the needs of the age.

What is needed to ensure the unity of the nation, social peace and economic development is an education system suitable to raising young people for the age of science, who are enlightened, confident, tolerant, self-renewing, inquisitive, analytical, problem-solving, equipped with common sense, subscribing to national and universal values and passionate about Turkish culture and civilization.

The Turkish Foundation of Education Volunteers was founded to contribute to raising such a generation and to offer them the opportunity of a better education.

* From the letter Suna Kıraç had sent to leading business people in 1995 to recruit financial and moral support for the TEGV.

Suna Kıraç, *Ömrümden Uzun İdeallerim Var* (My Ideals, Longer than my Lifetime), Suna and İnan Kıraç Foundation Publications, Istanbul, 2006, p. 212

SUNA KIRAÇ: "WHY I BECAME AN EDUCATION VOLUNTEER"

Because I am determined to live and fight in this country.

I wish to be criticized, not be a critic.

I decided to do, not talk.

I was first immersed in the education issues of our country seven years ago with our Koç High School, and four years later with Koç University.

Launching into an area I thought I knew well made me realize I knew nothing.

Why did I become an education volunteer? Because Robert College had taught me mindfulness and consistency in expressing my ideas, and to reveal my position. It had taught me to choose the path that required courage. To never fear the allegations of "wild, mad, big-headed or ambitious", to avoid mediocrity or becoming a "yes man".

Today is the anniversary of the March 27 local elections. The results were predicted for some sections of society, and a surprise for others; one thing they did was to mobilize non-governmental organizations, albeit briefly. Faxes were sent and meetings arranged. Thankfully a good deal of these activities focused on education. We must continue to gather these efforts so that they are determined and effective; we must never lose our enthusiasm. We must look back and assess what we could have achieved in the past year, what we actually did achieve, and where we failed.

Economic difficulties can be overcome, just as political crises can be resolved.

What can't be done is to repair a society whose children have been dispossessed.

Today, 33% of our population is at elementary and secondary school age. The leaders of the future will rise from this group. (State Institute of Statistics, 1990 figures)

Today, this group is at the stage when value sets and behavioral patterns are formed. They will have the correct impact on the future of the country so long as they receive high quality education in the correct direction. Should they fail to receive correct direction, our country will face far greater challenges than it does today.

Suna Kıraç, *Ömrümden Uzun İdeallerim Var*, pp. 213-14

Tekay, Mesrure *(b. December 19, 1955, Gaziantep)*, educator and director who served as director of Koç Primary School (*see* Koç School) from 1998 to 2013.

She graduated from the Gaziantep Private College in 1973, received a degree in English language and literature from Gazi University in 1976 and completed postgraduate studies in education technology at Hacettepe University in 1980. Tekay taught English at Ankara Private Yükseliş High School (1980-85) and Ankara Private İlkadım High School (1985-87), and served as head of the English department, deputy director and director of Ankara Private İlkem High School (1989-94). She became the founding director of Ankara İhsan Doğramacı Foundation Bilkent Private Elementary School in 1994, where she served until

1998 when she was appointed as the founding director of Koç Primary School. She remained in this position until her retirement in 2013. At present, she serves as a project consultant at the Koç Model School(*) run by the Vehbi Koç Foundation(*).

Tekin, Oğuz *(b. 8 April 1958, Ankara)*, archaeologist, historian of Antiquity and academician; director of AKMED(*) since January 2017.

In 1982, Tekin obtained a degree in classical archaeology from the Istanbul University (IU) Faculty of Letters, where he took up a position as assistant in the Department of Ancient History in 1984. He received a master's degree in 1987 and PhD in 1991. He became associate professor in 1993 and a professor in 1999. He served as deputy dean of the IU Faculty of Letters (2000-2004), and head of the Department of Ancient History (2006-2016). Professor Tekin moved to the Koç University (*) Department of Archaeology and Art History at the start of 2017, at the same time taking on the directorship of AKMED.

Prof. Tekin also contributes to the "Sylloge Nummorum Graecorum Turkey" and the "Corpus Ponderum Antiquorum et Islamicorum" projects as editor and writer. Alongside his research on numismatics, Tekin's expertise in markets and commercial weights and measures in antiquity has led to the publication of numerous books and articles. His *Eski Yunan ve Roma Tarihi'ne Giriş* (Introduction to the History of Ancient Greece and Rome, 2008) won the Best University Textbook award from the Turkish Academy of Sciences (TÜBA) in 2011.

His published titles include *Antik Numismatik ve Anadolu (1992;* Ancient Numismatics and Anatolia), *Antik Anadolu Numismatiği Bibliyografyası* (1993; Bibliography of Ancient Anatolian Numismatics), *Yapı Kredi Koleksiyonu Grek ve Roma Sikkeleri* (1994; Greek and Roman Coins in the Yapı Kredi Collection),

Eskiçağ'da Para (1995; Money in Antiquity), *Eskiçağ'da İstanbul* (1996; Istanbul in Antiquity), *Yapı Kredi Koleksiyonu Bizans Sikkeleri* (1999; Byzantine Coins in the Yapı Kredi Collection), *Sivas Definesi: VI. Mithradates Dönemi Pontos ve Paphlagonia Kentlerinin Bronz Sikkeleri* (1999; The Sivas Treasure: Bronze Coins of the Cities of Pontos and Paphlagonia in the Reign of Mithrades VI), *Sadberk Hanım Müzesi Antik Sikkeler Kataloğu* (2003; Catalog of Ancient Coins in the Sadberk Hanım Museum), *Eski Anadolu ve Trakya; Ege Göçlerinden Roma İmparatorluğu'nun İkiye Ayrılmasına Kadar* (2007; Ancient Anatolia and Thrace, from Migrations around the Aegean through to the Division of the Roman Empire), *Eskiçağ'da İstanbul'da Balık ve Balıkçılık* (2010; Fish and Fishing in Ancient Istanbul), *Konuşan Paralar: Tarih Boyunca Anadolu Kentleri ve Sikkeleri* (2012; Money Talks: Anatolian Cities and Their Coinage throughout History), *Tarih Boyunca İstanbul'da Sikke Darbı ve Sikkeler* (2013; Minting and Coins in Istanbul throughout History) and *Balance Weights in the Aegean World. Classical and Hellenistic Periods* (2016).

TEMA, full name TÜRKİYE EROZYONLA MÜCADELE, AĞAÇLANDIRMA VE DOĞAL VARLIKLARI KORUMA VAKFI (TURKISH FOUNDATION FOR COMBATING SOIL EROSION, FOR REFORESTATION AND THE PROTECTION OF NATURAL HABITATS), non-governmental organization aiming to protect Turkey's nature from soil erosion in particular. Its principal objectives include combating soil erosion as well as reforestation and protection of natural habitats.

Its formation in 1992 by Hayrettin Karaca, the founder of the Karaca Arboretum, and Tekfen Holding's founding partner Nihat Gökyiğit, was supported by Vehbi Koç(*). The Vehbi Koç Foundation(*) (VKV) joined TEMA in reforestation projects from 1992 onwards and became a regular donor in 2001. All founding costs of the Fatih Woodland TEMA Vehbi Koç Nature and Culture Center(*) in Otağtepe, Kavacık, Istanbul were also met by the VKV.

TEMA was founded in September 1992 after the first Earth Summit held in June earlier that year in Rio de Janeiro, Brazil; its principal purpose was to raise social awareness of the danger of erosion and desertification that threatens Turkey's environment and to ensure that this struggle becomes an official policy. Its slogan "Don't Let Turkey Become a Desert" successfully raised public awareness around the country. Since that date TEMA has been fighting desertification as well as carrying out reforestation, carbon capture, biological diversity conservation, rural development and climate-related projects. It also conducts awareness raising and education programs aimed at pupils of all ages from elementary through to high schools.

In 2012, TEMA won the inaugural Land for Life Award presented by the Secretariat of the United Nations Convention to Combat Desertification.

TESEV, full name TÜRKİYE EKONOMİK VE SOSYAL ETÜDLER VAKFI (TURKISH ECONOMIC AND SOCIAL STUDIES FOUNDATION), strategic studies institution founded in 1994, which is among the civil society organizations supported by the Vehbi Koç Foundation(*).

TESEV goes back to the Economic and Social Studies Conference Delegation pioneered by Dr. Nejat F. Eczacıbaşı in 1961 and known as the Conference Delegation for short. At the time, it not only created debate in a variety of topics but also endeavored to facilitate decision-making processes through its activities and publications. The need to develop policies based on the findings that emerged in the 1990s triggered the transformation of the Conference Delegation in 1994 into TESEV, a "strategic study institution" based on the wealth and accumulation of past experience. Between its founding in 1994 and 2004, TESEV published substantial reports on poverty, economy and sectoral policies. At the start of 2004, a decision was taken to focus on democratization, good governance, transparency and foreign policy. Consequently, consultation councils and program teams were formed and funding sources diversified and broadened.

As of February 2015, when the new board took over, TESEV's new research areas were redefined as democratization, good governance, social inequalities and inclusion, sustainable cities and foreign policy.

Today, it aims to expand the diversity of research topics by leveraging the wealth of scholars within and without TESEV. A research network bringing together the world of academia and society at large has been created to this end. The research results are published as policy notes and reports are conveyed to stakeholders via a variety of channels.

A 2017 report on global think tanks ranked TESEV 77th worldwide (39th on the non-US table) in impact on public policy, 34th in the best external relations and public engagement programs, 44th in the science and technology table, 8th in the Middle East and North Africa, 27th among think tanks with the most significant impact on public policy and 42nd among the institutions that make the best use of media.

TEV *see* **Turkish Education Foundation**

Third Sector Foundation of Turkey Conference *see* **New Approaches in Civil Society Conference**

Third Sector Foundation of Turkey *see* **TÜSEV**

Tiniç, Seha M(ehmet) *(b. 23 November, 1941, Istanbul)*, academician who served as president of Koç University(*) (KU) from 1993 to 2001.

In 1964, he obtained a degree in business administration from Robert College(*) Undergraduate Department (today's Boğaziçi University). After completing a master's degree at the University of Tulsa, USA, he lectured at the Middle East Technical University Faculty of Economics and Administrative Sciences, Department of Business Administration (1966-67). He received a doctorate in business from Cornell

University, USA in 1970. He lectured as associate professor (1970-73) and professor (1973-85) in the University of Alberta, Canada. He also served as guest lecturer at Dartmouth College, USA (1976-77) and the University of British Columbia, Canada (1978-79) and worked at the University of Texas School of Business Management (1985-93). Tiniç contributed to the foundation of KU, where he was appointed as president in 1993, a position he held until the middle of 2001.

Member of American Finance Association, Western Finance Association (President, 1984-85), American Economic Association and Finance Management Association, Tiniç has published over 30 papers on finance as well as several books including, *Investing in Securities: An Efficient Markets Approach* (1979) and *Solutions Manual for Investing in Securities: An Efficient Markets Approach* (1979; with Richard R. West).

Tohum *see* Koç School

Topkapı Palace Museum, establishment at Topkapı Palace, Istanbul, the site of a vast variety of works of art including countless treasures of the Ottoman dynasty. One of the leading and richest museums in the world, it won the inaugural Vehbi Koç Award(*) in 2002 for its effective role in promoting Turkish culture and history, organizing

scholarly conferences, adopting innovative steps to transform in line with contemporary approaches to museum management and taking urgent measures in the wake of the August 17, 1999 earthquake.

Erected by Mehmed II (the Conqueror) between 1460 and 1478 and expanded by other sultans, Topkapı Palace served as the administrative center of the Ottoman Empire and the official residence of Ottoman emperors for nearly 380 years until Abdülmecid (r. 1839-61) moved to Dolmabahçe Palace in 1856.

It was first opened to visitors as a museum during the reign of Abdülmecid when the British Ambassador was shown around the treasury. In time, it became customary to do so, and glazed showcases to protect these articles were constructed under Abdülaziz (r. 1861-76). The proposal to open the Imperial Treasury to visitors twice a week after the proclamation of the Second Constitutional Monarchy was never actually carried out. A decree issued in April 1924 brought the palace under the Istanbul Directorate of Antiquities, and following some minor repairs and administrative reorganization, the Topkapı Palace Museum opened on October 9, 1924. Comprehensively restored after decades of repairs, the palace today operates under the Turkish Ministry of Culture and Tourism.

The Topkapı Palace Museum starts at the Second Courtyard accessed through the Gate of Salutation. Royal carriages from the eighteenth and nineteenth centuries are on display in the Imperial Stables. This courtyard also houses the Domed Chamber where Turkish tiles are displayed, and the Imperial Treasury which holds weaponry. The china section of the Imperial Kitchens is one of the richest in the museum. Porcelains from China constitute one of the rarest collections in their field in the world, along with Japanese, European and Ottoman porcelain all of which were in use in the court. The confectionery section of the kitchen displays the metal pots and pans, coffee sets and gilded utensils used in daily life.

The Gate of Felicity leads to the Third Courtyard; to the left is the Dormitory of the White Eunuchs, where embroideries are currently on display. The Dormitory of the Campaigners is the site of imperial garments, while the Butler's Dormitory houses the permanent exhibition of imperial portraits. The two most important spaces in the Third Courtyard are the Treasury and the Pavilion of the Holy Mantle. The Treasury contains a wide range of objects, including everyday items of gold and silver adorned with a variety of precious stones, sultans' aigrettes, throne hangings, richly decorated weaponry such as sword sheaths, bow cases, quivers and coats of armor, shisha pipes, oil lamps, writing sets, unpolished precious stones, the famous Spoonmaker's Diamond and

(FROM LEFT TO RIGHT) **Prof. Talat Sait Halman, Filiz Çağman, director of the Topkapı Sarayı Museum, Semahat Arsel, İstemihan Talay, Minister of Culture, and Rahmi M. Koç at the award ceremony**

a variety of thrones. The Pavilion of the Holy Mantle, in the meanwhile, displays a large number of sacred items brought back from Egypt by Selim I (the Grim), including the Prophet Mohammad's mantle. The Third Courtyard is also home to a large imperial tent, a number of clocks and calligraphic works.

In addition to these sections displaying specific items, many other parts of the palace are open as museum-spaces, the most important of which is the Harem comprising some 400 rooms scattered around long, narrow corridors and compact courtyards. The Audience Chamber, the Library of Ahmed III, the Circumcision Room, and the Baghdad, Revan and Sofa Pavilions show diverse aspects of Ottoman court life.

Tosun, Kemal *(b. 1923, Chania, Crete, Greece, d. September 18, 1993, Istanbul)*, economist and academician who served on the Vehbi Koç Foundation(*) Board of Directors from 1975 to 1978.

In 1946, he obtained a degree from the Istanbul University (IU) Faculty of Economics, where he took up a position as assistant lecturer in business administration in 1948. He received a doctorate in 1951 and continued with postgraduate studies in business and public administration at the London School of Economics, UK (1952-53) and the University of Minnesota University, USA (1953-54). In 1959, he was appointed associate professor in the Deparment of Business Management at the IU Faculty of Economics, and following his research at Harvard University, USA (1961-62), he became a professor in 1964. In 1968, Professor Tosun moved to the IU Faculty of Business Department of Management and Organization, where he served as dean for several years (1974-77, 1985-88 and 1988-89). Between 1977 and 1989, he was the director of the Institute of Business Administration. His principal publications include *İşletme ve Müesseselerde Sevk ve İdare* (1961; Direction and Management in Businesses and Institutions), *İşletmeYönetimi, Genel Esaslar* (1966; Business Management, General Principles) and *Yönetim ve İşletme Politikası* (1990; Management and Administration Policies).

Tourism Development and Education Foundation *see* **TUGEV**

trust *(tesis)*, term used instead of "foundation" in the period between the 1926 Turkish Civil Code (Türk Medeni Kanunu; TMK) until the 1967 Foundations Code No. 903.

Criticisms of alleged abuses of the pious foundation system predated the declaration of the Republic by some way, and debates on the need for new regulations on their legal status had long been on the agenda. As controversy raged in the Republican era, new regulations were introduced to the TMK in order to centralize administration and liquidate foundations operating outside their remit. These regulations were listed in Articles 73 through to 81 of the Act and used the term "trust" rather than "foundation" to designate "the allocation of certain properties to specific purposes." The preference for trust was explained by pointing out the additional sense of "retention and inhibition" implied by the word "foundation", the suggestion being that the obstruction of economic potential in Islamic societies inhibited the economic development of these societies. Past abuses by pious foundations constituted another reason for this preference.

In the 41-year period between 1926 and 1967, 202 trusts were founded. The comperatively low number of "trusts" formed during this period can be attributed to the economic conditions of the period as well as the regulations and inspections of the TMK. Of these early trusts, 165 (83 %) were still active in 2009.

According to the TMK, trusts were established by a "trust deed" or "testament"; those of the "*mazbut*" (fixed) type were administered by the Directorate General of Foundations, whereas the "*mülhak*" (inheritable) were administered by the founders and their heirs. The Act classified trusts as either "family trusts" or "pious trusts". In addition, there were facilities established for purposes of "education" and "health" etc.

This type of establishment was defined as "foundation" in the 1967 Foundations Act. (*see also* foundation)

trustee *see* **foundation**

TUGEV, full name TURİZM GELİŞTİRME VE EĞİTİM VAKFI (TOURISM DEVELOPMENT AND EDUCATION FOUNDATION), non-governmental organization aiming to develop tourism and support the training of qualified personnel for the sector in Turkey. It was founded in 1984 by 14 entrepreneurs including Vehbi Koç(*) and Semahat Arsel(*) and four organizations. Vehbi Koç has also served as vice president of the foundation.

TUGEV has particularly contributed to the training of highly qualified personnel in the tourism sector and to the development of congress tourism. Its wide range of activities includes: student and instructor training at the OTEM Hotel and Training Center in Kemer, Antalya; certificate programs in conjunction with Boğaziçi, Uludağ and Trakya universities; consultation services for state institutions about tourism training; running courses at different levels; and organizing conferences and activities to guide public opinion. The foundation has specific activities to promote Istanbul more effectively, especially as a location for congress tourism, engaging in multidimensional planning, marketing and performance monitoring. Due to the efforts of Istanbul Congress and Visitor Bureau (ICVB) formed by TUGEV in 1997, Istanbul has now become one of the leading destinations for the conference sector.

Turkish Economic and Social Studies Foundation *see* **TESEV**

Turkish Education Foundation (Türk Eğitim Vakfı, TEV), a non-governmental organization run for the benefit of the public, founded with the aim of ensuring that successful but financially disadvantaged young people have access to an education. It was established on May 4, 1967 by 205 philanthropists led by Vehbi Koç(*), Nejat Eczacıbaşı, the rector of Istanbul University, Professor Ekrem Şerif Egeli, and the rector of Istanbul Technical University, Professor Bedri Karafakioğlu. TEV's most important goal is "to enable people to produce and use knowledge"; its most important outlook is "to provide environments where people can harness their abilities to contribute towards humanity and help achieve the ideal of a modern Turkey".

The foundation's highest decision-making and supervisory body is the board of trustees and the highest executive body is the board of directors. The first chair of the board of directors was Nejat Eczacıbaşı (1963-71), followed by Vehbi Koç (1971-93), Aydın Bolak(*) (1993-2001), Ömer Dinçkök (2001-04), Rona Yırcalı (2004-07), Ömer M. Koç(*) (2007-16) and Rona Yırcalı for a second time (2016-). Based in Istanbul, the foundation has branches in 12 cities, including Adana, Ankara, Bursa, Eskişehir, Izmir, Kayseri and Trabzon. The TEV also receives support from the Vehbi Koç Foundation(*); its sources of income comprise legacy gifts contingent upon the donor's death, grants and donations from people and institutions, and donations made by purchasing TEV wreaths.

TEV provides scholarships for "successful but financially struggling students attending technical and industrial vocational high school, vocational college, college, or studying for undergraduate, master's or doctoral degrees". Scholarship students are selected by scholarship committees arranged by the educational institutions themselves and attended by a representative of TEV. In addition, a number of scholarships are allocated annually to disabled or orphaned students who have earned a higher education place, or children from families who have been affected by natural disasters. While scholarship students will continue to receive their scholarships until the end of their studies, scholarships are removed for those who are unsuccessful, are in receipt of a scholarship from another institution, or do not meet the criteria for the TEV scholarship.

Scholarship students who reach the level specified by the Home Scholarships and Awards Code also receive "Success Awards". In 2007, 40 years after the foundation was established, it began awarding

Vehbi Koç with students who won scholarships for international study from the Turkish Education Foundation (1983)

"Scholarships for Outstanding Success" to support the leaders of the future. TEV was the first organization to do this in Turkey. In addition to supporting its scholarship students financially, TEV also engages in social activities to support their social development.

TEV's scholarships for studies in Turkey are non-repayable but, as a general rule, scholarship students agree to make a monetary or moral contribution to TEV once they have graduated and begun their careers, or they agree to provide a TEV scholarship to at least one other student as an obligation of conscience if they have the means to do so in future. The students provide a document confirming that they have accepted the obligation.

Since 1969, TEV has also provided postgraduate scholarships for studies abroad. When scholarship students complete their studies abroad, they are obligated to return home and pay back the sum they received from TEV during the course of their studies. TEV provides these scholarships in cooperation with the governments of Germany, France and Singapore and public and private institutions in Denmark, Italy, Spain and Japan.

TEV allocates approximately one million dollars to its scholarship fund annually and this is increased to three million dollars by contributions from partner institutions.

TEV has introduced a female dormitory project to meet the needs of those young women who arrive in large cities for their university education, ensuring they receive modern, safe and comfortable housing. These dormitories, located in Ankara, Izmir and Trabzon, accept both funded and fee-paying students.

Since its foundation, TEV has provided approximately 237,600 scholarships for studies in Turkey and 1,821 scholarships for studies abroad. Additionally, it has built a kindergarten, 15 elementary schools, an Anatolian high school, an Anatolian High School for Fine Arts, two Vocational High Schools in Healthcare, three student dormitories, a multi-purpose community center (Batman), an apprenticeship center (Tekirdağ) and a library. The İnanç Türkeş Private High School has also operated as part of TEV since 2001.

In 1995 and 1998, TEV was declared "Foundation of the Year in the Educational Field". Another of its educational projects is the "Turkey's Moneybox for Van" campaign, started by a partnership between TEV and Turkcell following the 2011 Van earthquake and run under the auspices of the Ministry of Education; it was cited as a global model by the UN. TEV's other projects include the "Project-planning for Teachers Project" and "Leadership for Teachers Program". TEV also organized the "First International Gifted and Talented Education Symposium" on September 23-24, 2010, in collaboration with Koç University(*) and Ministry of Education. It also supports the "7 is Too Late" campaign, led by AÇEV(*).

THE STORY OF TEV IN THE WORDS OF VEHBİ KOÇ

I've always believed that education is deeply important for a country to develop quickly. It's crucial to provide this support to young people who wish to study but lack the financial means to do so. The state actually provides a number of scholarships, but in my view, it's wrong to expect everything from the state. With this in mind, I set my mind to the need for a facility to provide scholarships for students in higher education. I consulted with trusted friends, particularly late Ahmed Dallı, on how this should be achieved. No matter who we spoke to, there was a great deal of interest and finally, in 1967, the Turkish Education Foundation was established. When the Foundations Law was passed, the foundation took on its current form.

The foundation had 205 founding members. When it was first founded, Dr. Nejat Eczacıbaşı was chair of the board of directors and I assumed the role after him; in 1971 we switched places. Now (1973), I'm the chair and Nejat Bey is vice chair.

In 1968, I traveled around 22 cities to raise awareness of the foundation outside of Istanbul and, in each city center, I spoke to leading businessmen and directors, explaining the purposes of the foundation. I asked for support for the foundation.

Since the TEV was established, it has attracted great interest from the public and been of immense benefit for the education of young people. I think that as time passes, it will be even more beneficial.

In 1972, we decided to collect capital funds to ensure the continuity of the foundation. For the first time in my life, I put myself out, approaching large institutions and leading businessmen to ask for support.

Not one of them turned me down. My friends in the foundation did the same and we succeeded in collecting five million lira of foundation capital, 900,000 of which came from the Koç Group. One of TEV's sources of income is legacy donations. Citizens who believe in the cause agree to donate their wealth to the foundation after they die. Another reasonably new source of income is the Flower Fund.

Vehbi Koç, *Hayat Hikâyem (My Life Story)*, 4th edition, Vehbi Koç Foundation Publications, Istanbul 1983, pp. 121

Turkish Family Health and Planning Foundation (TÜRKİYE AİLE SAĞLIĞI VE PLANLAMASI VAKFI, TAPV), also known as the TURKISH FAMILY PLANNING FOUNDATION or the TAP FOUNDATION, a foundation which supports a balanced population growth in line with Turkey's economic and social development. It is one of the civil society organizations supported by the Vehbi Koç Foundation(*).

TAPV was founded in November 1985 by business people, union leaders, academics, the chair of the Union of Chambers and Commodity Exchanges of Turkey and the chair of the Confederation of Turkish Tradesmen and Craftsmen under the leadership of Vehbi Koç(*). The foundation, which began its work in January 1986, aims to improve the quality of life of individuals, particularly young people, families and society as a whole. Its area of work includes reproductive, sexual and mother and baby health, and improving the social status of women in families and society.

TAPV aims to provide families with the necessary information, materials and services required to ensure that they have the number of children that they choose. It prepares educational materials, gathers data and carries out research to educate the public and those working in related fields about family planning.

In 1988, the foundation began its Family Planning Campaign. The Ministry of Health and Turkish Radio and Television (TRT) worked in partnership to create a TV series, films and documentaries on the subject. It also funded the production of a film dealing with related issues, *Berdel* (1990). The film, directed by Atıf Yılmaz, won numerous awards, including the 1991 Global Media Award from the Population Institute based in the USA.

In partnership with the Ministry of Health and various institutions, TAPV established family planning clinics in Bursa, Diyarbakır, Istanbul, Izmir and Mardin. Studies on reproductive health and family planning were carried out in Ankara, Istanbul, Izmir, Denizli and Trabzon. In 1995, the Developing Support for Women Group (KİDOG) was founded together with 19 non-governmental organizations to work for women's education, health and legal rights. It developed programs about reproduction and sexuality for young people. Today, it leads programs on healthy motherhood, sexual and women's health, working with teenagers and young people. As part of the "For My Country" project initiated by Koç Holding(*) in 2006, TAPV was among the groups active around the theme "I Support Gender Equality", which was adopted for the 2015-17 period.

TAPV received the 1994 United Nations (UN) Population Award for its work on managing population growth.

Turkish Foundation for Combating Soil Erosion, for Reforestation and the Protection of Natural Habitats *see* **TEMA**

Turkish Foundation of Educational Volunteers *see* **TEGV**

Turkish Marine Environment Protection Association *see* **DenizTemiz Association/TURMEPA**

Turkish Mathematics Association, a civil society organization founded in 1948 to ensure the development and proliferation of disciplines relating to mathematics in Turkey. Its activities aim to increase the contribution of mathematics and mathematicians to economic, social and technological matters and to increase the appeal of mathematics education in secondary and higher education, while at the same time improving teaching standards and effectiveness. The Vehbi Koç Foundation(*) funded the 2017 edition of the association's semi-academic publication *Matematik Dünyası* (World of Mathematics), which addresses high school levels and above, and sponsored the participation of academics in conferences in related fields.

The association was founded by a group of mathematicians from Istanbul University and Istanbul Technical University, including professors Cahit Arf, Nüzhet Gökdoğan, Mustafa İnan and Nazım Terzioğlu. It also provides scholarships for the mathematicians of the future and represents Turkey at the International Mathematical Union and the European Mathematical Society.

Turkish Nurses Association, a non-governmental organization which aims to ensure that nursing is an autonomous profession that serves the community and delivers a highly-skilled, trustworthy service. It has received regular support from the Vehbi Koç Foundation(*) (VKV) since 2005. The association was represented in the Nursing Committee, which was created within the VKV in late 1974 to manage the Nursing Fund(*).

In August 1933, the Community of Turkish Nurses was founded in Istanbul by voluntary nurses; Esma Deniz, who graduated among the second wave of graduates from the Admiral Bristol Nursing School in 1924, was appointed as chair. The community underwent a reorganization in July 1943 and was renamed the Turkish Nurses Association. In June 1949, it became a member of the International Council of Nurses. The association's headquarters, which were based in Istanbul from 1933 to 1973, moved to Ankara in March 1973. Today, the association has 17 branches.

In addition to the association's own publications, it has also published a series of handbooks in collaboration with the VKV.

TURMEPA *see* **DenizTemiz Association/ TURMEPA**

Tüfekçioğlu, Nevzat *(b. October 2, 1941, Bursa)*, financier and manager. He served on the Vehbi Koç Foundation(*) (VKV) Board of Directors from 2002 to 2003.

After completing his secondary education at Bursa High School for Boys in 1959, Tüfekçioğlu studied finance and economics at Ankara University Faculty of Political Sciences, graduating in 1963. He became assistant accountant at the Ministry of Finance in the same year, followed by accountant in 1966. In 1974, he left this post and began working in the Auditing and Financial Control Group at Koç Holding(*). After serving as coordinator, vice president and president, he retired in 2002. Tüfekçioğlu played an important role in the founding of Koç University(*) and today serves on the board of directors of numerous companies and foundations, including the Suna and İnan Kıraç Foundation(*), Kıraça Holding and NASAMER(*). He has also served as a consultant at the VKV since 2010.

Türkoğlu, Abdullah *(b. 1914, Niğde - d. March 31, 1989, Istanbul)*, economist and academic. He served on the Vehbi Koç Foundation(*) (VKV) Board of Directors from 1969 to 1975.

After completing his secondary education at Afyon High School, Türkoğlu graduated from the Faculty of Political Sciences (now Ankara University Faculty of Political Sciences) in 1938. He worked at the Ministry of Finance (1938-43). He later went to Switzerland where he received a doctorate from the University of Zurich's Department of Economics in 1949 and began working as an assistant at Istanbul University Faculty of Economics in the same year. In 1953, he became an associate professor, rising to professor in 1961. In 1968, he was elected dean of the Faculty of Economics. He spearheaded the foundation of the faculty's Institute for Economic Geography and Tourism in 1969. He was also a member of the teaching staff at Istanbul Private College for Economic and Commercial Sciences. In 1969, he joined the VKV Board of Directors and continued in the role until 1975. Professor Türkoğlu retired in 1984 and published several books, including *İktisadi Coğrafya I* (1958, 1979; Economic Geography I) and *Endüstri Ham Maddeleri ve Enerji Kaynakları* (1965; Industrial Raw Materials and Energy Sources).

TÜSEV, full name TÜRKİYE ÜÇÜNCÜ SEKTÖR VAKFI (THIRD SECTOR FOUNDATION OF TURKEY), an organization founded by 23 of Turkey's leading civil society organizations, including the Vehbi Koç Foundation(*) (VKV). It aims to develop the legal, financial and functional infrastructure of the third sector, which is composed of voluntary groups and non-profit organizations, such as foundations and associations, working for the public good. TÜSEV receives regular support from the VKV and is a member of numerous international bodies concerned with the third sector, including the European Foundation Centre (EFC) and the World Alliance for Citizen Participation (CIVICUS).

TÜSEV activities fit specific program themes: the Civil Society Law Reform program aims to promote a more suitable and facilitative infrastructure for foundations and associations; the Social Investment Program creates an infrastructure for social investment and philanthropy, promoting models and mechanisms which ensure transfer of funds to non-governmental organizations (NGOs), improving the legal and financial infrastructure related to social enterprises and promoting social enterprises; the International Relations and Networking Program tries to create common platforms for sharing good practices and experiences, raise awareness of civil society in Turkey on an international level and develop relationships by creating opportunities for cooperation; the Research and Publications Program aims to increase the visibility of the third sector, identify positive or negative trends and create a suitable environment in which to develop civil society.

The "Civil Society Index Project" (STEP), initiated by CIVICUS in 60 countries worldwide, was led by TÜSEV in Turkey from 2004 to 2006 and repeated between 2009 and 2011. As part of the project, civil society was examined under the key headings of structure, impact, environment and values; the results of the research and analysis were compiled in a report and published by TÜSEV.

Numerous meetings were organized as part of the Social Entrepreneurship Project, which was set up in 2009 by TÜSEV with support and collaboration from the British Council. The initiative aims to promote and encourage social entrepreneurship in Turkey.

The TÜSEV Civil Society Monitoring project began in 2011. The annual monitoring reports published as part of the project discuss developments in civil society in Turkey, including its strong points and impact, also making comparisons with findings from previous years.

The Monitoring Enabling Environment for Civil Society Development project was set up in December 2012 in partnership between the European Network of National Associations (ENNA) and the European Center for Not-for-Profit Law (ECNL) with financial support from the European Union. The project was introduced simultaneously in the West Balkans and Turkey and coordinated by the Balkan Civil Society Development Network (BCSDN); subsequent reports were published in 2013 and 2014 discussing civil society and its development in Turkey and other countries. Further related reports on Turkey and the region were published in 2015 and 2016.

The Civil Society Public Cooperation Project, led in partnership with the Civil Society Development Center (STGM) and the YADA Foundation, is supported by the European Union and aims to create an ongoing dialogue between civil society and the state, increasing the participation of NGOs in social debates and decision-making processes.

Various activities are run as part of the Donate for Change project, which aims to develop the culture of donating money in Turkey. The "Individual Giving and Philanthropy in Turkey Research", led by Ali Çarkoğlu and Erdem Aytaç, was supported by six leading Turkish foundations, including the VKV, and a report detailing the results was published in 2016.

The results of TÜSEV projects, research and studies are published in print and online and also shared via its social media accounts under the name TÜSEV Atölye.

The New Approaches in Civil Society Conference, held in Istanbul from November 21-22, 2013 marked the occasion of the twentieth anniversary of TÜSEV's foundation. It received support from the VKV and Sabancı Foundation and took as its theme "the next ten years in civil society".

TÜSEV New Approaches in Civil Society Conference *see* **New Approaches in Civil Society Conference**

U
UĞ – UN

Uğurbil, Kamil *(b. July 11, 1949, Tire)*, scientist awarded the Vehbi Koç Award(*) for health in 2016. He won recognition for his studies into the brain, carried out using a magnetic resonance imaging technique (MRI) which he developed.

After attending elementary school in Tire, Prof. Uğurbil went to middle school at Izmir Maarif College (now Bornova Anatolian High School) and completed his secondary education at Robert College(*). He continued his studies in the USA, receiving a physics degree from Columbia University, New York, in 1971, followed by master's and doctorate degrees from the same university in 1974 and 1977 respectively. After working at AT&T Bell Laboratories (1977-79), he served on the academic staff of Columbia University Department of Biochemistry (1979-82). In 1982, he began working at Minnesota University Department of Biochemistry as an associate professor. He has served at Minnesota University since 1985, a professor in the radiology, neurology and medicine departments. Prof. Uğurbil has served as founding director of the university's interdisciplinary Magnetic Resonance Research Center since 1991 and also as director of the Max Planck Institute for Biological Cybernetics (2003-06). He currently works as a consultant at the National Magnetic Resonance Research Center at Bilkent University in Ankara.

Prof. Uğurbil received the Vehbi Koç Award in 2016 for "developing pioneering new technologies for understanding how the brain works using magnetic resonance" and describes his main field of interest as "developing methods of screening neurological activity, particularly brain activity, using ultra-high field MRI technology". He aims to "develop our understanding of brain function by combining these procedural and technical developments with neurological practices relating to human and animal brains". The development of equipment and screening methods used for this purpose form an important part of his work. High-resolution MRI technology developed as a result of Prof. Uğurbil's research has enabled a better understanding of numerous diseases, such as Alzheimer's and depression, and facilitated the development of treatments. This technology has recently been used in studies mapping connections in the human brain as part of the Human Connectome project, for which Prof. Uğurbil was the principal researcher. Professor Uğurbil has published over

Prof. Kamil Uğurbil at the award ceremony with Ömer M. Koç

300 scientific papers relating to his research, which have been referenced over 30,000 times.

Uğurbil has received numerous awards, including the Gold Medal from the International Society of Magnetic Resonance in Medicine and the Richard R. Ernst Medal (Swiss Federal Institute of Technology - ETH, Zurich). He was elected a member of the American Academy of Arts and Sciences in 2005, the US National Academy of Medicine in 2007 and the US National Academy of Inventors in 2014. He was also one of 15 members of the BRAIN (Brain Research through Advancing Innovative Biotechnologies) Initiative, one of the Obama administration's top-priority projects.

UNHCR Syrian Refugee Educational Program, the provision of teaching and learning materials in Turkish and Arabic to

education units in refugee camps in Turkey in 2015, in accordance with a protocol signed between the Vehbi Koç Foundation(*) and the United Nations High Commissioner for Refugees (UNHCR). Teaching and learning materials supplied through the project, such as alphabet sets, maps, anatomical diagrams, abacuses, cell diagrams and periodic tables, were used at temporary education centers attended by approximately 8,000-10,000 Syrian students.

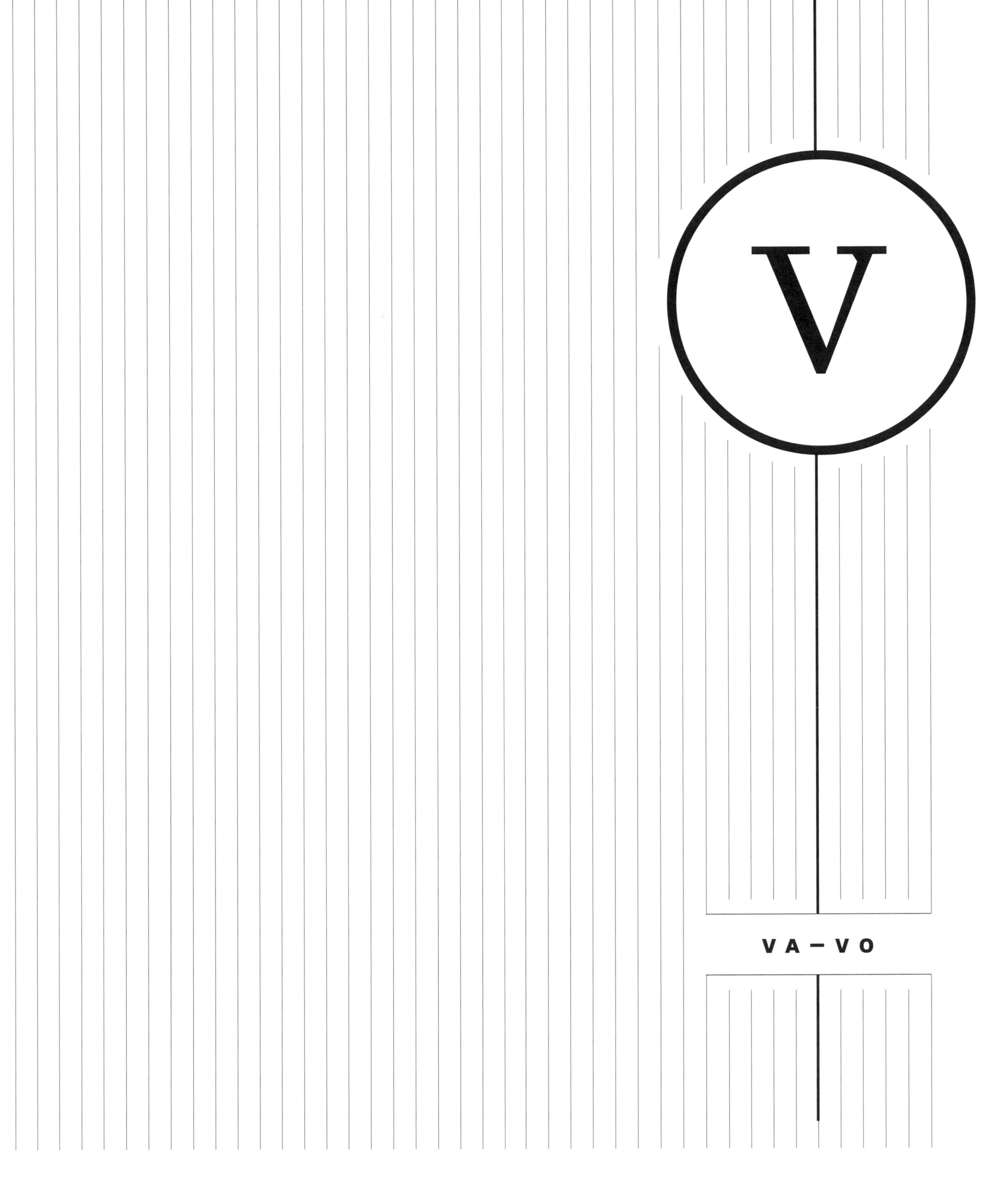

VA—VO

Van Koç Elementary and Middle School *see* **17 Schools Project**

Vehbi Koç Ankara Studies Research Center *see* **VEKAM**

Vehbi Koç Award, an award given since 2002 to individuals or organizations "who have made an important contribution to the development of Turkey and the Turkish people" in the fields of culture, education or health. The individual or institution who is to receive the $100,000 award, funded and coordinated by the Vehbi Koç Foundation(*) (VKV), is selected by the VKV Board of Directors from three candidates recommended by a jury formed of leading scientists and experts in the respective field. The members of the jury change every year in keeping with the award field. The aim of the Vehbi Koç Award is to "promote and reward exemplary services that add value to society". The award is given every year in a ceremony in February during events to commemorate the life of Vehbi Koç(*).

VEHBİ KOÇ AWARDS

YEAR	FIELD	PERSON/ORGANIZATION
2002	Culture	Topkapı Palace Museum(*)
2003	Education	AÇEV(*) (Mother Child Education Foundation)
2004	Health	Bilkent University Faculty of Science Department of Molecular Biology and Genetics (*)
2005	Culture	Fazıl Hüsnü Dağlarca(*)
2006	Education	Nuri Okutan(*)
2007	Health	Prof. Aziz Sancar(*)
2008	Culture	Prof. Mehmet Özdoğan(*)
2009	Education	Prof. Türkan Saylan(*)
2010	Health	Prof. Turgay Dalkara(*)
2011	Culture	Prof. Filiz Ali(*) and Ayvalık International Music Academy(*) (AIMA)
2012	Education	Prof. Nermin Abadan Unat(*)
2013	Health	Prof. Gökhan Hotamışlıgil(*)
2014	Culture	Prof. Zeynep Çelik(*)
2015	Education	Prof. Ali Nesin(*) and Nesin Mathematics Village(*)
2016	Health	Prof. Kamil Uğurbil(*)
2017	Culture	Prof. Zeynep Ahunbay(*)
2018	Education	Prof. Yılmaz Büyükerşen(*)

The old (2002-15) **and new** (2016 and later RIGHT) **Vehbi Koç Award figurines**

The new figurine is "a clear 3D structure that represents work related to health, education and culture. At the top of the figurine column, there are three volutes facing out in three directions symbolizing the accumulation of knowledge in the three subjects and its value and reward in the three aspects of life."

Vehbi Koç Foundation (VKV), a foundation established in Istanbul by Vehbi Koç(*) to provide social and cultural services. Following the completion of the preparatory stages of the foundation and the granting of tax immunity by the Turkish Cabinet, the VKV was officially established with the signing of the Foundation Deeds on January 17, 1969. It was the first private foundation established in the Republican era. From its headquarters in Istanbul, it engages in educational, health and cultural initiatives. The board of directors, the foundation's main management body, consisted of 11 people between 1969 and 1996. Other than Vehbi Koç, the board included four members of the Koç family(*), the CEO of Koç Holding(*), two members selected by the Koç Holding Board of Directors and "recognized for financial and economic expertise", two university professors, one legal expert, and the CEO or deputy chief executive of Türkiye İş Bankası A.Ş. The elected members carry out the role for three years and are eligible for re-election after this time. The board has remained the same, composed of 10 members, since Vehbi Koç's death. The executive committee, selected from among the members of the board of directors, is formed of three people.

The foundation's main source of income

was the Main Wealth Fund formed at the start of its operations and income from other funds formed with donations from the Koç family and Koç Holding.

In the early years of the fund, it established facilities such as student dormitories, libraries and clinics and handed these over to the relevant public institutions. At the start of the 1980s, it moved towards carrying out well-organized, securely-funded projects. Realizing that it was as important to keep these works going as it was to create them, VKV began taking responsibility for running the facilities it had established and by doing so aimed to keep the service quality at these institutions at a consistently high level. The organizations that the foundation took a role in establishing and/or running are:

Education: The Koç School(*) (high school, 1988; primary school comprising kindergarten, elementary school and middle school, Istanbul, 1998), Koç University(*) (Istanbul, 1993) and the Koç Elementary Schools (various cities 1998-2008) (*see* 17 School Project).

Health: SANERC(*) (the Semahat Arsel Nursing, Education and Research Center, Istanbul, 1992), the American Hospital(*) (Istanbul, 1995), the MedAmerican Medical Center(*) (Istanbul, 1997), the Koç University School of Nursing(*) (Istanbul, 1999), the Koç University School of Medicine (Istanbul, 2010), KUİYEM(*) (Koç University First Aid Education Center, Istanbul, 2010) and the Koç University Hospital(*) (Istanbul, 2014).

Culture: The Sadberk Hanım Museum(*) (Istanbul, 1980), VEKAM(*) (the Vehbi Koç Ankara Studies Research Center, 1994), the Ankara Orchard House(*), AKMED(*) (the Suna and İnan Kıraç Research Center for Mediterranean Civilizations, Antalya, 1996), the Kaleiçi Museum(*) (Antalya, 2000), ANAMED(*) (the Koç University Research Center for Anatolian Civilizations Istanbul, 2005), TANAS(*) (Art Gallery, Berlin, 2008-2013), Arter(*) (Space For Art, Istanbul, 2010) and the Vehbi Koç Foundation Ford Otosan Gölcük Culture and Community Center(*) (2010).

The VKV supports talented students with limited financial means through educational scholarships given mostly to vocational high school and university students with the aim of creating equality of opportunity in education. The fundamentals of the running and usage of the educational scholarships are set out in the Foundation Deeds (*see* Vehbi Koç Foundation Educational Scholarships). Up to the present day, over 50,000 students have been awarded VKV scholarships. The foundation puts volunteers from among Koç Group(*) employees in touch with the scholarship winners to help support them in their educational lives.

In addition, the VKV runs the Koç Model School(*) and Vocational Education: A Crucial Matter for the Nation(*) projects, and supports other projects concerning education, health and culture together with various other institutions and civil society organizations.

INSTITUTIONS, ACTIVITIES AND PROJECTS SUPPORTED BY VKV

Civil Society Bodies

Boğaziçi University Foundation(*) (BÜVAK)
Darülaceze(*)
DenizTemiz Association/TURMEPA(*)
ERG(*) (Education Reform Initiative)
Geyre Foundation(*)
HeCe Education, Culture and Mutual Aid Foundation(*)
İnönü Foundation(*)
Nesin Foundation(*)
TEGV(*) (Turkish Foundation of Educational Volunteers)
TEMA(*) (Turkish Foundation for Combating Soil Erosion, for Reforestation and the Protection of Natural Habitats)
TESEV(*) (Turkish Economic and Social Studies Foundation)
Turkish Nurses Association(*)
Turkish Mathematics Association(*)
TÜSEV(*) (Third Sector Foundation of Turkey)
Village Teachers' Communication and Mutual Aid Society(*)

Institutions

Ankara University School of Medicine Vehbi Koç Eye Hospital(*)
Ankara University Vehbi Koç Dormitory(*)
Atatürk Library(*)
Boğaziçi University Superdorm(*)
Galatasaray University Suna Kıraç Library(*)
Haydarpaşa Numune Education and Research Hospital Vehbi Koç Emergency Medical Center(*)
Middle East Technical University Vehbi Koç Dormitory(*)
Robert College Suna Kıraç Hall(*)
Semahat-Dr. Nusret Arsel Education Park(*)
Sevgi-Erdoğan Gönül Education Park(*)
Suna-İnan Kıraç Education Park(*)
Vehbi Koç Foundation Vocational and Technical Anatolian High School(*)

Activities and Projects

Adıyaman University Faculty of Education Vehbi Koç Building(*)
"Anatolia is Reading" Book Project(*)
Ankara University Mustafa V. Koç Research Center for Maritime Archaeology(*)
ATARC BOUN Cultural Heritage Project(*)
Boğaziçi European School of Politics(*)
Claros Excavations(*)
European Youth Parliament(*)
Fisherwomen of the Aegean Project(*)
Foundation for the Training and Care of Children with Intellectual Disabilities(*)
Greek-Turkish Youth Orchestra(*)
Hierapolis Excavations(*)
International Sevgi Gönül Byzantine Studies Symposium(*)
Istanbul Biennial(*)
Istanbul Jazz Festival(*)
İdil Biret Documentary(*)
Karşıyaka Elementary School Library (*)
Kocaeli University VKV Ford Otosan İhsaniye Vocational College for Automotive Technologies(*)
Sagalassos Excavations(*)
Saint Euphemia Church Restoration(*)
Science Academy Young Scientists Program (BAGEP) Scholarship Award(*)
17 Schools Project(*)
Sivas Kangal Koç Anatolian High School(*)
Social Entrepreneurship Development Program (see KUSIF)
Soma Underground Training Pit Project(*)
Teachers Network Project(*)
UNHCR Syrian Refugee Educational Program(*)
Vehbi Koç Foundation Van Teachers' Housing Complex(*)
Village Schools Exchange Network(*)
Vocational Education: A Crucial Matter for the Nation (MLMM) Project(*)
Whole School Support Project for the Integration of Refugee Children(*)
Zengibar Castle Excavations(*)

The VKV Vehbi Koç Award(*) program began in 2002 and aims to "promote and reward exemplary services that add value to society". The award is given "every year to people or organizations that have made an important contribution to the development of Turkey and the Turkish people in the fields of culture, education or health."

The VKV and the Koç family have received numerous awards in recognition of their work: World Monuments Fund Hadrian Award(*) (2007), Carnegie Foundation Medal of Philanthropy(*) (2009), BNP Paribas Grand Prix for Individual Philanthropy(*) (2011), Iris Foundation Award for Outstanding Contribution to the Decorative Arts(*) (2012), Ankara University Medal of Philanthropy(*) (2015).

THE STORY OF THE FOUNDING OF THE VKV BY VEHBİ KOÇ...

I owe a debt to God, to my country, to my co-operation with my dear colleagues and to my love of work for the success I have achieved in my lifetime. As the companies we had set up in the Koç Group developed, two big goals ripened in my mind. One of these was to reorganize the companies we had worked on for many years, in order to ensure their continuity and efficiency. That was why we established our holding company. My second aim was to corporatize our donations and philanthropic services, thus ensuring that they would continue after me. This second goal was achieved when I founded the Vehbi Koç Foundation.

I signed the articles of association for the Vehbi Koç Foundation in the presence of a notary on January 17, 1969. The witnesses were Hulki Alisbah and Aydın Bolak, who had both put a lot of work into it. In this plain ceremony carried out before my family and colleagues, I donated 12 million lira worth of shares to the Foundation in the name of Koç Holding. From now on, the foundation would be able to engage in philanthropic services with its own income.

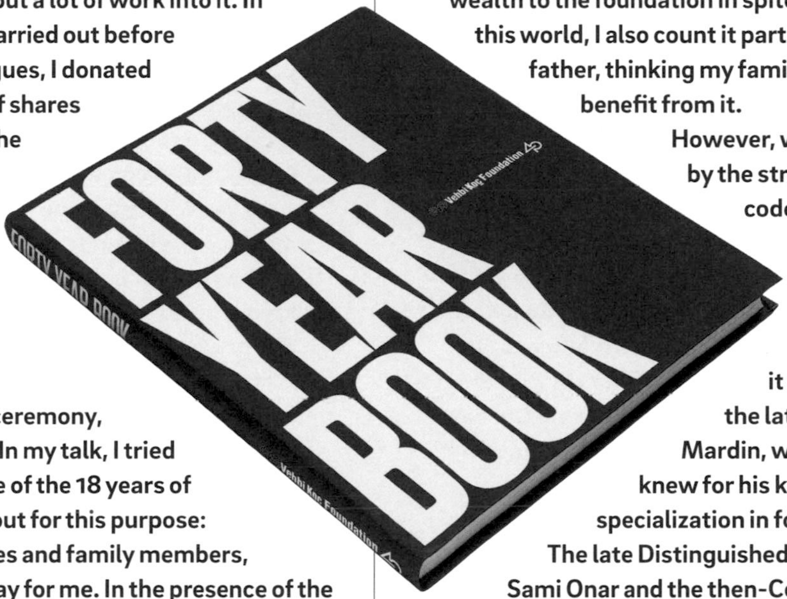

After the signing ceremony, I gave the talk below. In my talk, I tried to explain the timeline of the 18 years of work we had carried out for this purpose:

"My dear colleagues and family members,

Today is a happy day for me. In the presence of the notary Kemal Türkoğlu and witnesses, I have signed the deeds of the foundation that I have long been trying to establish. In my life from now on, I will work to ensure this foundation is well run and achieves its purposes. I expect and request of family members and colleagues who succeed me to do the same. In relation to this, I wish to mention briefly how the idea of a foundation came about and the history of the establishment of the foundation.

My father was a trustee of the İbadullah Foundation, which my ancestors founded in Ankara. I obtained the Koç family tree through the foundation files held at the Directorate General of Foundations. I have seen how many able businessmen have been raised in Turkey, how they have established big trading-houses and how after their founders' deaths those trading-houses have quickly gone to ruin and been lost. Today you will not find a single century-old company in our country. I have seen on my travels to the great countries of Europe and America how many large establishments there are and particularly how there are thousands of charitable foundations of all sizes in America. I also learned how Henry Ford, the founder of the Ford Company with which I have been working since 1928, established the Ford Foundation in order to keep his enterprise alive.

I explained my thoughts on establishing this type of foundation to Mr. Hulki Alisbah, who joined our enterprise in the last months of 1949. I had various conversations with the late Cafer Tüzel, who was our legal advisor at the time. Mr. Alisbah prepared the Foundation Deeds Project that you see today while on a ferry trip we took on the Black Sea in 1951, and this can be counted as the beginning of our efforts to establish a foundation.

In surrendering a significant portion of my wealth to the foundation in spite of the vagaries of this world, I also count it part of the duties of a father, thinking my family may in the future benefit from it.

However, we were all surprised by the strict rules in the civil code preventing family foundations from carrying out philanthropic works. We thought it necessary to consult the late Professor Ebülula Mardin, whom everyone knew for his knowledge and specialization in foundation affairs. The late Distinguished Professor Sıddık Sami Onar and the then-Commercial Court President, Professor Tahir Çağa, also joined him in giving advice.

After this committee investigated the legal regulations and the Deeds Project we had prepared, they confirmed the impossibility of a foundation that the family could benefit from to the degree we had expected, informing us that the only possibility was to take advantage of the minimum contribution allowed to the family under the "waged" rule. In this case, it would have meant accepting that they would be deprived of the wealth I had earnt as the result of my arduous labor to ensure their future, and I didn't think that I had the right to do that. Or the "reserved share" would increase in proportion to the size of the foundation and this would mean that a foundation of the size we had hoped for was impossible. Meanwhile, a commission formed of Supreme Court members and professors were engaged at the Ministry of Justice to amend the Civil Code. The relevant clauses of the Civil Code referring to foundations as "trusts" (*tesis*) were very unclear and incomplete, so we approached both the government and the commission to alter the system in a way compatible with the charitable foundation traditions in our country that went back for centuries. I told this two or three times to the Prime Minister of the time, Adnan Menderes, and he agreed and ordered the Minister of Justice to get in contact.

These communications took such a long time that the late Cafer Tüzel and Hulki Alisbah met with two different Ministers of Justice. We explained our thoughts and we gave them the project we had prepared, but no positive outcomes arose from all our administrative and legal efforts.

I repeated my administrative attempts after the 1960 revolution. Ferit Melen, who was then the Minister of Finance, took a great interest and ordered the Ministry of Finance Chief Legal Advisor to find a formula that would fit what was required. The Ministries of Finance and Justice wrote to one another, and yet in the end, the lawyers did not reach a positive result for the Civil Code and its faltering provisions.

At that time, along with others, Aydın Bolak, a parliamentarian for Balıkesir who is now a signatory witness to the deeds, prepared a bill changing clauses of the Civil Code relating to foundations. Aydın Bolak systematically prepared for this. First of all, he consulted with Ankara University, setting up a seminar and debate at the Faculty of Law for this purpose. At the seminar, everyone from professors to their youngest assistants openly debated ideas; it was indeed at this seminar that the word "foundation", an old expression which accurately described this type of institution, replaced the word "trust" in the Civil Code.

While all these official formalities were completed, we continued our work on developing our foundation deeds. In 1966, we presented them to a large scholarly and legal group, consisting of Cevat Fehmi Başkut, Aydın Bolak, Professor Tahir Çağa, Professor Nurettin Çuhadar, Ahmed Dallı, Distinguished Professor Ekrem Şerif Egeli, Distinguished Professor Sıddık Sami Onar, Kemal Türkoğlu, Professor Süheyl Ünver and Bülent Yazıcı for investigation. On the basis of the observations of this group, we rewrote many of the provisions of the deeds. We investigated foundations such as those of Ford, Philips, Thyssen, and Rockefeller in Europe and America and we tried to advance even further based on those ideas at our meetings. After this, the bill to be presented to the Turkish Grand National Assembly (TGNA) was debated at a temporary commission. It was put on the TGNA's agenda and accepted in the final days as the election process was finishing. Thus, the draft was prevented from becoming obsolete. Finally, the law passed through the Senate in 1967 and was published on July 24, 1967 in issue no. 903 of the *Resmî Gazete* (Official Gazette). Despite this, the establishment of our foundation was postponed for one and a half more years. The reason for this was that the law had left many provisions on this issue to the regulations. Despite the law ordering them to be published within six months, the consultations at the Council of State still went on.

The law made it necessary for foundations to secure a cabinet decision in order to benefit from a tax exemption. In our application to benefit from this provision, which was applicable to our foundation, we first needed to wait for the regulations and later to ask for the consent of various ministries, leading it to be finished very late. Finally, on December 28, 1968 with Cabinet decision 6/11114 our foundation was granted an exemption and at last the final text that we have signed today came about. As I have shown above, the work we began in 1951 came to fruition 18 years later.

If you want to be successful at something, you must work without fear and you must never stop chasing it. That is what we did. I count it my duty in your presence to thank Aydın Bolak, who was to a large extent responsible for this law being passed. I am sure of this: that many other businessmen will establish this type of foundation and that the country will gain much from them.

To end, I would like to wish that this foundation is propitious for the Koç family and group, for the country and for its people. I know that it is my duty to express in your presence my heartfelt thanks to all of my colleagues who have carried out work for this foundation's establishment, most of all Mr. Alisbah, who worked so long for it. I ask of God that it will enjoy good luck, and I send good wishes to all of you with love and respect. I ask that this talk be read out at the first board of directors meeting of the Vehbi Koç Foundation and that it feature in the first minutes."

Thus, the foundation I had intended to set up for years was finally established. From the day it was set up, this foundation has given scholarships to students and has also given mass aid in education and health.

The foundation now donates in its own name with its own revenues. When the foundation's income is insufficient to do something, I support it. I will try to continue this work while I remain well.

Vehbi Koç, *Hayat Hikâyem* (*My Life Story*), 4th Edition, Vehbi Koç Foundation Publications, Istanbul, 1983, pp. 123-26

BEQUEST

Praise be to Almighty God, who with His will enabled me to perform charitable works during my lifetime with pleasure, and granted me the means to continue after my death.

In the belief that the Turkish Nation will continue to exist as long as the world endures, regardless of the difficulties that might occur, my wish was to establish this Foundation in perpetuity. Thus, I have based this endowment on a commercial entity that will be able to adapt itself to the requirements of the day rather than on properties dependent on economic conditions and natural disasters. I have chosen to set up this endowment with the shares of Koç Holding. These are made up of numerous commercial and industrial enterprises, and therefore less subject to risk. This Foundation, that I have established by the Grace and Kindness of God, I entrust first of all to my heirs and to their succeeding generations, to my business colleagues and to the Government of the Republic of Turkey. I call upon all my heirs, my close acquaintances, my business colleagues, my fellow citizens who may be involved in this Foundation, and the officials who will assume its administration, to accept this endowment as a bequest made to the Turkish Nation, to protect it, and strive with their best intention to achieve its original aims. I request the auditing authorities of the State and, when necessary, its authorized agencies, courts and judiciary, never to depart from the dictates of their conscience when making decisions, lest this Foundation suffer harm and be diverted from its aims. I have brought this enterprise into being as a result of a lifetime of effort and sincere desire.

I pray that God will regard it worthy of His Protection and grant it success.

Vehbi Koç

VKV BOARD OF DIRECTORS (1969-2016)

23.05.1969

- Vehbi Koç
  Chair
- Aydın Bolak
  Deputy chair
- Suna Kıraç
  General Secretary
- Rahmi M. Koç
  Member
- Semahat Arsel
  Member
- Sevgi Gönül
  Member
- Cahit Yücel
  Member
- Hulki Alisbah
  Member
- İsak de Eskinazis
  Member
- Prof. Kemal Oğuzman
  Member
- Prof. Abdullah Türkoğlu
  Member

1970 - 1974

- Vehbi Koç
  Chair
- Aydın Bolak
  Deputy chair
- Semahat Arsel
  Member
- Rahmi M. Koç
  Member
- Sevgi Gönül
  Member
- Suna Kıraç
  Member
- Prof. Kemal Oğuzman
  Member
- Prof. Abdullah Türkoğlu
  Member
- Cahit Yücel
  Member
- Hulki Alisbah
  Member
- İsak de Eskinazis
  Member

1974

- Vehbi Koç
  Chair
- Aydın Bolak
  Deputy chair
- Semahat Arsel
  Member
- Rahmi M. Koç
  Member
- Sevgi Gönül
  Member
- Suna Kıraç
  Member
- Prof. Kemal Oğuzman
  Member
- Prof. Abdullah Türkoğlu
  Member
- Talat Orhon
  Member
- Hulki Alisbah
  Member
- İsak de Eskinazis
  Member

1975 - 1978

- Vehbi Koç
  Chair
- Aydın Bolak
  Deputy chair
- Semahat Arsel
  Member
- Rahmi M. Koç
  Member
- Sevgi Gönül
  Member
- Suna Kıraç
  Member
- Prof. Kemal Oğuzman
  Member
- Prof. Kemal Tosun
  Member
- Talat Orhon
  Member
- Hulki Alisbah
  Member
- İsak de Eskinazis
  Member

1978 - 1980

- Vehbi Koç — *Chair*
- Aydın Bolak — *Deputy chair*
- Semahat Arsel — *Member*
- Rahmi M. Koç — *Member*
- Sevgi Gönül — *Member*
- Suna Kıraç — *Member*
- Prof. Kemal Oğuzman — *Member*
- Prof. İlhan Akın — *Member*
- Talat Orhon — *Member*
- Hulki Alisbah — *Member*
- İsak de Eskinazis — *Member*

1981

- Vehbi Koç — *Chair*
- Aydın Bolak — *Deputy chair*
- Semahat Arsel — *Member*
- Rahmi M. Koç — *Member*
- Sevgi Gönül — *Member*
- Suna Kıraç — *Member*
- Prof. Kemal Oğuzman — *Member*
- Prof. İlhan Akın — *Member*
- Hulki Alisbah — *Member*
- İsak de Eskinazis — *Member*
- Necdet Şardağ — *Member*

1982 - 1985

- Vehbi Koç — *Chair*
- Aydın Bolak — *Deputy chair*
- Semahat Arsel — *Member*
- Rahmi M. Koç — *Member*
- Sevgi Gönül — *Member*
- Suna Kıraç — *Member*
- Prof. Kemal Oğuzman — *Member*
- Prof. İlhan Akın — *Member*
- Hulki Alisbah — *Member*
- İsak de Eskinazis — *Member*
- Oral Çobanoğlu — *Member*

1985 - 1986

- Vehbi Koç — *Chair*
- Aydın Bolak — *Deputy chair*
- Semahat Arsel — *Member*
- Rahmi M. Koç — *Member*
- Sevgi Gönül — *Member*
- Suna Kıraç — *Member*
- Prof. Kemal Oğuzman — *Member*
- Prof. İlhan Akın — *Member*
- Fahir İlkel — *Member*
- İsak de Eskinazis — *Member*
- Ünal Korukçu — *Member*

1987

- Vehbi Koç — *Chair*
- Aydın Bolak — *Deputy chair*
- Semahat Arsel — *Member*
- Rahmi M. Koç — *Member*
- Sevgi Gönül — *Member*
- Suna Kıraç — *Member*
- Prof. Kemal Oğuzman — *Member*
- Prof. İlhan Akın — *Member*
- Fahir İlkel — *Member*
- İsak de Eskinazis — *Member*
- Ünal Korukçu — *Member*

1987 - 1993

- Vehbi Koç — *Chair*
- Aydın Bolak — *Deputy chair*
- Semahat Arsel — *Member*
- Rahmi M. Koç — *Member*
- Sevgi Gönül — *Member*
- Suna Kıraç — *Member*
- Prof. Kemal Oğuzman — *Member*
- Prof. İlhan Akın — *Member*
- Fahir İlkel — *Member*
- Can Kıraç — *Member*
- Ünal Korukçu — *Member*

1993

- Vehbi Koç — *Chair*
- Aydın Bolak — *Deputy chair*
- Semahat Arsel — *Member*
- Rahmi M. Koç — *Member*
- Sevgi Gönül — *Member*
- Suna Kıraç — *Member*
- Prof. Kemal Oğuzman — *Member*
- Prof. İlhan Akın — *Member*
- Fahir İlkel — *Member*
- İnan Kıraç — *Member*
- Ünal Korukçu — *Member*

1994

- Vehbi Koç — *Chair*
- Aydın Bolak — *Deputy chair*
- Semahat Arsel — *Member*
- Rahmi M. Koç — *Member*
- Sevgi Gönül — *Member*
- Suna Kıraç — *Member*
- Prof. Kemal Oğuzman — *Member*
- Prof. İlhan Akın — *Member*
- Tamer Şahinbaş — *Member*
- İnan Kıraç — *Member*
- Ünal Korukçu — *Member*

1995

- Vehbi Koç — *Chair*
- Aydın Bolak — *Deputy chair*
- Semahat Arsel — *Member*
- Rahmi M. Koç — *Member*
- Sevgi Gönül — *Member*
- Suna Kıraç — *Member*
- Prof. Kemal Oğuzman — *Member*
- Prof. İlhan Akın — *Member*
- Tamer Şahinbaş — *Member*
- İnan Kıraç — *Member*

- Ünal Korukçu
  Member

1996

- Vehbi Koç
  Chair
- Aydın Bolak
  Deputy chair
- Semahat Arsel
  Member
- Rahmi M. Koç
  Member
- Sevgi Gönül
  Member
- Suna Kıraç
  Member
- Prof. Mahmut Birsel
  Member
- Prof. İlhan Akın
  Member
- Tamer Şahinbaş
  Member
- İnan Kıraç
  Member
- Ünal Korukçu
  Member

1997

- Semahat Arsel
  Chair
- Rahmi M. Koç
  Deputy chair
- Aydın Bolak
  Deputy Chair
- Suna Kıraç
  Member
- Sevgi Gönül
  Member
- İnan Kıraç
  Member
- Prof. Üstün Ergüder
  Member
- Prof. Mahmut Birsel
  Member
- Ünal Korukçu
  Member
- Evren Artam
  Member

1998

- Semahat Arsel
  Chair
- Rahmi M. Koç
  Deputy chair
- Aydın Bolak
  Başkan Vekili
- Suna Kıraç
  Member
- Sevgi Gönül
  Member
- Temel Atay
  Member
- Prof. Üstün Ergüder
  Member
- Prof. Mahmut Birsel
  Member
- Ünal Korukçu
  Member
- Evren Artam
  Member

1999 - 2002

- Semahat Arsel
  Chair
- Rahmi M. Koç
  Deputy chair
- Aydın Bolak
  Başkan Vekili
- Suna Kıraç
  Member
- Sevgi Gönül
  Member
- Temel Atay
  Member
- Prof. Mahmut Birsel
  Member
- Prof. Üstün Ergüder
  Member
- Ersin Özince
  Member
- Evren Artam
  Member

2002 - 2003

- Semahat Arsel
  Chair
- Rahmi M. Koç
  Deputy chair
- Suna Kıraç
  Member
- Sevgi Gönül
  Member
- Temel Atay
  Member
- Bülend Özaydınlı
  Member
- Prof. Mahmut Birsel
  Member
- Prof. Üstün Ergüder
  Member
- Ersin Özince
  Member
- Nevzat Tüfekçioğlu
  Member

2004 - 2006

- Semahat Arsel
  Chair
- Rahmi M. Koç
  Deputy chair
- Suna Kıraç
  Member
- Mustafa V. Koç
  Member
- Ömer M. Koç
  Member
- Temel Atay
  Member
- Bülend Özaydınlı
  Member
- Prof. Mahmut Birsel
  Member
- Prof. Üstün Ergüder
  Member
- Ersin Özince
  Member

2007 - 2009

- Semahat Arsel
  Chair
- Rahmi M. Koç
  Deputy chair
- Suna Kıraç
  Member
- Mustafa V. Koç
  Member
- Ömer M. Koç
  Member
- Temel Atay
  Member
- Bülent Bulgurlu
  Member
- Prof. Mahmut Birsel
  Member
- Prof. Üstün Ergüder
  Member
- Ersin Özince
  Member

2010

- Semahat Arsel
  Chair
- Rahmi M. Koç
  Deputy chair
- Suna Kıraç
  Member
- Mustafa V. Koç
  Member
- Ömer M. Koç
  Member
- Temel Atay
  Member
- Turgay Durak
  Member
- Prof. Mahmut Birsel
  Member
- Prof. Üstün Ergüder
  Member
- Ersin Özince
  Member

2011 - 2012

- Semahat Arsel
  Chair
- Rahmi M. Koç
  Deputy chair
- Suna Kıraç
  Member
- Mustafa V. Koç
  Member
- Ömer M. Koç
  Member
- Temel Atay
  Member
- Turgay Durak
  Member
- Prof. Mahmut Birsel
  Member
- Prof. Dr. Üstün Ergüder
  Member
- Adnan Bali
  Member

2013

- Semahat Arsel
  Chair
- Rahmi M. Koç
  Deputy chair
- Mustafa V. Koç
  Member
- Ömer M. Koç
  Member
- İpek Kıraç
  Member
- Temel Atay
  Member

- Turgay Durak
  Member
- Prof. Mahmut Birsel
  Member
- Prof. Üstün Ergüder
  Member
- Adnan Bali
  Member

2014

- Semahat Arsel
  Chair
- Rahmi M. Koç
  Deputy chair
- Mustafa V. Koç
  Member
- Ömer M. Koç
  Member
- İpek Kıraç
  Member
- Temel Atay
  Member
- Turgay Durak
  Member
- Prof. Fehmi Celal Erkut
  Member
- Prof. Üstün Ergüder
  Member
- Adnan Bali
  Member

2015

- Semahat Arsel
  Chair
- Rahmi M. Koç
  Deputy chair
- Mustafa V. Koç
  Member
- Ömer M. Koç
  Member
- İpek Kıraç
  Member
- Temel Atay
  Member
- Levent Çakıroğlu
  Member
- Prof. Fehmi Celal Erkut
  Member
- Prof. Üstün
- Ergüder
  Member
- Adnan Bali
  Member

2016

- Semahat Arsel
  Chair
- Rahmi M. Koç
  Deputy chair
- Ömer M. Koç
  Member
- Ali Y. Koç
  Member
- İpek Kıraç
  Member
- Temel Atay
  Member
- Levent Çakıroğlu
  Member
- Prof. Fehmi Celal Erkut
  Member
- Prof. Üstün Ergüder
  Member
- Adnan Bali
  Member

Vehbi Koç Foundation American Hospital *see* **American Hospital**

Vehbi Koç Foundation Educational Scholarships, a scholarship program begun in 1969 by the Vehbi Koç Foundation(*) (VKV) with the aim of providing equal of opportunity in education to talented young people with insufficient financial resources. Over 50,000 students have so far benefited from VKV's educational scholarships, which have been available since the program began. Program scholarships are mostly given on an annual basis to vocational high school and university students.

Students who continue on to undergraduate programs at state universities can have their costs covered by VKV through University Scholarships; nursing students benefit from Nursing Scholarships; Boğaziçi University and Istanbul Technical University assistants can receive Assistant Scholarships; vocational school students can benefit from Vocational Educational Scholarships, which are made up of donations from Koç Holding(*) companies, (Fiat Laboratory, and Yapı Kredi Bank, scholarships). The top three most successful graduates of the Koç elementary schools that are part of the 17 Schools Project(*) benefit from non-repayable 17 Schools Success Scholarships. In addition, there are scholarship opportunities for successful children of Koç Group employees studying at university or vocational high schools whose family incomes fall below a certain level.

The VKV Educational Scholarships Portal was formed at www.vkv.org.tr in order to provide a transparent and sustainable applications infrastructure, and from the 2014-2015 academic year onwards, it began to take applications online.

In addition, scholarship programs for successful students with insufficient financial means are available from other VKV institutions, Koç University(*), Koç School(*), VEKAM(*), AKMED(*) and ANAMED(*).

Vehbi Koç Foundation Ford Otosan Gölcük Culture and Community Center, a culture, arts and sports center established in 2011 by the Vehbi Koç Foundation(*) in collaboration with Ford Otosan. The center provides an environment for the development of the social, cultural and artistic lives of the local people. Established on a 2.7-hectare plot with 4,700 square meters of inside space, it serves an average of 100,000 Gölcük residents a year with an auditorium, VIP hall, exhibition hall, art workshops, sports hall, fitness salon, dance studio, an observatory, restaurant and garden.

The auditorium plays host to free classical music, traditional music, world music and jazz music concerts, as well as talks with musical figures, dance performances, and theatrical performances for adults and children. The program is arranged around a different theme every month. Picture and photographic exhibitions of the works of selected artists are held in the center's exhibition hall. Artistic workshops, which are held every month, provide the opportunity for local people to try out different types of art according to their talents and hobbies. Since the center was founded, these have included adult workshops on model boat making, paper marbling, painting, ceramics, patchwork, Turkish folk music, Turkish classical music and *bağlama* (a string instrument); children's activities have covered ceramics, painting, puppetry, mask-making and chocolate making workshops. As part of the "Artists of Industry" project, bodywork and painting experts working at the Ford Otosan factory produced sculptures out of sheet metal and waste materials. In addition, the center hosts panels, seminars and educational events. The Ford Otosan Beyond Disability Theater Club, which has been carrying out activities aimed at hearing-impaired people since 2013, won the Jury Special Award at the 13th Direklerarası Audience Awards the same year and continues under the umbrella of the center's project for promoting sign language.

The center's sports hall includes indoor and outdoor basketball courts, tennis courts, fitness and pilates salons, as well as a dance studio. The indoor basketball court serves as the home court of basketball and volleyball teams belonging to Ford Otosan workers, Gölcük Municipality and schools from the area. At the fitness salon, which has all the necessary equipment for healthy living and body building, Ford Otosan workers can work out for free with regular exercise programs prepared by experienced instructors. Also in the sports hall dance studio are courses in various types of dance, including Latin dance, given by experienced instructors. Pilates classes are held in the same studio.

The observatory allows visitors to look down on the Gulf of İzmit, an important bird migration path, and watch the wetlands within the Ford Otosan grounds and 152 different types of birds.

The center was designed and constructed according to ecological principles, and its renewable copper, wood and brick architecture was awarded the 2011 Arkitera Employers' Prize and 2012 National Architectural Structure Discipline Award. The center's open areas, with their striking natural beauty, include healthy walking tracks for visitors. The human figures made of rope by sculptor Kaya Özköprülü in the garden have become a symbol of the center.

Vehbi Koç Foundation Ford Otosan Van Teachers' Housing Complex, a modern housing complex constructed with the help of the Vehbi Koç Foundation(*) and Ford Otosan in Kalecik village after the earthquake disaster in Van in 2011. The complex, built with the aim of repairing the damage to educators and educational life in the area, was completed in 2012 in only five months. The housing complex is composed of four three-story buildings, making a total of 128 apartments. The apartments are one or two bedroom and fitted

out with white goods from Arçelik. The 10,000 square meter housing complex grounds include a social facility, indoor and outdoor sports areas, a green area and a car park.

Vehbi Koç Foundation Koç High School Suna Kıraç Story Competition *see* **Suna Kıraç Inter-School Short Story Competition**

Vehbi Koç Foundation Koç Private Primary and High School *see* **Koç School**

Vehbi Koç Foundation Publications, books published by the Vehbi Koç Foundation(*) (VKV). The first book published by the VKV was Vehbi Koç's autobiographic work entitled *Hayat Hikâyem* in 1973 (*My Life Story,* 1977). in 1973. Over the years, this has been followed by other publications in the fields of autobiography, culture, art, history, and health. In addition, it has contributed to the preparation and printing of many special publications and exhibition catalogs in relevant subject areas. From 2012 onwards, the VKV has published its annual reports every year in February in Turkish and English under the name *Vehbi Koç Vakfi Faaliyet Raporu/Vehbi Koç Foundation Annual Report.*

VKV PUBLICATIONS*

- Akman, Renan ve Tüzün, Gürel, *Vehbi Koç Foundation Encyclopedia,* 2019
- Arsel, Semahat, *Eskimeyen Tatlar: Türk Mutfak Kültürü/Timeless Tastes: Turkish Culinary Culture,* 1996
- Berker, Nadire ve Yalçın,Selim, *Osman Cevdet Çubukçu: Tıbbiye'nin ve Bir Tıbbiyeli'nin Öyküsü* (Medical Schools and the Story of a Medical Student), 2003
- Birol, Leman et al., *İç Hastalıkları Hemşireliği* (Internal Diseases Nursing), 1989
- *Çeviker, Gülsevim, Amiral Bristol Hemşirelik Okulu 1920-1999* (The Story of the Admiral Bristol Nursing School 1920-1999), 2011
- Dokur, Suna (ed.), *Forty Year Book,* 2010
- Falconi, Ilaria and Kuneralp, Sinan, *Palazzo Gamberini: Türkiye'nin Roma Büyükelçiliği/Palazzo Gamberini: Ambasciata di Turchia in Roma,* 2013
- Fuerest, Elinor V. et al., *Hemşireliğin Temel İlkeleri* (The Fundamentals of Nursing), 1979
- Gönül, Sevgi, *Sevgi'nin Diviti* (From Sevgi's Pen), 2011
- Hofling, Charles K. et al., *Hemşirelikte Ana Psikiyatrik Kavramlar* (Core Psychiatric Concepts in Nursing), 1981
- Karamani, Arzu and Öztuncay, Bahattin (ed.), *Gün Işığında İstanbul'un 8000 Yılı: Marmaray, Metro, Sultanahmet Kazıları/In the Light of Day: 8000 Years of Istanbul through Marmaray, Metro, Sultanahmet Excavations,* 2007
- Koç, Vehbi, *Hatıralarım Görüşlerim Öğütlerim,* 1987/ *Recollections, Observations, Counsel,* 1991
- Koç, Vehbi, *Hayat Hikâyem,* 1973/*My Life Story: The Autobiography of a Turkish Businessman,* 1977
- Kolay, Selçuk et al., *Derinlerden Yansımalar: Çanakkale Savaşı Batıkları/Echoes From The Deep: Wrecks of the Dardanelles Campaign,* 2013 (with the Aydın Şahenk Foundation)
- Korre-Zogpraphou, Katerina, *The Iznik Ceramics of the Monastery of Panaghia Panakhrantou,* 2012
- Ödekan, Ayla (ed.), *"Kalanlar" - 12. ve 13. Yüzyıllarda Türkiye'de Bizans/"The Remnants" - 12th and 13th Centuries Byzantine Objects in Turkey,* 2007
- *Öztuncay, Bahattin, Robertson, Osmanlı Başkentinde Fotoğrafçı ve Hakkâk-Ömer M. Koç Koleksiyonu/Robertson, Photographer and Engraver in the Ottoman Capital-Ömer M. Koç Collection,* 2013
- *Öztuncay, Bahattin (ed.), I. Dünya Savaşı'nda İttifak Cephesinde Savaş ve Propaganda/ Propaganda and War, The Allied Front during the First World War,* 2015
- *Öztuncay, Bahattin, Bâki Muhabbet-Ömer M. Koç Koleksiyonu* (Eternal Conversation-The Ömer M. Koç Collection), 2016
- *Öztuncay, Bahattin, Youssouf Bey, The Charged Portraits of Fin-de-Siècle Pera, Ömer M. Koç Collection,* 2017
- Turan, İlhami, *Osmanlı Kıyafetleri: Fenerci Mehmed Albümü/Ottoman Costume Book: Fenerci Mehmed,* 1986
- *Üçok, Ayşe, Koç Ailesinin Yaşamı: Sadberk Hanım* (Koç Family Life: Sadberk Hanım), 2006
- Yıldırım, Nuran, *Savaşlardan Modern Hastanelere Türkiye'de Hemşirelik Tarihi* (From War to Modern Hospitals, The Story of Nursing in Turkey), 2014
- Wieck, King, *Hemşirelik Teknikleri El Kitabı* (Nursing Methods Handbook), 1983

*The publications of organizations affiliated to the VKV are listed under their own entries.

Vehbi Koç Foundation Vocational and Technical Anatolian High School, formerly known as the Sarıyer Vehbi Koç Foundation High School, a vocational and technical high school found on the street Meserburnu Caddesi in Sarıyer, Istanbul. The new building was constructed by Vehbi Koç(*) in 1976, and the educational institution has long been provided with financial support by the Vehbi Koç Foundation(*) (VKV).

The old school building, which was

constructed in the 1880s, was handed over to the Istanbul Municipality by its owner and was opened in 1944 as a middle school. From 1966 onwards, education continued in the same building as a high school. When the needs of the building, damaged over time, became too expensive to meet, today's new school building was constructed on the land behind it with the support of Vehbi Koç. The historical building, which has gone through renovations, was for years used for administrative purposes and as a Teachers' Lodge. The school, which had long operated under the name of the Sarıyer Vehbi Koç Foundation High School, was turned into a hospitality and tourism vocational high school in the 2012-13 school year and the other building was given to the school for use as a practice hotel.

In the 2014-15 academic year, the school was turned into a vocational and technical Anatolian high school.

Vehbi Koç Science, Art and Literature Prize Contest, an initiative begun by the Vehbi Koç Foundation(*) to distribute prizes to citizens of the Turkish Republic based on topics chosen every year in the fields of the sciences, literature, social sciences and art. "Just as these prizes could be awarded as the result of a contest, they could equally be awarded without a competition for someone who creates a work of copyright or who is involved in a creative endeavour."

In 1973, the topic of the first prize contest was "Legal, administrative, economic and financial precautions necessary to alleviate difficulties in the establishment, operation and development of foundations subject to the Civil Code from the perspective of problems that have emerged or could in future." The first prize in this contest was awarded to Dr. Ahmet İşeri. It was decided that the second contest, held in 1975, would aim to keep Turkish handicrafts alive and that its topic would be the art of procelain tiles. In line with this aim, tile-making courses for young people were organized under the tutelage of Professor Muhsin Demironat in Kütahya and a prize was awarded to the person producing the best work, which was Hakkı Ermumcu for his porcelain tile panels.

From 1980 onwards, the funds allocated for the Science, Art and Literature Prizes were used to support a variety of inititatives and events: bookbinding (1980), the tile course and competition held in Kütahya (1983), the excavations at Aphrodisias (1985), and the promotion of an album of Ottoman clothing by Fenerci Mehmed Efendi (1986) in Turkey and abroad. In 1988, the fund was used to buy artworks from a variety of artists.

VEKAM, full name KOÇ UNIVERSITY VEHBİ KOÇ ANKARA STUDIES RESEARCH CENTER, a research-implementation establishment linked to Koç University(*) that carries out interdisciplinary research and academic work on Ankara's urban development, as well as on the social and economic history, culture and cultural heritage of Ankara and its surroundings. It also supports other research and projects in these fields. It was set up in 1994 in an orchard house belonging to Vehbi Koç(*) in Keçiören, Ankara.

The orchard house, which was built at the end of the nineteenth century and bought from Marshall Fevzi Çakmak in 1923, was for many years used as the summer home of the Koç family(*). Vehbi Koç spent a large part of his life here and all of his children were born in this house, which is one of the few remaining examples of its type and has legal status as a Priority Protected Immovable Cultural Asset. The house, which was restored in the years 1992 and 1993, was transferred to the Vehbi Koç Foundation to host a research and archive institution for academic work on Ankara, and in 1994, it opened as the Vehbi Koç Ankara Studies Research Center. VEKAM aims to compile all forms of information and documents relating to Vehbi Koç and Ankara, while also carrying out research, academic work and projects relating to Ankara. It was affiliated with Koç University in 2014 and renamed the Koç University Vehbi Koç Ankara Studies Research Center.

With its library and archive hosting rich sources of information, VEKAM acts as the city memory of Ankara. From the day it opened, it added all types of publications relating to Ankara to its collection, including rare books, and became the first stop for urban research on Ankara.

The library collection includes travelogues, original novels written in local and foreign languages, the memoirs of foreign diplomats who served in Ankara, publications containing historical and cultural research on Ankara, reports published by local administrations, professional unions and chambers of commerce, and local periodical publications. The library also hosts the Ali Esat Bozyiğit Collection, which contains special sources on folk culture.

The VEKAM offers rich content and various types of materials to researchers in the Vehbi Koç Collection, which shines a light on Turkey's economic history, and the Ankara Collection, where all forms of information about Ankara can be found. The Vehbi Koç Collection contains documents and photographs about Vehbi Koç's years of activity in Ankara, documentary films about his life, and newspaper clippings including important news and commentary from between the years 1956 and 1993. The Ankara Collection includes materials such as Ankara engravings, photographs and postcards, family albums donated by Ankara families, city plans from different eras of Ankara's history, maps, and documentary films. The collection also contains study books, school curriculums, grade slips, diplomas, the yearbooks of the foremost educational institutions of the age and photographs of leading educators and students from the 1923-45 period. The *Cumhuriyet Kıraatları* (Republic Readings) series is one of the collection's original examples.

From 2013, VEKAM has published the *Journal of Ankara Studies*(*), an interdisciplinary, peer-reviewed journal containing original articles and short pieces in Turkish and English on the historical, cultural, political and economic development of the city of Ankara and the urban problems of our day.

The VEKAM institution has undertaken numerous projects, including the "Age of Reason", the "Orchard Houses Social History", the "Ankara Districts Cultural Heritage", the "Five Ankaras", the "Standards of Research, Documentation and Preservation for the Cultural Heritage of Civil Architecture between 1930-1980 in Ankara" and "Local Content in Cloud Europeana". VEKAM has organized exhibitions in different venues in Ankara, Istanbul and Izmir, and has been holding conferences on topics related to urban history and culture since March 2014. In 2015, it began to award prizes for research with the aim of supporting new academic work about Ankara and its surroundings, and in 2016 it began the VEKAM Library and Archives Research Awards program. In the same year, it signed an agreement with the Skilliter Centre for Ottoman Studies at Cambridge University to develop a three-year joint project on the socioeconomic history of Ottoman Anatolia. Three symposiums took place as part of the project: "Disease and Disaster in Ottoman Anatolia" (2016), "Trade and Production in Ottoman Anatolia" (2017) and "Social Life in Ottoman Anatolia" (2018).

See also Ankara Orchard House

VEKAM PUBLICATIONS

- **Anameriç, Hakan and Rukancı, Fatih, *Posta Pullarında Başkent Ankara (1922-2008)* (The Capital City Ankara in Postage Stamps),** *İstanbul, 2011*
- **Ayaokur, Alev, *Müzelerde Bilgi Yönetimi,* (Information Management in Museums),** *Ankara, 2014*
- **Bayraktar, Nuray (ed.), *Korumada Sivil Mimarlık* (Civilian Architecture in Conservation),** *Ankara, 2014*
- **Bayraktar, Nuray (ed.), *Tarih Yazımında Sivil Mimarlık Çalıştay Notları* (Civil Architecture in Historiography Workshop Notes)** *Ankara, 2014*
- **Bayraktar, Nuray (ed.), *Sivil Mimari Bellek, Ankara 1930-1980* (Civil Architectural Memory, Ankara: 1930-1980)** *Ankara, 2017*
- **Berkes, Turgut (ed.), *Geçmişten Geleceğe Kitabın Serüveni, Bildiriler* (Book's Quest: From Past to Future, Papers)** *Ankara, 2011*
- **Berkes, Turgut (ed.), *Türkiye'de Arşivler ve Arşivcilik Uygulamaları* (Archives and Archive Management in Turkey),** *Ankara, 2011*
- **Cengizkan, Ali, *Koçzâde Ahmet Vehbi Bey ve Bir İnşaatın Öyküsü: Ankara Hukuk Mektebi* (Koçzâde Ahmet Vehbi Bey and a Construction Story; Ankara Law School),** *Ankara, 2004*
- **Gençkaya, F. Ömer, *Eğitimin Başkenti Ankara,*** *İstanbul, 2008***/ *Ankara, Capital of Education,*** *Ankara 2011*
- **Kaçar, Ayşe Duygu, *Kültür/Mekân: Gazi Orman Çiftliği, Ankara* (Culture/Space: Gazi Forest Farm, Ankara),** *Ankara, 2015*
- **Kolektif, *Eski Dostlar Aramızda: Reklamlarda Ankara***

1935-1967/Among Old Friends: Advertisements on Ankara 1935-1967, Ankara, 2007
- Kolektif, *Geçmişten Geleceğe Türkiye'de Müzecilik IV-Bir Açık Hava Müzesi: Ankara ve Çevresi* (The Past and Future of Museology in Turkey IV-An Open Air Museum: Ankara and its Surroundings), Ankara 2010
- Köksal, Yonca and Polatel, Mehmet (ed.), *Avrupa Arşivlerinde Osmanlı İmparatorluğu* (The Ottoman Empire in the Archives of Europe), Ankara, 2014
- Kunstadter, M. Melissa (ed.), *Ankara Palas'ın Unutulmaz GecelerindenSahneler/ Scenes from the Unforgettable Nights of Ankara Palace*, Ankara, 2006
- Niyazioğlu, Sinan, *İroni ve Gerilim: İkinci Dünya Savaşı Yıllarında İstanbul ve Ankara'da Savaş Algısı/ Irony and Tension: Perception of War in Istanbul and Ankara during the Second World War*, Ankara, 2016
- Oğuz, Esin Sultan (ed.), *İhtisas Kütüphaneleri Paneli* (Specialized Libraries Panel), Ankara, 2007
- Önen, B. Zeynep (ed.), *80 Yılda Devr-i Türkiye: 80 Kare Ankara/Around Turkey in 80 Years: Ankara in 80 Frames*, Ankara, 2004
- Önen, B. Zeynep et al. (ed.), *Geçmişten Geleceğe Türkiye'de Müzecilik I-Sempozyum* (The Past and Future of Museology in Turkey I- Symposium), Ankara, 2008
- Önen, B. Zeynep and Türkyılmaz, Mehtap (ed.), *Geçmişten Geleceğe Türkiye'de Müzecilik II-Eğitim, İşletmecilik ve Turizm* (The Past and Future of Museology in Turkey II- Education, Management and Tourism), Ankara, 2009
- Önen, B. Zeynep (ed.), *Geçmişten Geleceğe Türkiye'de Müzecilik III-Ankara'da Müze, Müzede Ankara* (The Past and Future of Museology in Turkey III-Museums in Ankara, Ankara in Museums), Ankara, 2009
- Önen, B. Zeynep and Türkyılmaz, Mehtap (ed.), *Türkiye'de Arşivler ve Arşivcilik Uygulamaları* (Archives and Archive Management in Turkey), Ankara, 2011
- Önen, B. Zeynep and Türkyılmaz, Mehtap (ed.), *Geçmişten Geleceğe Kitabın Serüveni* (Book's Quest: From Past to Future), Ankara, 2011
- Sönmez, Savaş, *Ankaralı Bulmacalar* (Ankara Crosswords), Ankara, 2005, 2016
- Şimşek, G. Hüseyin and Palancı, Necmettin (ed.), *Ankara Halk Türküleri ve Oyun Havaları Nota Kitabı* (Ankara Folk and Dance Songs Notation) Ankara, 2001
- Tanyer, Turan, *Cumhuriyet Dönemi Ankara'sının Sosyal Hayatından Sahneler*, Ankara, 2006/*Scenes from the Social Life of Ankara during the Early Republican Period*, Ankara, 2016
- Toklu, Gürkan et al. (ed.), *Ankara İli Beslenme Alışkanlıkları ve Mutfak Kültürü Sempozyum Bildirileri ve Katalog* (Food Culture and Cuisine in the Ankara Region, Symposium Papers), Ankara, 1999
- Toygar, Kamil and Berkok, Nimet (ed.), *Ankara Mutfak Kültürü ve Yemekleri*, (Ankara Cuisine and Dishes) Ankara, 1999
- Türkyılmaz, Mehtap et al. (ed.), *Kur(t)uluş. 1923*, Ankara, 2013
- Türkyılmaz, Mehtap et al. (ed.), *Cumhuriyet'i O'nu O Cumhuriyet'ini Büyüttü... Vehbi Koç (1901-1996)/ A Son and a Pioneer of the Republic... Vehbi Koç (1901-1996)*, Ankara, 2013
- Türkyılmaz, Mehtap and Kırcı, A. Beril (ed.), *19. Yüzyıldan 20. Yüzyıla Osmanlı İmparatorluğu: Mücadele-Koleksiyoncuların Seçkisi/Ottoman Empire from 19th to 20th Century: Struggle-Collectors' Selection*, Ankara, 2015
- Uysal, Y. Yeşim et al., *Sivil Mimari Bellek: Ankara 1930-1980* (Civil Architectural Memory, Ankara 1930-1980), Ankara, 2014
- Yenişehirlioğlu, Filiz and Yücel, Gözde Çerçioğlu (ed.), *Weaving the History: Mystery of a City, Sof* Ankara, 2018
- Yıldırım, Ayşe Ege, *Anadolu'dan Bir Tanık: Bengüboz'un Objektifinden Mudurnu'da Erken Cumhuriyet Dönemi/Eyewitness from Anatolia: Mudurnu in the Early Republican Era through the Lens of Bengüboz*, Ankara, 2016
- Yıldırım, Bülent et al. (ed.), *Ankara'da Yayımlanan Süreli Yayınlar Kaynakçası: 1923-2015* (Bibliography of Periodicals Published in Ankara), Ankara, 2016

VEKAM EXHIBITIONS

- 19 May, Youth and Sports Day: Republic and the Youth *(May 16–30, 2002)*
- Elegance of the Breeze: Fans and Purses from 18th Century *(October 19, 2002–October 11, 2003)*
- Republic Day: Atatürk and the Republic *(October 28–November 2, 2002)*
- Celebrations for the 83rd Anniversary of Atatürk's Arrival in Ankara *(December 26,2002)*
- Ankara: Reflections on 80 Years *(July 8, 2003)*
- Age of Turkey in the 80th Year of the Republic: Age of Reason: Educational Documents *(October 24, 2003–January 30, 2004)*
- Enchanting World of Silver: Filigree Arts in Beypazari *(March 6–25, 2004)*
- Ankara in Spring: Unforgettable Joy and Recreation Places *(April 13–15, 2004)*
- Unbearable Lightness of Silk: Silk Point Laces And Hand-Woven Textiles of Nallıhan *(May 8–28, 2004)*
- Archaeological Excavations in Ankara: Footsteps of History *(June 30–September 20, 2004)*
- Silent Voice of Eternal Lands: Silk Point Laces of Nallıhan and Their Use in Daily Life *(October 8–November 25, 2004; October 22–November 19, 2004)*
- I Produce Therefore I Am - I: Women Who Work in Keçiören *(March 8–27, 2005)*
- Ankara in Literature: Ankara Books *(March 28–April 14, 2005)*
- Around Turkey in the 82 Years of the Republic Ankara in 100 Frames *(April14–21, 2005)*
- Embroidery and Filigree Arts in Anatolia: Selected Pieces of Beypazari Embroidery and Filigree Works *(June 9–July 9, 2005)*
- A Plain Man: Vehbi Koç and His Awards and Personal Items *(September 19–December 19, 2005)*
- Past, Present, and Eternity: Angora Wool Products and Cultural Assets of Ayaş *(October 1–29, 2005)*
- Education in the Birth of Modern Turkey, in the 82nd Year of the Republic Documents and Visual Memories *(November 12–December 26, 2005)*
- Scenes from Ankara's Social Life in the Republican Period *(May 6–August 6, 2006)*
- Scenes from Unforgettable Nights of Ankara Palas *(November 3–10, 2006; November 13–29, 2006; December 8, 2006–February 27, 2007)*
- Among Old Friends: Advertisements on Ankara *(1935–67) (March 17, 2007)*
- Meeting with Ulus I: A Day in the Life of Victory Monument *(November 9, 2007–February 28, 2008)*
- Human(Ity) / Exhibition *(November 18–23, 2007)*
- Honey, Would You Like to Take a Peek on My Collection? *(February 13–24, 2008)*
- Meeting with Ulus - II: Through the Lens of Time: Ankara Castle and Hanlar Quarter *(May 21, 2008)*
- Happy New Year: Old Calendars, New Year and Festival Post Cards *(December 24, 2008–May 9, 2009)*
- Check Out Ankara's Stones: Examples of the Buildings in the Foundation Era *(January 8–24, 2009)*
- The Road of the Republican Revolution – Atatürk Boulevard Exhibition *(February 9–March 14, 2009)*
- Golds of Ankara *(May 21–28, 2009)*
- Monuments of the Republic – I *(June 3–10, 2009)*
- Postage Stamps Depicting Ankara, the Capital (1922–2008) *(October 20–23, 2009; November 17, 2009)*
- Dance of Memories *(18 January–5 March2010)*
- Ankara Train Station Wandering Around in the Country *(15 October–12 November 2010; 10–17 January 2011)*
- A Son and a Pioneer of the Republic... Vehbi Koç (1901–1996)... *(February 24, 2012)*
- Kur(t)uluş. 1923 *(January 21–March 27, 2014)*
- Antioch on the Orontes: Initial Research on the City Of Mosaics *(June 15–September 20, 2014)*
- Ankara: Streets and Citizens from the Ottoman Empire to the Turkish Republic *(December 7, 2014–January 2, 2015; October 15–17, 2015; January 16–27, 2017)*
- Ottoman Empire from the 19th to 20th Century: Struggle *(April 25– May 20, 2015; April 17–28, 2017)*
- A Monumental Work from Mongolia, the Vast Country *(May 22, 2015–March 31, 2016)*
- Josephine's Fragments *(March 30–June 16, 2016)*
- Eyewitness from Anatolia: Mudurnu in the Early Republican Era Through the Lens of Bengüboz *(April 19–30, 2016, Ankara; July 12–30, 2016, Istanbul)*
- Civil Architectural Memory: Ankara: 1930–1980 *(November 29–December 15, 2014, December 19–30, 2016, Ankara; September 21–October 6, 2016, Izmir)*
- Irony and Tension / Perception of War in Istanbul and Ankara During the Second World War Years *(November 17–December 5, 2016)*
- Scent and the City *(January 6–March 31, 2018)*
- Weaving History: Mystery of a City, Sof *(May 12–September 16, 2018)*

KOÇ FAMILY MEMORIES AT THE FAMILY'S ORCHARD HOUSE IN KEÇIÖREN

I used to look with envy at the carts, horses, clothes and dresses of the residents of Keçiören who went past us every day. Most of these Christians sold their houses after leaving Ankara. My father bought the house and garden now in Keçiören from Marshall Fevzi Çakmak in 1923 for 2,900 Turkish lira. This is our current home in Keçiören... My four children were born in Keçiören. So we have great memories of this house in Keçiören. We stayed in this house over summer up until 1954.

Vehbi Koç

Can Dündar, *Özel Arşivinden Belgeler ve Anılarıyla Vehbi Koç* (Vehbi Koç through Documents and Memoirs from his Private Archive), 5th Edition, Doğan Kitap, Istanbul, p. 21

My father bought this orchard house in 1923. We four siblings were all born in this house, in the same room, on the same bedstead, in the corner room upstairs. My late mother would always come here at the start of the summer and would always stay two months, before going back to Büyükdere in Istanbul. Our house had wonderful Ankara pears, brilliant apricots, unostentatious but tasty crisp apples and very sweet grapes. In those days, doctor Yusuf Hikmet lived behind us. Later on, Ankara parliamentarian Fevzi Daldal moved into that house. Opposite us was Hatice. Her grandson Atilla is there now. Down past the orchard was Recep Peker's magnificent mansion and next to that was the parliamentarian Mr. Ekrem's house. In short, we were surrounded by very upright neighbors. If my memory is correct, when the house was first bought it went through some restoration. After that it had various repairs, and finally there was a large restoration to bring it to the condition you see today. Marshall Fevzi Çakmak, a hero of the National Struggle, also lived here, making the house even more special for us.

Rahmi M. Koç

http://vekam.org.tr/upload/userfiles/files/rahmikoç.pdf

When I look at the old days, I recall that we lived in one of the rare houses to have electricity, because at our friends' houses they ate their evening meals under the light of kerosene lamps. There were blackout curtains. There was also a shelter that still remains there that I was afraid to even pass by. In our house's safe we kept quinine rather than jewelry, gold or money.

You could find nothing to eat in Ankara in winter. We spent all summer in this orchard house preparing for winter. We collected apples and pears and lined them up in the store for eating in winter—in Ankara local jargon we *made a spread*. We would line up okra and eggplants on strings and leave them to dry in the sun. Trees like this apricot tree you see on the ground lined both sides like a two-sided crown. But we were only able to save one of them. We would collect the apricots and make dried fruit; we would collect tomatoes and make tomato paste.

There was a wire cupboard in the kitchen. I spent my childhood in this house with lips purple from blackcurrants and hands blackened by walnuts. My most important role was to shake a tin under the trees and scare away the birds from eating the cherries. And my favorite time was towards evening, holding a corner of a sheet opened under that mulberry tree in the corner to catch the mulberries as our butler shook the tree. I can count many, many other such memories.

Sevgi Gönül

http://vekam.org.tr/upload/userfiles/files/sevgigönül.pdf

Our house was a two-story, plaster-and-wood, typical Ankara orchard house. It had an orchard and garden of around 24,000 square meters. Up the stone stairs on the front side there was a big green iron door which at that time seemed stately. The most important characteristics of the door were its sliding lock and the twin handles on the outside. It led to a large stone anteroom with rooms opening out onto it. On the top floor, there was a second big anteroom that was used as a parlor and a dining room and had bedrooms opening onto it.

We would wander around in the open air of the big garden and eat sweet and sour cherries and mulberries off the trees. We would play rope games and hopscotch in the garden. We spent our days riding bikes, playing ball, climbing trees and playing families under them. We would collect fresh fruit and vegetables. Blind man's buff and puss-in-the-corner were a part of our lives. Our gardener Abdullah Ağa would go up a tree and shake it with his feet, and we would watch as the green-shelled walnuts and the ripe mulberries fell onto a sheet below.

My father, who as the head of the household was deeply worried by the Second World War, built a big shelter with two entrances in our house garden in Keçiören. As he told us, he kept this shelter well-equipped throughout the entire war, and he maintained his cautious attitude until the end of the war. The shelter was kept ready to be used at any time for a long while. As the country was saved from entering the war, over time the shelters filled with sand and water and fell into ruin. Every shelter would end up with a little hill above it that looked like a minibus.

On Ramadan evenings we would go up on this tiny hill and shout "The lamp is burning!" Also during Ramadan, the sound of the drum for sahur would be heard towards the morning, but it never scared us. Our raven-black nanny, Sevim, would scare us by saying "the boogymen are coming" when we wouldn't sleep. At the same time, the poplar trees in the garden in front of our door would shake with a whispering sound, striking fear into our little hearts.

The nights at the orchard house were just as scary as the days were lovely and fun. In those days, there was no modern garden lighting. The orchard and garden were lit with tiny bulbs.

I will never forget one adventure I had in the orchard. Despite being a careful and cautious child, I still liked to take risks now and again. What I was most interested in was "how to go down steps on a bicycle". Every day I was more intrigued. One day I began to go down the stone steps on my tricycle. I don't remember the rest very clearly. When I opened my eyes my head was half sewn up, and I was surrounded by a doctor, my mother and all the women in my family. My interest had come at the cost of a scar.

Although our family were financially well-off, we lived like a traditional Turkish family. When we went to the orchard house in September and October, we would dry fruit and vegetables for the winter, making tomato paste out of tomatoes, pickles out of cucumbers and drying eggplants by pinning them to a piece of string to be made into a kind of dolma (stuffed vegetable) that was called "Aleppo dolma". We used to line up the "pale pears", that were then known as winter pears, in a room next to the outhouse, and we would dry the apricots and line them up in the orchard house to make a kind of stewed fruit that the Ankara people would call "*zerdali kurusu*".

We used to make natural jam, that was stacked in lots of pots. There was never any waste. We made the most of every blessing from God. My mother kept quinine, absorbent cotton and iodine in a locked cupboard. In the environment of depravation during and after the war, quinine was a medicine that was valuable enough to keep in the safe, because the country was suffering an epidemic of malaria and typhus. The pencils we used in school would be sharpened with a knife so that there would be no waste. We used to walk to school. My father banned us from going by automobile.

At that time, toys were very limited. Wooden houses, wax dolls, straw baby strollers, slingshots for boys... That was all. We learned to be happy with those things. We didn't seek happiness in material things. In essence, there was neither great wealth as a country or as individuals. My big brother's slingshots were regularly confiscated. When he found the place where the slingshots had been hidden in a cupboard in the orchard house, he would shout "We've found a mine! A mine!" That was wealth for us!

Suna Kıraç

Suna Kıraç, *Ömrümden Uzun İdeallerim Var* (My Ideals, Longer than my Lifetime), Suna and İnan Kıraç Foundation Publications, Istanbul, 2006, pp. 27–29

Venice Biennial Pavilion of Turkey, a space allocated to the Turkish Pavilion for the 2014–34 period at Arsenale (a shipyard), one of the main venues for the Venice Biennial. Due to this initiative led by the Istanbul Foundation for Culture and Arts (İKSV) with the contribution of 21 sponsors, including the Vehbi Koç Foundation(*), Turkey has

been able to adopt a long-term space at the Venice Biennial, considered to be one of the most important contemporary art and architecture events in the world. As a result of this space, Turkey was able to take part in the Venice Biennial International Architecture Exhibition with a national pavilion for the first time in 2014.

Village Schools Exchange Network (Köy Okulları Değişim Ağı, KODA), is a non-governmental organization founded in 2016 to support holistic, high-standard education suited to rural conditions at village schools. During the 2017-18 academic year, the Vehbi Koç Foundation(*) contributed towards KODA's work, which aims to develop teachers in rural schools, empowering them both personally and professionally, while developing and implementing child-centered, innovative model practices to raise educational standards. As part of this initiative, teacher's gatherings, summer camps and other festivities were organized at 10 schools in the provinces of Kastamonu, Mardin, Muş and Samsun. Monthly workshops arranged at pilot rural schools provided support for children's academic, emotional and cognitive development.

Village School Teachers' Communication and Mutual Aid Society, a civil society organization which supports rural teachers and students and encourages education and teaching for adults living in villages. It has received support since 1975, in accordance with the provisions of the Vehbi Koç Foundation(*) (VKV) official articles of foundation.

The society was founded in Istanbul in 1962 with the aim of providing some regularity to the individual aid donated to poorly equipped rural schools and the poor and abandoned students in them. Over the years, the society has helped provide hundreds of schools with books, clothes, shoes, teaching materials, sports and other equipment, computers, fax machines and projectors, and when requested has established libraries of 2,500-3000 books.

VKV *see* **Vehbi Koç Foundation**

VKV Contemporary Art Collection *see* **Arter**

Vocational Education: A Crucial Matter for the Nation Project,

known in Turkish as MESLEK LİSESİ MEMLEKET MESELESİ (MLMM), initiated by Koç Holding(*) on June 21, 2006 to mark the 80th anniversary of the company's founding with support from the Ministry of National Education and the Vehbi Koç Foundation(*) (VKV).

The aims of the "Promotion of Vocational-Technical Education Program" are: "to support successful elementary school graduates with limited opportunities to attend vocational high schools that provide training to enter industry, IT and service sectors; and to provide internship opportunities to nurture qualified technical staff with the knowledge, skills and competencies required in the current economy." The project aims to "create an awareness of the importance of vocational and technical education for the nation's economy, sow the seeds of cooperation between the state and the business world, and incentivize young people to seek out vocational education."

As part of the project, the VKV with the support of Koç Holding companies plans to support 8,000 vocational high school students for seven years with "internship scholarships" and by contributing to a variety of programs dedicated to their personal and professional development. Over time the project developed with a vocational school coaching system, development modules, and training labs, transforming into an overall "school-business collaboration" strategy which has become a model practice for bridging the gap between the educational and business worlds. Hundreds of employees from Koç Holding companies have worked on a volunteer basis with vocational high school administrators in their local areas to allocate scholarships through the program. Later on they provided personal and professional development coaching to the scholarship winners.

As a part of the project, students who choose a career path in a related field are given the opportunity to do an internship at Koç Holding companies paired with their schools. Those who are successful are given priority in their job applications to Koç Holding companies.

Tüpraş, Migros, Tofaş, Otokoç and Ford Otosan have established school labs to provide additional support in specialized fields. Tofaş and Ford Otosan, in particular, aim to find employees through their pre-employment training programs for middle school, high school, and industrial vocational high schools.

Micro-projects run by some Koç Holding companies also aim to improve the professional skills of young people, increase their employability and fill the gaps in areas where there are skills shortages.

EXAMPLES OF VOCATIONAL EDUCATION PROJECT MICRO-PROJECTS CARRIED OUT BY KOÇ HOLDING COMPANIES:

- **Arçelik AŞ: Domestic Electrical Appliances Technical Training Program**
- **Türk Traktör: Agricultural Machinery Training Program**
- **Ford Otosan: İnönü Ford Cargo Technical Training Program**
- **Otokar: Welding Training Workshop**
- **Tüpraş: Opening of the Machinery Technology Site at the Körfez Technical and Industrial Vocational College**
- **Aygaz: Life Workshop with Aygaz**
- **Düzey: Target Vocational High School Students with Düzey**
- **Koçtaş: I Love My Vocation: I'm Interning at Koçtaş**

From 2008 to 2011, the project ran competitions for 10th grade scholarship students with the following themes: "I'm Successful, I'm a Vocational School Student" (2008), "Let's Shape Our Future" (2009), "The Future of Vocational Education is Your Future!" (2010), "Do You Also Have Ideas About the Future of Vocational Education?" (2011). Scholarship students could enter the competitions with academic essays, presentations or visual designs and the 20 winners were invited to the Koç University(*) campus in Istanbul during the summer for a week-long personalized education and tour program.

As part of the program, which drew attention for its implementation of a "positive discrimination" policy towards female students, 21 Koç Holding companies in different capacities and sectors and over 500 employees volunteered to work with the 8,000 vocational school students from 264 vocational schools.

Once the scholarship targets were met, from 2010 onwards the project entered a new stage, aiming to mobilize different stakeholders by developing a comprehensive model for sharing experiences at corporate, sectoral and national levels. The "Collaboration for Quality in Vocational Education" project began on December 20, 2010, to disseminate the experiences and achievements of the project and improve the quality of vocational training throughout the country. Implemented in partnership with the Education Reform Initiative (ERG)(*), the project aimed to stimulate necessary policy changes through interactive participation. After its completion in 2012, a summary document, "Quality Strategy in Vocational and Technical Education" and much of the research was shared with the public.

In 2011, the Koç Holding companies' employee volunteer project, "Vocational High School Mentors," was chosen as Europe's best volunteer program. In the following year, in order to ensure the continuity of the "Vocational Education" program's vision, it was transferred to the Turkish business sector under the leadership of the Private Sector Volunteers Association (ÖSGD). In addition to supporting the vocational personal development of high school students, the program also cultivated the volunteering spirit among employees. From 2012 to 2017, 53 ÖSGD member businesses and about 1,100 volunteers participated in the project, which reached 8,000 students in 101 vocational schools across 14 cities, provided internships to 612 students and employment to 27. In 2013, the film and book *Bizim Hikâyemiz* (Our Stories) were produced to narrate the story of the Vocational Education: A Crucial Matter for the Nation Project from its beginnings. In the book, all the participating stakeholders, school teachers, students, Koç Holding businesses, and VKV employees present their experiences of the project before and after its implementation.

The Program for Developing School-Business Partnerships(*) that emerged from "Collaboration for Quality in Vocational Education" was implemented from 2015 onwards.

Voice, an in-house school magazine produced by Koç School(*). Following the decision to release a regular, periodical publication in 2001, *Voice* was initially published in the form of a colorful bulletin and was later published in the form of a magazine for the first time in 2004. Published by the school's Communications Office, the magazine features news from the school, information about student events, essays and student articles for its audience of students, teachers, school staff and alumni. *Voice* was published twice a year for the first ten years (Autumn/Winter and Spring/Summer editions) and has been published once a year since 2015.

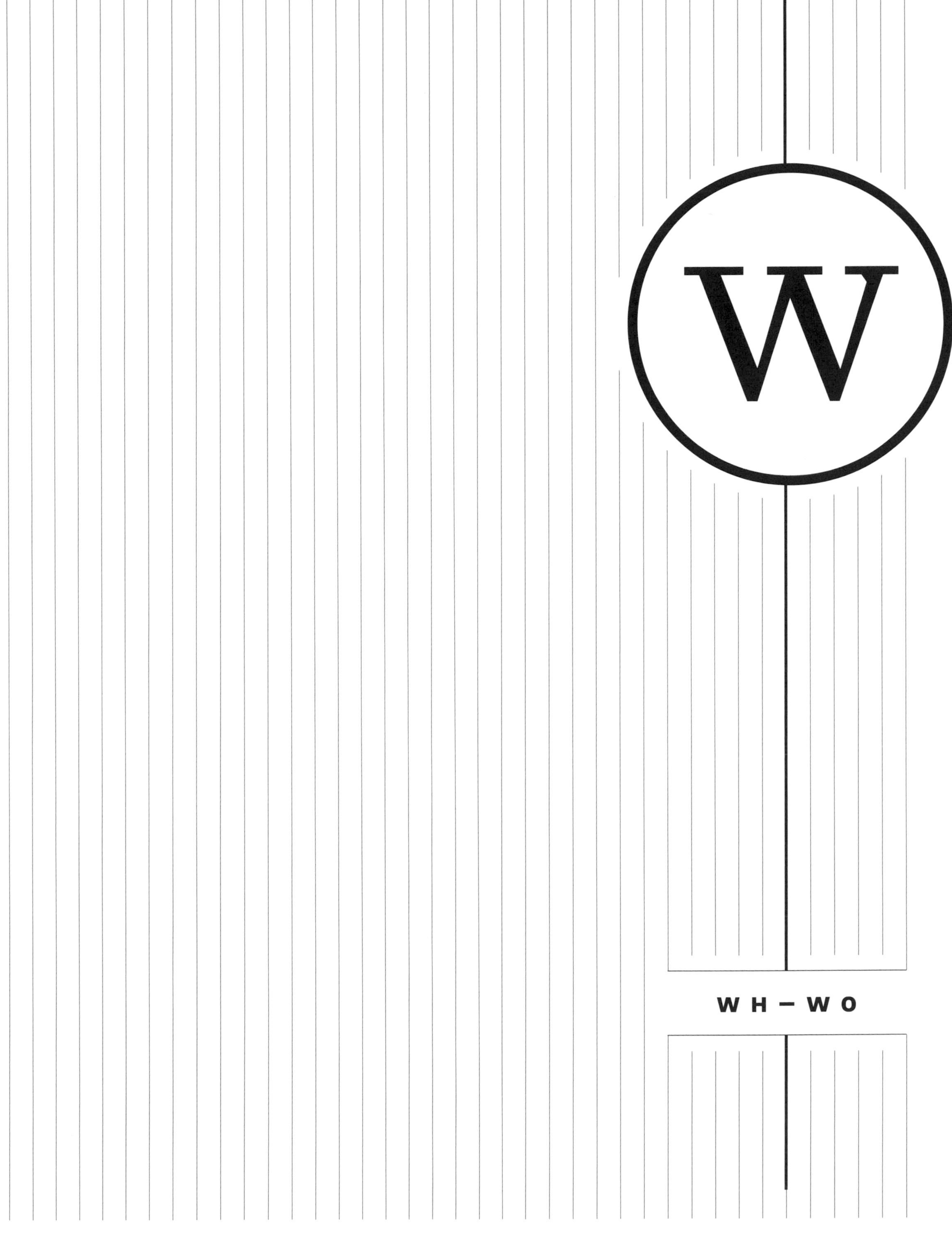
W
WH – WO

Whole School Support Project for the Integration of Refugee Children, project aiming to ease the integration of refugee children into their host society through education. Based in Turkey, the project is run in partnership with a Netherlands-based foundation with support from the Vehbi Koç Foundation(*), which acts as a local facilitator providing help with communication and delivery.

The first stage was a pilot study that aimed to ease integration of Syrian refugee children studying in Turkish state schools through providing information for teachers and parents as well as supporting students. The pilot project was carried out in Sultanbeyli, Istanbul by the Association for Positive Behavior Development (ODGEDER) with the support of the Sultanbeyli Municipality and District Directorate of National Education. The project included a template for building and strengthening student, teacher, parent, administrative and guidance services, together with surveys, polls and training seminars to help provide guidance and counseling to meet student needs.

Winkler, Warren H. *(b. April 1, 1928, St. Louis, Missouri, USA – d. February 25, 2019, Istanbul),* physician who served at the American Hospital(*) as chief physician (1967–94) and general director (1967–90).

Winkler served in the US Navy for two years towards the end of World War II, before studying for an undergraduate degree at Elmhurst College (1947–50). From 1951 to 1955, he studied medicine at Michigan University, completing his internship in Traverse City, Michigan in 1956.

In 1956, Dr. Winkler was appointed to a rural health center in Talas, Kayseri, by the American Board of Commissioners for Foreign Missions, but before accepting the role, he spent two years specializing in surgery at McNeal Hospital in Chicago (1956–58). Dr. Winkler's book, *Two Doctors on One Journey* (2014), details the years he spent in Talas from 1959 to 1965.

In 1965, Dr. Winkler joined the academic staff at Johns Hopkins School of Public Health (Baltimore, Maryland) and taught there for one academic year. In the following year, he was sent to Turkey by Johns Hopkins University to act as a consultant to the Turkish Ministry of Health and was made director of the local health project in Muş as part of this role.

In 1967, Dr. Winkler was offered the role of chief physician at the American Hospital in Istanbul. He accepted on the basis that he could work part-time, subsequently spending two years traveling between Istanbul and Muş to fulfil the two separate roles simultaneously. In 1968, he brought his family to Istanbul and devoted all his time to managing the American Hospital. Dr. Winkler served as chief physician of the American Hospital for more than 25 years. In 1990, he passed the role of general director on to George D. Rountree(*). In 1994, he left his position as chief physician, but continued to work at the American Hospital.

Dr. Winkler's 28-year period of service at the American Hospital was an era of rapid development. Following the addition of five annexes to the main building, the hospital expanded from an area of 2,640 square meters to 14,255 square meters, the number of medical departments rose from seven to 37 and the number of physicians rose from 42 to 143. Over time, the American Hospital developed into a medical center due to the importance given to outpatient services and preventative care programs.

World Monuments Fund Hadrian Award, award established in 1988 by a New York-based international nonprofit organization, the World Monuments Fund. Founded for the protection of architecture and cultural heritage worldwide, the fund aims to encourage work in the field. The award, given annually to those playing a leading role in the development and protection of art and architecture worldwide, takes its name from the Roman Emperor Hadrian, who carried out a number of important architectural projects during his rule, 117-138 BCE. In 2007, the prize was awarded to the Koç family(*) in recognition for its contribution to the protection of Turkey's rich cultural heritage and support given to culture and art through the Vehbi Koç Foundation(*).

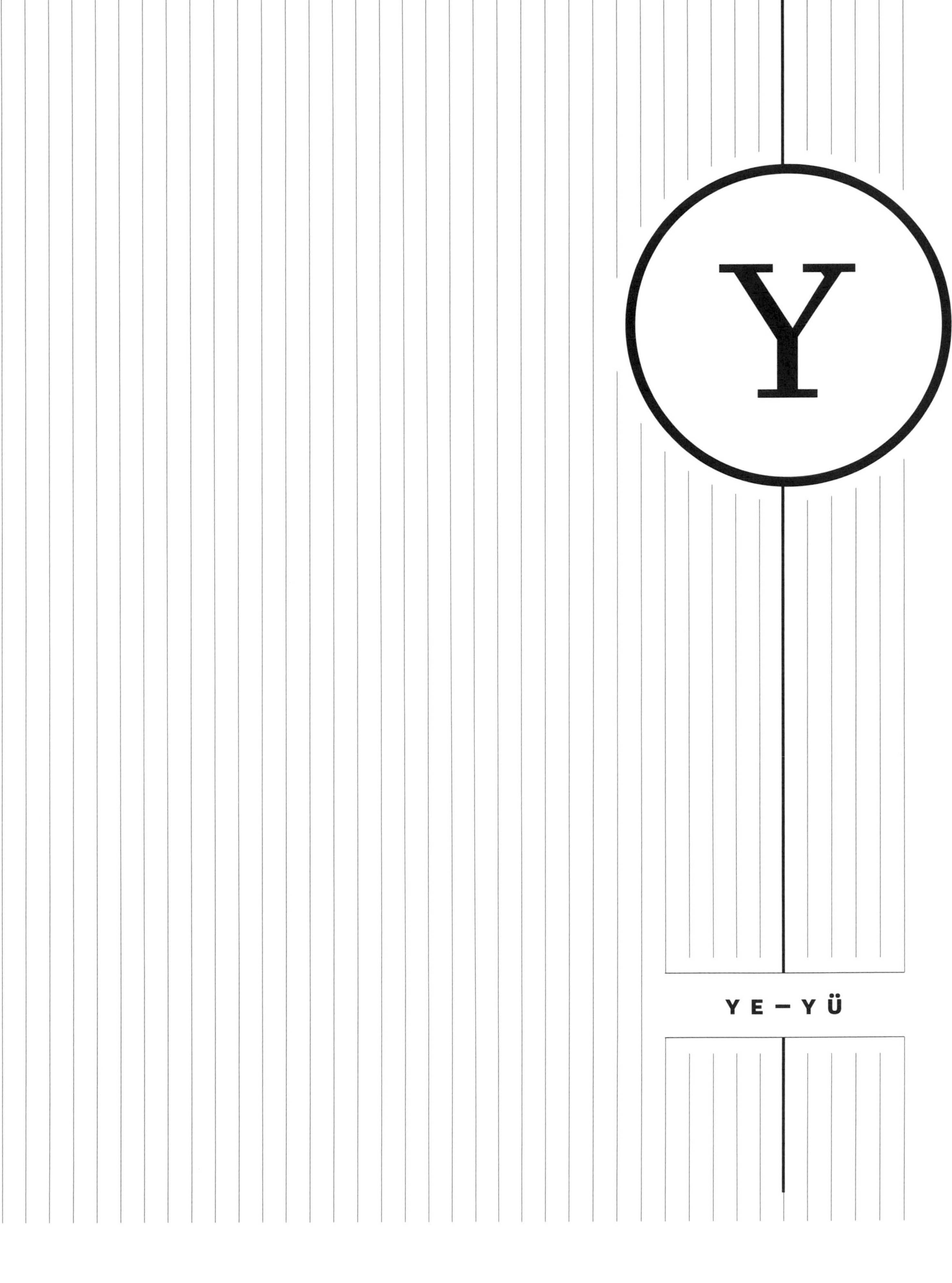

YE—YÜ

Yenişehir Koç Middle School
see **17 Schools Project**

Yenişehirlioğlu, Filiz *(b. February 10, 1949)*, academician. She has served as the director of VEKAM(*) since 2014.

After completing her secondary education at the American College for Girls (*see* Robert College) in Arnavutköy, she went on to study archeology and history of art at Sorbonne University in Paris, graduating in 1971. She received a master's degree (1973) and a doctorate (1981) in Islamic archeology and art history from the same university. From 1975 to 1986, she was a member of the teaching staff at Hacettepe University (HU). In 1986, she traveled to the USA and worked as a visiting lecturer on the Aga Khan Program for Islamic Architecture at Harvard University. In 1990, Prof. Yenişehirlioğlu became a professor at HU and continued to spend her academic life lecturing on Ottoman art and architecture. From 1995 to 1998, she was a visiting fellow at the Faculty of Oriental Studies at Cambridge University, UK. After returning to Turkey, she taught at the HU Department of Archeology and Art History until 2003. In 2003, she transferred to Başkent University, where she founded the Faculty of Fine Arts, Design and Architecture and became dean. In 2014, while serving as a member of the teaching staff at Koç University(*) Department of Archeology and Art History, she was made director of VEKAM, which is affiliated with the university.

In addition to her academic duties, Prof. Yenişehirlioğlu also served as a member of the UNESCO Cultural Heritage National Commission (1987–92 and 2002–2006) and was president of the Association of Art Historians in Anatolia (2001–03). She was made a Knight in the Order of Arts and Letters by the French Ministry of Culture in 1991 and received the Italian Adelaide Ristori Award in 1992. In addition to other publications, Prof. Yenişehirlioğlu has written the following books: *Les grandes lignes de l'évolution du programme décoratif en céramique des édifices ottomans au cours du XVIème siècle* (1985), and *Türkiye Dışında Osmanlı MimariYapıtları* (Ottoman Architectural Works Outside of Turkey; 1989). Books she has produced in collaboration with other writers include: *Ali Saim Ülgen Çizimleri ile Mimar Sinan veYapıları* (Mimar Sinan and His Buildings with Drawings by Ali Saim Ülgen; 1989) and *Mersin Evleri* (Mersin Houses; 1995). A study edited by Prof. Yenişehirlioğlu, titled *Akdeniz Uygarlıkları Sanatı* (The Art of Mediterranean Civilizations) was published in 2012.

Yıldırım, Erdal *(b. April 26 1966, Rize)*, engineer and director. He has served as the president of the Vehbi Koç Foundation(*) (VKV) since 1997.

After completing his secondary education at Kabataş High School, Istanbul (1981), Yıldırım studied mechanical engineering at Boğaziçi University (BU), graduating in 1987. He worked in the tourism sector (1987–91), before serving as secretary general of the BU Alumni Association (1991–97). He assumed his current position as president of the VKV in 1997. Yıldırım is also a member of the board of directors at the Suna and İnan Kıraç Foundation(*), TEMA(*) and TÜSEV(*), and a member of the board of trustees at the Boğaziçi University Foundation(*) and TEGV(*).

Yıldırım completed a master's degree in philanthropy at Indiana University in 2005. In 2012, he published a book, *BanaYönetim Kurulunu Söyle, Sana Kim Olduğunu Söyleyeyim* (Tell Me the Board of Directors and I'll Tell You...), which is used as a resource for volunteers and professionals working in non-governmental organizations. After publishing the autobiographical work, *Ateşin Üstünden Atladım* (Jumping Over the Fire; 2016), he published *Az mı Gittik, Uz mu Gittik? Yeni Vakıfların 50Yıllık Hikâyesi* (Have We Travelled Little, Have We Travelled Well? The 50 Year Story of New Foundations; 2017).

Yılmazyavuz, (Timur) Cengiz *(b. December 1, 1967, Ereğli, Zonguldak)*, operations engineer and director. He served as deputy general director at the American Hospital(*) between 2012 and 2018.

After completing his secondary education at Beşiktaş Anatolian High School in Istanbul in 1984, Yılmazyavuz studied at the Department of Industrial Engineering at Istanbul Technical University (ITU), graduating in 1988. He also completed a master's degree in industrial engineering at the ITU Graduate School of Science, Engineering and Technology in 1991. He served as assistant audit coordinator at Koç Holding(*) (1989–2000), and as assistant general manager at Mako AŞ, a Koç Holding company (2000–02). Yılmazyavuz took on the role of deputy general director of the American Hospital in 2002, leaving this position in 2018.

Yücel, Cahit *see* **Vehbi Koç Foundation**

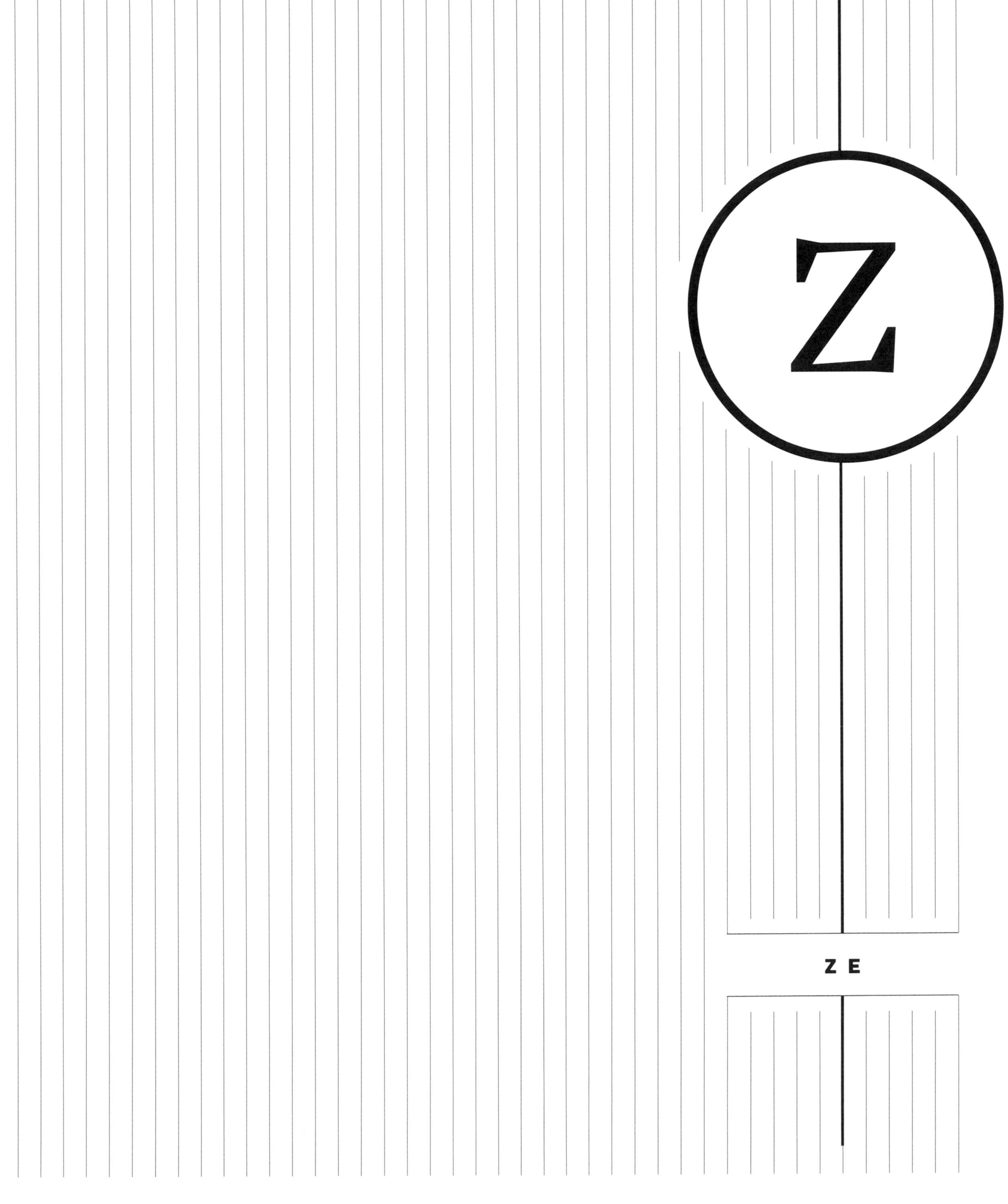
Z
Z E

Zekeriyaköy Family Health Center, full name ZEKERİYAKÖY PRIVATE AMERICAN FAMILY HEALTH CENTER, an outpatient clinic founded in 2013 by the American Hospital(*) to provide health services to people living in Zekeriyaköy, Kilyos, Maslak, Sarıyer and the surrounding areas.

The center was open 24 hours a day, seven days a week and offered regular health tests and check-ups, diagnosis and treatment of chronic and acute health problems, minor surgical interventions, vaccinations for adults, babies and children, travel medicine consulting services, monitoring for children's health and diseases, all forms of laboratory tests, ECGs, radiology and ultrasound services, ambulance services, homecare and treatment services. On certain days of the week, American Hospital specialists in orthopedics, surgery, gynecology and obstetrics, dermatology, allergies, physical therapy/ rehabilitation and diet attended to patients at the center.

The center ceased operations in late 2014.

Zengibar Castle Excavations, excavation works carried out on the ancient settlement of Isaura Nea, near the village of Hacılar in the Bozkır district of Konya. Excavations began in the area under the supervision of the archaeologist Dr. Osman Doğanay in 2010 and have received support from the Vehbi Koç Foundation(*) since 2014.

The archaeological site, now known as Zengibar Castle, is located on a hill measuring 1,800 meters in height, surrounded by cliffs on three sides. The area was controlled by the Roman Empire in 78 BCE and fell under the jurisdiction of the Galatian King Amyntas. Hoping to crush a people's rebellion, Amyntas destroyed the city of Isaura, which was located on a hill near the district of modern-day Bozkır, and had a new city with the same name built close by. After Amyntas' death in 25 BCE, the region once again fell under Roman rule. The city was home to 10,000 people in Roman times and was surrounded by four kilometers of wall supported by bastions. The wall can be entered from the south via the Acropolis gate and from the west via the City gate. The Triumphal Arch of Hadrian, located in the center of the city, comprises an arch connected by two piers. Next to the arch lies a building used as a basilica in Roman times. The city contains a large number of sepulchers and necropolises. The sepulchers and fortifications are covered in reliefs.

Zengibar Castle was discovered in 1837 by the British traveler and geologist W. J. Hamilton. In the late 1920s, a group led by the art historian and archaeologist Heinrich Swoboda determined the characteristics of a large number of structures in the city and attempt to reconstruct a number of them. The ruins were officially registered following a decision by the Konya Culture and Natural Heritage Preservation Board in 1988 and its borders as the Grade I and III Protected Site were defined in 2006.

VEHBİ KOÇ FOUNDATION ENCYCLOPEDIA

EDITORIAL BOARD
Renan Akman
Bülent Erkmen
Seçil Kınay
Gürel Tüzün
Erdal Yıldırım

AUTHORS
Renan Akman
Gürel Tüzün

CONCEPT AND DESIGN CONSULTANT
Bülent Erkmen

TRANSLATION
Paula Darwish

COPY-EDITOR
Defne Karakaya

BOOK DESIGN
Kerem Yaman, *BEK*

PREPRESS
BEK Tasarım

RESEARCH ASSISTANTS
Zeynep Otluoğlu Dursun
Nazlı Başak Örgüt

PROJECT COORDINATOR
Seçil Kınay, *Vehbi Koç Foundation*

PRINTED BY
Ofset Filmcilik ve Matbaacılık
Sanayi ve Ticaret A.Ş.
Çağlayan Mahallesi
Şair Sokak No: 4 Kağıthane - İstanbul
www.ofset.com
Certificate No: 12326

1st Print
Istanbul, April 2019

ISBN 978-975-7078-50-0